GREAT BOOKS OF THE WESTERN WORLD

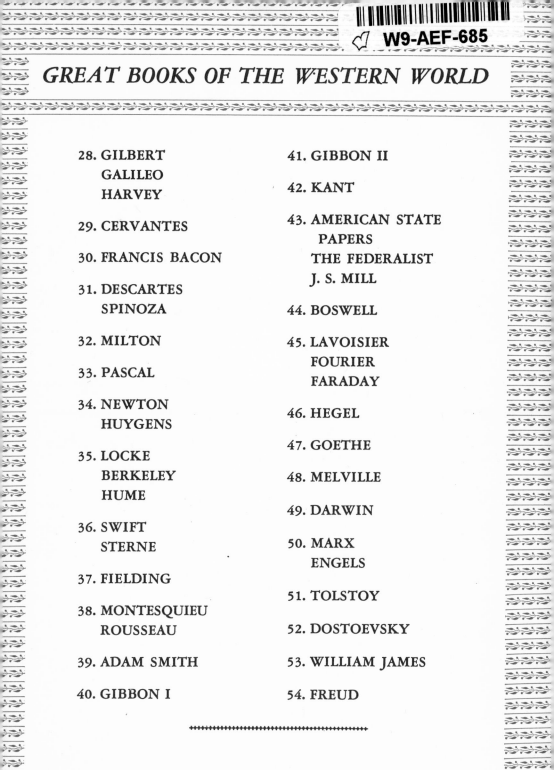

28. GILBERT
    GALILEO
    HARVEY

29. CERVANTES

30. FRANCIS BACON

31. DESCARTES
    SPINOZA

32. MILTON

33. PASCAL

34. NEWTON
    HUYGENS

35. LOCKE
    BERKELEY
    HUME

36. SWIFT
    STERNE

37. FIELDING

38. MONTESQUIEU
    ROUSSEAU

39. ADAM SMITH

40. GIBBON I

41. GIBBON II

42. KANT

43. AMERICAN STATE
    PAPERS
    THE FEDERALIST
    J. S. MILL

44. BOSWELL

45. LAVOISIER
    FOURIER
    FARADAY

46. HEGEL

47. GOETHE

48. MELVILLE

49. DARWIN

50. MARX
    ENGELS

51. TOLSTOY

52. DOSTOEVSKY

53. WILLIAM JAMES

54. FREUD

GREAT BOOKS
OF THE WESTERN WORLD

ROBERT MAYNARD HUTCHINS, *EDITOR IN CHIEF*

21.

DANTE

THE DIVINE COMEDY OF DANTE ALIGHIERI

TRANSLATED BY

CHARLES ELIOT NORTON

◆ ◆ ◆

WILLIAM BENTON, *Publisher*

ENCYCLOPÆDIA BRITANNICA, INC.

CHICAGO · LONDON · TORONTO · GENEVA · SYDNEY · TOKYO · MANILA

By arrangement with Houghton Mifflin Company

THE UNIVERSITY OF CHICAGO

The Great Books
is published with the editorial advice of the faculties
of The University of Chicago

©

1952
BY ENCYCLOPÆDIA BRITANNICA, INC.
NINETEENTH PRINTING, 1971
COPYRIGHT UNDER INTERNATIONAL COPYRIGHT UNION

ALL RIGHTS RESERVED UNDER PAN AMERICAN AND UNIVERSAL COPYRIGHT CONVENTIONS BY ENCYCLOPÆDIA BRITANNICA, INC.

Library of Congress Catalog Card Number: 55–10329
International Standard Book Number: 0–85229–163–9

BIOGRAPHICAL NOTE

DANTE, 1265 – 1321

DANTE ALIGHIERI was born in Florence about the middle of May, 1265. The city, then under its first democratic constitution, was sharply divided between the Papal party of the Guelphs and the Imperial party of the Ghibellines. Dante's family were adherents of the Guelph faction, and when Dante was only a few months old, the Guelphs obtained decisive victory at the Battle of Benevento. Although of noble ancestry, the Alighieri family was neither wealthy nor particularly prominent.

It seems probable that Dante received his early education at the Franciscan school of Santa Croce. He evidently owed much to the influence of Brunetto Latini, the philosopher and scholar who figured largely in the councils of the Florentine commune. Before twenty, he began writing poetry and became associated with the Italian poets of the "sweet new style," who exalted their love and their ladies in philosophical verse. Dante's "lady," whom he celebrated with singular devotion, was a certain Beatrice. According to Boccaccio's life of Dante, she was Beatrice Portinari, daughter of a Florentine citizen, who married a wealthy banker, and died when she was but twenty-four. Dante first sang of Beatrice in the *Vita Nuova* (1292), a sequence of poems with prose comment in which he recounts the story of his love, of the first meeting when they were both nine years of age, the exchange of greetings which passed between them on May Day, 1283, and of Beatrice's death in 1290.

Upon turning thirty, Dante became actively involved in Florentine politics. The constitution of the city was based upon the guilds, and Dante, upon his enrolment in the guild of physicians and apothecaries, which also included book dealers, became eligible for office. He participated in the deliberations of the councils, served on a special embassy, and in 1300 was elected one of the six priors that governed the city. The former struggle between the Guelphs and Ghibellines had appeared in new form in the conflict between the Whites and the Blacks. As one of the priors, Dante seems to have been influential in the move to lessen factionalism by banishing from Florence the rival leaders, including among the Blacks his wife's relative, Corso Donati, and among the Whites his "first friend," the poet, Guido Cavalcanti. Despite the opposition of Dante and the White leaders to Papal interference in Florentine affairs, Pope Boniface VIII in 1301 invited Charles of Valois, brother of King Philip of France, to enter Florence to settle the differences between the two factions. Actually he assisted the Blacks to seize power, and more than six hundred Whites were condemned to exile. In 1302 Dante, with four others of the White party, was charged with corruption in office. He was condemned to pay a fine of five thousand florins within three days or lose his property, exiled for two years, and denied the right ever again to hold public office. Three months later, upon his refusal to pay the fine, Dante was condemned to be burned alive if he should come within the power of the republic.

"After it was the pleasure of the citizens of the most beautiful and most famous daughter of Rome, Florence, to chase me forth from her sweet bosom," Dante writes of his exile in the *Convivio*, "I have gone through almost every region to which this tongue of ours extends, showing against my will the wound of fortune." It is recorded that Dante attended a meeting at San Godenzo, where an alliance was formed between the Whites in exile and the Ghibellines, but he does not seem to have been present in 1304 when the combined forces were defeated at Lastra. Perhaps he had already separated himself from the "evil and foolish company" of his fellow-exiles, "formed a party by himself," and found his "first refuge and hostelry" at the court of the Della Scalas in Verona. Probably during the following years he spent time at Bologna and later at Padua, where Giotto is said to have entertained him. Toward the end of 1306 he was the guest of the Malaspinas in Lunigiana and acted as their ambassador in making peace with the Bishop of Luni. Sometime after this date he may have visited Paris and attended the university there.

During the early years of his exile Dante appears to have studied in those subjects which gained him the title of philosopher and theologian as well as poet. In the *Convivio*, probably written between 1305 and 1308, he tells how, after the death of Beatrice, he turned to Cicero's *De Amicitia* and the *Consolatio Philosophiae* of Boethius, which awoke in him the love of philosophy. To sing its praises he began his *Convivio*, which he intended to be a kind of treasury of universal knowledge in the form of poems connected by lengthy prose commentaries. At the same time he worked upon the *De Vulgari Eloquentia*, a Latin treatise in which he defended the use of Italian as a literary language.

The election of Henry of Luxemburg as emperor in 1308 stirred Dante's political hopes. When Henry entered Italy in 1310 at the head of an army, Dante in an epistle to the princes and people of Italy hailed the coming of a deliverer. At Milan he paid personal homage to Henry as his sovereign. When Florence, in alliance with King Robert of Naples, prepared to resist the emperor, Dante in a second epistle denounced them for their obstinacy and prophesied their doom. In a third epistle he upbraided the Emperor himself for his delay and urged him on against Florence. It was probably during this period that he wrote his *De Monarchia*, an intellectual defense of the emperor as the sovereign of the temporal order. The death of Henry in 1313, after a year or so of ineffectual fighting, brought an end to the political aspirations of Dante and his party.

The city of Florence in 1311 and again in 1315 renewed his condemnation.

After Henry's death, Dante passed the rest of his life under the protection of various lords of Lombardy, Tuscany, and the Romagna. According to one tradition, he retired for a time to the monastery of Santa Croce di Fonte Avellana in the Appenines, where he worked on the *Divine Comedy*, which may have been planned as early as 1292. He was almost certainly for a time at the court of Can Grande della Scala, to whom he dedicated the *Paradiso*. In 1315 Florence issued a general recall of exiles. Dante refused to pay the required fine and to "bear the brand of oblation," feeling that such a return would derogate from his fame and honor. To the end of his life he appears to have hoped that his *Comedy* would finally open the gates of the city to him.

The last few years of the poet's life were spent at Ravenna, under the patronage of Guido da Polenta, a nephew of Francesca da Rimini. Dante's daughter, Beatrice, was a nun in that city, and one of his sons held a benefice there; his wife seems to have resided in Florence throughout his exile. Dante was greatly esteemed at Ravenna and enjoyed a congenial circle of friends. Here he completed the *Divine Comedy* and wrote two eclogues in Latin which indicate that a certain contentment surrounded his closing days. Returning from a diplomatic mission to Venice on behalf of his patron, he caught a fever and died September 14, 1321. He was buried at Ravenna before the door of the principal church, with the highest honors, and "in the habit of a poet and a great philosopher."

CONTENTS

PURGATORY

CONTENTS

·: HELL :·

CANTO I

1. MIDWAY upon the journey of our life I found myself in a dark wood, where the right way was lost.[1] Ah! how hard a thing it is to tell what this wild and rough and difficult wood was, which in thought renews my fear! So bitter is it that death is little more. But in order to treat of the good that I found in it, I will tell of the other things that I saw there.

10. I cannot well report how I entered it, so full was I of slumber at that moment when I abandoned the true way. But after I had reached the foot of a hill,[2] where that valley ended which had pierced my heart with fear, I looked upward, and saw its shoulders clothed already with the rays of the planet[3] which leads man aright along every path. Then was the fear a little quieted which had lasted in the lake of my heart through the night that I had passed so piteously. And even as one who with spent breath, issued forth from the sea upon the shore, turns to the perilous water and gazes, so did my mind, which still was flying, turn back to look again upon the pass which never left person alive.

28. After I had rested a little my weary body, I again took my way along the desert slope,[4] so that the firm foot was always the lower. And lo! almost at the beginning of the steep a she-leopard,[5] light and very nimble, which was covered with a spotted coat. And she did not withdraw from before my face, nay, hindered so my road that I often turned to go back.

37. The time was the beginning of the morning, and the Sun was mounting up with those stars that were with him when the Love Divine first set in motion those beautiful things;[6] so that the hour of the time and the sweet season were occasion to me of good hope concerning that wild beast with the dappled skin; but not so that the sight which appeared to me of a lion[7] did not give me fear. He appeared to be coming against me, with his head high and with ravening hunger, so that it appeared that the air was affrighted at him; and a she-wolf,[8] which in her leanness seemed laden with all cravings, and ere now had made many folk to live forlorn,—she brought on me so much heaviness, with the fear that came from sight of her, that I lost hope of the height. And such as is he who gains willingly, and the time arrives which makes him lose, so that in all his thoughts he laments and is sad, such did the beast without peace make me, which, coming on against me, was pushing me back, little by little, thither where the Sun is silent.

61. While I was falling back to the low place, one who appeared faint-voiced through long silence presented himself before my eyes. When I saw him in the great desert, "Have pity on me!" I cried to him, "whatso thou be, whether shade or real man." He answered me: "Not man; man once I was, and my parents were Lombards, and both Mantuans by country. I was born *sub Julio*, though late, and I lived at Rome under the good Augustus, at the time of the false and lying gods. I was a poet, and sang

[6] It was a common belief, which existed from early Christian times, that the spring was the season of the Creation. By the Julian calendar, March 25 was the date of the vernal equinox, and to it was assigned the Annunciation and the Crucifixion. March 25 was thus what may be called the ideal Good Friday. But in the year 1300 the actual Good Friday fell on April 8. This is the date which Dante, following the calendar of the Church, adopted for that of his journey.

[7] The lion is the type of pride.

[8] The wolf is the type of avarice. Cf. Jeremiah, 5. 6. These three beasts correspond with the triple division of sins into those of incontinence, of violence, and of fraud (see Canto xi).

[1] The action of the poem begins on the night before Good Friday of the year 1300; cf. Canto xxi. 112-114. Dante was thirty-five years old. The dark wood is the forest of the world of sense.

[2] The hill is the type of the true course of life.

[3] According to the Ptolemaic system, the sun was a planet.

[4] Cf. Matthew, 7. 14.

[5] The leopard is the type of the temptations of the flesh.

of that just son of Anchises[1] who came from
Troy, after proud Ilion had been burned. But
thou, why dost thou return to such great annoy?
Why dost thou not ascend the delectable moun-
tain which is the source and cause of all joy?"

79. "Art thou then that Virgil and that fount
which pours forth so broad a stream of speech?"
replied I with bashful front to him: "O honor
and light of the other poets! may the long study
avail me and the great love, which have made
me search thy volume! Thou art my master
and my author; thou alone art he from whom
I took the fair style that has done me honor.
Behold the beast because of which I turned;
help me against her, famous sage, for she makes
my veins and pulses tremble."

91. "It behoves thee to hold another course,"
he replied, when he saw me weeping, "if thou
wouldst escape from this savage place; for this
beast, because of which thou criest out, lets not
any one pass along her way, but so hinders him
that she kills him; and she has a nature so
malign and evil that she never sates her greedy
will, and after food has more hunger than be-
fore. Many are the animals with which she
wives, and there shall be more yet, until the
hound shall come that will make her die of
grief. He shall not feed on land or pelf, but
wisdom and love and valor, and his birthplace
shall be between Feltro and Feltro. Of that
low Italy shall he be the salvation, for which
the virgin Camilla died, and Euryalus, Turnus
and Nisus of their wounds.[2] He shall hunt her
through every town till he shall have put her
back again in Hell, there whence envy first
sent her forth.

112. "Wherefore I think and deem it for thy
best that thou follow me, and I will be thy
guide, and will lead thee hence through the
eternal place where thou shalt hear the despair-
ing shrieks, shalt see the ancient spirits woeful
who each proclaim the second death.[3] And
then thou shalt see those who are contented in
the fire,[4] because they hope to come, whenever
it may be, to the blessed folk; to whom if thou

wouldst then ascend, there shall be a soul[5]
more worthy than I for that. With her I will
leave thee at my departure; for that Emperor
who reigns thereabove wills not, because I was
rebellious[6] to His law, that through me any
one should come into His city. In all parts He
governs and there He reigns: there is His city
and His lofty seat. O happy the man whom
thereto He elects!" And I to him: "Poet, I be-
seech thee by that God whom thou didst not
know, in order that I may escape this ill and
worse, that thou lead me thither where thou
now hast said, so that I may see the gate of St.
Peter,[7] and those whom thou reportest so af-
flicted."

136. Then he moved on, and I held behind
him.

CANTO II

1. THE day was going, and the dusky air was
taking the living things that are on earth from
their fatigues, and I alone was preparing to
sustain the war alike of the journey and of the
woe, which my memory that errs not shall re-
trace.

7. O Muses, O lofty genius, now assist me!
O memory that didst inscribe that which I saw,
here shall thy nobility appear!

10. I began: "Poet, who guidest me, consider
my power, if it be sufficient, before thou trust
me to the deep pass. Thou sayest[8] that the par-
ent of Silvius while still corruptible went to
the immortal world and was there in the body;
and truly if the Adversary of every ill was
courteous to him, it seems not unmeet to the
man of understanding, thinking on the high
effect that should proceed from him, and on
the who and the what;[9] for in the empyrean
heaven he was chosen for father of revered
Rome and of her empire; both which (would
one say truth) were ordained for the holy place
where the successor of the greater Peter has his
seat. Through this going, whereof thou givest
him vaunt, he learned things which were the
cause of his victory and of the papal mantle.
Afterward the Chosen Vessel[10] went thither to

---

[1] Aeneas. Cf. *Aeneid,* i. 544.
[2] Camilla and Turnus died for Italy fighting against
the Trojans; Euryalus and Nisus died on the Trojan
side (*Aeneid*).
[3] Cf. Revelation, 20. 10. 14; 21. 8; St. Augustine,
City of God, xiii. 8.
[4] That is, contented in the purifying pains of Purga-
tory, by which they are made fit for Paradise.

[5] Beatrice.
[6] See Canto iv. 36.
[7] See *Purgatory,* Canto ix. 127.
[8] See *Aeneid.* vi.
[9] God was thus gracious to him as the Father of the
Roman people (the "who"), and founder of the Ro-
man Empire (the "what").
[10] St. Paul. Cf. Acts, 9. 15, and II Corinthians, 12, 1-4.

bring thence comfort to that faith which is the beginning of the way of salvation. But I, why go I thither? or who concedes it? I am not Aeneas, I am not Paul; neither I nor others believe me worthy of this; wherefore if I yield myself to go, I fear lest the going may be mad. Thou art wise, thou understandest better than I speak."

37. And as is he who unwills what he willed, and by reason of new thoughts changes his purpose, so that he withdraws wholly from what he had begun, such I became on that dark hillside: because in my thought I abandoned the enterprise which had been so hasty in its beginning.

43. "If I have rightly understood thy speech," replied that shade of the magnanimous one, "thy soul is hurt by cowardice, which often-times encumbers a man so that it turns him back from honorable enterprise, as false seeing does a beast when it shies. In order that thou loose thee from this fear I will tell thee why I came, and what I heard at the first moment that I grieved for thee. I was among those who are suspended, and a Lady blessed and beauti-ful called me, such that I besought her to com-mand. Her eyes were more shining than the star, and she began to say to me sweet and clear, with angelic voice, in her speech:

58. " 'O courteous Mantuan soul! of whom the fame yet lasts in the world, and shall last so long as motion continues, my friend, and not of fortune, is so hindered on his road upon the des-ert hillside that he has turned for fear, and I am afraid, through that which I have heard of him in heaven, lest he be already so astray that I may have risen late to his succor. Now do thou move, and with thy ornate speech and with whatever is needful for his deliverance, assist him so that I may be consoled thereby. I am Beatrice who make thee go. I come from a place whither I desire to return. Love moved me, that makes me speak. When I shall be before my Lord, I will often praise thee to Him.'

75. "Then she was silent, and thereon I be-gan: 'O Lady of Virtue! through whom alone the human race excels all contained within that heaven which has the smallest circle,[1] thy com-mand so pleases me that to obey it, were it al-ready done, were slow to me. There is no need for thee further to open to me thy will; but tell me the reason why thou dost not beware of descending down here into this centre, from the ample place whither thou burnest to return.'

85. " 'Since thou wishest to know so inward-ly, I will tell thee briefly,' she replied to me, 'wherefore I fear not to come here within. One need be afraid only of those things that have power to do one harm, of others not, for they are not fearful. I am made by God, thanks be to Him, such that your misery touches me not, nor does the flame of this burning assail me. A gentle Lady[2] is in heaven who feels compassion for this hindrance whereto I send thee, so that she breaks stern judgment there above. She summoned Lucia[3] in her request, and said, "Thy faithful one now has need of thee, and I commend him to thee." Lucia, the foe of every cruel one, moved and came to the place where I was, seated with the ancient Rachel."[4]

103. " 'She said, "Beatrice, true praise of God, why dost thou not succor him who so loved thee that for thee he came forth from the vulgar throng? Dost thou not hear the pity of his plaint? Dost thou not see the death that com-bats him on the stream where the sea has no vaunt?" Never were persons in the world swift to do their good, or to fly their harm, as I, after these words were uttered, came down here from my blessed seat, putting my trust in thy upright speech, which honors thee and them who have heard it.'

115. "After she had said this to me, weeping she turned her lucent eyes, whereby she made me more quick to come. And I came to thee thus as she willed. I withdrew thee from before that wild beast which took from thee the short way on the beautiful mountain. What is it then? Why, why dost thou hold back? why dost thou harbor such cowardice in thy heart? why hast thou not daring and assurance, since

---

[1] The heaven of the moon, the innermost of the nine revolving heavens, the nearest to the earth.

[2] The Virgin Mary, never spoken of by name in Hell.

[3] As an allegorical figure she is the symbol, as her name indicates, of illuminating Grace.

[4] Rachel was adopted by the Church as the type of the contemplative life, in which the soul devotes itself to the consideration of the things of God and so has a foretaste of the felicity of heaven. Beatrice, the type of instruction in the divine mysteries, is therefore rightly at Rachel's side.

three such blessed Ladies care for thee in the court of Heaven, and my speech pledges thee such good?"

127. As the flowerets, bent and closed by the chill of night, when the sun brightens them erect themselves all open on their stem, so I became with my drooping courage, and such good daring ran to my heart that I began like a person enfreed: "O compassionate she who succored me, and courteous thou who didst speedily obey the true words that she addressed to thee! Thou by thy words hast so disposed my heart with desire of going, that I have returned to my first intent. Now go, for one sole will is in us both: thou leader, thou lord, and thou master."

141. Thus I said to him; and when he moved on, I entered along the deep and savage road.

CANTO III

1. "THROUGH me is the way into the woeful city; through me is the way into the eternal woe; through me is the way among the lost people. Justice moved my lofty maker: the divine Power, the supreme Wisdom and the primal Love made me. Before me were no things created, save eternal, and I eternal last. Leave every hope, ye who enter!"[1]

10. These words of obscure color I saw written at the top of a gate; whereat I: "Master, their meaning is dire to me."

13. And he to me, like a person well advised: "Here it behoves to leave every fear; it behoves that all cowardice should here be dead. We have come to the place where I have told thee that thou shalt see the woeful people, who have lost the good of the understanding."

19. And when he had put his hand on mine with a cheerful look, wherefrom I took courage, he brought me within to the secret things. Here sighs, laments, and deep wailings were resounding through the starless air; wherefore at first I wept thereat. Strange tongues, horrible utterances, words of woe, accents of anger, voices high and faint, and sounds of hands with them, were making a tumult which whirls always in that air forever dark, like the sand when the whirlwind breathes.

31. And I, who had my head girt with horror,

said: "Master, what is that which I hear? and what folk is it that seems so overcome with its woe?"

34. And he to me: "The wretched souls of those who lived without infamy and without praise maintain this miserable mode. They are mingled with that caitiff choir of the angels, who were not rebels, nor were faithful to God, but were for themselves. The heavens chased them out in order to be not less beautiful, nor does the deep Hell receive them, for the damned would have some boast of them."

43. And I: "Master, what is so grievous to them, that makes them lament so bitterly?"

45. He answered: "I will tell thee very briefly. These have not hope of death; and their blind life is so debased, that they are envious of every other lot. Fame of them the world permits not to be; mercy and justice disdain them. Let us not speak of them, but do thou look and pass on."

52. And I, who was gazing, saw a banner, which, whirling, ran so swiftly that it seemed to me disdainful of any pause, and behind it came so long a train of folk, that I should never have believed death had undone so many. After I had recognized some among them, I saw and knew the shade of him who made, through cowardice, the great refusal.[2] At once I understood and was certain, that this was the sect of the caitiffs displeasing to God and to his enemies. These wretches, who never were alive, were naked, and much stung by gad-flies and by wasps that were there; these streaked their faces with blood, which, mingled with tears, was gathered at their feet by loathsome worms.

70. And when I gave myself to looking onward, I saw people on the bank of a great river; wherefore I said: "Master, now grant to me that I may know who these are, and what rule makes them appear so ready to pass over, as I discern through the faint light." And he to me: "The things will be clear to thee, when we shall stay our steps on the sad shore of Acheron." Then with eyes ashamed and downcast, fearing lest my speech might be troublesome to him, far as to the river I refrained from speaking.

[1] Cf. Aquinas, *Summa Theologica*, Part I, Q 45, A 6; Part I, Q 39, A 8.

[2] Probably Pope Celestine V, who, after having held the papacy for five months in 1294, abdicated.

82. And behold! coming toward us in a boat, an old man, white with ancient hair, crying: "Woe to you, wicked souls! hope not ever to see the Heavens! I come to carry you to the other bank, into the eternal darkness, into heat and into frost. And thou who art there, living soul, depart from these that are dead." But when he saw that I did not depart, he said: "By another way, by other ports thou shalt come to the shore, not here, for passage; a lighter bark must carry thee."[1]

94. And my Leader to him: "Charon, vex not thyself; it is thus willed there where is power for that which is willed; and ask no more." Thereon were quiet the fleecy jaws of the ferryman of the livid marsh, who round about his eyes had wheels of flame.

100. But those souls, who were weary and naked, changed color and gnashed their teeth, soon as they heard his cruel words. They blasphemed God and their parents, the human race, the place, the time and the seed of their sowing and of their birth. Then, all of them bitterly weeping, drew together to the evil bank, which awaits every man who fears not God. Charon the demon, with eyes of glowing coal, beckoning to them, collects them all; he beats with his oar whoever lingers.

112. As in autumn the leaves depart one after the other, until the bough sees all its spoils upon the earth, in like wise the evil seed of Adam throw themselves from that shore one by one, at signals, as the bird at his recall. Thus they go over the dusky wave, and before they have landed on the farther side, already on this a new throng is assembled.

121. "My son," said the courteous Master, "those who die in the wrath of God, all come together here from every land; and they are eager to pass over the stream, for the divine justice spurs them so that fear is turned to desire. A good soul never passes this way; and therefore if Charon fret at thee, well mayest thou now know what his speech signifies."

130. This ended, the gloomy plain trembled so mightily, that the memory of the terror even now bathes me with sweat. The tearful land gave forth a wind that flashed a crimson light which vanquished all sensation in me, and I fell as a man whom slumber seizes.

[1] Cf. *Aeneid*, vi. 298ff., 326ff.

CANTO IV

1. A HEAVY thunder broke the deep sleep in my head, so that I started up like a person who is waked by force, and, risen erect, I moved my rested eye round about, and looked fixedly to distinguish the place where I was. True it is, that I found myself on the brink of the woeful valley of the abyss which collects a thunder of infinite wailings. It was so dark, deep, and cloudy, that, though I fixed my sight on the depth, I did not discern anything there.

13. "Now let us descend here below into the blind world," began the Poet all deadly pale, "I will be first, and thou shalt be second."

16. And I, who had observed his color, said: "How shall I come, if thou fearest, who art wont to be the comfort to my doubting?" And he to me: "The anguish of the folk who are here below paints on my face that pity which thou takest for fear. Let us go on, for the long way urges us."

23. Thus he placed himself, and thus he made me enter into the first circle[2] that girds the abyss. Here, as one listened, there was no lamentation but that of sighs which made the eternal air to tremble; this came of the woe without torments felt by the crowds, which were many and great, of infants and of women and of men.

31. The good Master to me: "Thou dost not ask what spirits are these that thou seest. Now I would have thee know, before thou goest farther, that these did not sin; and though they have merits it suffices not, because they did not have baptism, which is part of the faith that thou believest; and if they were before Christianity, they did not duly worship God: and of such as these am I myself. For such defects, and not for other guilt, are we lost, and only so far harmed that without hope we live in desire."

43. Great woe seized me at my heart when I heard him, because I knew that people of much worth were suspended in that limbo.

46. "Tell me, my Master, tell me, Lord," I began, with wish to be assured of that faith which vanquishes every error, "did ever anyone who afterwards was blessed go forth from here, either by his own or by another's merit?"

51. And he, who understood my covert

[2] Limbo (Lat. *limbus*, edge, hem, border).

speech, answered: "I was new in this state when I saw a Mighty One come hither crowned with sign of victory. He drew out hence the shade of the first parent, of Abel his son, and that of Noah, of Moses the law-giver and obedient, Abraham the patriarch, and David the King, Israel with his father and with his offspring, and with Rachel, for whom he did so much, and many others; and He made them blessed: and I would have thee know that before these, human spirits were not saved."

64. We ceased not going on because he spoke, but all the while were passing through the wood, the wood, I mean, of crowded spirits; nor yet had our way been long from the place of my slumber, when I saw a fire, which overcame a hemisphere of darkness.[1] We were still a little distant from it, yet not so far but that I could in part discern that honorable folk possessed that place.

73. "O thou who honorest both science and art, who are these, who have such honor that it separates them from the manner of the others?" And he to me: "The honorable renown of them which sounds above in thy life wins grace in heaven which thus advances them."

79. At this a voice was heard by me: "Honor the loftiest Poet! his shade returns which had departed." When the voice had stopped and was quiet, I saw four great shades coming to us; they had a semblance neither sad nor glad.

85. The good Master began to say: "Look at him with that sword in hand who comes before the three, even as lord; he is Homer, the sovereign poet; the next who comes is Horace, the satirist; Ovid is the third, and the last is Lucan. Since each shares with me the name which the single voice sounded, they do me honor, and in that do well."

94. Thus I saw assembled the fair school of that Lord of the loftiest song who soars above the others like an eagle. After they had discoursed somewhat together, they turned to me with sign of salutation; and my Master smiled thereat. And far more of honor yet they did me, for they made me of their band, so that I was the sixth amid so much wisdom. Thus we went on as far as the light, speaking things concerning which silence is becoming, even as was speech there where I was.

106. We came to the foot of a noble castle, seven times circled by high walls,[2] defended round about by a fair streamlet. This we passed as if hard ground; through seven gates[3] I entered with these sages; we came to a meadow of fresh verdure. People were there with slow and grave eyes, of great authority in their looks; they spoke seldom, and with soft voices. Thereon we withdrew ourselves upon one side, into an open, luminous, and high place, so that they all could be seen. There before me upon the green enamel were shown to me the great spirits, whom for having seen I inwardly exalt myself.

121. I saw Electra with many companions, among whom I recognized Hector and Aeneas, Cæsar in armor, with his gerfalcon eyes; I saw Camilla and Penthesilea, on the other side I saw the King Latinus, who was sitting with Lavinia his daughter. I saw that Brutus who drove out Tarquin; Lucretia, Julia, Marcia, and Cornelia; and alone, apart, I saw the Saladin. When I raised my brows a little more, I saw the Master of those who know,[4] seated amid the philosophic family: all regard him, all do him honor. Here I saw Socrates and Plato, who in front of the others stand nearest to him; Democritus, who ascribes the world to chance; Diogenes, Anaxagoras, and Thales, Empedocles, Heraclitus, and Zeno; and I saw the good collector of the qualities, Dioscorides, I mean;[5] and I saw Orpheus, Tully, and Linus, and moral Seneca, Euclid the geometer, and Ptolemy, Hippocrates, Avicenna, and Galen, and Averrhoës, who made the great comment.[6] I cannot report of all in full, because the long

---

[1] The fire may be the symbol of the partial light afforded by philosophy to the virtuous heathen.

[2] The castle is the symbol of the abode of Philosophy, or human wisdom unenlightened by revelation; its seven high walls may perhaps signify the four moral and three intellectual virtues—prudence, temperance, fortitude, and justice; understanding, knowledge, and wisdom, all which could be attained by the virtuous heathen. Cf. Aquinas, *Summa Theologica*, Part I-II, Q65, A2.

[3] The seven gates may typify the seven liberal arts of the *trivium* and the *quadrivium*, by which names the courses of instruction in them were known in the schools of the Middle Ages. The *trivium* included grammar, logic, and rhetoric; the *quadrivium*, music, arithmetic, geometry, and astronomy.

[4] Aristotle.

[5] Dioscorides, a physician in Cilicia, of the first century A. D., wrote, in his treatise *De materia medica*, of the qualities of plants.

[6] On Aristotle.

theme so drives me that many times the speech comes short of the fact.

148. The company of six is reduced to two. By another way the wise guide leads me out from the quiet into the air that trembles, and I come into a region where is nothing that can give light.

CANTO V

1. THUS I descended from the first circle down into the second, which girdles less space, and so much more woe that it goads to wailing. There stands Minos horribly, and snarls: he examines the transgressions at the entrance; he judges, and he sends according as he entwines himself. I mean, that when the ill born soul comes there before him, it confesses itself wholly, and that discerner of the sins sees what place of Hell is for it; he girds himself with his tail so many times as the grades he wills that it be sent down. Always many of them stand before him; they go, in turn, each to the judgment; they speak and hear, and then are whirled below.

16. "O thou that comest to the woeful inn," said Minos to me, when he saw me, leaving the act of so great an office, "beware how thou enterest, and to whom thou trustest thyself; let not the amplitude of the entrance deceive thee." And my Leader to him: "Wherefore dost thou too cry out? Hinder not his fated going; thus is it willed there where is power for that which is willed; and ask no more."

25. Now the notes of woe begin to make themselves heard by me; now I am come where much wailing smites me. I had come into a place mute of all light, that bellows as the sea does in a tempest, if it be combated by contrary winds. The infernal hurricane which never rests carries along the spirits with its rapine; whirling and smiting it molests them.[1] When they arrive before its rush, here are the shrieks, the complaint, and the lamentation; here they blaspheme the divine power. I understood that to such torment are condemned the carnal sinners who subject the reason to the appetite. And as their wings bear along the starlings in the cold season in a large and full troop, so did that blast the evil spirits; hither, thither, down, up it carries them; no hope ever comforts them,

neither of repose, nor of less pain.

46. And as the cranes go singing their lays, making in air a long line of themselves, so I saw come, uttering wails, shades borne along by the aforesaid strife. Wherefore I said: "Master, who are these folk whom the black air so castigates?"

52. "The first of those of whom thou wishest to have knowledge," said he to me then, "was empress of many tongues. She was so abandoned to the vice of luxury that lust she made licit in her law, to take away the blame into which she had been brought. She is Semiramis, of whom it is read that she succeeded Ninus and had been his wife; she held the land which the Sultan rules. That other is she[2] who, for love, slew herself, and broke faith to the ashes of Sichaeus; next is Cleopatra, the luxurious. See Helen, for whom so long a time of ill revolved; and see the great Achilles, who fought to the end with love. See Paris, Tristan—" and more than a thousand shades whom love had parted from our life he showed me, and, pointing to them, named to me.

70. After I had heard my Teacher name the dames of eld and the cavaliers, pity overcame me, and I was well nigh bewildered. I began: "Poet, willingly would I speak with those two that go together, and seem to be so light upon the wind."[3] And he to me: "Thou shalt see when they are nearer to us, and do thou then pray them by that love which leads them, and they will come." Soon as the wind sways them toward us, I lifted my voice: "O wearied souls, come to speak with us, if Another[4] deny it not."

82. As doves, called by desire, with wings open and steady, come through the air borne by their will to their sweet nest, these issued from the troop where Dido is, coming to us through the malign air, so strong was the compassionate cry.

88. "O living creature, gracious and benign, that goest through the black air visiting us who stained the world blood-red, if the King of the universe were a friend we would pray Him for thy peace, since thou hast pity on our perverse

---

[1] Cf. Wisdom of Solomon, 11. 16.

[2] Dido.

[3] These two are Francesca da Rimini, daughter of the lord of Ravenna, and her lover, Paolo, the brother of her husband, the son of the lord of Rimini.

[4] The name of God is never spoken by the spirits in Hell.

ill. Of what it pleases thee to hear, and what to speak, we will hear and we will speak to you, while the wind, as now, is hushed for us. The city where I was born sits upon the sea-shore, where the Po, with his followers, descends to have peace. Love, which quickly lays hold on gentle heart, seized this one for the fair person that was taken from me, and the mode still hurts me. Love, which absolves no loved one from loving, seized me for the pleasing of him so strongly that, as thou seest, it does not even now abandon me. Love brought us to one death. Cain awaits him who quenched our life." These words were borne to us from them.

109. Soon as I had heard those injured souls I bowed my face, and held it down so long until the Poet said to me: "What art thou thinking?" When I replied, I began: "Alas! how many sweet thoughts, how great desire, led these unto the woeful pass." Then I turned me again to them, and spoke, and began: "Francesca, thy torments make me sad and piteous to weeping. But tell me, at the time of the sweet sighs, by what and how did love concede to thee to know thy dubious desires?" And she to me: "There is no greater woe than the remembering in misery the happy time, and that thy Teacher knows. But if thou hast so great desire to know the first root of our love, I will do like one who weeps and tells.

127. "We were reading one day, for delight, of Lancelot, how love constrained him. We were alone and without any suspicion. Many times that reading urged our eyes, and took the color from our faces, but only one point was it that overcame us. When we read of the longed-for smile being kissed by such a lover, this one, who never shall be divided from me, kissed my mouth all trembling. Gallehaut was the book, and he who wrote it.[1] That day we read no farther in it."

139. While the one spirit said this, the other was so weeping that through pity I swooned as if I had been dying, and fell as a dead body falls.

CANTO VI

1. AT the return of my mind, which had closed itself before the pity of these two kinsfolk, that wholly confounded me with sadness,

I see around me new torments and new tormented souls wherever I move, and wherever I turn, and wherever I gaze.

7. I am in the third circle, that of the eternal, accursed, cold, and heavy rain: its rule and quality are never new. Coarse hail, and dark water, and snow pour down through the tenebrous air; the earth which receives them stinks. Cerberus, a cruel and strange beast, with three throats barks dogwise above the people that are here submerged. He has red eyes, a greasy and black beard, and a big belly, and paws armed with nails: he claws the spirits, bites, and rends them. The rain makes them howl like dogs; of one of their sides they make a screen for the other; the wretched profane ones[2] often turn themselves.

22. When Cerberus, the great worm, observed us, he opened his mouths, and showed his fangs to us; not a limb had he that he held still. And my Leader opened wide his hands, took some earth, and with full fists threw it into his ravenous gullets. As is the dog that baying craves, and becomes quiet when he bites his food, and is intent and struggles only to devour it, such became those filthy faces of the demon Cerberus, who so thunders at the souls that they would fain be deaf.

34. We were passing over the shades whom the heavy rain subdues, and were setting our feet upon their vain show which seems a body. They all of them were lying on the ground, except one which raised itself to sit, soon as it saw us passing in front. "O thou who art led through this Hell," it said to me, "recognize me, if thou canst; thou wast made before I was unmade." And I to it: "The anguish which thou hast, perchance withdraws thee from my memory, so that it seems not that I ever saw thee. But tell me who thou art, that art set in a place so woeful, and with such a punishment, that if any other be greater, none is so displeasing."

49. And he to me: "Thy city which is so full of envy that already the sack runs over, held me in it, in the bright life. You, citizens, called me Ciacco;[3] for the pernicious fault of gluttony, as thou seest, I am broken by the rain: and I, wretched soul, am not alone, for all these en-

---

[1] In the Romance, it was Gallehaut that prevailed on Guenever to give a kiss to Lancelot.

[2] Cf. Philippians, 3. 19.
[3] Ciacco, an abbreviation of Jacopo, seems, in popular speech, to have been the term for *hog*.

dure like punishment for like fault": and he spoke not a word more. I answered him: "Ciacco, thy distress so weighs upon me, that it invites me to weeping; but tell me, if thou knowest, to what will come the citizens of the divided city; if any one in it is just; and tell me the cause why such great discord has assailed it."

64. And he to me: "After long contention they will come to blood, and the sylvan party will chase out the other with much injury. Then afterwards within three suns it behoves that this shall fall, and the other surmount by means of the force of a certain one who just now is tacking. It will hold high its front long time, keeping the other under heavy weights, however it may lament and be shamed thereat. There are two just men, but they are not heeded there; Pride, Envy, and Avarice are the three sparks that have inflamed their hearts."[1] Here he made ending of the grievous sound.

77. And I to him: "I would that thou instruct me further, and that of more speech thou make a gift to me. Farinata and Tegghiaio who were so worthy, Jacopo Rusticucci, Arrigo, and Mosca, and the others who set their minds on well-doing, tell me where they are, and make me to know of them, for great desire urges me to learn if Heaven sweeten them, or Hell envenom them."

85. And he: "They are among the blacker souls: different sin weighs them down toward the bottom; if thou descend so far, thou mayst see them. But when thou shalt be in the sweet world I pray thee that thou bring me to the memory of others: more I say not to thee, and more I answer thee not." Thereon he twisted his straight eyes awry, looked at me a little, and then bent his head, and fell with it level with the other blind.

94. And the Leader said to me: "He rouses up no more on this side the sound of the angelic trump. When the hostile Power shall come, each one will find again his dismal tomb, will resume his flesh and his shape, will hear that which through eternity reverberates."

[1] This prophecy relates to the dissensions of the Whites and the Blacks by which Florence was rent. The "sylvan party" was that of the Whites, who were mainly Ghibellines. By the "one who just now is tacking" Dante probably refers to Pope Boniface VIII. In the overthrow of the Whites Dante's own fortunes were involved.

100. Thus we passed along with slow steps through the foul mixture of the shades and of the rain, touching a little on the future life; wherefore I said: "Master, these torments will they increase after the great Sentence, or be less, or will they be just as burning?" And he to me: "Return to thy science,[2] which declares that in proportion the thing is more perfect the more it feels the good, and so the pain. Though this accursed folk never can attain to true perfection, it expects thereafter to be more than now."

112. We took a circling course along that road, speaking far more than I repeat; and came to the point where the descent is. Here we found Pluto, the great enemy.

CANTO VII

1. *"Pape Satan, pape Satan aleppe,"* began Pluto with his clucking voice. And that gentle Sage, who knew everything, said to comfort me: "Let not thy fear hurt thee; for, whatever power he have, he shall not take from thee the descent of this rock." Then he turned to that swollen lip and said: "Be silent, accursed wolf![3] consume thyself inwardly with thine own rage: not without cause is this going to the depth; it is willed on high, there where Michael wrought the vengeance for the proud rape." As sails swollen by the wind fall in a heap when the mast snaps, so fell to earth the cruel wild-beast.

16. Thus we descended into the fourth hollow, taking more of the woeful bank which insacks the evil of the whole universe. Ah, justice of God! who heaps up so many new travails and penalties as I saw? And why does our guilt so ruin us? As does the wave, yonder upon Charybdis, which is broken on that which it encounters, so needs must here the people counterdance.

25. Here I saw many more people than elsewhere, both on the one side and the other, with great howls rolling weights by force of chest. They struck against each other, and then there each wheeled round, rolling back, crying: "Why holdest thou?" and "Why flingest thou away?" Thus they turned through the dark circle on either hand to the opposite point, still crying out at each other their opprobrious

[2] The teaching of Aristotle; see *Ethics*, x. 4.
[3] Cf. *Hell*, i. 49, and *Purgatory*, xx. 10.

measure; then each wheeled round, when he had come through his half circle to the other joust.

36. And I, who had my heart as it were pierced through, said: "My Master, now declare to me what folk this is, and if all these tonsured ones on our left were clerks."

40. And he to me: "Each and all of these were so asquint in mind in the first life that they made no spending in it with due measure. Clearly enough their voice bays it forth, when they come to the two points of the circle where the contrary fault divides them. These were clerks who have no hairy covering on their heads, and Popes and Cardinals, in whom avarice practices its excess."

49. And I: "Master, among such as these I ought surely to recognize some who were polluted with these evils."

52. And he to me: "Thou harborest a vain thought; the undiscerning life that made them foul now makes them dim to all discernment. Forever will they come to the two buttings; these will rise from the sepulchre with closed fist, and these with shorn hair. Ill-giving and ill-keeping have taken from them the beautiful world, and set them to this scuffle; what that is, I adorn not words for it. Now, son, thou canst see the brief jest of the goods that are committed to Fortune, for which the human race struggle with each other; for all the gold that is beneath the moon, or that ever was, could not of these weary souls make a single one repose."

67. "Master," said I to him, "now tell me further, this Fortune, on which thou touchest to me, what is it, which has the goods of the world so in its clutches?"

70. And he to me: "O foolish creatures, how great is that ignorance which harms you! I would have thee now receive my opinion concerning her. He whose wisdom transcends all, made the heavens, and gave them their guides, so that every part shines on every part, distributing equally the light. In like wise for the splendors of the world, He ordained a general ministress and guide, who should from time to time transfer the vain goods from race to race, and from one blood to another, beyond the resistance of human wit. Wherefore one race rules, and another languishes, pursuant to her

judgment, which is hidden like the snake in the grass. Your wisdom has no withstanding of her: she foresees, judges, and pursues her reign, as theirs the other gods. Her permutations have no truce; necessity compels her to be swift, so often comes he who obtains a turn. This is she who is so set upon the cross, even by those who ought to give her praise, giving her blame amiss and ill report. But she is blessed and hears this not: with the other Primal Creatures glad she turns her sphere, and blessed she rejoices. Now let us descend at once to greater woe: already every star is sinking that was rising when I set out, and too long stay is forbidden."

100. We crossed the circle to the other bank, above a fount that bubbles up and pours out through a trench which proceeds from it. The water was far darker than perse; and we, in company with the dusky waves, entered down through a strange way. This dismal little stream, when it has descended to the foot of the malign gray slopes, makes a marsh that is named Styx. And I, who was standing intent to gaze, saw muddy people in that swamp, all naked and with look of hurt. They were smiting each other, not with hand only, but with the head, with the chest, and with the feet, mangling one another piecemeal with their teeth.

115. The good Master said: "Son, now thou seest the souls of those whom anger overcame; and also I will that thou believe for certain that under the water are folk who sigh, and make this water bubble at the surface, as thine eye tells thee wherever it turns. Fixed in the slime, they say: 'Sullen were we in the sweet air that is gladdened by the Sun, bearing within ourselves the sluggish fume; now we are sullen in the black mire.' This hymn they gurgle in their throats, for they cannot speak with entire words."

127. Thus we circled a great arc of the foul fen, between the dry bank and the slough, with eyes turned on those who guzzle the mire. We came at length to the foot of a tower.

CANTO VIII

1. I SAY, continuing, that, long before we were at the foot of the high tower, our eyes went upward to its top by reason of two flamelets that we saw set there, while another was giving sig-

nal back from so far off that the eye could hardly catch it. And I turned me to the Sea of all wisdom; I said: "This one, what says it? and what answers that other fire? and who are they that made it?" And he to me: "Upon the turbid waves already thou mayst discern that which is expected, if the fume of the marsh hide it not from thee."

13. Bowstring never urged arrow from itself that ran so swift a course through the air, as a little vessel which at that instant I saw coming through the water toward us, under the guidance of a single boatman, who cried out: "Now art thou arrived, fell soul?"

19. "Phlegyas,[1] Phlegyas, this time thou criest out in vain," said my Lord, "thou shalt not have us longer than only while crossing the slough." As one who listens to some great deception that has been practiced on him, and then repines thereat, such became Phlegyas in his gathered anger.

25. My Leader descended into the bark and then he made me enter after him, and only when I was in did it seem laden. Soon as my Leader and I were in the boat, the antique prow goes its way, cutting more of the water than it is wont with others.

31. While we were running through the dead channel, one full of mud set himself before me, and said: "Who art thou that comest before thine hour?" And I to him: "If I come, I do not stay; but who art thou that art become so foul?" He answered: "Thou seest that I am one who laments." And I to him, "With lamenting and with sorrow, accursed spirit, do thou remain, for I know thee, though thou be all filthy." Then he stretched to the boat both his hands, whereat the wary Master thrust him back, saying: "Away there, with the other dogs!"

43. Then he clasped my neck with his arms, kissed my face, and said: "Indignant soul, blessed be she who bore thee! That was an arrogant person in the world; no goodness is there that adorns his memory; so is his shade furious here. How many now up there are held great kings who shall lie here like swine in mire, leaving of themselves horrible dispraises!"

52. And I: "Master, I should much like to see him soused in this broth before we depart from the lake." And he to me: "Before the shore lets itself be seen by thee thou shalt be satisfied; it is fitting that thou enjoy such a desire." A little after this I saw such rending of him by the muddy folk that I still praise God therefor, and thank Him for it. All cried: "At Filippo Argenti!" and the raging Florentine spirit turned upon himself with his teeth. Here we left him; so that I tell no more of him.

65. But on my ears a wailing smote, whereat forward intent I unbar my eye. And the good Master said: "Now, son, the city draws near that is named Dis,[2] with its heavy citizens, with its great throng." And I: "Master, already in the valley therewithin I clearly discern its mosques vermilion, as if they were issuing from fire." And he said to me: "The eternal fire that blazes there within displays them red as thou seest in this nether Hell."

76. We at last arrived within the deep ditches which encompass that disconsolate city. The walls seemed to me to be of iron. Not without first making a great circuit did we come to a place where the boatman loudly shouted to us: "Get ye out, here is the entrance."

82. Upon the gates I saw more than a thousand of those rained down from heaven who angrily were saying: "Who is this, that without death goes through the realm of the dead folk?" And my wise Master made a sign of wishing to speak secretly with them. Then they shut in a little their great scorn, and said: "Come thou alone, and let him be gone who so boldly entered on this realm. Alone let him return on the mad path: let him try if he can; for thou, who hast escorted him through so dark a region, shalt remain here."

94. Think, Reader, if I was discomforted at the sound of the accursed words, for I did not believe ever to return hither.

97. "O my dear Leader, who more than seven times hast restored to me security, and drawn me from deep peril that stood confronting me, leave me not," said I, "thus undone; and, if the passing farther onward be denied us, let us together quickly retrace our steps." And that Lord who had led me thither said to me: "Fear not, for no one can take from us our

---

[1] Phlegyas, a king of the Lapithae, enraged with Apollo for the violation of his daughter, set fire, in his impious wrath, to the temple, at Delphi, of the god, who slew him with his arrows.

[2] Cf. *Aeneid*, vi. 127.

passage, by Such an one is it given to us. But here await me, and comfort thy dejected spirit and feed on good hope, for I will not leave thee in the nether world."

109. So the sweet Father goes away, and here abandons me, and I remain in suspense; and yes and no contend within my head. I could not hear what he proffered to them, but he had not staid there with them long, when vying with each other they ran back within. These our adversaries closed the gates on the breast of my Lord, who remained without, and turned back to me with slow steps. He had his eyes upon the ground, and his brows were shorn of all hardihood, and he was saying with sighs: "Who has denied to me the houses of woe?"

121. And he said to me: "Because I am wroth, be not thou dismayed, for I shall win the contest, whoever circle round within for the defence. This their insolence is not new, for of old they used it at a less secret gate, which still is found without a bolt.[1] Above it thou didst see the dead inscription; and already, on this side of it, is descending the steep, passing without escort through the circles, One such that by him the city shall be opened to us."

CANTO IX

1. THAT color which cowardice painted outwardly on me when I saw my Guide turn back, repressed more speedily his own new color. He stopped attentive, like a man that listens, for the eye could not lead him far through the black air, and through the dense fog.

7. "Yet it shall be for us to win the fight," began he, "unless—— Such an one offered herself to us.[2] Oh how long it is to me till Another arrive here!"

10. I saw well how he covered up the beginning with the rest that came after, which were words different from the first; but nevertheless his speech gave me fear, because I drew his broken phrase perchance to a worse meaning than it held.

16. "Into this depth of the dismal shell does any one ever descend from the first grade who has for penalty only hope cut off?"[3]

19. This question I put, and he answered

[1] A like resistance had been offered to Christ on his descent to Hell.
[2] Beatrice.
[3] See *Hell*, iv. 41.

me: "Seldom it happens that any one of us makes the journey on which I am going. It is true that another time I was down here, conjured by that cruel Erichtho[4] who was wont to call back shades into their bodies. Short while had my flesh been bare of me, when she made me enter within that wall, in order to draw thence a spirit of the circle of Judas. That is the lowest place, and the darkest, and the farthest from the Heaven which encircles all. I know the road well; therefore assure thyself. This marsh which breathes out the great stench girds round the woeful city wherein now we cannot enter without anger."

34. And more he said, but I have it not in mind, because my eye had wholly attracted me toward the high tower with the ruddy summit, where in an instant were uprisen suddenly three infernal Furies, stained with blood, who had the limbs of women and their action, and were girt with greenest hydras. They had for hair little serpents and cerastes,[5] wherewith their savage brows were bound.

43. And he, who well recognized the handmaids of the queen[6] of the eternal lamentation, said to me: "Behold the fell Erinnyes; this is Megaera on the left side, she who wails on the right is Alecto, Tisiphone is in the middle": and therewith he was silent.

49. With her nails each was tearing her breast; they were beating themselves with their hands, and crying out so loud that I pressed close to the Poet through dread. "Let Medusa come, so we will make him of stone," they all said, looking downward; "ill was it we avenged not on Theseus his assault."[7]

55. "Turn thee round backwards, and keep thy sight closed, for if the Gorgon show herself, and thou shouldst see her, no return upward would there ever be."[8] Thus said the

[4] Erichtho, a sorceress of Thessaly, at the desire of Sextus, the son of Pompey, on the night before the battle of Pharsalia, conjured up one of his dead soldiers to foretell its issue.
[5] Horned snakes. See *Paradise Lost*, x. 525.
[6] Proserpine.
[7] Theseus, failing to rescue Proserpine, was kept in the lower world till delivered by Hercules, in defiance of the power of Hades.
[8] Medusa, who should turn Dante to stone, that is, should harden his heart to the influences of the Divine grace, may be the type of the sin of *desperatio*, despair of the mercy of God. See Aquinas, *Summa Theologica*, Part II-II, Q 20, A 3.

Master, and he himself turned me, and trusted not to my hands but with his own he also blinded me.

61. O ye who have sound understandings, regard the doctrine that is hidden under the veil of the strange verses!

64. And already across the turbid waves was coming a crash of a sound full of terror, at which both the shores trembled. Not otherwise it was than of a wind, impetuous by reason of the opposing heats, which strikes the forest, and without any stay shatters the branches, beats down and carries them away; forward, laden with dust, it goes superb, and makes the wild beasts and the shepherds fly.

73. My eyes he loosed, and said, "Now direct the nerve of sight across that ancient scum, there yonder where that fume is most bitter."

76. As the frogs before the hostile snake all vanish through the water, till each huddles on the ground, I saw more than a thousand destroyed souls flying thus before One, who on foot was passing over the Styx with soles unwet. From his face he was removing that thick air, waving his left hand oft before him, and only with that trouble he seemed weary. Well I perceived that he was a messenger from Heaven, and I turned me to the Master, and he made sign that I should stand quiet and bow down to him. Ah, how full of disdain he seemed to me! He came to the gate and with a little rod he opened it, for it had no resistance.

91. "O outcasts from Heaven! folk despised," began he upon the horrible threshold, "whence is this overweening harbored in you? Wherefore do ye kick against that Will from which its end can never be cut short, and which many a time has increased your woe? What avails it to butt against the fates? Your Cerberus, if ye remember well, still bears his chin and his throat peeled therefor."¹ Then he turned back over the filthy road, and said no word to us, but wore the semblance of a man whom other care constrains and stings, than that of him who is before him.

104. Then we moved our feet toward the city, secure after his holy words. We entered there within without any strife: and I, who had desire to observe the condition which such a stronghold locks in, soon as I was within,

send my eye round about, and I see on every hand a great plain full of woe and of cruel torment.

112. As at Arles, where the Rhone stagnates, as at Pola, near the Quarnaro which shuts Italy in and bathes her borders, the sepulchres make all the place uneven; so did they here on every side, save that the manner was more bitter here; for among the tombs flames were scattered, by which they were so wholly heated that no art requires iron more so. All their lids were lifted; and such dire laments were issuing forth from them as truly seemed of wretches and of sufferers.

124. And I: "Master, who are these folk that, buried within those coffers, make themselves heard with their woeful sighs?" And he to me: "Here are the heresiarchs with their followers of every sect, and the tombs are much more laden than thou thinkest. Like with like is buried here, and the monuments are more and less hot."

132. And after he had turned to the right hand, we passed between the torments and the high battlements.

CANTO X

1. Now, along a solitary path between the wall of the city and the torments, my Master goes on, and I behind his shoulders.

4. "O virtue supreme," I began, "that through the impious circles dost turn me according to thy pleasure, speak to me and satisfy my desires. The folk that are lying in the sepulchres, might they be seen? all the lids are now lifted, and no one keeps guard."

10. And he to me: "All will be locked in when they shall return here from Jehoshaphat with the bodies which they have left on earth.² Upon this side Epicurus with all his followers, who make the soul mortal with the body, have their burial place. Therefore as to the request that thou makest of me, thou shalt soon be satisfied here within; and also as to the desire of which thou art silent to me." And I: "Good Leader, I hold not my heart hidden from thee except in order to speak little; and not only now hast thou disposed me to this."

22. "O Tuscan, who goest thy way alive through the city of fire, speaking thus mod-

¹ See *Aeneid*, vi. 395-6.

² Cf. Joel, 3. 2, 12.

estly, may it please thee to stop in this place. Thy mode of speech makes manifest that thou art native of that noble fatherland to which perchance I was too molestful." Suddenly this sound issued from one of the coffers, wherefore in fear I drew a little nearer to my Leader. And he said to me: "Turn thee: what art thou doing? See there Farinata who has risen erect; all from the girdle upwards wilt thou see him."[1]

34. I had already fixed my face on his, and he was straightening himself up with breast and front as though he had Hell in great scorn. And the bold and ready hands of my Leader pushed me among the sepulchres to him, saying: "Let thy words be clear."

40. When I was at the foot of his tomb, he looked at me a little, and then, as though disdainful, asked me, "Who were thy ancestors?" I, who was desirous to obey, concealed it not from him, but disclosed it all to him; whereon he raised up his brows a little, then said: "They were fiercely adverse to me and to my forefathers and to my party, so that at two times I scattered them." "If they were driven out, they returned from every side," replied I to him, "both the one and the other time, but yours have not learned well that art."

52. Then there arose to sight alongside of this one, a shade uncovered far as to the chin: I think that it had risen on its knees. It looked round about me, as if it had desire to see if another were with me, but when its expectancy was quite spent, weeping it said: "If through this blind prison thou goest by reason of loftiness of genius, where is my son? and why is he not with thee?" And I to him: "I come not of myself; he who waits yonder is leading me through here, whom perchance your Guido had in disdain."[2]

64. His words and the mode of the punishment had already read to me the name of this one; wherefore my answer was so full.

67. Suddenly straightening up, he cried: "How didst thou say, 'he had'? lives he not still? does not the sweet light strike his eyes?" When he became aware of some delay that I

made before answering, he fell again supine, and appeared no more outside.

73. But that other magnanimous one, at whose instance I had stayed, changed not aspect, nor moved his neck, nor bent his side. "And if," he said, continuing his first discourse, "they have ill learned that art, it torments me more than this bed. But the face of the Lady who rules here[3] will not be rekindled fifty times ere thou shalt know how much that art weighs. And, so mayest thou return to the sweet world, tell me wherefore is that people so pitiless against my party in its every law?"

85. Thereon I to him: "The rout and the great carnage which colored the Arbia red cause such prayer to be made in our temple." After he had, sighing, shaken his head, "In that I was not alone," he said, "nor surely without cause would I have moved with the others; but I was alone there, where it was agreed by every one to destroy Florence, he who defended her with open face."

94. "Ah! so may your seed ever have repose," I prayed to him, "loose for me that knot, which has here entangled my judgment. It seems, if I hear rightly, that ye see in advance that which time is bringing with it, and as to the present have another way." "We see," he said, "like him who has bad light, the things that are far from us, so much the supreme Ruler still shines on us; when they draw near, or are, our intelligence is wholly vain, and, if another report not to us, we know nothing of your human state; wherefore thou canst comprehend that our knowledge will be utterly dead from that moment when the gate of the future shall be closed."

109. Then, as compunctious for my fault, I said: "Now, then, you will tell to that fallen one that his son is still conjoined with the living, and if just now I was dumb to answer, make him know that I was so because I was already thinking in the error which you have solved for me."[4]

115. And now my Master was recalling me, wherefore more hastily I prayed the spirit that he would tell me who was with him. He said

---

[1] Farinata degli Uberti was the head of the Ghibelline party in Tuscany for many years, about the middle of the thirteenth century.

[2] Guido Cavalcanti, Dante's first friend, was charged with the same sin of unbelief as his father.

[3] Proserpine, identified with Hecate, and hence with the Moon.

[4] Guido Cavalcanti died in August, 1300; his death was an event too near at hand at the time of Dante's journey to be known to his father.

to me: "Here I lie with more than a thousand; here within is the second Frederick[1] and the Cardinal,[2] and of the others I am silent."

121. Thereon he hid himself; and I turned my steps toward the ancient Poet, reflecting on that speech which seemed hostile to me. He moved on, and then, thus going, he said to me: "Why art thou so disturbed?" And I satisfied him as to his question. "Let thy memory preserve that which thou hast heard against thyself," that Sage bade me, "and now give heed here—" and he raised his finger: "When thou shalt be in presence of the sweet radiance of her whose beautiful eye sees everything, from her thou shalt learn the journey of thy life." Then to the left he turned his step.

134. We left the wall, and went toward the middle by a path that strikes into a valley which even up there was making its stench displeasing.

CANTO XI

1. Upon the edge of a high bank which great rocks broken in a circle made, we came above a more cruel pen. And here, because of the horrible excess of the stench which the deep abyss throws out, we drew aside behind the lid of a great tomb, whereon I saw an inscription which said: "I hold Pope Anastasius, whom Photinus drew from the right way."[3]

10. "It behoves that our descent be slow, so that the sense may first accustom itself a little to the dismal blast, and then it will be of no concern." Thus the Master, and I said to him: "Some compensation do thou find that the time pass not lost." And he: "Behold, I am thinking of that. My son, within these rocks," he began then to say, "are three lesser circles from grade to grade, like those which thou art leaving. All are full of accursed spirits; but, in order that hereafter the sight alone may suffice thee, hear how and wherefore they are in bonds.

22. "Of every wickedness that acquires hate in heaven injury is the end, and every such end afflicts others either by force or by fraud. But

because fraud is an evil peculiar to man, it more displeases God; and therefore the fraudulent are the lower, and woe assails them more.

28. "The first circle[4] is wholly of the violent: but because violence is done to three persons, it is divided and constructed in three rounds. To God, to one's self, to one's neighbor may violence be done; I say to them and to their belongings, as thou shalt hear with plain discourse. By violence, death and grievous wounds are inflicted on one's neighbor; and on his substance ruins, burnings, and harmful extortions. Wherefore the first round torments homicides, and every one who smites wrongfully, all despoilers and plunderers, in various troops.

40. "Man may lay violent hands upon himself and on his goods; and, therefore, in the second round it behoves that he repent without avail who deprives himself of your world, gambles away and dissipates his property, and laments there where he ought to be joyous.

46. "Violence may be done to the Deity, by denying and blaspheming Him in the heart, and by contemning nature and His bounty: and therefore the smallest round seals with its signet both Sodom and Cahors,[5] and him who, contemning God, speaks from his heart.

52. "The fraud, by which every conscience is stung, man may practice on one that confides in him, or on one that has no stock of confidence. This latter mode seems to destroy only the bond of love which nature makes; wherefore in the second circle nest hypocrisy, flatteries, and he who bewitches, falsity, robbery, and simony, panders, barrators, and such like filth.

61. "By the other mode that love is forgotten which nature makes and that which is thereafter added, whereby special confidence is created. Hence, in the smallest circle, where is the point of the universe, upon which Dis sits, whoso betrays is consumed forever."

67. And I: "Master, full clearly thy discourse proceeds, and full well divides this pit, and the people that possess it; but, tell me, they of the fat marsh, and they whom the wind drives, and they whom the rain beats, and they who encounter with such rough tongues, why are

[1] Frederick II, Emperor from 1212 to 1250.
[2] Ottaviano degli Ubaldini, a fierce Ghibelline.
[3] A confused tradition charged Pope Anastasius II (496-498), with having been led by Photinus of Thessalonica into heretical opinions concerning the divinity of Christ.
[4] The first circle below, the seventh in the order of Hell.
[5] Cahors, a town in southern France, noted in the Middle Ages for the usurious practice of its inhabitants.

they not punished within the ruddy city[1] if God be wroth with them? and if he be not so, why are they in such plight?"

76. And he said to me: "Why does thy wit so wander beyond its wont? or thy mind, where else is it gazing? Dost thou not remember those words with which thy Ethics treats in full of the three dispositions that Heaven abides not; incontinence, wickedness, and mad bestiality, and how incontinence less offends God, and incurs less blame?[2] If thou consider well this doctrine, and bring to mind who are those that up above suffer punishment outside, thou wilt see clearly why they are divided from these felons, and why less wroth the divine vengeance hammers them."

91. "O Sun that healest every troubled vision, thou dost content me so, when thou solvest, that doubt, not less than knowledge, pleases me; yet turn thee a little back," said I, "to where thou sayest that usury offends the Divine Goodness, and loose the knot."

97. "Philosophy," he said to me, "points out to him who understands it, not only in one part alone, how Nature takes her course from the Divine Intellect and from Its art. And if thou note thy Physics[3] well thou wilt find, after not many pages, that your art follows her so far as it can, as the disciple does the master, so that your art is as it were grandchild of God. From these two, if thou bring to mind Genesis at its beginning,[4] it behoves mankind to gain their life and to advance. But because the usurer holds another way, he contemns Nature in herself, and in her follower, since upon other thing he sets his hope. But follow me now, for to go on pleases me; for the Fishes are quivering on the horizon, and the Wain lies quite over Caurus,[5] and far onwards is the descent of the steep."

CANTO XII

1. THE place where we came to descend the bank was alpine, and, because also of what was there, such that every eye would be shy of it.

4. As is that downfall which, on this side of Trent, struck the Adige on its flank, either by earthquake or through failure of support,—for from the top of the mountain, whence it started, to the plain, the cliff has so tumbled down that it might afford some path to one that were above—such was the descent of that ravine: and on the edge of the broken chasm was outstretched the infamy of Crete, that was conceived in the false cow. And when he saw us he bit himself even as one whom wrath rends inwardly. My Sage cried out toward him: "Perchance thou believest that here is the Duke of Athens,[6] who up in the world gave thee thy death? Get thee gone, beast, for this one does not come instructed by thy sister, but he goes to behold your punishments."

22. As is that bull which breaks his halter at the instant he has just received his mortal stroke, and cannot go, but plunges this way and that, I saw the Minotaur do the like.

26. And he watchful cried: "Run to the pass; while he is in a rage it is well that thou descend." So we took our way down over the discharge of those stones, which often moved under my feet because of the novel burden.

31. I was going along thinking, and he said: "Thou art thinking perhaps on this ruin which is guarded by that bestial wrath which I just now quelled. Now I would have thee know that the other time when I descended here below into the nether hell, this cliff had not yet fallen. But in truth, if I discern aright, a little ere He came, who levied the great spoil on Dis from the uppermost circle,[7] on all sides the deep foul valley trembled[8] so that I thought the universe felt love whereby, as some believe, the world has oft-times been converted into chaos:[9] and, at that moment, this ancient rock here and elsewhere made such downfall. But fix thine eyes below, for the river of blood is near, in which everyone who does harm by violence to others is boiling."

49. Oh blind cupidity,[10] both guilty and mad, which so spurs us in the short life, and then, in

---

[1] Of Dis.

[2] Cf. Aristotle, *Ethics,* vii. 1.

[3] Cf. Aristotle, *Physics,* ii. 2.

[4] Cf. Genesis, 3. 19.

[5] The sign of the Fishes precedes that of the Ram, and, as the Sun was in the latter sign, the time indicated is about 4, or from 4 to 5 A. M. Caurus, the northwest wind, here stands for that quarter of the heavens.

[6] Cf. *Canterbury Tales*, "The Knight's Tale," 860-62.

[7] See Canto iv. 52-63, *supra.*

[8] Cf. Matthew, 27. 51.

[9] It was the doctrine of Empedocles that Love and Hate were powers to whose conflicting influences the actual condition of the sensible world is due.

[10] See *Paradise*, xv. 3; xxvii. 121; *De Monarchia*, i. 11, 70.

17

52. I saw a broad ditch, according as my Guide had said, bent in an arc, as that which embraces all the plain. And between the foot of the bank and it, Centaurs were running in a file, armed with arrows, as they were wont in the world to go to the chase. Seeing us descending, each stopped, and from the troop three detached themselves, with bows and darts first selected. And one cried from afar: "To what torment are ye coming, ye who descend the slope? Tell it from there; if not, I draw the bow." My Master said: "We will make answer unto Chiron near by there: to thy hurt was thy will ever thus hasty."

67. Then he touched me, and said: "That is Nessus, who died for the beautiful Dejanira, and himself wrought vengeance for himself; and that one in the middle, who is gazing on his own breast, is the great Chiron who nurtured Achilles; that other is Pholus, who was so full of wrath. Round about the ditch they go by thousands, shooting with their arrows whatever soul lifts itself from the blood more than its crime has allotted to it."

76. We drew near to those fleet wild beasts. Chiron took a shaft, and with the notch put his beard back upon his jaws. When he had thus uncovered his great mouth he said to his companions: "Are ye aware that the one behind moves what he touches? thus are not wont to do the feet of the dead." And my good Leader, who was now at his breast, where the two natures are conjoined, replied: "He is indeed alive, and thus alone it behoves me to show him the dark valley: necessity leads him and not delight. One who withdrew from singing hallelujah committed unto me this new duty; he is no robber, nor I a fraudulent soul. But, by that Power through which I move my steps along so savage a road, give to us one of thine, to whom we may keep close, who may show us where the ford is, and may carry this one on his back, who is not a spirit that can go through the air."

97. Chiron turned upon his right breast, and said to Nessus: "Turn, and guide them thus, and if another troop encounter you, make it give way."

100. We moved on with the trusty escort along the edge of the crimson boiling, in which the boiled were uttering loud shrieks. I saw folk under it up to the brow, and the great Centaur said: "These are tyrants who laid hold on blood and plunder. Here they bewail their merciless misdeeds: here is Alexander, and cruel Dionysius who made Sicily have woeful years. And that forehead which has such black hair is Azzolino,[1] and that other who is blond is Opizzo of Este,[2] who of a truth was slain by his stepson up there in the world."

113. Then I turned me to the Poet, and he said: "Let him now be first for thee, and I second." A little further on the Centaur stopped above a folk who far as the throat seemed to come out from that boiling stream. He showed to us at one side a solitary shade, and said: "He cleft, in the bosom of God, the heart that still is honored on the Thames."[3] Then I saw folk, who were holding their heads, and even all their chests, out of the stream; and of these I recognized many. Thus more and more that blood sank down, until it cooked only the feet: and here was our passage of the foss.

127. "As on this hand, thou seest that the boiling stream continually diminishes," said the Centaur, "so I would have thee believe that on this other it lowers its bed more and more, until it comes round again to where it behoves that tyranny should groan. The divine justice here goads that Attila who was a scourge on earth, and Pyrrhus and Sextus; and forever milks the tears which with the boiling it unlocks from Rinier of Corneto and from Rinier Pazzo,[4] who made such warfare upon the highways."

139. Then he turned back and repassed the ford.

CANTO XIII

1. NESSUS had not yet reached the yonder bank when we set forward through a wood which was marked by no path. Not green

[1] Azzolino (or Ezzelino) III da Romano, son-in-law of the Emperor Frederick II, and his vicar in northern Italy.
[2] Opizzo II of Este, Marquis of Ferrara. See Canto xviii. 56, *supra; Purgatory*, v. 77.
[3] In 1271, Prince Henry, son of Richard, Earl of Cornwall, was stabbed, during Mass, in the church of St. Sylvester at Viterbo, by Guy of Montfort, to avenge the death of his father, Simon, Earl of Leicester. Henry's heart was placed in a golden cup, on a column, at the head of London Bridge.
[4] Two noted highway robbers.

leaves were there, but of a dusky color, not smooth boughs but gnarled and tangled, not fruits but thorns with poison. Those savage wild-beasts that hold in hate the tilled places between Cecina and Corneto [1] have no thickets so rough or so dense.

10. Here the foul Harpies make their nests, who chased the Trojans from the Strophades with dismal announcement of future calamity.[2] They have broad wings, and human necks and faces, feet with claws, and the great belly feathered. They make lament on the strange trees.

16. And the good Master began to say to me: "Before thou enterest farther, know that thou art in the Second Round,[3] and wilt be, till thou shalt come to the horrible sand. Therefore look well around, and so shalt thou see things that would take credence from my speech."

22. I heard wailings uttered on every side, and I saw no one who made them, wherefore, all bewildered, I stopped. I believe that he believed that I believed that all these voices issued from amid those trunks from people who because of us had hidden themselves. Therefore said the Master: "If thou break off any twig from one of these plants, the thoughts thou hast will all be cut short."

31. Then I stretched my hand a little forward and plucked a little branch from a great thorn-bush, and its trunk cried out: "Why dost thou break me?" When it had become dark with blood it began again to cry: "Why dost thou tear me? hast thou not any spirit of pity? Men we were, and now we are become stocks; truly thy hand ought to be more pitiful had we been souls of serpents."

40. As from a green log that is burning at one of its ends, and drips from the other, and hisses with the air that is escaping, so from that broken twig came out words and blood together; whereon I let the tip fall, and stood like a man who is afraid.

46. "If he had been able to believe before," replied my Sage, "O injured soul, what he has seen only in my verse,[4] he would not have stretched out his hand on thee; but the incredible thing made me prompt him to an act which weighs on me myself. But tell him who thou

wast, so that, by way of some amends, he may refresh thy fame in the world above, whereto it is allowed him to return."

55. And the trunk:[5] "Thou dost so allure me with sweet speech, that I cannot be silent, and may it not burden you, that I am enticed to talk a little. I am he who held both the keys of the heart of Frederick, and who turned them, locking and unlocking so softly, that from his secrets I kept almost every one. Fidelity so great I bore to the glorious office, that I lost my sleep and my pulse thereby. The harlot, that never from the abode of Cæsar turned her strumpet eyes,—the common death and vice of courts,—inflamed all minds against me, and they, inflamed, did so inflame Augustus that my glad honors turned to dismal sorrows. My mind, through scornful disgust, thinking to escape scorn by death, made me unjust toward my just self. By the strange roots of this tree I swear to you, that I never broke faith to my lord who was so worthy of honor. And if one of you returns to the world, let him comfort my memory which yet lies prostrate from the blow that envy gave it."

79. He paused a little, and then, "Since he is silent," said the Poet to me, "lose not the hour, but, if more please thee, speak and enquire of him." Whereon I to him: "Do thou ask him further of what thou thinkest may satisfy me, for I cannot, such great pity fills my heart."

85. Therefore he began again: "So may this man do for thee freely that which thy speech prays for, spirit incarcerate, may it please thee yet to tell us how the soul is bound within these knots, and tell us, if thou canst, if from such limbs any soul is ever loosed."

91. Then the trunk puffed strongly, and soon the wind was changed into this voice: "Briefly shall ye be answered. When the ferocious soul departs from the body wherefrom itself has torn itself, Minos sends it to the seventh gulf. It falls into the wood, and no part is chosen for it, but where fortune flings it there it sprouts like a grain of spelt; it rises in a sapling and to a wild plant: the Harpies, feeding then upon its leaves, give pain, and to the pain a window. Like the others we shall go for our spoils, but

---

[1] Respectively a river and a town in Tuscany.
[2] See *Aeneid*, iii. 210-257.
[3] Of the Seventh Circle.
[4] See *Aeneid*, iii. 19ff.

[5] The spirit who speaks is Pier delle Vigne, the private secretary and confidential minister of Frederick II. Cf. Canto x. 110, *supra*.

not, however, that any one may revest himself with them, for it is not just for one to have that of which he deprives himself. Hither shall we drag them, and through the melancholy wood shall our bodies be suspended, each on the thorn-tree of its molested shade."

109. We were still attentive to the trunk, believing that it might wish to say more to us, when we were surprised by an uproar, like one who perceives the wild boar and the chase coming toward his post, and hears the beasts and the crash of the branches. And behold, two on the left hand, naked and scratched, flying so hard that they broke through every barrier of the wood. The one in front was shouting: "Haste now! haste thee, Death!" and the other, who seemed to himself too slow: "Lano, thy legs were not so nimble at the jousts of the Toppo";[1] and since perhaps his breath was failing, of himself and of a bush he made a group. Behind them the wood was full of black bitches, ravenous and running like greyhounds that had been slipped from the leash. On him who had squatted they set their teeth and tore him piecemeal, then carried off those woeful limbs.

130. My Guide then took me by the hand, and led me to the bush, which was weeping in vain through its bleeding fractures. "O Jacomo of Sant' Andrea," it was saying, "what has it vantaged thee to make of me a screen? What blame have I for thy wicked life?" When the Master had stopped above it, he said: "Who wast thou, who through so many wounds blowest forth with blood a woeful speech?"

139. And he to us: "O souls that are arrived to see the shameful ravage that has thus disjoined my twigs from me, collect them at the foot of the wretched bush. I was of the city which for the Baptist changed her first patron;[2] wherefore he will always make her sorrowful with his art. And were it not that at the passage of the Arno some semblance of him still remains, those citizens who afterwards rebuilt it upon the ashes that were left by Attila[3] would

have done the work in vain.[4] I made a gibbet for myself of my own house."

CANTO XIV

1. BECAUSE the love of my native place constrained me, I gathered up the scattered twigs and gave them back to him who was already faint-voiced.

4. Thence we came to the confine, where the second round is divided from the third, and where a horrible mode of justice is seen.

7. To make the new things clearly manifest, I say that we had reached a plain which rejects every plant from its bed. The woeful wood is a garland round about it, even as the dismal foss to that. Here, on the very edge, we stayed our steps. The floor was an arid and dense sand, not made in other fashion than that which of old was trodden by the feet of Cato.[5]

16. O vengeance of God, how much shouldst thou be feared by every one who reads that which was manifest to my eyes!

19. I saw many flocks of naked souls, that were all weeping very miserably, and divers law seemed imposed upon them. Some folk were lying supine on the ground, some were seated all crouched up, and others were going about continually.[6] Those who were going around were the more numerous, and those the less so who were lying down under the torment, but they had their tongues more loosed by the pain.

28. Over all the sand, with a slow falling, were raining down dilated flakes of fire, as of snow on alps without a wind. As the flames which Alexander in those hot parts of India saw falling upon his host, unbroken to the ground, wherefore he took care to trample the soil by his troops, because the vapor was better extinguished while it was single; so was descending the eternal heat whereby the sand was kindled, like tinder beneath the steel, for doubling of the dole. The dance of the wretched hands was ever without repose, now there, now here, shak-

---

[1] Lano was slain in flight at the defeat of the Sienese by the Aretines, near the Pieve del Toppo. He and Jacomo were notorious spendthrifts.

[2] The first patron of Florence was Mars; a fragment of a statue of whom stood till 1333 at the head of the Ponte Vecchio. See *Paradise,* xvi. 145-147.

[3] Totila, not Attila, besieged Florence, and, according to false popular tradition, burned it.

[4] Under these words lies a satirical reference to the devotion of the Florentines to money-making. Dante means, says Benvenuto da Imola, "that after Florence gave up Mars, that is, fortitude and valor in arms, and began to worship the Baptist alone, that is, the florin, on which is the figure of the Baptist, they met with misfortune in their wars."

[5] On his march across the Libyan desert.

[6] Cf. Canto xi. 49-51, *supra.*

ing off from them the fresh burning.

43. I began: "Master, thou that overcomest everything, except the obdurate demons, who at the entrance of the gate came out against us, who is that great one that seems not to heed the fire, and lies despiteful and twisted, so that the rain seems not to ripen him?"

49. And that same one[1] who was aware that I was asking my Leader about him, cried out: "Such as I was alive, such am I dead. Though Jove weary out his smith, from whom in wrath he took the sharp thunderbolt wherewith on my last day I was smitten, or though he weary out the others, turn by turn, in Mongibello[2] at the black forge, crying, 'Good Vulcan, help, help!' even as he did at the fight of Phlegra,[3] and hurl on me with all his might, he should not have thereby glad vengeance."

61. Then my Leader spoke with force so great, that I had never heard him so vehement: "O Capaneus, in that thy pride is not extinct, art thou the more punished; no torment save thine own rage would be a pain adequate to thy fury."

67. Then he turned round to me with better look, saying: "That was one of the Seven Kings who besieged Thebes, and he held, and it seems that he holds God in disdain, and it seems that he little prizes Him; but as I said to him, his own despites are very due adornments for his breast. Now come behind me, and take heed still not to set thy feet upon the scorched sand, but keep them always close to the wood."

76. In silence we came to where a little brook, the redness of which still makes me shudder, gushes forth from the wood. As from the Bulicame[4] a rivulet issues, which then the sinful women share among them, so that went down across the sand. Its bed and both its sloping banks were made of stone, and the margins on the side, wherefore I perceived that the crossing was there.

85. "Among all else that I have shown to thee, since we entered through the gate whose

threshold is denied to no one, nothing has been discerned by thine eyes so notable as is the present stream which deadens all the flamelets above it."[5] These words were of my Leader, wherefore I prayed him, that he would bestow on me the food of which he had bestowed on me the desire.

94. "In mid sea lies a wasted land," said he then, "which is named Crete, under whose king the world of old was chaste. A mountain is there which of old was glad with water and with leaves, which is called Ida; now it is desert, like a thing outworn. Rhea chose it of old for the trusty cradle of her little son, and, the better to conceal him when he wailed, caused cries to be made there.[6] Within the mountain a great old man stands upright, who holds his shoulders turned towards Damietta, and gazes at Rome as if his mirror. His head is formed of fine gold, and his arms and breast are pure silver; then far as to the fork he is of brass; from there downward he is all of chosen iron, save that his right foot is of baked earth, and he stands erect on that more than on the other.[7] Every part except the gold is cleft with a fissure that drips tears, which, collected, perforate that cavern. Their course is from rock to rock into this valley; they form Acheron, Styx, and Phlegethon; then their way is down through this narrow channel till, where there is no more descending, they form Cocytus, and what that pool is, thou shalt see; therefore here it is not told."

121. And I to him: "If the present stream flows down thus from our world, why does it appear to us only at this border?"

[5] See Canto xv. 3, infra.

[6] To prevent Saturn from hearing the cries of the infant Jupiter, whom, had he known him to be alive, he would have sought to devour, in order to avert the fulfillment of the prophecy that he would be dethroned by one of his children.

[7] This image is taken directly from the dream of Nebuchadnezzar (Daniel, 2. 31-33). It is the type of the historic life of man, with its back to the past, its face toward Rome—the centre of the actual world. Its upper parts of metal represent the Golden, Silver, Bronze, and Iron ages, according to the fancy of the poets. The two legs are generally interpreted as the symbols of the Empire and the Church; the right leg, on which the image rests the most, being the type of the Church. Its foot of baked earth: possibly may refer to the element of weakness in the papacy from the earthly character of the Popes. The tears of the sinful and suffering generations of man form the rivers of Hell.

[1] Capaneus, one of the seven kings who besieged Thebes. He, having mounted the walls, defied Jupiter, who slew him with a thunderbolt.

[2] Mt. Etna.

[3] The battle between the gods and the giants, in the vale of Phlegra, in Thessaly.

[4] A hot spring near Viterbo, frequented as a bath, the use of a portion of which was assigned to "sinful women."

124. And he to me: "Thou knowest that the place is circular, and though thou art come far, always to the left in descending toward the bottom, thou hast not yet turned through the whole circle; wherefore if a new thing appears to us, it ought not to bring wonder to thy face."

130. And I again: "Master, where are Phlegethon and Lethe found, for of the one thou art silent, and the other thou sayest is formed by this rain?"

133. "In all thy questions truly thou pleasest me," he answered, "but the boiling of the red water should well solve one that thou askest.[1] Lethe thou shalt see, but outside of this ditch, there where the souls go to lave themselves, when the fault repented of has been removed." Then he said, "Now it is time to quit the wood; take heed that thou come behind me; the margins which are not burning afford way, and above them every vapor is extinguished."

CANTO XV

1. Now one of the hard margins bears us on, and the fume of the brook overshadows so that it saves the water and the banks from the fire. As the Flemings, between Wissant and Bruges, fearing the flood that rushes toward them, make the bulwark whereby the sea may be routed; and as the Paduans along the Brenta, in order to defend their towns and their castles, ere Chiarentana[2] feel the heat—in such like were these made, though neither so high nor so thick had the master, whoever he was, made them.

13. We were now so remote from the wood that I could not have seen where it was though I had turned backward, when we encountered a troop of souls which was coming alongside the bank, and each of them was looking at us, as a man is wont to look at another at evening under the new moon; and they so sharpened their brows toward us as the old tailor does on the needle's eye.

22. Thus eyed by that company, I was recognized by one who took me by the hem, and cried out: "What a marvel!" And when he stretched out his arm to me, I fixed my eyes on his baked aspect so that his scorched visage did not prevent the recognition of him by my intelligence; and bending down my own to his face, I answered: "Are you here, Ser Brunetto?"[3] And he: "O my son, let it not displease thee if Brunetto Latini turns back a little with thee, and lets the train go on." I said to him: "With all my power I pray this of you, and if you will that I sit down with you I will do so, if it please him there, for I go with him." "O son," said he, "whoever of this herd stops for an instant, lies afterwards a hundred years without fanning himself when the fire smites him; therefore go onward: I will come at thy skirts, and then I will rejoin my band which goes lamenting its eternal penalties."

43. I dared not descend from the road to go level with him, but I held my head bowed like one who goes reverently. He began: "What fortune or destiny leads thee down here before thy last day? and who is this that shows the road?"

49. "There above, in the bright life," I answered him, "I went astray in a valley, before my time was full. Only yesterday morning I turned my back on it: this one appeared to me as I was returning to it, and he is leading me homeward again along this path."

55. And he to me: "If thou follow thy star, thou canst not miss the glorious port, if, in the fair life, I discerned aright: and if I had not so untimely died, seeing heaven so benignant to thee, I would have given thee cheer in thy work. But that ungrateful malignant people which descended from Fiesole of old, and still smacks of the mountain and the rock, will make itself hostile to thee because of thy good deeds; and it is right, for among the bitter sorb-trees it befits not the sweet fig to bear fruit. Old report in the world calls them blind; it is an avaricious, envious, and proud folk; from their customs take heed that thou cleanse thyself. Thy fortune reserves such honor for thee that the one party and the other shall have hunger for thee: but far from the goat shall be the grass. Let the Fiesolan beasts make litter of themselves, and let them not touch the plant, if any spring yet upon their dungheap, in which the holy seed may revive of those Romans who remained there when it became the nest of so much wickedness."

79. "If my entreaty were all fulfilled," replied

[1] Cf. *Aeneid*, vi. 556.
[2] The mountain regions north of the Brenta.
[3] Brunetto Latini, one of the most learned and able Florentines of the thirteenth century.

I to him, "you would not yet be placed in banishment from human nature; for in my mind is fixed, and now fills my heart, the dear, good, paternal image of you, when in the world hour by hour you taught me how man makes himself eternal; and how much I hold it in gratitude, it behoves that while I live should be discerned in my speech. That which you tell of my course I write, and reserve it with other text[1] to be glossed by a Lady, who will know how, if I attain to her. Thus much would I have manifest to you, that I, provided my conscience chide me not, for Fortune, as she wills, am ready. Such earnest is not strange unto my ears; therefore let Fortune turn her wheel as pleases her, and the churl his mattock."

97. My Master thereupon turned backward to his right, and looked at me; then said: "He listens well who notes it."

100. Not the less for this do I go on speaking with Ser Brunetto, and I ask, who are his most noted and most eminent companions. And he to me: "To know of some is good, of the others it will be laudable for us to be silent, for the time would be short for so much speech. In brief, know that all were clerks, and great men of letters and of great fame, defiled in the world by one same sin. Priscian goes along with that disconsolate crowd, and Francesco d' Accorso;[2] and thou couldst also have seen there, hadst thou had hankering for such scurf, him who was translated by the Servant of Servants from the Arno to the Bacchiglione, where he left his ill-strained nerves.[3] Of more would I tell, but my going on and my speech cannot be longer, for I see yonder a new smoke rising from the sand. Folk come with whom I must not be. Let my Treasure,[4] in which I still am living, be commended to thee, and more I ask not."

121. Then he turned back, and seemed of those who run across the plain at Verona for

the green cloth, and of these he seemed the one that wins, and not he that loses.

CANTO XVI

1. I was now in a place where the resounding of the water which was falling into the next circle was heard, like that hum which the beehives make, when three shades together separated themselves, as they ran, from a troop that was passing under the rain of the bitter torment. They came toward us, and each cried out: "Stop thou, who by thy garb seemest to us to be one from our wicked city!"

10. Ah me! what wounds I saw upon their limbs, recent and old, burnt in by the flames; it grieves me still for them but to remember it.

13. My Teacher gave heed to their cries; he turned his face toward me, and: "Now wait," he said; "to these one should be courteous, and were it not for the fire which the nature of the place shoots forth, I should say that haste better befitted thee than them."

19. As we stopped, they began again the old verse,[5] and when they had reached us they all three made a wheel of themselves. As champions, naked and oiled, are wont to do, watching for their grip and their vantage, before they exchange blows and thrusts, thus, wheeling, each directed his face on me, so that his neck was making continuous journey in contrary direction to his feet.

28. "And if the wretchedness of this soft place bring us and our prayers into contempt," began one, "and our darkened and scorched aspect, let our fame incline thy mind to tell us who thou art, that so securely rubbest thy living feet through Hell. He whose tracks thou seest me trample, although he go naked and stripped of skin, was of greater degree than thou thinkest. He was grandson of the good Gualdrada; his name was Guido Guerra, and in his life he did much with wisdom and with the sword. The other who treads the sand behind me is Tegghiaio Aldobrandi, whose reputation should be cherished in the world above. And I, who am set with them on the cross, was Jacopo Rusticucci,[6] and surely my savage wife

[1] See *supra*, Canto vi. 64ff; x. 80ff.
[2] Priscian, the famous grammarian of the sixth century; Francesco, a jurist of much repute in his time, who taught at Oxford and at Bologna, and died in 1294.
[3] Andrea de' Mozzi, bishop of Florence, because of his scandalous life was translated by Boniface VIII to the less conspicuous bishopric of Vicenza, through which city the Bacchiglione runs. He died in 1296.
[4] That is, *Li Livres dou Tresor*, Brunetto's chief literary work.

[5] The wonted burden of their lamentation. See xiv. 20, *supra*.
[6] Cf. *supra*, Canto vi. 79, 80. Tegghiaio and Guido Guerra were illustrious Florentines of the thirteenth century. The good Gualdrada was the daughter of

more than aught else injures me."

46. If I had been sheltered from the fire I should have cast myself below among them, and I believe that the Teacher would have permitted it; but because I should have been burnt and baked, fear overcame my good will which made me greedy to embrace them.

52. Then I began: "Not contempt, but grief, did your condition fix within me, such that slowly will it be all divested, soon as this my Lord said to me words by which I bethought me that such folk as ye are were coming. I am of your city; and I have always rehearsed and heard with affection your deeds and honored names. I am leaving the gall, and going for sweet fruits promised to me by my veracious Leader; but far as to the centre I needs must first descend."

64. "So may thy soul long direct thy limbs," replied he then, "and so may thy fame shine after thee, say if courtesy and valor abide in our city as of wont, or if they have quite gone forth from it? For Guglielmo Borsiere, who is in torment with us but short while, and is going yonder with our companions, afflicts us greatly with his words."

73. "The new people and the sudden gains have engendered pride and excess, Florence, in thee, so that already thou weepest therefor." Thus I cried with uplifted face, and the three, who understood this for answer, looked one at the other, as one looks at truth.

79. "If other times it costs thee so little," replied they all, "to satisfy others, happy thou if thus thou speakest at thy pleasure. Wherefore, if thou escapest from these dark places, and returnest to see again the beautiful stars, when it shall rejoice thee to say, 'I have been,' mind thou tell of us to the people." Then they broke the wheel, and in flying their swift legs seemed wings.

88. An amen could not have been said so quickly as they had disappeared: wherefore it seemed well to my Master to depart. I followed him, and we had gone little way before the sound of the water was so near to us, that had we spoken we had scarce been heard. As that river which first from Monte Viso holds its own course toward the east, on the left flank of the Apennine,—which is called Acquacheta up

above, before it sinks down into its low bed, and at Forlì has lost that name—reverberates in falling from the alp with a single leap there above San Benedetto, where ought to be shelter for a thousand; thus, down from a precipitous bank, we found that dark water resounding, so that in short while it would have hurt the ears.

106. I had a cord girt around me, and with it I had once thought to take the leopard of the painted skin.[1] After I had loosed it wholly from me, as my Leader had commanded me, I reached it to him gathered up and coiled. Whereon he turned toward the right, and threw it, somewhat far from the edge, down into that deep gulf. "And surely," said I to myself, "it must be that some novelty respond to the novel signal which the Master so follows with his eye."

118. Ah! how cautious ought men to be near those who see not only the deed, but with their wisdom look within the thoughts! He said to me: "That which I await will soon come up, and what thy thought is dreaming must soon discover itself to thy sight."

124. A man ought always to close his lips so far as he can to that truth which has the aspect of falsehood, because without fault it causes shame; but here I cannot be silent, and Reader, I swear to thee, by the notes of this comedy— so may they not be void of lasting grace—that I saw through that thick and dark air a shape marvelous to every steadfast heart come swimming upwards, like as he returns who goes down sometimes to loose an anchor that grapples either a rock or aught else which is hidden in the sea, who stretches upward, and draws in his feet.

CANTO XVII

1. "BEHOLD the wild beast with the pointed tail, that passes mountains, and breaks walls and weapons; behold him that infects all the world."[2] Thus began my Leader to speak to me; and he beckoned to him that he should come to shore near the end of the marbles we had walked on. And that loathsome image of

---

Messer Bellincione Berti, referred to in Cantos xv. and xvi. of *Paradise*

[1] The leopard of Canto i. 32. The cord symbolises the ascetic vows or whatsoever else on which Dante had formerly relied to capture and subdue the beast.

[2] Dante makes Geryon the type and image of Fraud, thus allegorizing the triple form (*Aeneid*, vi. 289; viii. 292).

fraud came onward, and landed his head and his bust, but did not draw up his tail on the bank. His face was the face of a just man (so benignant the skin it had outwardly), and all his trunk was of a serpent; he had two paws, hairy to the armpits; his back and his breast and both his sides were painted with nooses and rings. Tartars or Turks never made cloth with more colors of groundwork and pattern, nor were such webs laid on the loom by Arachne.

19. As sometimes boats lie on the shore, and are partly in water and partly on the ground, and as yonder, among the gluttonous Germans, the beaver settles himself to make his war,[1] so lay that worst of beasts upon the edge of stone which closes in the sand. In the void all his tail was quivering, twisting upwards its venomous fork, which in guise of a scorpion armed the point.

28. The Leader said: "Now needs must our way bend a little toward that wicked beast which is couching yonder." Therefore we descended on the right hand side and took ten steps upon the verge in order completely to avoid the sand and the flamelets. And when we had come to him, I see, a little farther on, people sitting upon the sand near to the empty space.[2]

37. Here the Master said to me: "In order that thou mayst carry away quite full experience of this round, now go and see their condition. Let thy talk there be brief; until thou returnest I will speak with this beast, that it may concede to us its strong shoulders."

43. Thus, further up along the extreme head of that seventh circle, all alone I went where the sad people were sitting. Their woe was bursting forth through their eyes; now here, now there they made help with their hands, sometimes against the vapors, and sometimes against the hot soil. Not otherwise do the dogs in summer, now with muzzle, now with paws, when they are bitten either by fleas, or flies, or gadflies. When I set my eyes on the face of certain of those on whom the grievous fire falls, I did not recognize one of them; but I perceived that from the neck of each was hanging a pouch,

which had a certain color and a certain device,[3] and therewith it seems their eye is fed. And as I come gazing among them, I saw upon a yellow purse azure which had the face and bearing of a lion.[4] Then as the current of my look proceeded, I saw another, red as blood, display a goose whiter than butter.

64. And one, who had his little white sack marked with an azure and gravid sow,[5] said to me: "What art thou doing in this ditch? Now get thee gone: and since thou art still alive, know that my neighbor, Vitaliano, will sit here at my left side. With these Florentines am I, a Paduan; often they stun my ears, shouting: 'Let the sovereign cavalier come who will bring the pouch with the three beaks.'"[6] Then he twisted his mouth, and thrust out his tongue, like an ox that licks its nose. And I, fearing lest longer stay might vex him who had admonished me to stay but little, turned back from these weary souls.

79. I found my Leader, who had already mounted upon the croup of the fierce animal, and he said to me: "Now be thou strong and courageous; henceforth the descent is by such stairs; mount thou in front, for I wish to be between, so that the tail cannot do harm."

85. As is he who has the shivering fit of the quartan so near that his nails are already pale, and he is all of a tremble only looking at the shade, such I became at these uttered words: but his exhortations wrought shame in me, which in presence of a good lord makes a servant strong.

91. I seated myself on those huge shoulders. "So do," I wished to say, but the voice came not as I thought, "that thou embrace me." But he who other time had succored me, in other chance, soon as I mounted, clasped me and sustained me with his arms; and he said: "Geryon, move on now; let thy circles be wide, and thy descending slow; consider the novel burden that thou hast."

100. As the little vessel goes from its place, backward, backward, so he thence withdrew;

---

[3] The blazon of their arms, by which Dante learns who they are, ignobly borne upon the purse.
[4] The armorial bearings of the Gianfigliazzi, a Guelf family of Florence; the next were those of the Ubriachi, Ghibellines, also of Florence.
[5] The arms of the Scrovigni of Padua.
[6] Giovanni Buiamonte of Florence, another notorious usurer.

[1] With his tail in the water to attract his prey, as was popularly believed.
[2] See Canto xi. 94-111, *supra*.

and when he felt himself quite at play, he turned his tail to where his breast had been, and moved it stretched out like an eel, and with his paws gathered the air to himself. Greater fear I do not think there was when Phaëton abandoned the reins, whereby heaven, as is still apparent,[1] was scorched; nor when the wretched Icarus felt his loins unfeathering by the melted wax, his father crying to him: "Ill way thou holdest," than mine was, when I saw that I was in the air on every side, and saw every sight vanished, except that of the beast. It goes along swimming slowly, slowly, wheels and descends, but I perceive it not, save for the wind upon my face, and from below.

118. I heard now on the right hand the gulf making beneath us a horrible din; wherefore I stretch out my head, with my eyes downward. Then I became more terrified at the precipice, because I saw fires and heard laments; whereat I, trembling, all the closer cling. And I saw then, for I had not seen them before, the descending and the circling, by the great evils which were drawing near on divers sides.

127. As the falcon which has been long on wing, that, without sight of lure or bird, makes the falconer say: "Ah me, thou stoopest!" descends weary, whence it started swiftly, through a hundred circles, and alights disdainful and sullen far from its master; so Geryon set us at the bottom, at the very foot of the rough hewn rock, and, disburdened of our persons, vanished as arrow from the bowstring.

CANTO XVIII

1. THERE is a place in Hell called Malebolge,[2] all of stone and of the color of iron, as is the circular wall that environs it. Right in the middle of this malign field yawns a very wide and deep pit, the structure of which I will tell of in its place. That belt, therefore, which remains between the pit and the foot of the high hard bank is circular, and it has its bed divided into ten valleys. Such a figure as where, for guard of the walls, very many moats encircle castles, the place where they are presents, such image did these make here. And as in such strongholds from their thresholds to the outer bank are little bridges, so from the base of the cliff ran crags which traversed the embankments and the moats far as the pit which cuts them off and collects them.

19. In this place we found ourselves, shaken off from the back of Geryon; and the Poet held to the left, and I moved on behind. On the right hand I saw new woe, new torments, and new scourgers, with which the first pouch was replete. At its bottom were the sinners naked; on this side the middle they came facing us;[3] on the further side along with us, but with greater steps. As the Romans, because of the great host in the year of the Jubilee,[4] have taken means for the passage of the people over the Bridge, so that on one side all have their front toward the Castle, and go to Saint Peter's, and on the other rim toward the Mount.[5]

34. Along the gloomy rock, on this side and on that, I saw horned demons with great whips, who were beating them cruelly from behind. Ah, how they made them lift their heels at the first blows! truly not one waited for the second, or the third.

40. While I was going on, my eyes were encountered by one, and I said straightway thus: "Ere now for sight of him I have not fasted"; wherefore to shape him out I stayed my feet, and the sweet Leader stopped with me, and assented to my going somewhat back. And that scourged one thought to conceal himself by lowering his face, but it availed him little, for I said: "Thou that castest thine eye upon the ground, if the features that thou bearest are not false, art Venedico Caccianimico; but what brings thee to such stinging Salse?"[6]

52. And he to me: "Unwillingly I tell it, but thy plain speech compels me, which makes me remember the old world. I was he who brought

---

[1] In the Milky Way.
[2] In the Eighth Circle the sinners are punished who belong to the first of the two classes of the fraudulent (see Canto xi. 52-66), that is, those who practised deceit upon persons who had no ground for special confidence in them. Its bed, which slopes gradually from the wall that environs it to the central pit of Hell, is occupied by ten deep concentric valleys, called *bolge*. *Bolgia* signifies, literally, a budget, or pouch; and *Malebolge*, evil pouches.

[3] In their long circling course round the *bolgia*, the panders, going in opposite direction to the poets, came facing them; on the further side the seducers were taking the contrary course.
[4] The first year of Jubilee: 1300.
[5] The Bridge and Castle of Sant' Angelo; the "Mount" is the Capitoline Hill.
[6] *Salse*, the name of a ravine near Bologna, into which the bodies of criminals were thrown.

the beautiful Ghisola[1] to do the will of the Marquis, however the shameful tale may be reported. And not the only Bolognese do I weep here; nay, this place is so full of them, that so many tongues are not now taught between Savena and the Reno to say *sipa*,[2] and if of this thou wishest assurance or testimony, bring to mind our avaricious breasts." As he spoke thus a demon struck him with his thong and said: "Begone, pander, here are no women for coining."

67. I rejoined my Escort; then with few steps we came to where a crag jutted from the bank. We ascended it easily enough, and turning to the right upon its ridge, from those eternal encircling walls we departed.

73. When we were there where it opens below to give passage to the scourged, the Leader said: "Wait, and let the sight strike on thee of these others born to ill, of whom thou hast not yet seen the face, because they have gone along together with us."

79. From the old bridge we looked at the train that was coming toward us on the other side, and which the scourge in like manner drives on. The good Master, without my asking, said to me: "Look at that great one who is coming, and seems not to shed a tear for pain. What royal aspect he still retains! He is Jason, who by courage and by wit despoiled the Colchians of their ram. He passed by the isle of Lemnos, after the bold pitiless women had given all their males to death. There with tokens and with ornate words he deceived Hypsipyle, the maiden, who first had deceived all the others. There he left her big with child, and lonely; such guilt condemns him to such torment; and also for Medea is vengeance wrought. With him goes whoever in such wise deceives. And let this suffice to know of the first valley, and of those that it holds in its fangs."

100. We were now where the narrow path intersects with the second embankment, and makes of that abutments for another arch. From there we heard people whining in the next pouch, and puffing with their muzzles, and beating themselves with their palms. The banks were encrusted with a mould by the breath from below which sticks on them, and was making quarrel with the eyes and with the nose. The bottom is so hollowed out that no place suffices us for seeing it, without mounting to the crown of the arch where the crag rises highest. Hither we came, and thence I saw down in the ditch people plunged in a filth that seemed to have come from human privies.

115. And while I am searching down there with my eye, I saw one with his head so foul with ordure that it was not apparent whether he were layman or clerk. He shouted to me: "Why art thou so greedy to look more at me than at the other filthy ones?" And I to him: "Because, if I remember rightly, ere now I have seen thee with dry hair, and thou art Alessio Interminei of Lucca; therefore I eye thee more than all the rest." And he then, beating his pate: "Down here the flatteries wherewith I never had my tongue cloyed have submerged me."

127. Hereupon my Leader said to me: "Mind thou push thy look a little further forwards so that thou mayest quite reach with thine eyes the face of that dirty and disheveled wench, who is scratching herself there with her nasty nails, and now is crouching down and now standing on foot. She is Thais the harlot, who answered her paramour when he said: 'Have I great thanks from thee?'—'Nay, marvelous.' And herewith let our sight be satisfied."

CANTO XIX

1. O Simon Magus,[3] O wretched followers, because ye, rapacious, do prostitute for gold and silver the things of God which ought to be the brides of righteousness, now it behoves for you the trumpet sound, since ye are in the third pouch.

7. We were now at the next tomb,[4] having mounted on that part of the crag which hangs plumb just over the middle of the ditch. O Supreme Wisdom, how great is the art which Thou dost display in heaven, on earth, and in the evil world! and how justly does Thy Power apportion!

13. Upon the sides and upon the bottom, I saw the livid stone full of holes all of one size,

---

[1] His own sister; the Marquis was one of the Esti of Ferrara. Venedico was a man of note, and for a time *podestà* of Pistoia.
[2] Bologna lies between the Savena and the Reno; *sipa* is the Bolognese provincialism for *sia*.

[3] See Acts, 8. 9-24.
[4] The next *bolgia*.

and each was circular. They seemed to me not less wide nor larger than those that in my beautiful Saint John are made for place of the baptizers;[1] one of which, not many years ago, I broke for the sake of one who was stifling in it: and let this be the seal to undeceive all men.

22. Forth from the mouth of each were protruding the feet of a sinner, and his legs up to the calf, and the rest was within. Both the soles of all of them were on fire, because of which their joints were twitching so hard that they would have snapped ropes and withes. As the flaming of things oiled is wont to move only on the outer surface, so was it there from the heels to the toes.

31. "Who is he, Master, who torments himself, twitching more than the others his consorts," said I, "and whom a ruddier flame is sucking?" And he to me: "If thou wilt that I carry thee down there by the bank which is the more sloping, from him thou shalt know of himself and of his wrongs." And I: "Whatever pleases thee is to my liking: thou art Lord, and knowest that I part me not from thy will, and thou knowest that which is unspoken."

40. Then we went upon the fourth embankment, turned, and descended on the left hand, down to the bottom pierced with holes, and narrow. The good Master set me not yet down from his haunch, till he brought me to the cleft of him who was thus lamenting with his shanks.

46. "O wretched soul, whoso thou art, that keepest upside down, planted like a stake," I began to say, "say a word, if thou canst." I was standing like the friar who confesses the perfidious assassin, who, after he is fixed, recalls him, in order to delay his death.

52. And he[2] cried out: "Art thou already standing there? Art thou already standing there, Boniface? By several years the writing lied to me. Art thou so quickly sated with that having, for which thou didst not fear to seize by guile the beautiful Lady,[3] and then to do her outrage?"

58. Such I became as those who, through not comprehending that which is replied to them, stand as if mocked, and know not what to answer.

61. Then Virgil said: "Tell him quickly, I am not he, I am not he that thou thinkest." And I answered as was enjoined on me; whereat the spirit writhed violently both his feet; then, sighing and with tearful voice, he said to me: "What then dost thou want of me? If to know who I am concern thee so much that thou hast therefore come down the bank, know that I was vested with the Great Mantle:[4] and verily I was a son of the She-Bear,[5] so eager to advance the cubs, that up there I put wealth, and here myself, into the purse. Beneath my head are the others that preceded me in simony, dragged down flattened through the fissures of the rock. Down there shall I in my turn sink, when he shall come whom I believed that thou wast, then when I put my sudden question; but already the time is longer that I have cooked my feet, and that I have been thus upside down, than he will stay planted with his feet red; for after him will come from westward, a shepherd without law,[6] of uglier deed, such as befits to cover him and me. A new Jason will he be, of whom it is read in Maccabees;[7] and as to that one his king was compliant, so to this one he who rules France shall be."

88. I know not if here I was too foolhardy that I answered him only in this strain: "Pray now tell me, how much treasure did our Lord require of Saint Peter before he placed the keys in his keeping? Surely he asked nothing save: 'Follow thou me.'[8] Nor did Peter or the others take gold or silver of Matthias, when he was chosen by lot to the place which the guilty soul had lost.[9] Therefore stay thou, for thou art

---

[1] "My beautiful Saint John" is the Baptistery of Florence.

[2] This is Nicholas III, Pope from 1277 to 1280, "the first Pope, or one of the first," says Villani, "in whose court simony was openly practiced." He takes Dante to be Boniface VIII, but Boniface was not to die till 1303.

[3] The Church, which Boniface had seized by guile,

through the deceit that he was charged with practising on Celestine V in order to obtain the papacy.

[4] The papal mantle. Cf. Canto ii. 27, *supra.*

[5] Nicholas was of the Orsini family, whose cognizance was a she-bear, *orsa.*

[6] Bertrand de Goth, a Gascon, was elected Pope in 1305 and died in 1314, little more than ten years after the death of Boniface. In 1309 Clement transferred the papal see to Avignon; this was a deed "without law," and he was beside noted for cupidity, simony, and licentiousness. Cf. *Paradise,* xxx. 142-148.

[7] See II Maccabees, 4. Clement was "compliant" to Philip IV.

[8] See Matthew, 16. 19, and John, 21. 19-22.

[9] See Acts, 1. 15-26.

rightly punished, and guard well the ill-gotten money that made thee bold against Charles.[1] And were it not that reverence for the supreme keys which thou heldest in the glad life even now forbids it to me, I would use still heavier words; for your avarice afflicts the world, trampling down the good and exalting the bad. Ye shepherds the Evangelist had in mind, when she that sitteth upon the waters was seen by him to fornicate with kings: she that was born with the seven heads, and from the ten horns had argument, so long as virtue pleased her spouse.[2] Ye have made you a god of gold and silver:[3] and what else is there between you and the idolaters save that they worship one, and ye a hundred? Ah Constantine! of how much ill was mother, not thy conversion, but that dowry which the first rich Father took from thee!"[4]

118. And, while I was singing these notes to him, whether anger or conscience stung him, he was kicking hard with both his feet. I believe, indeed, that it pleased my Leader, with so contented look did he all the while give heed to the sound of the true words uttered. Thereupon with both his arms he took me, and when he had me wholly on his breast, remounted along the way whereby he had descended. Nor did he tire of holding me clasped to him, till he had thus borne me up to the top of the arch which is the passage from the fourth to the fifth embankment. Here he gently laid down his burden, gently because of the rugged and steep crag, which would be a difficult pass for goats. Thence another great valley was discovered to me.

CANTO XX

1. OF a new punishment it behoves me to make verses, and give material to the twenti-

eth canto of the first lay, which is of the submerged.

4. I was now wholly in position to look into the uncovered depth which was bathed with tears of anguish, and I saw folk come, silent and weeping, along the great circular valley, at the pace which the litanies make in this world. As my sight descended lower on them, each appeared marvelously distorted between the chin and the beginning of the chest; for their face was turned toward their reins, and they must needs go backwards, because looking forward was taken from them. Perhaps indeed by force of palsy some one has been thus completely twisted, but I never saw it, nor do I believe it can be.

19. So may God let thee, Reader, gather fruit from thy reading, now think for thyself how I could keep my face dry, when close at hand I saw our image so contorted that the weeping of the eyes bathed the buttocks along the cleft. Truly I wept, leaning on one of the rocks of the hard crag, so that my Guide said to me: "Art thou even yet among the other fools? Here pity lives when it is quite dead. Who is more criminal than he who brings passion to the Divine Judgment?[5] Lift up thy head, lift up, and see him[6] for whom the earth opened before the eyes of the Thebans, whereat they all shouted: 'Whither art thou rushing, Amphiaraus? Why dost thou leave the war?' And he stopped not from falling headlong down far as Minos, who lays hold on every one. Look, how he has made a breast of his shoulders! Because he wished to see too far before him, he looks behind and goes a backward path.

40. "Behold Tiresias,[7] who changed semblance, when from male he became female, transforming all his members; and afterwards he was obliged to strike again with his rod the

[1] Charles of Anjou. The Pope was charged with having been bribed to favor the conspiracy to expel the French from Sicily, which came to a head, more than a year after his death, in the Sicilian Vespers, in March, 1282.
[2] Cf. Revelation, 17. The woman here stands for the Church; her seven heads may be interpreted as the Seven Sacraments, and her ten horns as the Commandments; her spouse is the Pope.
[3] Cf. Hosea, 8. 4.
[4] The reference is to the so-called Donation of Constantine, the authenticity of which was generally believed in till, about 1450, its forgery was conclusively exposed.

[5] Cf. Aquinas, *Summa Theologica*, Part III, Suppl. Q 94, A 3, citing Psalms, 58. 10. Virgil has not rebuked Dante for feeling compassion for individual sinners suffering the penalty of sin (see Cantos v. 72, 93, 117; xv. 79; xvi. 52), but he rebukes him here for shedding tears at the mere sight of the punishment, which, being the evidence of the justice of God, ought not to awaken pity.
[6] Amphiaraus, one of the seven kings who besieged Thebes, an augur and prophet.
[7] The story as told by Ovid is that when Teresias struck the two serpents with his staff he was transformed to a woman, and that seven years later, when he saw them again, he struck them with his staff and became a man again.

two entwined serpents, ere he could regain his masculine plumage. He who has his back to this one's belly is Aruns,[1] who on the mountains of Luni (where grubs the man of Carrara who dwells below) had a cave for his abode among white marbles, whence for looking at the stars and the sea his view was not cut off.

52. "And she who with her loose tresses covers her breasts, which thou dost not see, and has on that side all her hairy skin, was Manto,[2] who roamed through many lands, then settled there where I was born; whereof it pleases me that thou listen a little to me. After her father had departed from life, and the city of Bacchus[3] had become enslaved, she wandered long while through the world. Up in fair Italy, at foot of the alp which shuts in Germany above Tyrol, lies a lake which is called Benaco.[4] By a thousand founts, I think, and more, between Garda and Val Camonica, Apennino[5] is bathed by the water which settles in that lake. A place is in the middle there, where the Trentine Pastor and he of Brescia and the Veronese might each give his blessing if he took that road.[6] Peschiera, a fair and strong fortress, to front the Brescians and Bergamasques, sits where the shore round about is lowest. There that which in the bosom of Benaco cannot stay must needs all pour forth, and it becomes a river down through green pastures. Soon as the water gathers head to run, it is no longer called Benaco, but Mincio, far as Governo, where it falls into the Po. It has no long course before it finds a flat, on which it spreads, and makes a marsh, and is apt at times in summer to be noisome.

82. "Passing that way, the savage virgin saw land in the middle of the fen, without culture and bare of inhabitants. There, to avoid all human fellowship, she stayed with her servants to practice her arts, and lived, and left there her body empty. Afterward the men who were scattered round about gathered to that place, which was strong because of the fen which it had on all sides. They built the city over those dead bones, and for her, who first had chosen the place, they called it Mantua, without other augury. Formerly its people were more thick within it, before the stupidity of Casalodi had been tricked by Pinamonte.[7] Therefore I instruct thee that if thou ever hearest that my city had other origin, no falsehood may defraud the truth."

100. And I: "Master, thy discourses are so certain to me, and so lay hold on my faith, that the others would be to me as spent coals. But tell me of the people who are going onward, if thou seest any one of them worthy of note; for only to that does my mind revert."

106. Then he said to me: "That one, who stretches his beard from his cheek over his dusky shoulders, was an augur when Greece was so emptied of males that they scarcely remained for the cradles, and with Calchas he gave the moment for cutting the first cable at Aulis. Eurypylus was his name, and thus my lofty Tragedy sings him in some place;[8] well thou knowest this, who knowest the whole of it. That other who is so spare in the flanks was Michael Scot,[9] who verily knew the game of magical deceptions. Behold Guido Bonatti,[10] behold Asdente,[11] who now would wish he had attended to his leather and his thread, but too late repents. Behold the wretched women who left the needle, the spool, and the spindle, and became fortune-tellers; they wrought spells with herbs and with image.

124. "But come on now, for already Cain with his thorns[12] holds the confines of both the hemispheres, and touches the wave below Seville; and already yesternight was the moon round; well shouldst thou remember it, for it did thee no harm sometimes in the deep wood." Thus he spoke to me, and we went on the while.

[1] An Etruscan soothsayer.

[2] The daughter of Tiresias, and herself a prophetess. Cf. *Aeneid*, v. 199.

[3] Thebes.

[4] Now the Lago di Garda.

[5] Not the chain of the Apennines, but said to be the proper name of a special mountain in this locality.

[6] A point in the lake where the three dioceses meet.

[7] The Count of Casalodi, being lord of Mantua about 1270, gave ear to the treacherous counsels of Messer Pinamonte de' Buonaccorsi, and after expelling many of the nobles was himself driven from the city, with great slaughter and dispersion of the chief families that had remained.

[8] Cf. *Aeneid*, ii. 114-115.

[9] A famous Scotch wizard; died about 1250.

[10] A famous astrologer of Forlì, in the thirteenth century.

[11] A shoemaker of Parma, noted for his soothsaying.

[12] The Man in the Moon, who, according to the Italian version of the old popular legend, was Cain, condemned to carry forever a bundle of thorns.

CANTO XXI

1. THUS from bridge to bridge we went, talking of other things, which my Comedy cares not to sing, and were holding the summit,[1] when we stopped to see the next cleft of Malebolge and the next vain lamentations; and I saw it wonderfully dark.

7. As in the Arsenal of the Venetians, in winter, the sticky pitch for paying their unsound vessels is boiling, because they cannot sail the sea, and, instead thereof, one builds him a new bark, and one caulks the ribs of that which has made many a voyage; one hammers at the prow, and one at the stern; another makes oars, and another twists cordage; and one patches the foresail and the mainsail—so, not by fire, but by divine art, a thick pitch was boiling there below, which belimed the bank on every side. I saw it, but saw not in it aught but the bubbles which the boiling raised, and all of it swelling up and again settling down compressed.

22. While I was gazing down there fixedly, my Leader, saying: "Beware! beware!" drew me to himself from the place where I was standing. Then I turned as one who is in haste to see that from which it behoves him to fly, and whom a sudden fear dismays, and who for seeing delays not to depart, and I saw behind us a black devil come running up along the crag. Ah! how fell he was in aspect, and how bitter he seemed to me in act, with his wings open, and light upon his feet! His shoulder, which was sharp and high, was laden by a sinner with both haunches, the sinews of whose feet he held clutched.

37. "O Malebranche[2] of our bridge," he said, "lo here, one of the Ancients of Saint Zita![3] put him under, for I am returning for still others to that city, which I have furnished well with them; every man there is a barrator, except Bonturo:[4] there, for money, out of Nay is made Ay." Down he hurled him and turned back along the hard crag, and never

mastiff loosed was in such haste to follow a thief.

46. That one sank under, and rose again doubled up, but the demons that had cover of the bridge cried out: "Here the Holy Face[5] has no place; here one swims otherwise than in the Serchio;[6] therefore, if thou dost not want our grapples, make no show above the pitch." Then they pricked him with more than a hundred prongs, and said: "Here thou must dance under cover, so that, if thou canst, thou mayst swindle secretly." Not otherwise do the cooks make their scullions plunge the meat with their hooks into the middle of the cauldron, so that it may not float.

58. The good Master said to me: "In order that it be not apparent that thou art here, squat down behind a jag, that thou mayst have some screen for thyself, and at any offence that may be done to me be not afraid, for I have knowledge of these things, because once before I was in such a wrangle."

64. Then he passed on beyond the head of the bridge, and when he arrived upon the sixth bank, he had need to have a steadfast front. With that fury and with that storm with which dogs run out upon the poor wretch who, where he stops, suddenly asks alms, they came forth from under the little bridge, and turned against him all their grapples. But he cried out: "Let no one of you be savage; before your hook take hold of me, let one of you come forward that he may hear me, and then take counsel as to grappling me." All cried out: "Let Malacoda[7] go"; whereon, while the rest stood still, one moved and came to him, saying: "What does this profit him?"

79. "Thinkest thou, Malacoda, to see me come here," said my Master, "safe hitherto from all your hindrances, except by Divine Will and propitious fate? Let me go on, for in Heaven it is willed that I show to another this wild road." Then was his arrogance so fallen that he let the hook drop at his feet, and said to the others: "Now he may not be struck."

88. And my Leader to me: "O thou that sittest asquat among the splinters of the bridge,

---

[1] The crown of the arch of the craggy bridge across the fifth *bolgia*.

[2] *Malebranche:* "Evil-claws."

[3] One of the *Anziani*, the chief magistrates of Lucca, whose special protectress was Santa Zita.

[4] Ironical; Bonturo was the chief barrator of them all.

[5] The *Santo Volto*, an image of Christ upon the cross, still venerated at Lucca.

[6] The river that runs not far from Lucca.

[7] *Malacoda:* "Evil-tail."

return now securely to me." Wherefore I moved and came swiftly to him; and the devils all pressed forward, so that I feared they would not keep compact. And thus I once saw the foot-soldiers afraid, who were coming out from Caprona under pledge,[1] seeing themselves among so many enemies. I drew close with my whole body to my Leader's side, and did not turn my eyes from their look, which was not good. They were lowering their forks, and one was saying to the other: "Wilt thou that I touch him on the rump?" and they were answering: "Yes, see that thou nick it for him." But that demon who was holding speech with my Leader turned round with all haste and said: "Quiet, quiet, Scarmiglione!"

106. Then he said to us: "Further advance along this crag is not possible, because the sixth arch lies all shattered at the bottom. And if it be still your pleasure to go forward, go on along this ridge; near by is another crag that affords a way. Yesterday, five hours later than this, completed one thousand two hundred and sixty-six years since the way was broken here.[2] I am sending thitherward some of these of mine, to see if any one is airing himself; go ye with them, for they will not be wicked. Come forward, Alichino and Calcabrina," he began to say, "and thou, Cagnazzo; and Barbariccia, do thou guide the ten. Let Libicocco go also, and Draghignazzo, tusked Ciriatto, and Graffiacane, and Farfarello, and mad Rubicante.[3] Search round about the boiling pitch; let these be safe far as the next crag, which all unbroken goes over these dens."

127. "O me! Master, what is this that I see?" said I; "pray, if thou knowest the way, let us go alone without escort, for as for myself I crave it not. If thou art as wary as thou art wont, does thou not see that they grin, and with their brows threaten harm to us?" And

[1] In August, 1289, the town of Caprona, on the Arno, surrendered to the Florentine troops, with whom Dante was serving.
[2] By the earthquake at the death of the Saviour, who, it was believed, was thirty-four years old at his crucifixion.
[3] Some of the names of these demons have as plain a significance as *Malacoda*; for example, *Cagnazzo* for *Cagnaccio*, "wretched dog"; *Barbariccia*, "crisp beard"; *Graffiacane*, "scratch dog"; while others suggest a meaning by their composition or their sound, as *Alichino*, "bent wing"; *Rubicante*, "rubicund"; *Scarmiglione*, "dishevelled," and so on.

he to me: "I would not have thee afraid; let them grin on at their will, for they are doing it at the boiled sufferers."

136. Upon the left bank they took a turn, but first each had pressed his tongue with his teeth toward their leader as a signal, and he had made a trumpet of his rump.

CANTO XXII

1. I HAVE seen ere' now horsemen moving camp, and beginning an assault, and making their muster, and sometimes retiring for their escape; I have seen foragers over your land, O Aretines, and I have seen the starting of raids, the onset of tournaments, and the running of jousts, now with trumpets, and now with bells, with drums, and with signals from strongholds, and with native things and foreign— but never to so strange a pipe did I see horsemen or footmen set forth, or ship by sign of land or star.

13. We were going along with the ten demons. Ah, the fell company! but in the church with the saints, and in the tavern with the gluttons. My attention was only on the pitch in order to see every condition of the pouch, and of the people that were burning in it.

19. Like dolphins, when by the arching of their back, they give a sign to the sailors to take heed for the safety of their vessel, so, now and then, to alleviate his pain, one of the sinners would show his back and hide it in less time than it lightens. And as at the edge of the water of a ditch the frogs lie with only their muzzle out, so that they conceal their feet and the rest of their bulk, so on every side were the sinners; but as Barbariccia approached so did they draw back beneath the boiling. I saw, and still my heart shudders at it, one waiting, just as it happens that one frog stays and another jumps. And Graffiacane, who was nearest over against him, hooked him by his pitchy locks, and drew him up so that he seemed to me an otter. (I knew now the name of every one of them; I had so noted them when they were chosen, and afterwards, when they called each other, had listened how.) "O Rubicante, see thou set thy claws upon his back so thou flay him," shouted all the accursed ones together.

43. And I: "My Master, contrive, if thou canst, to find out who is the luckless one come

into the hands of his adversaries." My Leader drew up to his side, and asked him whence he was, and he replied: "I was born in the kingdom of Navarre; my mother placed me in service of a lord, for she had borne me to a ribald, destroyer of himself and of his substance. Afterward I was of the household of the good King Thibault;[1] there I set myself to practice barratry, for which I pay reckoning in this heat."

55. And Ciriatto, from whose mouth protruded on either side a tusk, as of a boar, made him feel how one of them rips. Among evil cats had the mouse come; but Barbariccia clasped him in his arms, and said: "Stand off, while I clutch him," and turned his face to my Master. "Ask further," said he, "if thou desirest to know more from him, before another one undo him."

64. The Leader: "Then, tell now of the other sinners; knowest thou any one under the pitch who is Italian?" And he: "I parted a short while since from one who there beyond was a neighbor; would that with him I still were so covered that I should not fear claw or hook." And Libicocco said: "We have borne too much," and seized his arm with his grapple so that, tearing, he carried off a sinew of it. Draghignazzo, he too wished to give him a grip down at his legs, whereat their decurion turned round about with evil look.

76. When they were a little quieted, my Leader, without delay, asked him who was still gazing at his wound: "Who was he from whom thou sayst thou madest ill parting to come to shore?" And he replied: "It was Friar Gomita, he of Gallura,[2] vessel of every fraud, who held the enemies of his lord in hand, and dealt so with them that each of them praises him for it. Money he took, and let them smoothly off, so he says; and in his other offices besides he was no little barrator, but sovereign. With him frequents Don Michael Zanche of Logodoro,[3] and their tongues never feel

tired in talking of Sardinia. O me! see ye that other who is grinning: I would say more, but I fear lest he is making ready to scratch my itch." And the Grand Provost, turning to Farfarello, who was rolling his eyes as if to strike, said: "Get away there, wicked bird!"

97. "If ye wish to see or to hear Tuscans or Lombards," thereon began again the frightened one, "I will make some of them come; but let the Malebranche stand a little withdrawn, so that they may not be afraid of their vengeance, and I, sitting in this very place, for one that I am, will make seven of them come, when I shall whistle, as is our wont to do whenever one of us sets himself outside." Cagnazzo at this speech raised his muzzle, shaking his head, and said: "Hear the cunning trick he has devised for casting himself below!" Whereon he who had snares in great plenty answered: "Too cunning am I when I procure for my own companions greater sorrow." Alichino held not in, and, in opposition to the others, said to him: "If thou plunge, I will not come after thee at a gallop, but I will beat my wings above the pitch; let the ridge be left, and let the bank be a screen, to see if thou alone availest more than we."

118. O thou that readest, thou shalt hear a new sport! Each turned his eyes to the other side, he first who had been most averse to doing this. The Navarrese chose his time well, planted his feet firmly on the ground, and in an instant leaped, and from their purpose freed himself. At this, each of them was stung with his fault, but he most who was the cause of the loss; wherefore he started and cried out: "Thou art caught." But it availed little, for wings could not outstrip fear. The one went under, and the other, flying, turned his breast upward. Not otherwise the wild duck on a sudden dives under when the falcon comes near, and he returns up vexed and baffled. Calcabrina, angry at the flout, flying kept behind him, charmed that the sinner should escape, that he might have a scuffle; and when the barrator had disappeared he at once turned his claws upon his companion, and grappled with him above the ditch. But the other was indeed a full-grown sparrowhawk for clawing him well, and both of them fell into the middle of the boiling pool. The heat was a sudden un-

---

[1] Probably Thibault II, King of Navarre and brother-in-law of Saint Louis.

[2] Gallura, one of the four divisions of Sardinia, called judicatures, made by the Pisans, after their conquest of the island. Also see *Purgatory*, viii. 53. Friar Gomita was hanged for his frauds.

[3] Logodoro, another of the judicatures of Sardinia. Zanche was murdered about 1290, by his son-in-law Branca d' Oria; see Canto xxxiii. 134-147, *infra*.

grappler; but yet there was no rising from it, they had their wings so beglued. Barbariccia, in distress with the others of his troop, made four of them fly to the other side with all their forks, and very swiftly, on this side and that, they descended to their posts, and stretched their hooks toward the belimed ones, who were already cooked within the crust: and we left them thus embroiled.

CANTO XXIII

1. SILENT, alone, and without company, we were going on, one before, the other behind, as Minor Friars go along the way. My thought was turned by the present brawl upon the fable of Aesop, in which he told of the frog and the mouse; for *now* and *this instant* are not more alike than the one is to the other, if beginning and end be rightly coupled by the attentive mind.[1] And as one thought bursts out from another, so then from that was born another which made my first fear double. I was thinking in this wise: These through us have been put to scorn, and with such harm and trick as I believe must vex them greatly; if anger be added to ill-will, they will come after us more merciless than the dog to the hare which he snaps up.

19. Already I was feeling my hair all bristling with fear, and was backwards intent, when I said: "Master, if thou dost not speedily conceal thyself and me, I am afraid of the Malebranche; we have them already after us; I so imagine them that I already feel them." And he: "If I were of leaded glass, I should not draw to me thine outward image more quickly than I receive thine inward. Even now came thy thoughts among mine, with like action and like look, so that of both I made one sole counsel. If it be that the right bank lies so that we can descend into the next pouch, we shall escape from the imagined chase."

34. He had not yet finished reporting this counsel, when I saw them coming with wings spread, not very far off, with will to take us.

My Leader on a sudden took me, as a mother who is wakened by the noise, and sees the kindled flames close to her, who takes her son and flies, and, having more care of him than of herself, stays not so long as only to put on a shift: and down from the ridge of the hard bank, he gave himself supine to the sloping rock that closes one of the sides of the next pouch. Never ran water so swiftly through a duct, to turn the wheel of a land-mill, when it approaches nearest to the paddles, as my Master over that border, bearing me along upon his breast as his son and not as a companion. Hardly had his feet reached the bed of the depth below, when they were on the ridge right over us; but here there was no fear, for the high Providence that willed to set them as ministers of the fifth ditch deprived them all of power of departing thence.

58. There below we found a painted people who were going round with very slow steps, weeping, and in their semblance weary and subdued. They had cloaks, with hoods lowered before their eyes, fashioned of the cut which is made for the monks in Cologne. Outwardly they are gilded, so that it dazzles, but within all lead, and so heavy that those Frederick used to have put on were of straw.[2] O mantle wearisome for eternity!

68. We turned, still ever to the left hand, along with them, intent on their sad plaint. But because of the weight, that tired folk were coming so slowly that we had fresh company at every movement of the haunch. Wherefore I to my Leader: "Contrive to find some one who may be known by deed or name, and while thus going move thine eyes around." And one who heard the Tuscan speech cried out behind us: "Stay your feet, ye who run thus through the dusky air; perchance thou shalt have from me that which thou askest." Whereon my Leader turned and said: "Wait, and then proceed according to his pace." I stopped, and saw two show, by their look, great haste of mind to be with me, but their load and the narrow way retarded them.

85. When they had come up, awhile, with eye askance, they gazed at me without speaking a word; then they turned to one another,

---

[1] This fable, not among those now ascribed to Aesop, but included in a collection which went under his name, has it that the frog deceitfully induced the mouse, attached by a string to his leg, to trust himself to the water. The mouse was drowned, and a kite, seeing the body floating on the surface, seized it, and with it the frog still tied to it, and swallowed both.

[2] Emperor Frederick II caused leaden cloaks to be put on criminals, who were then burned to death.

and said one to the other: "This one seems alive by the action of his throat; and if they are dead, by what privilege do they go uncovered by the heavy stole?" Then they said to me: "O Tuscan, who to the college of the wretched hypocrites art come, hold it not in disdain to tell who thou art." And I to them: "I was born and grew up on the fair river of Arno, at the great town, and I am in the body that I have always had. But who are ye, from whom such woe distils, as I see, down along your cheeks? and what penalty is it that so glitters on you?"

100. And one of them replied to me: "The orange hoods are of lead so thick that the weights thus make their scales to creak. Jovial Friars[1] were we, and Bolognese; I named Catalano and he Loderingo, and together taken by thy city, as one man alone is usually chosen, in order to preserve its peace: and we were such as still is apparent round about the Gardingo."

109. I began: "O Friars, your ills"—but more I said not, for there struck my eye one crucified upon the ground with three stakes. When he saw me he writhed all over, blowing into his beard with sighs: and the Friar Catalano, who observed it, said to me: "That transfixed one, whom thou lookest at, counseled the Pharisees that it was expedient to put one man to torture for the people.[2] Traverse and naked is he on the path, as thou seest, and he first must needs feel how much whoever passes weighs. And in like fashion his father-in-law[3] is stretched in this ditch, and the others of that Council which for the Jews was seed of ill."

[1] Brothers of the Military and Conventual Order of Santa Maria, established in 1261, with knightly vows and high intent. From the laxity of their rules and their free life the nickname of "Jovial Friars" was given to them.

After the battle of Montaperti, the Ghibellines held the upper hand in Florence for more than five years. The defeat and death of Manfred early in 1266 shook their power and revived the hopes of the Guelfs. As a compromise, the Florentine Commune elected a *podestà* from each party; the Guelf was Catalono de' Malavolti, the Ghibelline, Loderingo degli Andalò both from Bologna. They were believed to have joined hands for their own gain, and to have favored the reviving Guelfs. The houses of the Uberti, a powerful Ghibelline family, were burned; these lay in the region of the city called the Gardingo, close to the Palazzo Vecchio.

[2] Caiaphas. See John, 11. 50.

[3] Annas; John, 18. 13, 14, 24.

124. Then I saw Virgil marvel over him that was outstretched in a cross so vilely in the eternal exile. Afterwards he addressed this speech to the Friar: "May it not displease you, if it be allowed you, to tell us if any opening lies on the right hand, whereby we two can go out hence without constraining any of the Black Angels to come to deliver us from this deep." He answered then: "Nearer than thou hopest is a rock that starts from the great encircling wall and spans all the savage valleys, save that at this one it is broken, and does not cover it. Ye will be able to mount up over the ruin that lies against the side, and heaps up at the bottom." My Leader stood a little while with bowed head, then said: "Ill did he who hooks the sinners yonder report the matter." And the Friar: "Of old at Bologna I used to hear tell of vices enough of the devil, among which I heard that he is a liar, and the father of falsehood."

145. Then my Leader went on, with great steps, disturbed a little with anger in his look; whereon I departed from the burdened ones, following the prints of the beloved feet.

CANTO XXIV

1. IN THAT part of the young year when the sun tempers his locks beneath Aquarius, and now the nights are passing to the south, when the hoar frost copies on the ground the image of her white sister, but the temper of her pen lasts little while, the rustic, whose provision fails, gets up and looks, and sees the plain all white, whereat he smites his thigh, returns indoors, and grumbles to and fro, like the poor wretch who knows not what to do; then goes out again and picks up hope, seeing the world to have changed face in short while, and takes his crook and drives forth his sheep to pasture. Thus my Master made me dismayed, when I saw his brow so disturbed, and thus speedily arrived the plaster for the hurt. For when we came to the ruined bridge, the Leader turned to me with that sweet look which I first saw at the foot of the mount. After taking some counsel with himself, looking first well at the ruin, he opened his arms, and laid hold of me. And as one who acts and considers, and seems always to provide in advance, so, lifting me up toward the top of a great rock, he was taking

note of another splinter, saying: "Grapple next on that, but try first if it be such that it can support thee."

31. It was no way for one clothed in a cloak, for we with difficulty, he light and I pushed up, could mount from jag to jag. And had it not been that on that precinct the bank was shorter than on the other side, I do not know about him, but I should have been completely vanquished. But because all Malebolge slopes toward the opening of the lowest well, the site of each valley imports that one side is higher than the other. We came, however, at length, to the point where the last stone is broken off. The breath was so milked from my lungs when I was up that I could no farther, nay, sat me down on first arrival.

46. "Henceforth it behoves thee thus to put off sloth," said the Master, "for, sitting upon down or under quilts, one comes not to fame, without which he who consumes his life leaves such vestige of himself on earth as smoke in air, or the foam on water: and therefore rise up, conquer thy panting with the soul that wins every battle, if it be not weighed down by its heavy body. A longer stairway needs must be ascended: it is not enough to have departed from these; if thou understandest me, now act so that it avail thee." Then I rose up, showing myself better furnished with breath than I felt, and said: "Go on, for I am strong and resolute."

61. Up along the crag we took the way, which was rugged, narrow, and difficult, and far steeper than the one before. I was going along speaking in order not to seem exhausted, when a voice, ill suited for forming words, came out from the next ditch. I know not what it said, though I was already upon the back of the arch which crosses here; but he who was speaking seemed moved to anger. I had turned downwards, but my living eyes could not go to the bottom, through the darkness: wherefore I said: "Master, see that thou get to the next girth, and let us descend the wall, for as from this place I hear and do not understand, so I look down and shape out nothing." "Other reply," he said, "I give thee not than the doing, for the becoming request ought to be followed by the deed in silence."

79. We descended the bridge at its head,

where it is joined with the eighth bank, and then the pouch was apparent to me. And I saw within it a terrible crowd of serpents,[1] and of such strange kind that the memory still curdles my blood. Let Libya with her sand vaunt herself no more; for though she bring forth chelydri, jaculi, and phareae, and cenchri with amphisboena, she never, with all Ethiopia, nor with the land that lies on the Red Sea, showed either so many or so malignant plagues.

91. Amid this cruel and most dismal swarm were running people naked and terrified, without hope of hole or heliotrope.[2] They had their hands tied behind with serpents, which fixed their tail and their head through the loins, and were twisted up in front.

97. And lo! at one, who was near our bank, darted a serpent that transfixed him there where the neck is knotted to the shoulders. Nor O nor I was ever so quickly written as he took fire and burnt, and needs must become all ashes as he fell; and when he was thus destroyed on the ground, the dust drew together of itself, and in an instant into that same one returned. Thus by the great sages it is affirmed that the Phœnix dies, and then is born again when she draws nigh to her five-hundredth year. In her life she feeds not on herb or grain, but only on tears of incense and amomum; and nard and myrrh are her last winding-sheet.

112. And as he who falls, and knows not how, by force of a demon that drages him to ground, or of other obstruction that binds the man when he rises and gazes around him, all bewildered by the great anguish that he has suffered, and as he looks, sighs; such was that sinner after he had risen. Oh power of God! how severe it is, that showers down such blows for vengeance!

121. My Leader then asked him who he was; whereon he answered: "I rained down from Tuscany short time ago into this fell gullet. Bestial life, and not human, pleased me, like a mule that I was.[3] I am Vanni Fucci, beast, and Pistoia was my fitting den." And I to my Leader: "Tell him not to slip away, and

---

[1] Cf. *Paradise Lost*, x. 540.
[2] A precious stone, of green color, spotted with red, supposed to make its wearer invisible.
[3] That is, a bastard; one of the Lazzari, a noble family of Pistoia. In 1293, he with two companions

ask what sin thrust him down here, for I have seen him a man of blood and of rages." And the sinner who heard did not dissemble, but directed toward me his mind and his face, and painted himself with dismal shame.

133. Then he said: "It grieves me more, that thou hast caught me in the misery where thou seest me, than when I was taken from the other life. I cannot refuse that which thou askest. I am put so far down because I was the thief in the sacristy with the fair adornments, and it was once falsely ascribed to another. But in order that thou enjoy not this sight, if ever thou shalt be forth of these dark places, open thine ears to my announcement, and hear: Pistoia first strips herself of Blacks, then Florence renovates her people and her fashions. Mars draws a vapor from Val di Magra which is wrapt in turbid clouds, and with impetuous and bitter storm there shall be fighting on the Pescian plain, whence it shall suddenly rend the mist, so that every White shall be smitten by it. And this I have said in order that it may grieve thee."

CANTO XXV

1. AT the end of his words the thief raised his hands with both the figs,[2] crying, "Take that, God! for at Thee I square them." From that time forth the serpents were my friends, for then one coiled about his neck, as if it said: "I will not have thee say more"; and another about his arms and bound him up anew,[3]

clinching itself so in front that he could not give a shake with them. Ah Pistoia! Pistoia! why dost thou not decree to make ashes of thyself, so that thou last no longer, since in evil-doing thou dost surpass thine own seed?[4] Through all the dark circles of Hell I saw no spirit so arrogant toward God, not even that one who fell down from the walls at Thebes.[5] He fled away, and spoke not a word more.

17. And I saw a Centaur full of rage come crying out: "Where is he, where is the obdurate one?" I do not believe Maremma[6] has so many snakes as he had upon his croup up to where our semblance begins. On his shoulders, behind the nape, a dragon with open wings was lying upon him, which sets on fire whomsoever it encounters. My Master said: "This is Cacus, who beneath the rock of Mount Aventine often made a lake of blood. He goes not on one road with his brothers, because of the fraudulent theft he committed of the great herd that he had in his neighborhood; for which his crooked deeds ceased under the club of Hercules, who perhaps dealt him a hundred blows with it, and he felt not ten of them."[7]

34. While he was thus speaking, and that one had run by, lo! three spirits came below us, of whom neither I nor my Leader was aware till when they cried out: "Who are ye?" by which our story was stopped, and we then gave heed only to them. I did not know them, but it happened, as it usually happens by some chance, that one had occasion to name another, saying: "Where can Cianfa have stayed?" Wherefore I, in order that my Leader might be attentive, put my finger upward from my chin to my nose.

46. If, Reader, thou art now slow to credit that which I shall tell, it will be no marvel, for I who saw it hardly admit it to myself. As I was holding my eyebrows raised upon them, lo! a serpent with six feet darts in front of one, and takes hold all over him. With its middle feet it clasped his paunch, and with its fore

---

broke into the sacristy of San Zeno, at Pistoia. They carried off what silver and jewels they could lay hands on. At length, when an innocent man was about to be punished for the crime, Fucci revealed the name of the receiver of the plunder, who was hanged, while he himself escaped punishment.

[1] These verses may be partially explained as follows: In May, 1301, Pistoia expelled the Blacks; many of them were received in Florence, and, in November, the Florentine Blacks, thus reinforced, drove the Priors of the White party from office, chose new Priors of their own party, and in the following January succeeded in driving from the city the great body of the Whites, of whom Dante was one. The "vapor" from Val di Magra was Moroello Malaspina, captain of the forces of the Blacks; for years there were "turbid clouds" of confusion, and much desultory fighting, the Whites suffering defeat after defeat. The Pescian plain probably denotes a district near Pistoia.

[2] A coarse gesture of contemptuous defiance, made by thrusting out the fist with the thumb between the fore and middle finger.

[3] See Canto xxiv. 94, *supra.*

[4] According to tradition, the first settlers of Pistoia were the remnants of Catiline's forces after his defeat and death, 62 B.C.

[5] Capaneus; see Canto xiv. 46-72, *supra.*

[6] The desolate and unwholesome district of Tuscany bordering the sea.

[7] Cf. *Aeneid,* viii. 193ff.

feet took his arms, then struck its teeth in one and the other cheek; its hind feet it spread out upon his thighs, and put its tail between them, and stretched it up behind along the reins. Ivy was never so bearded to a tree, as the horrible beast entwined its own through the other's limbs. Then they stuck together as if they had been of hot wax, and mingled their color; neither the one nor the other seemed now that which it had been; even as in advance of the flame, a dark color proceeds up along the paper which is not yet black, and the white dies away. The other two were looking on, and each cried: "O me! Agnèl, how thou changest! See, now thou art neither two nor one!"

70. Now were the two heads become one, when there appeared to us two countenances mixed in one face wherein the two were lost. The two arms were made of four strips; the thighs with the legs, the belly and the chest became members that were never seen before. Every original aspect was there canceled; two and none the perverted image appeared, and such it went away with slow step.

79. As the lizard under the great scourge of the dog-days, changing from hedge to hedge, seems a lightning-flash, if it cross the way, so seemed, coming toward the bellies of the two others, a little fiery serpent, livid, and black as a pepper corn. And it transfixed in one of them that part whereat our nourishment is first taken, then fell down stretched out before him. The transfixed one gazed at it, but said nothing; nay, with feet fixed, he began to yawn, just as if sleep or fever had assailed him. He looked at the serpent, and that at him; one through the wound, the other through its mouth, were smoking fiercely, and the smoke commingled.

94. Let Lucan henceforth be silent, where he tells of the wretched Sabellus and of Nasidius,[1] and let him wait to hear that which now is related. Let Ovid be silent concerning Cadmus and Arethusa,[2] for if, poetizing, he converts him into a serpent and her into a fountain, I grudge it not to him; for never did he transmute two natures front to front, so that both the forms were prompt to exchange their matter. They responded to one another in such wise, that the serpent cleft his tail into a fork, and the wounded one drew his feet together. The legs and the thighs along with them so stuck together, that in short while the juncture made no mark that was apparent. The cleft tail was taking on the shape that the other was losing, and its skin was becoming soft, and that of the other hard. I saw the arms entering through the armpits, and the two feet of the beast, which were short, lengthening out in proportion as the arms were shortening. Then the hinder feet, twisted together, became the member that man conceals, and the wretch from his had two stretched forth.

118. While the smoke veils the one and the other with a new color, and generates hair on the one part, and strips it from the other, the one rose up, and the other fell down, not however turning aside their pitiless lights, beneath which each was changing his muzzle. He who was erect drew his in toward the temples, and, from the too much material that came in there, the ears issued on the smooth cheeks; that which did not run back and was retained, of its superfluity made a nose for the face, and thickened the lips so much as was needful. He that was lying down drives his muzzle forward, and draws backward his ears into his head, as the snail does its horns. And his tongue, which before was united and fit for speech, cleaves itself, and the forked one of the other closes up; and the smoke stops. The soul that had become a brute fled hissing along the valley, and the other, speaking, sputters behind it. Then he turned on him his new shoulders, and said to the third, "I want that Buoso should run, as I have done, on his belly along this path."

142. Thus I saw the seventh ballast[3] change and transmute, and here let the novelty be my excuse, if my pen straggle a little. And although my eyes were somewhat confused, and my mind bewildered, those could not flee away so covertly but that I clearly distinguished Puccio Sciancato: and he it was who alone, of the three companions that came first, was not

---

[1] Sabellus, bitten by a little serpent in the Libyan desert, melts away "like snow under a hot South wind," and Nasidius, stung by a snake of another kind, swells until he bursts his armor.

[2] See *Metamorphoses*, iv. 575ff, and v. 507ff.

[3] The sinners in the seventh *bolgia*.

changed; the other[1] was he whom thou, Ga-
ville, weepest.

CANTO XXVI

1. REJOICE, Florence, since thou art so great
that thou beatest thy wings over sea and land,
and thy name is spread through Hell! Among
the thieves I found five such, thy citizens,
whereat shame comes to me, and thou dost not
mount unto great honor thereby. But, if near
the morning one dreams of the truth, thou
shalt feel within short time what Prato,[2] as
well as others, craves for thee. And if already
it were, it would not be too soon. So were it!
since surely it must be; for it will weigh the
more on me as the more I age.

13. We departed thence, and, up along the
stairs which the bourns[3] had before made for
our descent, my Leader remounted and drew
me. And pursuing the solitary way among the
fragments and the rocks of the craggy bridge,
the foot sped not without the hand. I sorrowed
then, and now I sorrow again when I direct
my mind to what I saw; and I curb my genius
more than I am wont, that it may not run un-
less virtue guide it; so that if a good star, or
better thing, have given me the good, I may
not grudge it to myself.

25. As many as the fireflies which, in the
season when he that brightens the world keeps
his face least hidden from us, the rustic, who
is resting on the hillside what time the fly
yields to the gnat, sees down in the valley,
perhaps there where he makes his vintage and
ploughs—with so many flames all the eighth
pit was gleaming, as I perceived so soon as I
was there where the bottom became apparent.
And as he[4] who was avenged by the bears saw
the chariot of Elijah at its departure, when the
horses rose erect to heaven,—for he could not
so follow it with his eyes as to see aught save
the flame alone, like a little cloud, mounting
upward,—thus each of those flames was mov-
ing through the gulley of the ditch, for not

one shows its theft, and every flame steals
away a sinner.

43. I was standing on the bridge, risen up
to look, so that, if I had not taken hold of a
rock, I should have fallen below without being
pushed. And my Leader, who saw me thus
intent, said: "Within these fires are the spir-
its; each is swathed by that wherewith he is
burnt." "My Master," I replied, "through hear-
ing thee am I more certain, but already I
deemed that it was so, and already I wished to
say to thee: Who is in that fire which comes
so divided at its top that it seems to rise from
the pyre on which Eteocles was put with his
brother?[5] He answered me: "Therewithin
Ulysses and Diomed are tormented, and thus
they go together in their punishment, as in
their wrath. And within their flame they groan
for the ambush of the horse which made the
gate whence the noble seed of the Romans is-
sued forth; within it they lament the artifice
whereby the dead Deidamia still mourns for
Achilles, and there they bear the penalty for
the Palladium."[6]

64. "If they have power to speak within
those sparks," said I, "Master, much I pray
thee, and repray, that my prayer avail a thou-
sand, that thou make not to me denial of
waiting till the horned flame come hither: thou
seest that with desire I bend me toward it."
And he to me: "Thy prayer is worthy of much
praise, and therefore I accept it; but mind that
thy tongue restrain itself. Leave speech to me,
for I have conceived that which thou wishest;
for, because they were Greeks, they would
perhaps be disdainful of thy words."

76. When the flame had come there where
it seemed to my Leader time and place, I heard
him speak to it in this form: "O ye, who are
two within one fire, if I deserved of you while

---

[1] Francesco Guercio de' Cavalcanti, slain by men
of the village of Gaville, in Valdarno, which mourns
for the cruel vengeance taken for his death.
  The three who had come first were the three Flor-
entine thieves, Agnello, Buoso, and Puccio.
[2] A Tuscan town ten miles from Florence.
[3] The projections of the rocky wall.
[4] Elisha. II Kings, 2. 9-24.

[5] Cf. Aeschylus, The Seven Against Thebes, and
Euripides, The Phoenician Maidens. Such was the
mutual hate of Eteocles and Polynices that, when
their bodies were burned on the same funeral pile,
the flames divided in two.
[6] It was through the stratagem of the wooden horse
that Troy was destroyed, and Aeneas was compelled
to lead forth his followers, the seed of the Romans.
Deidamia was the mother of a son by Achilles, and
when by the craft of Ulysses, accompanied by Diomed,
Achilles was discovered and persuaded to go to Troy,
she slew herself. The Palladium, the image of Athena,
on which the safety of Troy depended, was stolen by
the two heroes. Aeneid, ii. 163-170.

I lived, if I deserved of you much or little, when in the world I wrote my lofty verses, move not, but let one of you tell, whither, being lost, he went away to die." The greater horn of the ancient flame began to wag. murmuring, even as a flame that the wind wearies. Then waving its tip to and fro, as if it were the tongue that spoke, it cast forth a voice, and said:

90. "When I departed from Circe, who had detained me more than a year there near to Gaeta, before Aeneas had so named it,[1] neither fondness for my son, nor piety for my old father, nor the due love which should have made Penelope glad, could overcome within me the ardor which I had to become experienced of the world, and of the vices of men, and of their virtue. But I put forth on the deep, open sea, with one vessel only, and with that little company by which I had not been deserted. I saw one shore and the other as far as Spain, as far as Morocco and the island of Sardinia, and the others which that sea bathes round about. I and my companions were old and slow when we came to that narrow strait where Hercules set up his bounds, to the end that man should not put out beyond. On the right hand I left Seville, on the other I had already left Ceuta.

112. "'O brothers,' I said, 'who through a hundred thousand perils have reached the West, to this so brief vigil of your senses which remains wish not to deny the experience, following the sun, of the world that has no people. Consider your origin; ye were not made to live as brutes, but to pursue virtue and knowledge.'

121. "With this little speech I made my companions so keen for the voyage that hardly afterwards could I have held them back. And turning our stern to the morning, with our oars we made wings for the mad flight, always gaining on the left hand side.[2] The night saw now all the stars of the other pole, and ours so low that it rose not forth from the ocean floor. The light beneath the moon had been five times rekindled and as many quenched, since we had entered on the passage of the deep, when there appeared to us a mountain dark in the distance, and it seemed to me so high as I had never seen one.[3] We rejoiced, and soon it turned to lamentation, for from the new land a whirlwind rose and struck the fore part of the vessel. Three times it made her whirl with all the waters, the fourth it made her stern lift up and the prow go down, as pleased Another, till the sea had closed over us."

CANTO XXVII

1. THE flame was already erect and quiet, by reason of not speaking more, and already was going from us, with the permission of the sweet poet, when another, which was coming behind it, made us turn our eyes to its tip, by a confused sound that was issuing forth from it. As the Sicilian bull,[4] which bellowed first with the plaint of him (and that was right) who had shaped it with his tools, was wont to bellow with the voice of the sufferer, so that, although it was of brass, yet it appeared transfixed with the pain, so, through not at first having way or outlet from the fire, the disconsolate words were converted into its language. But when they had taken their course up through the point, giving to it in their passage that vibration which the tongue had given, we heard say: "O thou, to whom I direct my voice, and who just now wast speaking Lombard,[5] saying: 'Now go thy way, no more I urge thee:' although I may have arrived perhaps somewhat late, let it not irk thee to stop to speak with me; behold, it irks not me, and I am burning. If thou art but now fallen into this blind world from that sweet Italian land whence I bring all my sin, tell me if the Romagnoles[6] have peace or war; for I was of the mountains there, between Urbino and the chain from which Tiber is unlocked."[7]

---

[1] See *Aeneid*, vii. 1-4.
[2] In Dante's scheme of the Earth the southern hemisphere was a vast expanse of water, in which the only land was the Mountain of Purgatory (Canto xxxiv. 122-126), the antipodes of Jerusalem (*Purgatory*, iv. 68-71). The course of Ulysses and his companions after passing through the Pillars of Hercules was to the southwest, until they came in sight of the Mountain. See *Purgatory*, i. 132.

[3] Cf. *Paradise*, xxvi. 139; *Purgatory*, iii. 15.
[4] The brazen bull of Phalaris, tyrant of Agrigentum, made to hold criminals to be burned within it. Perillus, its inventor, was the first to suffer.
[5] See Canto i. 68, *supra*.
[6] The people of the Romagna. See *Purgatory*, xiv. 92.
[7] The spirit who speaks is that of the Ghibelline count, Guido da Montefeltro, the ablest and most famous warrior of his time in Italy.

31. I was still downward attent and leaning over, when my Leader touched me on the side, saying, "Speak thou, this is an Italian." And I, who already had my answer ready, without delay began to speak: "O soul, that art hidden down there, thy Romagna is not, and never was, without war in the hearts of her tyrants, but no open war have I left there now. Ravenna is as it has been for many years; the eagle of Polenta[1] is brooding there, so that he covers Cervia with his wings. The city that made some while ago the long struggle, and of the French a bloody heap, finds itself again beneath the green paws.[2] And the old mastiff and the new of Verrucchio,[3] who made the ill disposal of Montagna, make an auger of their teeth there where they are wont. The young lion of the white lair,[4] who changes side from summer to winter, rules the cities of Lamone and of Santerno. And she[5] whose flank the Savio bathes lives between tyranny and a free state, even as she sits between the plain and the mountain. Now I pray thee that thou tell us who thou art; be not harder than another has been, so may thy name hold front in the world."

58. After the fire had roared for a while according to its fashion, the sharp point moved to and fro, and then gave forth this breath: "If I believed that my reply were to a person who should ever return to the world, this flame would stand without more quiverings; but inasmuch as, if I hear truth, never did any one return alive from this depth, I answer thee without fear of infamy.

67. "I was a man of arms, and then I was a cordelier,[6] trusting, thus girt, to make amends; and surely my trust had come full but for the Great Priest,[7] whom ill befall! who set me back into my first sins; and how and wherefore, I will that thou hear from me. While I was that shape of bone and flesh which my mother gave me, my works were not leonine, but of the fox. All wily practices and covert ways I knew, and I so plied their art that the sound went forth to the end of the earth. When I saw me arrived at that part of my age where every one ought to strike the sails and coil up the ropes, what before was pleasing to me then was irksome to me, and I yielded me repentant and confessed. Ah wretched, alas! and it would have availed.

85. "The Prince of the new Pharisees having war near the Lateran,[8]—and not with Saracens nor with Jews, for every enemy of his was Christian, and not one of them had been to conquer Acre, or a trafficker in the land of the Soldan,—regarded in himself neither his supreme office, nor his Holy Orders, nor in me that cord which was wont to make those girt with it more lean; but as Constantine besought Sylvester within Soracte to cure his leprosy,[9] so this one besought me as master to cure the fever of his pride. He asked counsel of me, and I kept silence, because his words seemed drunken. And then he said to me: 'Let not thy heart mistrust; from this time forward I absolve thee, and do thou teach me to act so that I may throw Palestrina to the ground. I can lock and unlock Heaven, as thou knowest; wherefor the keys are two, which my predecessor held not dear.'[10] Then his weighty argu-

---

[1] Guido da Polenta had been lord of Ravenna since 1275. His shield bore an eagle. Cervia is a small coastal town near Ravenna.

[2] Forlì, where in 1282 Guido da Montefeltro had defeated, with great slaughter, a troop, largely of French soldiers, sent against him by Pope Martin IV. It was now ruled by the Ordelaffi, whose shield bore on its upper half a green demi-lion on a gold field.

[3] Verrucchio was a castle near Rimini, which had long been in possession of the Malatesta family. "The old mastiff and the new" were Malatesta de' Malatesti and his son Malatestino, lords of Rimini. In 1295 they had treacherously overpowered and murdered Montagna de' Parcitati, the head of the Ghibellines in Rimini.

[4] This is Maghinardo de' Pagani da Susinana, who bore on his shield a blue lion on a white field. He was a Ghibelline in Romagna, and a Guelf with the Florentines, says Villani. "Lamone" is Faenza, near the river of Lamone, and "Santerno" is Imola, by which the Santerno runs.

[5] The city of Cesena.

[6] In 1296 Guido, past seventy years old, entered the Franciscan Order, girding himself with its cord.

[7] Boniface VIII.

[8] With the Colonna family, whose stronghold was Palestrina, visible from the Lateran hill. In 1297 Boniface proclaimed a crusade against them; Palestrina was surrendered to him on false promises, and then demolished.

[9] It was for this service that Constantine was supposed to have made Pope Sylvester I "the first rich Father" (Canto xix. 117) by the famous "Donation" conveying to the Pope the sovereignty over Italy and the whole Western Empire. Sylvester, to escape from Constantine's previous persecution of the Christians, had taken refuge on Mount Soracte.

[10] Cf. Canto iii. 59-60, *supra*.

ments pushed me to where silence seemed to me the worst, and I said: 'Father, since thou dost wash me of that sin wherein I now must fall, long promise with short keeping will make thee triumph on the High Seat.'

112. "Francis came for me afterwards, when I was dead, but one of the black Cherubim said to him: 'Bear him not away; do me not wrong; he must come down among my drudges because he gave the fraudulent counsel, since which till now I have been at his hair; for he who does not repent cannot be absolved, nor can repentance and will exist together, because of the contradiction which does not allow it.' O me woeful! how I shuddered when he took me, saying to me: 'Perhaps thou didst not think that I was a logician.' He bore me to Minos; and he twisted his tail eight times round his hard back,[1] and, after he had bitten it from great rage, he said: 'This is one of the sinners of the thievish fire': wherefore here, where thou seest, I am lost, and going thus robed I am afflicted." When he had thus completed his speech the flame, sorrowing, departed, twisting and flapping its sharp horn.

133. We passed onward, I and my Leader, over the crag, far as to the next arch that covers the ditch in which the fee is paid by those who acquire their load by sundering.[2]

CANTO XXVIII

1. WHO, even with words unfettered, could ever tell in full, though many times narrating, of the blood and of the wounds that I now saw? Every tongue assuredly would come short, by reason of our speech and our memory which have small capacity to comprise so much.

7. If all the people were again assembled, that of old upon the storm-tossed land of Apulia lamented for their blood shed by the Trojans,[3] and in the long war that made such vast spoil of the rings,[4] as Livy writes, who does not err; together with those who, by resisting Robert Guiscard,[5] felt the pain of blows,

[1] See Canto v. 11-12.
[2] See Canto xi. 56.
[3] Cf. Canto xxvi. 60.
[4] The spoils—three bushels and a half of rings—of the battle of Cannæ, in the Second Punic War, which lasted more than fifteen years.
[5] The Norman conqueror and Duke of Apulia. He died in 1085.

and the others whose bones are still heaped up at Ceperano,[6] where every Apulian was false, and there by Tagliacozzo,[7] where the old Alardo conquered without arms—and one should show his limb pierced through, and one his lopped off, it would be nothing to equal the hideous mode of the ninth pouch.

22. Truly a cask by losing mid-board or stave is not so split open, as one I saw who was cleft from the chin to where the wind is broken; his entrails were hanging between his legs, his pluck was visible, and the dismal sack which makes ordure of what is swallowed. While I fix myself all on seeing him, he looked at me, and with his hands opened his breast, saying: "Now see how I rend myself; see how mangled is Mahomet. In front of me goes Ali[8] weeping, cleft in the face from chin to forelock; and all the others whom thou seest here were, when living, sowers of scandal and of schism, and therefore are they so cleft. A devil is here behind that fashions us so cruelly, putting again to the edge of the sword each of this throng when we have circled the doleful road; because the wounds are closed up before one passes again before him. But who art thou that art musing on the crag, perhaps to delay going to the punishment that has been adjudged on thine own accusations?"

46. "Death has not reached him yet," replied my Master, "nor does guilt lead him to torment him; but, in order to give him full experience, it behoves me, who am dead, to lead him down here through Hell, from circle to circle; and this is true, as that I speak to thee."

More than a hundred there were who, when they heard him, stopped in the ditch to look at me, forgetting the torment in their wonder.

55. "Now say then to Fra Dolcino,[9] thou who perhaps wilt shortly see the sun, if he wish

[6] There was no battle at Ceperano, but the defence of the bridge there over the Garigliano was treacherously abandoned, leaving the way open for Charles of Anjou to advance to Benevento, where in 1266, the great battle was fought which ended in the defeat and death of Manfred, king of Sicily. At this battle many of the Apulian barons proved traitors.
[7] Here, in 1268, Conradin, the nephew of Manfred, was defeated and taken prisoner by Charles of Anjou. The victory was won, not by arms, but by a stratagem devised by Count Erard (Alardo) de Valéry.
[8] Cousin and son-in-law of Mahomet, and himself the head of a schism.
[9] A heretic and reformer, who for two years main-

not speedily to follow me hither, so to arm himself with provisions that stress of snow may not bring the victory to the Novarese, which to gain otherwise would not be easy." Mahomet said to me this word, after he had lifted one foot to go on, then to depart he stretched it on the ground.

64. Another who had his throat pierced and his nose cut off close under his brows, and had but one ear only, having stopped to gaze, for wonder, with the others, before the others opened his gullet, which outwardly was all crimson, and said: "O thou whom guilt does not condemn, and whom I saw above in the land of Italy, if exceeding resemblance deceive me not, if ever thou return to see the sweet plain which slopes from Vercelli to Marcabò,[1] remember Pier da Medicina,[2] and make known to the two best men of Fano, to Messer Guido and likewise to Angiolello,[3] that, if our foresight here is not vain, they will be thrown out of their vessel and sunk near La Cattolica,[4] through the treachery of a fell tyrant. Between the islands of Cyprus and Majorca Neptune never saw so great a crime, not of the pirates, nor of the Argolic people.[5] That traitor who sees only with one eye, and holds the city[6] from sight of which one who is here with me would wish he had fasted, will make them come to parley with him; then will deal so that against the wind of Focara[7] they will not need vow or prayer."

91. And I to him: "Show to me and declare, if thou wishest that I carry up news of thee, who is he of the bitter sight?" Then he put his hand on the jaw of one of his companions, and opened the mouth of him, crying: "This is he, and he does not speak; this one, being banished stifled the doubt in Cæsar, affirming that the man prepared always suffered harm from delay." Oh, how aghast, with his tongue cut off in his throat, seemed to me Curio,[8] who had been so bold to speak!

103. And one who had both hands lopped off, lifting the stumps through the murky air so that the blood made his face foul, cried out: "Thou shalt bear in mind Mosca,[9] too, who said, alas! 'Thing done has a head,' which was the seed of ill for the Tuscan people." And I added for him: "And death to thine own race." Whereat he, accumulating woe on woe, went away like a person sorrowful and mad.

112. But I remained to look at the crowd, and saw a thing which, without more proof, I should be afraid only to tell, were it not that conscience reassures me, the good companion which emboldens man under the hauberk of feeling itself pure. I saw truly, and I seem to see it still, a trunk without a head going along, even as the others of the dismal herd were going. And it was holding its cut-off head by the hair, dangling it in hand like a lantern, and that was gazing on us, and saying: "O me!"

127. Of itself it was making a lamp for itself; and they were two in one, and one in two; how it can be He knows who so ordains. When he was right at foot of the bridge, he lifted his arm high with the whole head, in order to bring its words near to us, which were: "Now see the dire punishment, thou that, breathing, goest seeing the dead: see if any other be great as this! And that thou mayst carry news of me, know that I am Bertran de Born,[10] he that gave to the young king

---

tained himself in Lombardy against the forces of the Pope. Finally, being reduced by famine in time of snow, in 1307, he was taken captive and burnt at Vercelli.
[1] From the foot of the Alps to the Adriatic. Marcabo was a stronghold near the mouths of the Po.
[2] Medicina is a town between Bologna and Imola. Piero was a fosterer of discord among the lords of the cities of the Romagna.
[3] Guido del Cassero and Angiolello da Cagnano, treacherously drowned by order of the one-eyed Malatestino (Cf. Canto xxvii. 46).
[4] A small town on the Adriatic between Rimini and Pesaro.
[5] Cf. *Aeneid*, ii. 78.
[6] Rimini.
[7] A high foreland near La Cattolica, dreaded by mariners because of the dangerous squalls which often swept down from it.

[8] Curio the Tribune, banished from Rome, fled to Cæsar delaying at the Rubicon, and urged him to cross.
[9] In 1215 one of the Buondelmonti, plighted to a maiden of the Amidei family, broke faith, and engaged himself to one of the Donati. The relatives of the slighted girl took counsel how to avenge the affront, and Mosca de' Lamberti gave the ill advice to kill the young Buondelmonte, with the words: "Thing done has a head": it cannot be undone—it shows its head. The murder was the beginning of long woe to Florence, and of the division of her people into Guelfs and Ghibellines.
[10] The famous troubadour who incited young Prince Henry to rebel against his father, Henry II of England.

the ill encouragements. I made father and son rebels to each other. Ahithophel did not more with Absalom and with David by his wicked goadings. Because I divided persons thus united, I carry my brain, alas! divided from its source which is in this trunk. Thus the retribution is observed in me."

CANTO XXIX

1. THE many people and the divers wounds had so inebriated my eyes that they were fain to stay for weeping; but Virgil said to me: "What art thou still watching? why does thy gaze still rest down there among the dismal mutilated shades? Thou hast not done so at the other pits; consider, if thou thinkest to count them, that the valley circles two and twenty miles; and already the moon is beneath our feet;[1] the time is little now that is conceded to us, and other things are to be seen than these thou seest." "If thou hadst," replied I thereupon, "given heed to the reason why I was looking, perhaps thou wouldst have permitted me yet to stay."

16. Meanwhile my Leader was going on, and I was going behind him, now making my reply, and adding: "Within that hollow where I was now holding my eyes so fixedly, I believe that a spirit of my own blood is weeping for the guilt which costs so dear down there." Then said the Master: "Let not thy thought henceforth be broken upon him; attend to other things, and let him stay there; for I saw him at the foot of the little bridge, pointing thee out, and threatening fiercely with his finger, and I heard him called Geri del Bello.[2] Thou wert then so wholly occupied with him who of old held Hautefort[3] that thou didst not look that way; so he went off."

31. "O my Leader," said I, "that his violent death has not yet been avenged for him by any one who is a partner in the shame made him indignant; wherefore, as I deem, he went on without speaking to me, and thereby he has made me the more pitiful for him."

37. Thus we spoke as far as the first place on the crag which shows the next valley, if more light were there, quite to the bottom. When we were above the last cloister of Malebolge, so that its lay brothers could appear to our sight, divers lamentations pierced me, which had their arrows barbed with woe; wherefore I covered my ears with my hands.

46. Such suffering as there would be if, between July and September, the sick from the hospitals of Valdichiana and of Maremma and of Sardinia[4] were all in one ditch together, such was there here; and such stench came forth therefrom, as is wont to come from gangrened limbs. We descended upon the last bank of the long crag, ever to the left hand, and then my sight became livelier down toward the bottom, where the ministress of the High Lord—infallible Justice—punishes the falsifiers whom she registers here.

58. I do not believe it was a greater sorrow to see the whole people in Aegina sick, when the air was so full of harm that the animals, even to the little worm, all fell dead, and afterwards the ancient people, according as the poets hold for sure, were restored from seed of ants, then it was to see the spirits languishing in different heaps through that dark valley. One was lying on the belly, and one on the shoulders of another, and one, on all fours, was shifting himself along the dismal path. Step by step we went without speech, looking at and listening to the sick, who could not lift their persons.

73. I saw two seated leaning on each other, as pan is leaned against pan to warm, spotted from head to foot with scabs; and never did I see currycomb plied by stable-boy for whom his lord is waiting, or by one who stays awake unwillingly, as each was incessantly plying the bite of his nails upon himself, because of the great rage of his itching which has no other relief. And the nails were dragging down the scab, as a knife does the scales of bream, or of other fish that has them larger still.

85. "O thou, that art dismailing thyself with thy fingers," began my Leader unto one of them, "and who sometimes makest pincers of them, tell me if any Italian is among those who

[1] It was early in the afternoon.
[2] A first cousin of Dante's father. He was a harmful and quarrelsome person, who, having sown discord among the Sacchetti, was slain by one of them. After thirty years his death was avenged by his nephews, by the killing of one of the Sacchetti.
[3] Bertran de Born was lord of Hautefort.

[4] All haunts of malarial fever.

are here within, so may thy nails suffice thee eternally for this work." "Italians are we whom here thou seest so spoiled, both of us," replied one weeping, "but who are thou that askest of us?" And the Leader said: "I am one that descends with this living man down from ledge to ledge, and I intend to show Hell to him." Then their mutual support was broken; and each turned trembling to me, with others who heard him by rebound. The good Master drew quite close to me, saying: "Say to them what thou wilt"; and I began, since he wished it: "So may memory of you in the first world not steal away from the minds of men, but may it live under many suns, tell me who ye are, and of what folk; let not your unseemly and loathsome punishment fright you from disclosing yourselves unto me."

109. "I was of Arezzo," replied one of them, "and Albero of Siena had me put in the fire; but that for which I died does not bring me here. It is true that I said to him, speaking in jest, that I knew how to raise myself through the air in flight, and he, who had lively desire and little wit, wished that I should show him the art, and only because I did not make him Daedalus, caused me to be burned by one[1] who had him for son; but to the last pouch of the ten, Minos, to whom it is not allowed to err, condemned me by reason of the alchemy that I practiced in the world."

121. And I said to the Poet: "Now was ever people so vain as the Sienese? surely not so the French by much."

124. Whereon the other leprous one, who heard me, replied to my words: "Excepting Stricca, who knew how to make moderate spendings; and Niccolò, who first invented the costly use of the clove, in the garden where such seed takes root; and excepting the brigade in which Caccia of Asciano squandered his vineyard and his great wood, and Abbagliato showed his wit. But that thou mayst know who thus seconds thee against the Sienese, sharpen thine eye toward me so that my face may answer well to thee, so wilt thou see that I am the shade of Capocchio, who falsified the metals by alchemy; and thou shouldst recol-

lect, if I descry thee aright, how I was a good ape of nature."

CANTO XXX

1. AT the time when Juno was wroth because of Semele against the Theban blood, as she showed more than once, Athamas became so insane,[2] that seeing his wife come laden on either hand with her two sons, he cried out: "Spread we the nets, so that I may take the lioness and the young lions at the pass," and then he stretched out his pitiless talons, seizing the one who was named Learchus, and whirled him and dashed him on a rock; and she drowned herself with her other burden. And when Fortune turned downward the loftiness of the Trojans which dared all, so that together with his kingdom the king was undone, Hecuba, sad, wretched, and captive, after she saw Polyxena dead, and descried her Polydorus on the seastrand, she the doleful, frantic, barked like a dog, to such degree had grief distraught her mind.[3]

21. But neither furies of Thebes nor of Troy were ever seen in any one so cruel, not in goading beasts much less human limbs, as those I saw in two pale and naked shades who were running, biting, in the way that a boar does when he is let out from the sty. One came at Capocchio, and struck his tusks in the nape of his neck, so that dragging him it made his belly scratch along the solid bottom. And the Aretine,[4] who remained trembling, said to me: "That mad sprite is Gianni Schicchi, and he goes rabid dressing others thus." "Oh!" said I to him, "so may the other not fix its teeth on thee, let it not be weariness to thee to tell who it is before it breaks away from here." And he to me: "That is the ancient soul of infamous Myrrha, who became loving of her father beyond rightful love. She came thus to sinning with him by falsifying herself in another's form, even as the other, who goes off there, ventured, in order to gain the lady of the stud, to simulate in his own person Buoso Donati,

[1] The Bishop of Siena, under whose ecclesiastical jurisdiction Griffolino of Arezzo fell as a dealer in the black art.

[2] Athamas, King of Orchomenos, near Thebes, had two children by the sister of Semele, Ino. Both he and Ino had incurred the resentment of Juno.

[3] See Euripides, *Hecuba*.

[4] See Canto xxix. 109ff., *supra*.

making a will and giving to the will due form."[1]

46. And after the two rabid ones, upon whom I had kept my eye, had passed on, I turned it to look at the others of the evil born. I saw one shaped in fashion of a lute, had he only had his groin cut short at the part where man is forked. The heavy dropsy which, with its ill-digested humor, so unmates the members that the face does not correspond with the belly, was making him hold his lips open, as the hectic does, who for thirst turns one toward his chin, and the other upward.

58. "Oh ye, who are without any punishment, and I know not why, in this dismal world," said he to us, "behold and consider the misery of Master Adam. Living, I had enough of what I wished, and now, alas! I long for a drop of water. The little brooks that from the green hills of the Casentin run down into the Arno, making their channels cool and soft, stand ever before me, and not in vain; for their image dries me up far more than the malady whereby I strip my face of flesh. The rigid justice that scourges me draws occasion from the place where I sinned to set my sighs the more in flight. There is Romena, where I falsified the coin stamped with the Baptist, for which on earth I left my body burnt.[2] But if I could see here the miserable soul of Guido, or of Alessandro, or of their brother,[3] I would not give the sight for Fonte Branda.[4] One of them is here within already, if the raging shades who go around speak true; but what does it avail me who have my limbs bound? If I were only still so light that in a hundred years I could go one inch, I should already have set out along the path, seeking for him among this disfigured folk, although it circles round eleven miles, and has not here less than a half mile across. Because of them I am among such

a family; they induced me to strike the florins which had three carats of base-metal."

91. And I to him: "Who are the two poor wretches that are smoking like wet hands in winter, lying close to thy confines on the right?" "Here I found them," he answered, "when I rained down into this trough, and they have not since given a turn, and I do not believe they will give one to all eternity. One is the false woman who accused Joseph, the other is the false Sinon the Greek, from Troy:[5] because of their sharp fever they throw out such great reek."

100. And one of them, who took it ill perhaps to be named so darkly, with his fist struck him on his stiff paunch; it sounded as if it were a drum; and Master Adam struck him on the face with his arm which did not seem less hard, saying to him: "Though moving be taken from me because of my limbs which are heavy, I have an arm free for such need." Whereon he replied: "When thou wast going to the fire thou hadst it not thus ready; but so and more thou hadst it when thou wast coining." And he of the dropsy: "Thou sayest true of this, but thou wast not so true a witness there where thou wast questioned of the truth at Troy." "If I said false, thou didst falsify the coin," said Sinon, "and I am here for a single sin, and thou for more than any other demon." "Remember, perjurer, the horse," answered he who had the puffed up paunch, "and be it ill for thee that all the world knows it." "And for thee be ill the thirst wherewith thy tongue cracks," said the Greek, "and the putrid water that makes thy belly thus a hedge before thine eyes." Then the coiner: "Thy mouth gapes thus for its own harm as it is wont, for if I have thirst, and humor stuffs me, thou hast the burning, and the head that pains thee, and to lick the mirror of Narcissus thou wouldst not want many words of invitation."

130. I was wholly fixed in listening to them, when the Master said to me: "Now only look! for it wants but little that I quarrel with thee." When I heard him speak to me with anger, I turned me toward him with such shame that even yet it circles through my memory. And as is he who dreams of his harm, and, dreaming,

---

[1] Buoso Donati had died without making a will, whereupon his son suborned Gianni Schicchi, one of the Cavalcanti family, to personate the dead man in bed, and to dictate a will in his favor. This Gianni did, inserting, however, several clauses with bequests to himself, among which was that of a favorite mare or she-mule of Buoso's, reputed the best in Tuscany.
[2] A little village near the border of the Casentino bears the name of La Consuma, perpetuating the fact that here, in 1281, Master Adam was burnt alive by the Florentines, jealous for the purity of their florin.
[3] Counts of Romena.
[4] A spring in Romena.

[5] See *Aeneid*, ii. 57ff.

desires to dream, so that he longs for that which is, as if it were not, such I became, not being able to speak; for I desired to excuse myself, and all the while I was excusing myself, and never thought that I was doing it. "Less shame washes away a greater fault than thine has been," said the Master; "therefore disburden thyself of all sadness, and make reckoning that I am always at thy side, if again it happen that fortune find thee where people may be in a similar wrangle; for the wish to hear this is a base wish."

CANTO XXXI

1. ONE and the same tongue first stung me, so that it tinged both my cheeks, and then supplied the medicine to me. Thus do I hear that the lance of Achilles and of his father was wont to be cause first of a sad and then of a good gift.[1]

7. We turned our backs to the wretched valley, up over the bank that girds it round, crossing without any speech. Here it was less than night and less than day, so that my sight went little forward; but I heard a loud horn sounding, so that it would have made every thunder faint, and this directed my eyes, following its course counter to it, wholly to one place.

16. After the dolorous rout when Charlemagne lost the holy gest, Roland sounded not so terribly.[2] Short while I carried my head turned thitherward, when it seemed to me that I saw many high towers; whereon I: "Master, say, what city is this?" And he to me: "Because thou dost cross through the darkness from too far off, it happens that then thou dost err in thy imagining. Thou wilt see well, if thou drawest nigh there, how much the sense is deceived at a distance; therefore spur thyself on somewhat more." Then he took me tenderly by the hand, and said: "Before we go further forward, in order that the fact may seem less strange to thee, know that these are not towers, but giants, and they are in the pit round about the bank, from the navel downward, one and all of them."

34. As when the mist is dissipating, the look little by little shapes out what the vapor that thickens the air conceals, so, as I pierced the gross and dark air, as we drew nearer and nearer to the brink, error fled from me and fear grew upon me. For as above its circular enclosure Montereggione[3] crowns itself with towers, so with half their bodies the horrible giants, whom Jove still threatens from heaven when he thunders, betowered the bank which surrounds the pit.

46. And already I discerned the face of one of them, his shoulders, and his breast, and great part of his belly, and down along his sides both his arms. Nature, surely, when she left the art of such like living beings, did exceeding well to take such executioners from Mars: and though she repent not of elephants and of whales, he who looks subtly holds her therein more just and more discreet; for where the faculty of the mind is added to evil will and to power, the human race can make no defense against it. His face seemed to me long and huge as the pinecone of St. Peter's at Rome, and his other bones were in proportion with it; so that the bank, which was an apron from his middle downward, showed of him fully so much above, that three Frieslanders would have made ill vaunt to reach to his hair: for I saw of him thirty great spans down from the place where one buckles his cloak.

67. *"Rafel mai amech zabi almi,"* the fierce mouth, to which sweeter psalms were not befitting, began to cry. And my Leader toward him: "Foolish soul! Keep to thy horn, and with that vent thyself, when anger or other passion touches thee; seek at thy neck, and thou wilt find the cord that holds it tied, O soul confused! and see it lying athwart thy great breast." Then he said to me: "He accuses himself; this is Nimrod, because of whose evil thought one language only is not used in the world. Let us leave him alone, and not speak in vain; for such is every language to him, as his to others which is known to no one."

82. Then turning to the left, we made a longer journey, and at a crossbow-shot we found the next, far more fierce and larger. Who had been the master to bind him I cannot tell; but he had his right arm shackled behind, and the other in front, by a chain

---

[1] Cf. Shakespeare, 2 *Henry VI*, v. 1. 160. So, too, Chaucer, in *The Squire's Tale*, 10552-4.
[2] At Roncesvalles.

[3] The castle of Montereggione is not far from Siena.

which held him girt from the neck downward, so that upon his uncovered part it was wound as far as the fifth coil. "This proud one wished to make trial of his power against the supreme Jove," said my Leader, "wherefore he has such requital. Ephialtes[1] is his name, and he made his great endeavors when the giants caused fear to the Gods: the arms which he plied he moves nevermore."

97. And I to him: "If it may be, I would that my eyes might have experience of the measureless Briareus." Whereon he answered: "Hard by here thou shalt see Antaeus, who speaks, and is unfettered,[2] who will set us at the bottom of all sin. He whom thou wishest to see is much farther on, and is bound and fashioned like this one, save that he seems more ferocious in his look."

106. Never was earthquake so mighty that it shook a tower as violently as Ephialtes was quick to shake himself. Then more than ever did I fear death; and for it there had been no need of more than the fright, if I had not seen his bonds.

112. We then proceeded further forward, and came to Antaeus, who stood full five ells, besides his head, above the rock. "O thou that, in the fateful valley which made Scipio the heir of glory, when Hannibal with his followers turned his back, didst once bring a thousand lions for booty, and who hadst thou been at the high war of thy brothers, it seems that some still believe that the sons of the Earth would have conquered, set us below (and disdain not to do so) where the cold locks up Cocytus. Make us not go to Tityus, nor to Typhon; this man can give of that which is longed for here; therefore stoop, and twist not thy muzzle. He can yet restore fame to thee in the world; for he is living, and still expects long life, if Grace does not untimely call him to itself."

130. Thus said the Master: and he in haste stretched out those hands, of which Hercules once felt the mighty grip, and took my Leader. Virgil, when he felt himself taken up, said to me: "Come hither, so that I may take thee": then he did so that he and I were one bundle.

As the Carisenda[3] seems to the view, beneath its leaning side, when a cloud is going over it so that the tower hangs counter to it, thus seemed Antaeus to me who was watching to see him stoop; and it was a moment when I could have wished to go by another road. But lightly in the depth that swallows Lucifer with Judas he set us down; nor, thus stooping, did he there make stay, but like the mast of a ship he raised himself.

CANTO XXXII

1. IF I had rhymes both harsh and raucous, such as would befit the dismal hole on which all the other rocks thrust, I would press out more fully the juice of my conception; but since I have them not, not without fear I bring myself to speak; for to describe the bottom of the whole universe is no enterprise to take up in jest, nor for a tongue that cries mamma and papa. But may those Dames[4] aid my verse, who aided Amphion to enclose Thebes, so that the speech may not be diverse from the fact.

13. O ye, beyond all others, miscreated rabble, that are in the place whereof to speak is hard, better had ye here been sheep or goats!

16. When we were down in the dark pit beneath the feet of the giant, far lower, and I was still gazing at the high wall, I heard say to me: "Take heed how thou steppest; go so that thou trample not with thy soles the heads of thy wretched weary brothers." Whereat I turned, and saw before me, and under my feet, a lake which by reason of frost had semblance of glass and not of water.[5]

25. The Danube in Austria never made in winter so thick a veil for its current, nor the Don yonder under the cold sky, as there was here: for if Tambernich[6] had fallen on it, or Pietrapana,[7] it would not have given a creak

---

[1] See *Odyssey*, xi. 306-317.
[2] Because he took no part in the war of his brethren against the gods.
[3] The shorter but more inclined of the two famous leaning towers at Bologna.
[4] The Muses, who so endowed the lyre of Amphion that its sound charmed the rocks to move from Mount Cithaeron and build themselves up for the walls of Thebes.
[5] The lake of ice has four concentric rings: the first is Caina, where traitors to their kindred suffer penalty; the second is Antenora, for traitors to their country; the third is Ptolomea, for traitors to their guests; the fourth is Judecca, for the worst of all sinners, traitors to their benefactors.
[6] A mountain, the identity of which has not been settled.
[7] One of the Tuscan Apennines.

even at the edge. And as the frog lies to croak with muzzle out of the water, what time the peasant woman often dreams of gleaning, so, livid up to where shame appears, were the woeful shades within the ice, setting their teeth to the note of the stork. Every one held his face turned downward: from the mouth the cold and from the eyes the sad heart provides testimony of itself among them.

40. When I had looked round awhile, I turned to my feet, and saw two so close that they had the hair of their heads mixed together. "Tell me, ye who thus press tight your breasts," said I, "who are ye?" And they bent their necks, and after they had raised their faces to me, their eyes, which before were moist only within, gushed up through the lids, and the frost bound the tears between them, and locked them up again; clamp never girt board to board so strongly: and thereupon they, like two he-goats, butted one another, such anger overcame them.

52. And one who had lost both his ears by the cold, with his face still downward, said to me: "Why dost thou so mirror thyself on us? If thou wouldst know who are these two, the valley whence the Bisenzio descends belonged to their father Albert, and to them.[1] They issued from one body; and thou mayst search all Caina, and thou wilt not find shade more worthy to be fixed in ice; not he whose breast and shadow were broken by one self-same blow by the hand of Arthur;[2] not Focaccia;[3] not this one who so encumbers me with his head that I see no further, and who was named Sassol Mascheroni;[4] if thou art a Tuscan, thou now knowest well who he was. And that thou

mayst not put me to more speech, know that I was Camicion de' Pazzi,[5] and I await Carlino to exculpate me."

70. Then I saw a thousand faces made currish by the cold: whence a shudder comes to me, and will always come, at frozen pools.

73. And while we were going toward the centre to which all gravity collects, and I was trembling in the eternal chill, whether it was will, or destiny, or fortune I know not, but, walking among the heads, I struck my foot hard in the face of one. Wailing he railed at me: "Why dost thou kick me? If thou dost not come to increase the vengeance of Mont' Aperti, why dost thou molest me?" And I: "My Master, now wait here for me, so that by means of this one I may free me from a doubt,[6] then thou shalt make as much haste for me as thou wilt."

85. The Leader stopped; and I said to that shade who was still bitterly blaspheming: "Who art thou that thus chidest another?" "Now who art thou, that goes through the Antenora,"[7] he answered, "smiting the cheeks of others, so that if thou wert alive, it would be too much?" "I am alive, and it may be dear to thee," was my reply, "if thou demandest fame, that I set thy name among my other notes." And he to me: "For the contrary have I desire; take thyself hence, and give me no more trouble, for ill thou knowest to flatter on this swamp." Then I took him by the hair of the nape, and said: "It shall needs be that thou name thyself, or that not a hair remain upon thee here." Whereon he to me, "Though thou strip me of hair, I will not tell thee who I am, nor show it to thee, though thou fall a thousand times upon my head."

103. I had already twisted his hair in my

---

[1] Counts Napoleone and Alessandro degli Alberti; one was a Ghibelline, the other a Guelf. They quarrelled over their inheritance, and each seeking treacherously to kill the other, they were both slain. The Bisenzio is a little stream which falls into the Arno some ten miles west of Florence.
[2] Sir Mordred, the usurping treacherous son of King Arthur. At Dover they met in arms, and Arthur smote Mordred with such a thrust of his spear that, on its withdrawal, a ray of light passed through the wound.
[3] Focaccia de' Cancellieri of Pistoia. Enraged by a trifling offense committed by a boy, his cousin, he cut off the boy's hand, and then treacherously killed the boy's father. From this crime sprang the feud of the Blacks and the Whites, which, after raging in Pistoia, was introduced into Florence.
[4] Sassol Mascheroni murdered his nephew for an inheritance.

[5] Camicion de' Pazzi is reported to have betrayed and killed his kinsman Ubertino. Carlino was also a Pazzi. In 1302 the castle of Piantravigne was held by a body of the recently exiled Whites of Florence, with them Carlino. The castle was besieged by the Blacks, and Carlino for a bribe opened its gates to them.
[6] Dante suspects that the shade is that of Bocca degli Abati, the Florentine traitor, who, at the battle of Montaperti, in 1260, cut off the hand of the standard-bearer so that the standard fell, and the Guelfs of Florence, disheartened, were routed with frightful slaughter. See Canto x. 85-93.
[7] The second division of the ninth circle named after the Trojan who was said to have betrayed Troy.

hand, and had pulled out more than one tuft, he barking, with his eyes kept close down, when another cried out: "What ails thee, Bocca? Is it not enough for thee to make a noise with thy jaws, but thou must bark too? What devil is at thee?" "Now," said I, "I do not want thee to speak, accursed traitor, for to thy shame will I carry true news of thee." "Begone," he answered, "and tell what thou wilt; but be not silent, if thou go forth from here within, about him who now had his tongue so ready. He is lamenting here the silver of the French: I saw, thou canst say, him of Duera,[1] there where the sinners stand cold. Shouldst thou be asked who else was there, thou hast at thy side him of the Beccheria[2] whose gorge Florence cut. Gianni de' Soldanier[3] I think is farther on with Ganelon,[4] and Tribaldello[5] who opened Faenza when it was sleeping."

124. We had now departed from him, when I saw two frozen in one hole, so that the head of one was a hood for the other. And as bread is devoured for hunger, so the upper one set his teeth upon the other where the brain joins with the nape. Not otherwise Tydeus gnawed for despite the temples of Menalippus,[6] than this one was doing to the skull and the other parts. "O thou that by so bestial a sign showest hatred against him whom thou are eating, tell me the wherefore," said I, "with this compact, that if thou with reason complainest of him, I, knowing who ye are, and his sin, may yet make thee quits with him in the world above, if that with which I speak be not dried up."

[1] Buoso da Duera, commanding part of the Ghibelline forces in Lombardy opposed to the troops of Charles of Anjou, on their way to conquer the kingdom of Naples, in 1265, was believed to have been bribed to let them pass unmolested.
[2] Tesauro de' Beccheria, Abbot of Vallombrosa, beheaded by the Florentines in 1258, because of his treacherous dealings with the exiled Ghibellines.
[3] A Ghibelline of Florence who plotted against his own party.
[4] Ganelon caused the destruction of Charlemagne's rear guard at Roncesvalles, where Roland and Oliver perished. Cf. Chaucer, The Nun's Priest's Tale, 4417-8.
[5] To avenge a grudge against some of the Ghibellines of Bologna, who, being expelled, had found refuge in Faenza, in 1280, Tribaldello treacherously opened the gates to their enemies, who, entering, massacred many of them.
[6] Cf. Aeschylus, The Seven Against Thebes, 382ff.

CANTO XXXIII

1. FROM his savage repast that sinner raised his mouth, wiping it with the hair of the head that he had spoiled behind: then he began: "Thou wishest that I should renew a desperate grief which oppresses my heart already only in thinking, ere I speak of it. But, if my words are to be seed that may bear fruit of infamy for the traitor whom I gnaw, thou shalt see me speak and weep together. I know not who thou art, nor by what mode thou art come down here, but Florentine thou seemest to me truly when I hear thee. Thou hast to know that I was Count Ugolino and this one the Archbishop Ruggieri.[7] Now I will tell thee why I am such a neighbor. That, by the effect of his evil thoughts, I, trusting to him, was taken and then put to death, there is no need to tell; but what thou canst not have heard, that is, how cruel my death was, thou shalt hear, and shalt know if he has wronged me.

22. "A narrow slit in the mew, which from me has the title of Hunger, and in which others must yet be shut up, had already shown me through its opening many moons, when I had the bad dream which rent for me the veil of the future.

"This one appeared to me master and lord, chasing the wolf and his whelps upon the mountain because of which the Pisans cannot see Lucca. With lean, eager, and trained hounds, he had put before him at the front Gualandi with Sismondi and with Lanfranchi.[8] After short course, the father and his sons seemed to me weary, and it seemed to me I saw their flanks ripped by the sharp fangs.

37. "When I awoke before the morrow, I

[7] Ugolino della Gherardesca, Count of Donoratico, was for many years the most powerful citizen of Pisa. In 1285, he permitted his ambitious grandson, Nino dei Visconti, the "noble Judge Nino" (Purgatory, viii. 53), to share in the rule of the city. Discord soon broke out between them; each had his partisans, and the Guelf party was rent by this division. The Ghibellines saw their opportunity. Their chief, Archbishop Ruggieri degli Ubaldini, pretending friendship with Ugolino, joined forces with him to expel his grandson. The strength of the Guelfs being thus weakened, the Archbishop turned against the Count. After a great fight in the streets, the Count and two of his sons and two of his grandsons were taken prisoners. They were shut up in the tower of the Gualandi alla Sette Vie, and there were starved to death.
[8] Three of the chief Ghibelline families of Pisa.

heard my sons, who were with me, wailing in their sleep, and asking for bread. Truly thou art cruel if already thou dost not grieve, at thought of that which my heart was foreboding: and if thou dost not weep, at what art thou wont to weep? They were now awake, and the hour was drawing near at which food used to be brought to us, because of his dream each one was apprehensive. And I heard the door below of the horrible tower being nailed up; whereat I looked on the faces of my sons without saying a word. I did not weep, I was so turned to stone within. They were weeping; and my poor little Anselm said, 'Thou lookest so, father, what ails thee?'

52. "I shed no tear for that; nor did I answer all that day, nor the night after, until the next sun came forth upon the world. When a little ray made its way into the woeful prison, and I discerned by their four faces my own very aspect, I bit both my hands for woe; and they, thinking I did it through desire of eating, of a sudden raised themselves up, and said: 'Father, it will be far less pain to us if thou eat of us; thou didst clothe us with this wretched flesh, and do thou strip it off.' I quieted me then, not to make them more sad: that day and the next we all stayed dumb. Ah, thou hard earth! why didst thou not open? After we had come to the fourth day, Gaddo threw himself stretched out at my feet, saying: 'My father, why dost thou not help me?' Here he died: and, even as thou seest me, I saw the three fall one by one between the fifth day and the sixth; then I betook me, already blind, to groping over each, and for two days I called them after they were dead: then fasting was more powerful than woe."

76. When he had said this, with his eyes twisted, he seized again the wretched skull with his teeth, that were strong as a dog's upon the bone.

79. Ah Pisa! reproach of the people of the fair country where the *sì* doth sound,[1] since thy neighbors are slow to punish thee, let Caprara and Gorgona[2] move and make a hedge for Arno at its mouth, so that it may drown every person in thee; for even if Count Ugolino had

repute of having betrayed thee in thy strongholds, thou oughtest not to have set his sons on such a cross. Their young age, thou modern Thebes, made Uguccione and Il Brigata innocent, and the other two that my song names above.

91. We passed onward to where the ice roughly enswathes another folk, not turned downward, but all reversed. The very weeping allows not weeping there, and the grief, which finds a barrier on the eyes, turns inward to increase the anguish; for the first tears form a block, and like a visor of crystal fill all the cup beneath the eyebrow.

100. And although, as in a callus, all feeling, because of the cold, had ceased to abide in my face, it now seemed to me I felt some wind, wherefore I: "My Master, who moves this? Is not every vapor quenched here below?" Whereon he to me, "Speedily shalt thou be where thine eye, beholding the cause that rains down the blast, shall make answer to thee of this."

109. And one of the wretches of the cold crust cried out to us: "O souls so cruel that the last station has been given to you, lift from my eyes the hard veils, so that, before the weeping recongeal, I may vent a little the woe which swells my heart." Wherefore I to him: "If thou wishest that I succor thee, tell me who thou art, and if I relieve thee not, may I have to go to the bottom of the ice." He replied then: "I am Friar Alberigo;[3] I am he of the fruits of the bad garden, who here get back a date for a fig."[4] "Oh!" said I to him, "art thou then dead already?"

122. And he to me, "How my body may fare in the world above I have no knowledge. Such vantage hath this Ptolomea[5] that oftentimes the soul falls down here before Atropos

[3] Alberigo de' Manfredi of Faenza, one of the Jovial Friars (Canto xxiii. 103). Having received a blow from his younger brother Manfred, he pretended to forgive it, and invited him and his son to a feast. Toward the end of the meal he gave a preconcerted signal by calling out: "Bring the fruit," upon which his emissaries rushed in and killed the two guests.
[4] Am paid with overplus for my sin; a fig is the cheapest of Tuscan fruits; the imported date is more costly.
[5] The third ring of ice, named for that Ptolemy, Captain of Jericho, who, having invited them to a banquet, treacherously slew his father-in-law, the high-priest Simon and his two sons. I Maccabees, 16. 11-16.)

[1] Italy, whose language Dante calls *il volgare di sì*, the common tongue in which *sì* is the word for yes (*Convito*, i. 10).
[2] Two little islands near the mouth of the Arno, on whose banks Pisa lies.

has given motion to it.[1] And that thou mayst the more willingly scrape the glassy tears from my face, know that soon as the soul betrays, as I did, its body is taken from it by a demon, who thereafter governs it until its time be all revolved. It falls headlong into such cistern as this, and perhaps the body of the shade that is wintering here behind me still appears above. Thou shouldst know him if thou comest down but now; he is Ser Branca d' Oria,[2] and many years have passed since he was thus shut up." "I believe," said I to him, "that thou art deceiving me; for Branca d' Oria is not yet dead, and he eats, and drinks, and sleeps, and puts on clothes." "In the ditch of the Malebranche above," he said, "there where the sticky pitch is boiling, Michel Zanche[3] had not yet arrived, when this one left a devil in his stead in his own body, and in that of one of his next kin, who committed the treachery together with him. But now stretch hither thy hand; open my eyes for me." And I did not open them for him, and to be churlish to him was courtesy.[4]

151. Ah Genoese! men strange to all morality and full of all corruption, why are ye not scattered from the world? For with the worst spirit of Romagna[5] I found one of you, such that for his deeds he is already in soul bathed in Cocytus, and in body he appears still alive on earth.

CANTO XXXIV

1. "Vexilla regis prodeunt inferni[6] toward us; therefore look forward," said my Master; "see if thou discern him." As when a thick fog breathes, or when our hemisphere darkens to night, a mill which the wind is turning seems from afar, such a structure it seemed to me that I then saw.

8. Then, because of the wind, I drew me behind my Leader; for no other shelter was there. I was now (and with fear I put it into verse), there where the shades were wholly covered, and showed through like a straw in glass. Some are lying down; some are upright,

this one with his head, and that with his soles uppermost; another, like a bow, bends his face to his feet.

16. When we had gone so far forward that it pleased my Master to show me the creature which had the fair semblance, he took himself from before me and made me stop, saying: "Lo Dis! and lo the place where it is needful that thou arm thyself with fortitude!" How frozen and faint I then became, ask it not, Reader, for I do not write it, because all speech would be little. I did not die, and did not remain alive: think now for thyself, if thou hast a grain of wit, what I became, deprived of one and the other.

28. The emperor of the woeful realm issued forth from the ice from the middle of his breast; and I compare better with a giant, than the giants do with his arms. See now how great must be that whole which is conformed to such a part. If he was as fair as he now is foul, and lifted up his brows against his Maker, well should all tribulation proceed from him. Oh how great a marvel it seemed to me, when I saw three faces on his head! one in front, and that was crimson; the others were two, which were adjoined to this above the very middle of each shoulder, and they were joined up to the place of the crest; and the right seemed between white and yellow, the left was such in appearance as those who come from there whence the Nile descends.[7] Beneath each came forth two great wings, of size befitting so great a bird; sails of the sea I never saw such. They had no feathers, but their fashion was of a bat; and he was flapping them so that three winds were proceeding from him, whereby Cocytus was all congealed. With six eyes he was weeping, and over three chins were trickling the tears and bloody drivel. At each mouth he was crushing a sinner with his teeth, in manner of a heckle, so that he thus was making three of them woeful. To the one in front the biting was nothing to the clawing, whereby sometimes his back remained all stripped of the skin.

61. "That soul up there which has the great-

---

[1] Cf. Psalms, 55. 15. Also see Canto xi. 52-63, *supra*.
[2] A member of the famous Genoese house of Doria; murderer, about 1290, of his father-in-law, Michel Zanche, Governor of Logodoro, in Sardinia.
[3] See Canto xxii. 88.
[4] See Aquinas, *Summa Theologica*, Part III, Suppl., Q 94, A2.
[5] Friar Alberigo.
[6] "The banners of the King of Hell advance": *Vexilla regis prodeunt* are the first words of a hymn.

[7] The three faces exhibit the devilish counterpart of the attributes of the three persons of the Godhead, Impotence, Ignorance, and Hate (Cf. Canto iii. 5, 6); Hate scarlet with rage, Ignorance black with its own darkness, Impotence pale yellow with jealousy and envy.

est punishment," said the Master, "is Judas Iscariot, who has his head within, and plies his legs outside. Of the other two who have their heads downwards, he who hangs from the black muzzle is Brutus; see how he writhes and says not a word; and the other is Cassius, who seems so large-limbed. But the night is rising again; and now we must depart, for we have seen the whole."

70. As was his pleasure, I clasped his neck, and he took advantage of time and place, and when the wings were wide opened he caught hold on the shaggy flanks; down from shag to shag he then descended between the matted hair and the frozen crusts. When we were where the thigh turns just on the thick of the haunch, my Leader, with effort and stress of breath, turned his head to where he had had his shanks, and grappled to the hair like one who mounts, so that I believed we were returning again to hell.

82. "Cling fast hold," said the Master, panting like one weary, "for by such stairs must we depart from so great evil." Then he came forth through the cleft of a rock, and placed me upon its edge to sit; then stretched toward me his cautious step.

88. I raised my eyes, and thought to see Lucifer as I had left him, and I saw him holding his legs upward; and if I then became perplexed, let the dull folk suppose it, who see not what that point is which I had passed.[1]

94. "Rise up on foot," said the Master; "the way is long and the road is difficult, and already the sun returns to mid-tierce."[2]

97. It was no hallway of a palace where we were, but a natural dungeon which had a bad floor, and lack of light. "Before I tear myself from the Abyss," said I when I had risen up, "my Master, talk a little with me to draw me out of error. Where is the ice? and this one, how is he fixed thus upside down? and how in such short while has the sun made transit from evening to morning?"

106. And he to me: "Thou imaginest that thou still art on the other side of the centre, where I laid hold on the hair of the wicked Worm that pierces the world. On that side thou wast so long as I descended; when I turned, thou didst pass the point to which from every part all weighty things are drawn; and thou art now arrived beneath the hemisphere which is opposite to that which the great dry land covers, and beneath whose zenith the Man was slain who was born and lived without sin: thou hast thy feet upon a little circle which forms the other face of the Judecca. Here it is morning when it is evening there; and this one who made a ladder for us with his hair is still fixed even as he was before. On this side he fell down from heaven, and the earth, which before was spread out on this side, through fear of him made of the sea a veil, and came to our hemisphere; and perhaps to fly from him that land which appears on this side left here this vacant space and ran back upward."[3]

127. A place is there below, stretching as far from Beelzebub as his tomb extends, which is not known by sight, but by the sound of a rivulet which descends here along the hollow of a rock that it has gnawed with its winding and gently sloping course.[4] My Leader and I entered by that hidden road, to return into the bright world; and without care to have any repose, we mounted up, he first and I second, so far that through a round opening I saw some of the beautiful things which Heaven bears, and thence we issued forth again to see the stars.

---

[1] The centre of the universe; when Virgil had turned upon the haunch of Lucifer, the passage had been made from one hemisphere of the earth—the inhabited and known hemisphere—to the other where no living men dwell, and where the only land is the Mountain of Purgatory. In changing one hemisphere for the other there is a change of time of twelve hours, from about sunset to about sunrise. A second Saturday morning begins for the poets, and they pass nearly as long a time as they have been in Hell, that is, twenty-four hours, in traversing the long and hard way that leads to the surface of the hemisphere into which they have just entered.

[2] Tierce is the name given to the first three hours after sunrise. Mid-tierce consequently at the equinox is about half-past seven o'clock.

[3] Dante's conception appears to be, that at the Creation the southern hemisphere of the Earth was occupied by the dry land, while the northern was a hemisphere of waters, and that, at the fall of Lucifer on the southern hemisphere, the land recoiled in horror to the northern, forcing the waters of the latter to fill the place which it left void. At the same moment the interior of the globe into which Lucifer was hurled fled from him, and rising, amid the waters of the southern hemisphere, formed the solitary Mount of Purgatory.

[4] The streamlet of sin from Purgatory which finds its way back to Satan.

·: PURGATORY :·

CANTO I

1. To run over better waters the little vessel of my genius now hoists her sails, as she leaves behind her a sea so cruel; and I will sing of that second realm where the human spirit is purified, and becomes worthy to ascend to heaven.

7. But here let dead poesy rise again, O holy Muses, since I am yours, and here let Calliope somewhat mount up, accompanying my song with that sound of which the wretched Picae felt the stroke such that they despaired of pardon.[1]

A sweet color of oriental sapphire, which was gathering in the serene aspect of the mid sky, pure even to the first circle,[2] renewed delight to my eyes, soon as I issued forth from the dead air which had afflicted my eyes and my breast. The fair planet which incites to love was making all the Orient to smile, veiling the Fishes that were in her train. I turned me to the right hand, and gave heed to the other pole, and saw four stars, never seen save by the first people.[3] The heavens appeared to rejoice in their flamelets. O widowed northern region, since thou art deprived of beholding these!

28. When I had withdrawn from regarding them, turning me a little to the other pole, there whence the Wain had already disappeared, I saw close to me an old man alone, in aspect worthy of so much reverence that no son owes more to his father.[4] He wore his beard long and mingled with white hair, like his locks, of which a double list fell upon his breast. The rays of the four holy stars so adorned his face with light, that I saw him, as though the sun had been in front.

40. "Who are ye that, counter to the blind stream, have fled from the eternal prison?" said he, moving those venerable plumes. "Who has guided you? Or who was a lamp to you, issuing forth from the deep night which ever makes the infernal valley black? Are the laws of the abyss thus broken? or is a new design changed in heaven that, being damned, ye come to my rocks?"

49. My Leader then took hold of me, and with words, and with hands, and with signs, controlled to reverence my knees and brow. Then he answered him: "Of myself I came not; a Lady descended from Heaven, by reason of whose prayers I succored this man with my company. But since it is thy will that more of our condition be unfolded to thee, how it truly is, mine cannot be that this be denied to thee. This man has not yet seen his last evening, but through his folly was so near thereto that there was very little time to turn. Even as I have said, I was sent to him to rescue him, and there was no other way than this, along which I have set myself. I have shown to him all the guilty people; and now I intend to show him those spirits that purge themselves under thy ward. How I have brought him, it would be long to tell thee; from on high descends power which aids me to lead him to see thee and to hear thee. Now may it please thee to look graciously upon his coming. He goes seeking liberty,[5] which is so dear, as he knows who for it renounces life.

73. "This thou knowest; for death for its sake was not bitter to thee in Utica, where thou didst leave the vesture which on the great day shall be so bright. The eternal edicts are not violated by us, for this one is alive, and

---

[1] The nine daughters of Pieros of Emathia, who, contending in song with the Muses, were for their presumption changed to magpies.

[2] The horizon.

[3] Purgatory is in the southern hemisphere, and "the other" is the South pole. The four stars are the symbols of the cardinal virtues—Prudence, Temperance, Fortitude and Justice.

[4] Cato. Cf. *Aeneid,* viii. 670.

[5] Cf. Romans, 8. 21. See the last words of Virgil to Dante, at the end of Canto xxvii.

Minos does not bind me; but I am of the circle where are the chaste eyes of thy Marcia, who in her look still prays thee, O holy breast, that for thine own thou hold her. For her love, then, incline thyself to us; allow us to go on through thy seven realms:[1] I will report this grace from thee to her, if thou deignest to be mentioned there below."

85. "Marcia so pleased my eyes while I was on earth," said he then, "that whatsoever grace she wished from me, I did; now that she dwells on the other side of the evil stream,[2] she can move me no more, by that law which was made when thence I issued forth. But if a Lady of Heaven move and direct thee, as thou sayest, there is no need of flatteries; it may well suffice thee that thou ask me for her sake. Go then, and see thou gird this one with a smooth rush, and that thou wash his face so that thou cleanse it from all stain, for it were not befitting to go with eye dimmed by any cloud before the first minister that is of those of Paradise. This little island, round about at its very base, down there yonder where the wave beats it, bears rushes upon its soft ooze. No plant of other kind, that puts forth leaf or grows hard, can there have life, because it yields not to the shocks. Thereafter let not your return be this way; the Sun, which now is rising, will show you how to take the mountain by easier ascent."

109. On this he disappeared, and I rose up, without speaking, and drew me quite close to my Leader, and bent my eyes on him. He began: "Son, follow my steps; let us turn back, for from here this plain slopes to its low bounds."

115. The dawn was vanquishing the matin hour, which was flying before it, so that from afar I discerned the trembling of the sea. We went along over the solitary plain like a man who turns to the road which he has lost, and, till he find it, seems to himself to go in vain. When we were where the dew contends with the sun, and, through being in a place where there is shade, is little dispersed, my Master softly placed both his hands outspread upon the grass; whereon I, who was aware of his intent, stretched toward him my tearful cheeks:

then he wholly uncovered on me that color which hell had concealed.

130. We came, then, to the desert shore which never saw man navigate its waters who afterwards had experience of return. Here he girt me, even as pleased the other. O marvel! that such as he culled the humble plant, such it instantly sprang up again there whence he had plucked it.

CANTO II

1. THE sun had now reached the horizon whose meridian circle covers Jerusalem with its highest point; and the night which circles opposite to him was issuing forth from the Ganges with the Scales which fall from her hand when she exceeds;[3] so that where I was the white and red cheeks of the beautiful Aurora were becoming orange through too much age.

10. We were still alongside the sea, like folk who are thinking of their road, who go in heart and in body linger; and lo! as, at approach of the morning, Mars glows ruddy through the dense vapors, down in the west above the ocean floor, such appeared to me,—so may I again behold it!—a light along the sea coming so swiftly that no flight equals its motion. From which when I had a little withdrawn my eye to ask my Leader, again I saw it, brighter become and larger. Then on each side of it appeared to me a something, I knew not what, white, and beneath, little by little, another came forth from it.

25. My Master still said not a word, until the first white things appeared as wings; then, when he clearly recognized the pilot, he cried out: "Mind, mind thou bend thy knees: Lo! the Angel of God: fold thy hands: henceforth shalt thou see such officials. See how he scorns human instruments, so that he wills not oar, or other sail than his own wings, between such distant shores. See, how he holds them straight toward heaven, stirring the air with his eternal feathers, which are not changed like mortal hair."

---

[1] The seven circles of Purgatory.
[2] Acheron.

[3] Purgatory and Jerusalem are antipodal, and the Ganges or India was arbitrarily assumed to be their common horizon, the Western horizon to the one, the Eastern to the other. The night is here taken as the point of the heavens opposite the sun, and the sun being in Aries, the night is in Libra.

37. Then, as the Bird Divine came more and more toward us, the brighter he appeared; so that my eye endured him not near by, but I bent it down: and he came on to the shore with a little vessel, swift and light, so that the water swallowed naught of it. At the stern stood the Celestial Pilot, such that he seemed inscribed among the blest; and more than a hundred spirits sat within. *"In exitu Israel de Egypto"*[1] they all were singing together with one voice, with whatso of that psalm is after written. Then he made them the sign of the Holy Cross; whereon they all threw themselves upon the strand; and he went away swift as he had come.

52. The crowd which remained there seemed strange to the place, gazing round about, like one who makes essay of new things. The Sun, who with his bright arrows had chased the Capricorn from mid-heaven, was shooting forth the day on every side, when the new people raised their brows toward us, saying to us: "If ye know, show us the way to go to the mountain." And Virgil answered: "Ye perhaps believe that we are experienced of this place, but we are pilgrims, even as ye are. We came just now, a little while before you, by another way, which was so rough and difficult that the ascent henceforth will seem play to us."

67. The souls, who by my breathing had become aware that I was still alive, marvelling, became deadly pale. And as to hear news the folk press to a messenger who bears an olive branch, and no one shows himself shy of crowding, so all of those fortunate souls fastened themselves on my countenance, as if forgetting to go to make themselves fair.

76. I saw one of them drawing forward to embrace me with so great affection, that it moved me to do the like. O shades, empty save in aspect! Three times I clasped my hands behind it, and as often returned with them unto my breast. With wonder, I believe, I painted me; whereat the shade smiled and drew back, and I, following it, pressed forward. Gently it said, that I should pause; then I knew who it was, and I prayed it that it would stay to speak with me a little. It replied to me: "Even as I loved thee in the mortal body, so loosed from

it I love thee; therefore I stay; but wherefore art thou going?"

91. "My Casella, in order to return another time to this place where I am, do I make this journey," said I, "but from thee how has so much time been taken?"

94. And he to me: "No wrong has been done me if he who takes both when and whom it pleases him has many times denied to me this passage; for of a just will his own is made. For three months, indeed, he has taken with all peace whoso has wished to enter. Wherefore I, who had now turned to the seashore where the water of Tiber becomes salt, was benignantly received by him. To that outlet has he now directed his wing, because always those assemble there who towards Acheron do not descend."

106. And I: "If a new law take not from thee memory or practice of the song of love which was wont to quiet all my longings, may it please thee therewith somewhat to comfort my soul, which coming hither with its body is so wearied."

112. *"Love which in my mind discourses with me,"*[2] he then began so sweetly, that the sweetness still within me sounds. My Master, and I, and that folk who were with him, appeared so content as if naught else could touch the mind of any.

118. We were all fast and attentive to his notes; and lo! the venerable old man crying: "What is this, ye laggard spirits? What negligence, what stay is this? Run to the mountain to strip off the slough which lets not God be manifest to you."

124. As, when picking up grain or tares, the doves assembled at their feeding, quiet, without display of their wonted pride, if aught appear of which they are afraid, suddenly let the food alone, because they are assailed by a greater care, so I saw that fresh troop leave the song, and go towards the hillside, like one that goes, but knows not where he may come out: nor was our departure less speedy.

CANTO III

1. ALTHOUGH the sudden flight had scattered them over the plain, turned to the mount whereto reason spurs us, I drew up close to my

[1] "When Israel went out of Egypt." Psalms, 114.

[2] The first verse of a *canzone* by Dante.

trusty companion. And how should I have run without him? Who would have led me up over the mountain? He seemed to me of his own self remorseful. O conscience, upright and stainless, how bitter a sting to thee is little fault!

10. When his feet left the haste which mars the dignity of every act, my mind, which at first had been restrained, let loose its attention, as though eager, and I set my face against the hill which rises highest towards heaven from the sea. The sun, which behind was flaming ruddy, was broken in front of me by the figure which the staying of its rays upon me formed. When I saw the ground darkened only in front of me, I turned me to one side with fear of having been abandoned: and my Comfort, turning wholly round to me, began to say:

24. "Why dost thou still distrust? Dost thou not believe me with thee, and that I guide thee? It is already evening there where the body is buried within which I cast a shadow; Naples holds it, and from Brundusium it was taken: if in front of me there is no shadow now, marvel not more than at the heavens, of which the one obstructs not the other's radiance.[1] The Power, which wills not that how it acts be revealed to us, disposes bodies like this to suffer torments both of heat and cold. Mad is he who hopes that our reason can traverse the infinite way which One Substance in Three Persons holds. Be content, O human race, with the *quia*;[2] for if ye had been able to see everything, there had been no need for Mary to bear child: and ye have seen desiring fruitlessly men such that their desire would have been quieted, which is given them eternally for a grief. I speak of Aristotle and of Plato, and of many others." And here he bowed his front, and said no more, and remained disturbed.

46. We had come, meanwhile, to the foot of the mountain; here we found the cliff so steep that the legs would there be nimble in vain. Between Lerici and Turbìa[3] the most deserted, the most secluded path is a stairway easy and open, compared with that. "Now who knows on which hand the hillside slopes," said my Master, staying his step, "so that one who goes without wings may ascend?"

55. And while he was holding his face bent down, and was questioning his mind about the road, and I was looking up round about the rock, a company of souls appeared to me on the left hand, who were moving their feet towards us, and seemed not doing so, so slowly were they coming. "Lift," said I, "Master, thine eyes; behold on this side those who will give us counsel, if of thyself thou canst not have it." He looked at them, and with a relieved air replied: "Let us go thither, for they come slowly, and do thou confirm thy hope, sweet son."

67. That people was still as far—I mean after a thousand steps of ours—as a good thrower would cast with his hand, when they all pressed up to the hard masses of the high bank, and stood still and close, as one who goes in doubt stops to look.[4] "O ye who have made good ends, O spirits already elect," Virgil began, "by that peace which, I believe, is awaited by you all, tell us, where the mountain lies so that the going up is possible; for to lose time is most displeasing to him who knows most."

79. As the sheep come forth from the fold by ones, and twos, and threes, and the others stand timid, holding eye and muzzle to the ground; and what the first does the others also do, huddling themselves to it if it stop, silly and quiet, and wherefore know not; so I then saw the head of that fortunate flock moving to approach, modest in countenance and dignified in gait.

88. When those in front saw the light broken on the ground at my right side, so that the shadow was cast by me on the rock, they stopped, and drew somewhat back; and all the rest who were coming behind did the like, not knowing why. "Without your asking, I confess to you that this is a human body which ye see, whereby the light of the sun on the ground is cleft. Marvel not, but believe that not without power which comes from heaven does he seek to surmount this wall." Thus the Master:

---

[1] The nine concentric heavens are transparent.
[2] That is, be content to know that the thing is.
[3] Lerici and Turbìa are at the two ends of the Riviera.

[4] They stopped, surprised, at seeing Virgil and Dante advancing to the left, against the rule in Purgatory, where the course is always to the right, symbolizing progress in good.

and that worthy people said: "Turn, proceed before us, then"; with the backs of their hands making sign. And one of them began: "Whoever thou art, turn thy face as thou thus goest on; consider whether in the world thou didst ever see me?" I turned me toward him, and looked at him fixedly: blond was he, and beautiful, and of gentle aspect, but a blow had divided one of his eyebrows.

109. When I had humbly disclaimed having ever seen him, he said: "Now look!" and showed me a wound high upon his breast. Then he said, smiling; "I am Manfred,[1] grandson of the Empress Constance: wherefore I pray thee, that when thou returnest, thou go to my beautiful daughter,[2] mother of the honor of Sicily and of Aragon, and tell to her the truth if aught else be told. After I had my body broken by two mortal stabs, I rendered myself, weeping, to Him who pardons willingly. My sins were horrible, but the Infinite Goodness has such wide arms that it takes whatever turns to it. If the Pastor of Cosenza,[3] who was set on the hunt of me by Clement, had then rightly read this page in God, the bones of my body would still be at the head of the bridge near Benevento, under the protection of the heavy cairn. Now the rain bathes them, and the wind moves them forth from the kingdom, hard by the Verde, whither he transported them with extinguished light.

133. By their malediction one is not so lost that the Eternal Love cannot return, while hope has speck of green. True is it, that whoso dies in contumacy of Holy Church, though he repent him at the end, needs must stay outside, upon this bank, thirtyfold the whole time that he has been in his presumption, if such decree become not shortened through good prayers.

[1] The natural son of the Emperor Frederick II, and king of Sicily. Urban IV and Clement IV offered the throne of Sicily to Charles of Anjou, the brother of St. Louis. Charles, crowned king of Sicily at Rome, routed Manfred at Benevento. Manfred himself was slain in the battle.
[2] Constance, who married Peter III of Aragon. She had three sons, Alphonso, James, and Frederick. Alphonso succeeded his father in Aragon, and James in Sicily, but after the death of Alphonso, in 1291, James became king of Aragon, and Frederick king of Sicily.
[3] The archbishop of Cosenza, at command of Clement IV, took Manfred's body from its grave near Benevento, and threw it unburied on the bank of the Verde (now the Garigliano), separating the states of the Church from the kingdom of Naples.

See if hereafter thou canst make me glad, revealing to my good Constance how thou hast seen me, and also this prohibition; for here by means of those on earth much may be gained."[4]

CANTO IV

1. WHEN by reason of delights, or of pains which any capacity of ours may experience, the soul is wholly engaged by it, to any other faculty it seems no further to give heed: and this is counter to the error which believes that one soul above another is kindled within us.[5] And therefore, when a thing is heard or seen which may hold the soul intently turned to it, the time goes by, and the man perceives it not: for one faculty is that which listens, and another is that which keeps the soul entire; the latter is as it were bound, and the former is loose.

13. Of this I had true experience, hearing that spirit and wondering: for full fifty degrees had the sun ascended,[6] and I was not aware of it, when we came where those souls with one accord cried out to us: "Here is what you ask."

19. The man of the farm, when the grape is growing dark, often hedges up a larger opening with a forkful of his thorns, than was the passage from which my Leader and I behind him ascended alone, when the troop departed from us. One goes to Sanleo, and descends to Noli, one mounts up Bismantova[7] to its summit, with only feet; but here it behoves that one fly, I mean with the swift wings and with the feathers of great desire, behind that guide who gave me hope and made a light for me. We ascended through the cleft rock, and on each side the wall pressed close on us, and the ground beneath required both feet and hands.

34. When we were upon the upper edge of the high bank, on the open hillside: "My Master," said I, "what way shall we take?" And he to me: "Let no step of thine fall back, always win up behind me on the mountain, till some sage guide appear for us."

40. The summit was so high that it surpassed the sight; and the mountain-side far

[4] Cf. Aquinas, Summa Theologica, Part III, Suppl., Q 63, A 2.
[5] Cf. Ibid., Part I, Q 76, A 3.
[6] It was now about nine A.M.
[7] All these are places difficult of access.

steeper than a line from the mid quadrant to the centre. I was weary, when I began: "O sweet Father, turn and regard how I remain alone if thou stay not." "My son," said he, "far as here drag thyself on," pointing out to me a ledge a little above, which on that side circles all the hill. His words so spurred me, that I forced myself on, scrambling after him, until the belt was beneath my feet. There we both sat down, turning toward the east, whence we had ascended, for to look back is wont to encourage a man. I first turned my eyes to the low shores, then I raised them to the sun, and wondered that we were struck by it on the left. The Poet well perceived that I was all bewildered at the chariot of the light, where it was entering[1] between us and Aquilo.

61. Wherefore he to me: "If Castor and Pollux were in company with that mirror which sheds its light up and down, thou wouldst see the zodiac revolving ruddy still closer to the Bears, if it went not out of its old road.[2] How this can be, if thou wishest to be able to conceive, with collected thought imagine Zion and this mountain to stand upon the earth so that both have one sole horizon and different hemispheres; then thou wilt see, if thy intelligence right clearly heed, how the road which Phaëthon, to his harm, knew not how to drive, must needs pass this mountain on the one side, and that on the other."

76. "Surely, my Master," said I, "I never saw so clearly as I now discern, there where my wit seemed deficient, that the mid-circle of the supernal motion, which in a certain art is called Equator, and which always remains between the sun and the winter, is distant, for the reason that thou tellest, as far from here toward the north, as the Hebrews saw it toward the warm region. But, if it please thee, willingly would I know how far we have to go, for the hill rises higher than my eyes are able." And he to me: "This mountain is such, that ever at the beginning below it is hard, and the more one goes up, behold! the less it troubles

him; therefore when it shall seem to thee so pleasant, that the going up will be easy to thee as going down the current in a vessel, then wilt thou be at the end of this path; there mayst thou expect repose from toil: more I answer not, and this I know for true."

97. And as he ended his words, a voice near by sounded: "Perchance before then thou wilt be constrained to sit." At the sound of it each of us turned, and we saw at the left a great stone, of which neither he nor I had taken note before. Thither we drew; and there were persons who were reposing in the shadow behind the rock, as one through indolence sets himself to repose. And one of them, who seemed to me weary, was seated, and was clasping his knees, holding his face down low between them. "O sweet my Lord," said I, "look at him, who shows himself more indolent than if sloth were his sister." Then that one turned to us and gave heed, moving his look only up along his thigh, and said: "Now go thou up, for thou art valiant." I recognized then who he was, and that effort which was still quickening my breath a little, did not hinder my going to him, and after I had reached him, he scarcely raised his head, saying: "Hast thou clearly seen how the sun drives his chariot over thy left shoulder?"

121. His lazy acts and his short words moved my lips a little to a smile; then I began: "Belacqua,[3] henceforth I grieve not for thee, but tell me why thou art seated here? dost thou await a guide, or has only thy wonted mood recaptured thee?" And he: "Brother, what avails the going up? For the bird of God that sits at the gate would not let me go to the torments. It behoves that heaven first circle around me outside the gate, as long as it did in life, because I delayed my good sighs until the end; unless, before then, the prayer assist me which rises from a heart that lives in grace: what avails the other, which is not heard in heaven?"

136. And already the Poet was mounting up before me, and was saying: "Come on now: thou seest that the meridian is touched by the sun, and on the shore the night now covers Morocco with her foot."

---

[1] Dante, his face toward the east, was bewildered at seeing the sun on his left hand. Aquilo, the north wind, is put for the north.

[2] If the sun were in the sign of the Gemini—Castor and Pollux (which is nearer the constellations of the Bears than Aries, in which the sun now is)—it would make the zodiac ruddy still farther to the north.

[3] Belacqua was a Florentine, a maker of citherns and other musical instruments.

CANTO V

1. I HAD now parted from those shades, and was following the footsteps of my Leader, when behind me one, pointing his finger, cried out: "Look how the ray seems not to shine on the left hand of that lower one, and he seems to bear himself as if alive." I turned my eyes at the sound of these words, and I saw them watching, for marvel, only me, only me, and the light which was broken.

10. "Why is thy mind so caught," said the Master, "that thou slackenest thy going? What matters to thee that which is whispered here? Come on after me, and let the people talk. Stand like a firm tower that never wags its top for blowing of the winds: for always the man in whom thought on thought wells up removes from himself his mark, because one weakens the force of the other." What could I answer, save: "I come"? I said it, overspread somewhat with the color, which, at times, makes a man worthy of pardon.

22. And therewhile, across upon the mountain-side, a little in front of us, were coming people, singing *Miserere,* verse by verse. When they observed that I gave no place for passage of the rays through my body, they changed their song into a long and hoarse "Oh!" and two of them, in form of messengers, ran to meet us, and asked of us: "Make us acquainted with your condition." And my Master: "Ye can go back, and report to those who sent you, that the body of this one is true flesh. If, as I suppose, they stopped because of seeing his shadow, enough is answered them: let them do him honor and it may profit them."

37. Never did I see enkindled vapors at early night so swiftly cleave the clear sky, or the clouds of August at set of sun,[1] that these did not return up in less time; and, arrived there, they with the others wheeled round toward us, like a troop that runs without curb.

43. "These folk that press to us are many, and they come to pray thee," said the Poet; "yet do thou still go on, and in going listen." "O soul," they came crying, "that with those limbs with which thou wast born art on thy

way to be glad, a little stay thy step. Look if thou hast ever seen any one of us, so that thou mayst carry news of him to earth. Pray, why dost thou go on? Pray, why dost thou not stop? We all of old were slain by violence, and sinners up to the last hour; then light from Heaven made us mindful, so that both penitent and pardoning we issued forth from life at peace with God, who fills our hearts with the desire of seeing Him." And I: "Although I gaze upon your faces, I recognize no one; but if aught that I can do be pleasing to you, spirits wellborn, speak ye, and I will do it by that peace which makes me, following the feet of such a guide, seek it from world to world."

64. And one began: "Each of us trusts in thy good service, without thy swearing it, provided that want of power cut not off the will; wherefore I, who speak alone before the others, pray thee, if ever thou see that land which lies between Romagna and the land of Charles,[2] that thou be courteous to me with thy prayers in Fano, so that supplication may be well made in my behalf, that I may be able to purge away my grave offenses. Of that place was I; but the deep wounds, wherefrom issued the blood in which I had my seat,[3] were dealt me in the bosom of the Antenori,[4] there where I thought to be most secure; he of Este had it done, who held me in wrath far beyond what justice willed. But if, when I was overtaken at Oriaco, had fled toward La Mira,[5] I should still be yonder where men breathe. I ran to the marsh, and the reeds and the mire hampered me so that I fell, and there I saw a lake made by my veins upon the ground."

85. Then said another: "Ah! so may that desire be fulfilled which draws thee to the high mountain, with good piety do thou help mine. I was of Montefeltro, and am Buonconte.[6]

[1] The shooting stars in a clear sky, or the lightning in the clouds of August.

[2] The March of Ancona, between the Romagna and the kingdom of Naples, then held by Charles II, King of Naples and Count of Anjou. The speaker is Jacopo del Cassero, of the leading Guelf family in Fano. On his way to become Podestà of Milan, in 1298, he was assassinated by the minions of Azzo VIII of Este, whose enmity he had incurred.
[3] Cf. Leviticus, 17. 14.
[4] That is, in the territory of the Paduans, whose city was reputed to have been founded by Antenor.
[5] La Mira is a village on the bank of one of the canals of the Brenta between Padua and Venice. Oriaco is not far from it.
[6] Son of Count Guido da Montefeltro; cf. *Hell,*

Joan, or any other, has no care for me, where-
fore I go among these with downcast front."
And I to him: "What violence, or what chance
caused thee to stray so far from Campaldino,
that thy burial place was never known?"
"Oh!" replied he, "at foot of the Casentino[1]
crosses a stream, named the Archiano, which
rises in the Apennine above the Hermitage.[2]
Where its name becomes vain I arrived,
pierced in the throat, flying on foot, and
bloodying the plain. Here I lost my sight, and I
ended my speech with the name of Mary, and
here I fell, and my flesh remained alone. I will
tell the truth, and do thou repeat it among the
living. The Angel of God took me, and he of
Hell cried out, 'O thou from Heaven, why dost
thou rob me?[3] Thou bearest away for thyself
the eternal part of him for one little tear which
takes him from me; but of the rest I will make
other disposal.'

109. "Thou knowest well how in the air that
moist vapor is collected which turns to water
soon as it rises where the cold condenses it. He
joined that evil will, which seeks only evil,
with intelligence, and moved the mist and the
wind by the power that his nature gave.[4]
Then, when the day was spent, he covered the
valley with cloud, from Pratomagno to the
great chain,[5] and made the sky above so dense
that the pregnant air was turned to water. The
rain fell, and what of it the earth did not en-
dure came to the gullies, and as it gathered in
great streams it rushed so swiftly towards the
royal river that nothing held it back. The ro-
bust Archiano found my frozen body near its
mouth, and pushed it into the Arno, and
loosed on my breast the cross which I made of
myself when the pain overcame me. It rolled

me along its banks, and along its bottom, then
with its spoil it covered and girt me."

130. "Pray, when thou shalt have returned
unto the world, and rested from the long jour-
ney," the third spirit followed on the second,
"remember me, who am Pia.[6] Siena made me,
Maremma unmade me; he knows it, who, be-
fore wedding, had enringed me with his gem."

CANTO VI

1. WHEN the game of hazard is broken up, he
who loses remains sorrowful, repeating the
throws, and, saddened, learns; with the other
all the folk go along; one goes before, and one
plucks him from behind, and one at his side
brings himself to mind: he does not stop, and
listens to one and the other; the man to whom
he reaches forth his hand presses on him no
longer, and thus from the throng he defends
himself. Such was I in that dense crowd, turn-
ing my face to them this way and that; and,
promising, I loosed myself from it.

13. Here was the Aretine, who from the
fierce arms of Ghin di Tacco had his death;[7]
and the other who was drowned when
running in pursuit.[8] Here Federigo No-
vello[9] was praying with hands outstretched,
and he of Pisa, who made the good Mar-
zucco show himself strong.[10] I saw Count

[6] Pia is reported to have been put to death in her
husband's stronghold in the Tuscan Maremma.
[7] The Aretine was Messer Benincasa da Laterina, a
learned judge, who had condemned to death for their
crimes two relatives of Ghin di Tacco, the most fa-
mous highwayman of the day, whose headquarters
lay between Siena and Rome. Some time after, Messer
Benincasa sitting as papal auditor in Rome, Ghino
made his way to the tribunal, slew Benincasa, and
escaped unharmed.
[8] Another Aretine, of the Tarlati family. While pur-
suing or pursued by his enemies, his horse carried
him into the Arno, where he was drowned.
[9] Federigo, son of the Count Guido Novello, of
whom nothing is known but that he was slain in 1291,
near Bibbiena.
[10] Benvenuto says: "I have heard from the good
Boccaccio, whom I trust more than the others, that
Marzucco was a good man of the city of Pisa, who
had become a Franciscan friar, whose son was be-
headed by order of Count Ugolino, the tyrant, who
commanded that his body should remain unburied.
At a late hour his father humbly approached the
Count, and like a stranger unconcerned in the matter,
and without tears or other sign of grief, he said,
'Surely, my lord, it would be proper and to your honor
that that poor slain man should be buried, and not left
cruelly as food for dogs.' Then the Count, recognizing
him, said, astonished, 'Go, for thy patience overcomes

xxvii. Joan was his wife. He was the captain of the
Aretines at the battle of Campaldino (1289), where
he was slain.
[1] The Casentino is a "district in Tuscany comprising
the upper valley of the Arno, and the slopes of the
Etruscan Apennines."
[2] The monastery of Camaldoli, founded by St.
Romualdo of Ravenna, in 1012, the earliest house of
the Order of Reformed Benedictines which derives its
name from this locality.
[3] Cf. Hell, xxvii. 112-120.
[4] Cf. Aquinas, Summa Theologica, Part I, Q 110,
A 3.
[5] Pratomagno is the mountain ridge which forms
the western boundary of the Casentino; "the great
chain" is the main ridge of the Apennines.

Orso;[1] and the soul divided from its body by spite and by envy, as it said, and not for fault committed, Pierre de la Brosse,[2] I mean; and here let the Lady of Brabant have foresight, while she is on earth, so that for this she be not of the worse flock.

25. When I was free from each and all those shades who prayed only that someone else should pray, so that their becoming holy may be speeded, I began: "It seems to me, O Light of mine, that thou deniest expressly, in a certain text, that orison can bend decree of Heaven, and these folk pray only for this,—shall then their hope be vain? or is thy saying not rightly clear to me?"[3]

34. And he to me: "My writing is plain, and the hope of these is not fallacious, if it be well regarded with sound mind; for top of judgment vails not itself because a fire of love may, in one instant, fulfil that which he who is here installed must satisfy. And there where I affirmed this proposition, defect was not amended by a prayer, because the prayer was disjoined from God. However, in regard to matter of doubt so deep decide thou not, unless she tell it thee, who shall be a light between the truth and the understanding. I know not if thou understandest; I speak of Beatrice; thou shalt see her above, smiling and happy, upon the summit of this mountain."

49. And I: "My Lord, let us go on with greater speed, for now I am not weary as a while ago; and see how the hill now casts its shadow." "We will go forward with this day," he answered, "as much farther as is now possible for us; but the fact is otherwise than thou supposest. Before thou canst be there-above thou wilt see him return, who is now hidden by the hill-side so that thou dost not make his rays to break. But see there a soul which, stationed all alone, is looking toward

us; it will point out to us the speediest way."

61. We came to it. O Lombard soul, how lofty and disdainful didst thou hold thyself; and in the movement of thine eyes grave and slow! It said not anything to us, but let us go on, only eyeing us in manner of a lion when he is couching. Still Virgil drew near to it, praying that it would show to us the best ascent; and it made no answer to his request, but of our country and life enquired of us.

71. And the sweet Leader began: "Mantua" —and the shade, all in itself recluse, rose toward him from the place where first it was, saying: "O Mantuan, I am Sordello of thy city."[4] And they embraced each other.

76. Ah, servile Italy! hostel of grief! ship without pilot in great tempest; not lady of provinces, but a brothel! that noble soul was so ready, only at the sweet name of his native town, to give glad welcome here unto his fellow-citizen; and now in thee thy living men exist not without war, and of those whom one wall and one moat shut in one gnaws the other. Search, wretched one, around its shores, thy seaboard, and then look within thy bosom, if any part in thee enjoys peace! What avails it that for thee Justinian readjusted thy bridle, if the saddle be empty? Without this, the shame would be less. Ah folk, that oughtest to be devout and let Cæsar sit in the saddle, if thou rightly understandest what God notes for thee! Look how fell this wild beast has become, through not being corrected by the spurs, since thou didst put thy hand upon the rein.

97. O German Albert, who abandonest her that has become untamed and savage, and oughtest to bestride her saddle-bows, may a just judgment from the stars fall upon thy blood, and may it be so strange and manifest that thy successor may have fear thereat![5] For thou and thy father, held back up there by greed, have suffered the garden of the empire

my obduracy,' and immediately Marzucco went and buried his son."

[1] Count Orso, the son of Count Napoleone degli Alberti, was murdered by his cousin, the son of Count Alessandro. Cf. Hell, xxxii. 55-60.

[2] Pierre de la Brosse was chamberlain and confidant of Philip the Bold of France. He lost the king's favor and was hanged. It was believed that he had incurred the hatred of Mary of Brabant, Philip's second wife. As she lived till 1321, Dante's warning may have reached her ears.

[3] Cf. Aeneid, vi. 376.

[4] Sordello, who lived in the thirteenth century, left his native land and gave up his native tongue to live and write as a troubadour in Provence.

[5] Albert of Hapsburg, son of the Emperor Rudolph, was elected King of the Romans in 1298, but, like his father, never went to Italy to be crowned. He was murdered by his nephew, John the Parricide, in 1308, at Königsfelden. The successor of Albert was Henry VII of Luxemburg, who came to Italy in 1311 and was crowned at Rome in 1312. His death in 1313 ended Dante's hopes.

to become desert. Come thou to see the Montecchi and Cappelletti, the Monaldi and Filippeschi,[1] thou man without care, those already wretched, and these in dread. Come, cruel one, come, and see the distress of thy nobility, and cure their hurts; and thou shalt see Santafiora[2] how safe it is.

112. Come to see thy Rome, that weeps, widowed and alone, and cries day and night: "My Cæsar, wherefore dost thou not keep me company?" Come to see how the people love one another; and, if no pity for us move thee, come to be shamed for thine own renown! And if it be lawful for me, O Supreme Jove, who wast on earth crucified for us, are Thy just eyes turned aside elsewhere? Or is it preparation, which in the abyss of Thy counsel Thou art making, for some good utterly cut off from our perception? For the cities of Italy are all full of tyrants, and every churl that comes playing the partisan becomes a Marcellus.[3]

127. My Florence! surely thou mayst be content with this digression, which does not touch thee, thanks to thy people that takes such heed. Many have justice at heart, but shoot slowly, through not coming to the bow without deliberation; but thy people has it on the edge of its lips. Many reject the common burden, but thy people eagerly responds without being called, and cries, "I load myself." Now make thee glad, for thou hast truly wherefore: thou rich, thou at peace, thou wise! If I speak the truth, the fact does not hide it. Athens and Lacedæmon, that made the ancient laws and were so civilized, made in regard to living well but little sign, compared with thee that makest such fine-spun provisions, that what thou spinnest in October reaches not to mid-November. How often in the time that thou rememberest hast thou changed law, money, office, and custom, and renewed thy members; And if thou mind thee well and see the light, thou wilt see thyself resembling that sick woman, who can-

not find repose upon the feathers, but with her tossing seeks to ease her pain.

CANTO VII

1. AFTER the becoming and glad salutations had been repeated three and four times, Sordello drew back and said: "Who are you?" "Before the souls worthy to ascend to God were turned to this mountain,[4] my bones had been buried by Octavian; I am Virgil, and for no other sin did I lose heaven, but for not having faith"; thus then replied my Leader.

10. As is he who suddenly sees a thing before him whereat he marvels, and does and does not believe, saying: "It is, it is not,"—such seemed that shade, and then he bent down his brow, and humbly returned toward him, and embraced him where the inferior lays hold.[5]

16. "O glory of the Latins," said he, "through whom our language showed what it could do, O eternal honor of the place wherefrom I was, what merit or what grace shows thee to me? If I am worthy to hear thy words, tell me if thou comest from Hell, and from what cloister." "Through all the circles of the realm of woe," replied he to him, "am I come hither; the power of Heaven moved me, and with it I come. Not by doing, but by not doing have I lost the sight of the high Sun which thou desirest, and which by me was known too late. There is a place below not sad with torments but with darkness only, where the lamentations sound not as wailings, but are sighs; there I abide with the little innocents bitten by the teeth of death before they were exempt from human sin; there I abide with those whom the three holy virtues did not invest, but who without vice knew the others, and followed all of them.[6] But if thou knowest and canst, give us some direction whereby we may come more speedily to where Purgatory has its right beginning."

40. He replied: "A fixed place is not assigned for us; it is permitted me to go upward and around; so far as I can go, I join myself to thee as guide. But see how already the day declines, and to go up by night is not possible; therefore it is well to think of some fair sojourn. There

---

[1] The Montecchi were Ghibellines of Verona, the Cappelletti were Guelphs of Cremona, the Monaldi were Guelphs of Perugia, and the Filippeschi were Ghibellines of Orvieto.

[2] The Counts of Santafiora were once the most powerful Ghibelline nobles in the Sienese territory. Now their territories were full of lawlessness and misery.

[3] The Consul M. Claudius Marcellus was a bitter opponent of Cæsar.

[4] Cf. *Hell*, iv. 63.

[5] Cf. *Purgatory*, xxi. 130.

[6] Cf. *Hell*, iv; description of Limbo.

are souls yonder to the right, apart; if thou consentest to me I will lead thee to them, and not without delight will they be known to thee." "How is this?" was the answer, "would he who might wish to ascend by night be prevented by another, or could he not ascend because he had not the power?"

52. And the good Sordello drew his finger on the ground, saying: "See, only this line thou couldst not pass after the sun is gone; not, however, that aught else than the nocturnal darkness would give hindrance to going up; that hampers the will with impotence. One might, indeed, in the darkness turn downward, and walk the hillside wandering around, while the horizon holds the day shut up." Thereon my Lord, as if wondering, said: "Lead us, then, there where thou sayest one may have delight while waiting."

64. A short distance had we gone from that place, when I perceived that the mountain was hollowed out in like fashion as the valleys hollow them here on earth. "Yonder," said that shade, "will we go, where the hillside makes a lap of itself, and there will we await the new day." Now steep, now level, was a winding path that led us to a side of the dale, where its border more than half dies away. Gold and fine silver, and cochineal and pure white, Indian wood bright and clear blue, fresh emerald at the instant it is split, would each be vanquished in color by the herbage and by the flowers set within that valley, as by its greater the less is vanquished. Nature had not only painted there, but of sweetness of a thousand odors she made there one unknown and blended fragrance.

82. Here I saw souls who, because of the valley, were not visible from without, seated upon the green and upon the flowers, singing *Salve Regina*.[1]

[1] The beginning of an antiphon recited, during certain seasons of the year, at compline, the last service of the day, after sunset. The whole antiphon is as follows, and its appropriateness to the condition of these sinners is manifest: "Hail, Queen, mother of mercy! our life, our joy, our hope, hail! To thee we, exiled sons of Eve, do cry; to thee we sigh, groaning and weeping in this valley of tears. Come then, our Advocate, turn thy pitying eyes upon us, and show to us, after our exile, Jesus, the blessed fruit of thy womb. O clement, O pitiful, O sweet Virgin Mary! Pray for us, holy Mother of God, that we may be made worthy of the promises of Christ."

85. "Before the now diminished sun sink to his nest," began the Mantuan who had turned us thither, "do not desire that I guide you among these. From this bank ye will better discern the acts and countenances of each and all, than when received among them on the level below. He who sits highest and has the semblance of having neglected that which he should have done, and who moves not his mouth to the others' songs, was Rudolph the Emperor,[2] who might have healed the wounds that have slain Italy, so that too late is she called back to life by another. The next, who to appearance is comforting him, ruled the land where the water rises which the Moldau bears to the Elbe, and the Elbe to the sea. His name was Ottocar,[3] and in his swaddling-clothes he was better far than bearded Wenceslaus, his son, whom luxury and idleness feed.[4]

103. And that small-nosed one,[5] who seems close in counsel with him who has so benign an aspect,[6] died in flight and disflowering the lily; look there, how he beats his breast: see the next one who, sighing, has made with his hand a bed for his cheek. Father and father-in-law are they of the Pest of France;[7] they know his vicious and foul life, and thence comes the grief which so pierces them. He who looks so large-limbed,[8] and who accords in singing with him of the masculine nose,[9] wore girt the cord of every worth, and if the youth that is sitting behind him[10] had remained after him as king, truly the worth had gone from vessel to

[2] Rudolph of Hapsburg, first Emperor of the House of Austria, born in 1218, crowned Emperor at Aachen in 1273, died in 1291.
[3] Ottocar, King of Bohemia and Duke of Austria, was slain in battle against Rudolph in 1278.
[4] Cf. *Paradise*, v. 125.
[5] This is Philip III, the Bold, of France. Having invaded Catalonia, in a war with Peter III of Aragon, he was driven back, and died, on his disastrous retreat in 1285.
[6] Henry of Navarre, whose daughter Joan married Philip IV of France.
[7] Philip IV of France. Cf. *Hell*, xix. 87; *Purgatory*, xx. 91; xxxii. 152; xxxiii. 45; *Paradise*, xix. 118.
[8] Peter III of Aragon, the husband of Constance, daughter of Manfred (see Canto iii. 115, 143). In 1282, when the French were driven out of Sicily, Pedro was made king of Sicily.
[9] Charles of Anjou, king, by conquest, of Naples and Sicily. See Canto xx. 67-69.
[10] This youth is Alfonso, son of Peter III, who succeeded his father as king of Aragon, but died, twenty years old, in 1291.

vessel, which cannot be said of the other heirs: James and Frederick hold the realms;[1] the better heritage no one possesses.

121. Rarely does human goodness rise through the branches, and this He wills who gives it, in order that it may be claimed from Him.[2] To the large-nosed one also my words apply not less than to the other, Peter, who is singing with him; wherefore Apulia and Provence are now grieving.[3] The plant is as inferior to its seed, as, more than Beatrice and Margaret, Constance still boasts of her husband.[4] See the King of the simple life sitting there alone, Henry of England; he in his branches has a better issue.[5] That one who lowest among them is seated on the ground, looking upward, is William the Marquis,[6] for whom Alessandria and her war make Montferrat and Canavese mourn."

CANTO VIII

1. It was now the hour that turns back desire in those that sail the sea, and softens their hearts, the day when they have said to their sweet friends farewell, and which pierces the new pilgrim with love, if he hear from afar a bell that seems to deplore the dying day— when I began to render hearing vain, and to look at one of the souls, who, uprisen, besought attention with its hand. It joined and raised both its palms, fixing its eyes toward the east, as if it said to God, "For aught else I care not." *Te lucis ante*[7] so devoutly issued from his

mouth and with such sweet notes that it made me issue forth from my own mind. And then the others sweetly and devoutly accompanied it through all the hymn to the end, having their eyes on the supernal wheels. Here, reader, sharpen well thine eyes to the truth, for surely the veil is now indeed so thin that passing through within is easy.

22. I saw that army of the gentle-born silently thereafter gazing upward, as if in expectation, pallid and humble; and I saw two angels, issuing from on high and descending, with two flaming swords truncated and deprived of their points. Green as leaflets just now born was their raiment, which, beaten and blown by their green pinions, they trailed behind. One came to his station a little above us, and the other descended on the opposite bank, so that the people were contained between them. I clearly discerned in them their blond heads, but on their faces the eye was dazzled, as a faculty which is confounded by excess. "Both come from the bosom of Mary," said Sordello, "for guard of the valley, because of the serpent which will straightway come." Whereat I, who knew not by what path, turned me round, and, all chilled, drew close to the trusty shoulders.

43. And Sordello again: "Now let us go down among the great shades, and we will speak to them; well-pleasing will it be to them to see you." Only three steps I think that I descended and I was below; and I saw one who was gazing only at me as if he wished to recognize me. It was already the time when the air was darkening, but not so that between his eyes and mine it did not reveal that which it locked up before. Towards me he made, and I made towards him. Noble Judge Nino,[8] how much it pleased me when I saw that thou wast not among the damned! No fair salutation was silent between us; then he asked: "How long is it since thou camest to the foot of the mountain across the far waters?"

58. "Oh," said I to him, "from within the dismal places I came this morning, and I am in the first life, although in going thus I may gain the other." And when my answer was heard, Sordello and he drew themselves back, like

---

[1] The kingdoms of Aragon and Sicily; both James and Frederick, the two surviving sons of Peter III, were living when Dante thus wrote of them. (See Canto iii. 116.) The "better heritage" was their father's virtue.

[2] Cf. Chaucer, *Wife of Bath's Tale,* 6707-12.

[3] Apulia and Provence were grieving under the rule of Charles II, the degenerate son of Charles of Anjou.

[4] That is, possibly, Charles himself, the husband first of Beatrice of Provence and then of Margaret of Nevers, was inferior to Peter, the husband of Constance.

[5] Henry III of England (died 1272), father of Edward I.

[6] William, Marquis of Montferrat and Canavese. In a war with the Guelfs, who had risen in revolt in 1290, he was taken captive at Alessandria, and for two years, till his death, was kept in an iron cage.

[7] The opening words of a hymn sung at compline, the last service of the day:—"Before the close of light, we pray thee, O Creator, that through thy clemency, thou be our watch and guard."

[8] Nino (Ugolino) de' Visconti of Pisa was the grandson of Count Ugolino. He had held the judicature of Gallura, in Sardinia (see *Hell,* xxii. 81).

folk suddenly bewildered. The one turned to Virgil, and the other to one who was seated there, crying: "Up, Corrado,[1] come to see what God through grace has willed." Then, turning to me: "By that singular gratitude thou owest unto Him who so hides His own first wherefore that there is no ford to it, when thou shalt be beyond the wide waves, say to my Joan that she cry for me there where answer is made to the innocent. I do not think her mother[2] loves me longer, since she changed her white wimples, which she, wretched, needs must even now long for. Through her one may understand easily enough how long in woman the fire of love endures, if the eye or the touch does not often rekindle it. The viper[3] which leads afield the Milanese will not make for her so fair a sepulture as the cock of Gallura would have done." Thus he said, marked in his aspect with the stamp of that righteous zeal which glows with due measure in the heart.

85. My greedy eyes were going only to the sky, only there where the stars are slowest, even as a wheel nearest the axle. And my Leader: "Son, at what art thou gazing up there?" And I to him: "At those three torches with which the pole on this side is all aflame." And he to me: "The four bright stars which thou sawest this morning[4] are low on the other side, and these are risen where those were."

94. As he was speaking, lo! Sordello drew him to himself, saying: "See there our adversary!" and pointed his finger that he should look thither. At that part where the little valley has no barrier was a snake, perhaps such as gave to Eve the bitter food. Through the grass and the flowers came the evil streak, turning now and again its head to its back, licking like a beast that sleeks itself. I did not see, and therefore cannot tell, how the celestial falcons moved, but I saw well both one and the other in motion. Hearing the air cleft by their green wings the serpent fled, and the angels wheeled upward to their posts with equal flight.

109. The shade which had drawn close to the Judge when he exclaimed, through all that assault had not for a moment loosed its gaze from me. "So may the lantern which is leading thee on high find in thine own free will so much wax as is needed as far as to the enamelled summit," it began, "if thou knowest true news of Valdimacra[5] or of the neighboring region, tell it to me, for there I once was great. I was called Corrado Malaspina; I am not the elder,[6] but from him I am descended; to mine own I bore the love which is here refined." "Oh," said I to him, "through your lands I have never been, but where does man dwell in all Europe that they are not renowned? The fame that honors your house proclaims its lords, proclaims its district, so that he knows of them who never yet was there. And I swear to you, so may I go on high, that your honored race does not despoil itself of the praise of the purse and of the sword. Custom and nature so privilege it that though the guilty head[7] turn the world awry, alone it goes straight and scorns the evil way."

133. And he: "Now go, for the sun shall not return to rest seven times in the bed which the Ram covers and bestrides with all four feet, before this courteous opinion will be nailed in the middle of thy head with greater nails than the speech of another, if course of judgment be not arrested."

CANTO IX

1. THE concubine of old Tithonus was now gleaming white on the balcony of the east, forth from the arms of her sweet friend; her forehead was bright with gems set in the shape of the cold animal that strikes people with its tail.[8] And in the place where we were the night had taken two of the steps with which she ascends, and the third was already bending its wings downward, when I, who had somewhat of Adam with me, overcome by sleep, reclined

[1] Corrado, of the Guelf family of the Malaspina, lords of the Lunigiana, a district between Genoa and Pisa.
[2] Beatrice d' Este, who, in 1300, married, secondly, Galeazzo de' Visconti of Milan.
[3] The viper was the cognizance of the Visconti, the lords of Milan; the cock that of the Judicature of Gallura.
[4] Cf. Canto i. 23.

[5] The valley of the Magra, in the Lunigiana.
[6] The elder Corrado Malaspina was the husband of Constance, King Manfred's sister. The second Corrado was his grandson.
[7] Probably Rome as the seat of a corrupt papacy.
[8] By "the concubine of old Tithonus," Dante seems to intend the lunar Aurora, in distinction to the proper wife of Tithonus, Aurora, who precedes the rising Sun.

upon the grass, there where all five of us were already seated.

13. At the hour near the morning when the little swallow begins her sad lays,[1] perhaps in memory of her former woes, and when our mind, more a wanderer from the flesh and less captive to the thought, is in its visions almost divine,[2] in dream I seemed to see an eagle with feathers of gold poised in the sky, with wings spread, and intent to stoop. And I seemed to be there[3] where his own people were abandoned by Ganymede, when he was rapt to the supreme consistory. In myself I thought perhaps this bird strikes only here through wont, and perhaps from other place disdains to carry anyone upward in its feet. Then it seemed to me that, having wheeled a little, it descended terrible as a thunderbolt, and snatched me upwards far as the fire.[4] There it seemed that it and I burned, and the imagined fire so scorched that of necessity my sleep was broken.

34. Not otherwise Achilles shook himself—turning around his awakened eyes, and not knowing where he was, when his mother stole him away, sleeping in her arms, from Chiron to Scyros, thither whence afterwards the Greeks withdrew him[5]—than I started, as from my face sleep fled away; and I became pale, as does a man who, frightened, turns to ice. At my side was my Comforter alone, and the sun was now more than two hours high, and my face was turned toward the sea.

46. "Have no fear," said my Lord; "be reassured, for we are at a good point; restrain not, but put forth all thy strength. Thou art now arrived at Purgatory; see there the cliff that closes it round; see the entrance there where it appears divided. Short while ago, in the dawn that precedes the day, when thy soul was sleeping within thee upon the flowers wherewith

the place down yonder is adorned, came a lady, and said: 'I am Lucia;[6] let me take this one who is sleeping; thus will I assist him along his way.' Sordello remained, and the other noble forms: she took thee up, and as the day grew bright, she came upward, and I along her footprints. Here she laid thee down: and first her beautiful eyes showed me that open entrance; then she and slumber went away together."

64. Like a man who in perplexity is reassured, and who changes his fear into confidence after the truth is disclosed to him, so did I change; and when my Leader saw me free from disquiet, up along the cliff he moved on, and I behind, toward the height.

70. Reader, thou seest well how I exalt my theme, and therefore marvel not if I support it with more art.[7]

73. We drew near to it, and reached a place such that there, where at first there seemed to me to be a rift, like a cleft which divides a wall, I saw a gate, and three steps beneath for going to it, of divers colors, and a gatekeeper who as yet said not a word. And as I opened my eye upon him more and more, I saw him sitting on the upper step, such in his face that I endured it not.[8] And he had in his hand a naked sword, which so reflected the rays toward us that I often raised my sight in vain. "Tell it from there, what would ye?" he began to say: "Where is the guide? Beware lest the coming up be harmful to you."[9] "A lady from Heaven versed in these things," replied my Master to him, "only just now said to us: 'Go thither, here is the gate.'" "And may she speed your steps in good," began again the courteous gatekeeper, "come forward then unto our stairs."

94. Thither we came to the first great stair; it was of white marble so polished and smooth that I mirrored myself in it as I appear. The second, of deeper hue than perse, was of a rough and scorched stone, cracked lengthwise and athwart. The third, which uppermost lies massy, seemed to me of porphyry as flaming red as blood that spurts forth from a vein. Up-

---

[1] The allusion is to the story of Procne and Philomela, transformed the one into a swallow, the other into a nightingale.

[2] Cf. *Hell,* xxvi. 7.

[3] On Mount Ida.

[4] The sphere of fire by which, according to mediæval cosmography, the sphere of the air was surrounded.

[5] Statius tells how Thetis, to prevent Achilles from going to the siege of Troy, bore him, sleeping, away from his instructor, the centaur Chiron, and carried him to the Island of Scyros, where, though concealed in women's garments, Ulysses and Diomed discovered him.

[6] Cf. *Hell,* ii.

[7] See Aquinas, *Summa Theologica,* Part I-II, Q 113, A 6, 8.

[8] Aquinas, *Summa Theologica,* Part III. *Suppl.,* Q 8, A 1.

[9] Cf. Aquinas, *Summa Theologica,* Part III, Q 89, A 2.

on this the Angel of God held both his feet, sitting upon the threshold, which seemed to me stone of adamant.[1] Up over the three steps my Leader drew me with good will, saying: "Beg humbly that he undo the lock." Devoutly I threw myself at the holy feet; I besought for mercy's sake that he would open for me; but first upon my breast I struck three times. Seven P's he inscribed upon my forehead with the point of his sword,[2] and: "See that thou wash these wounds when thou art within," he said.

115. Ashes or earth dug out dry would be of one color with his vestment, and from beneath that he drew two keys. One was of gold and the other was of silver: first with the white and then with the yellow he so did to the gate, that I was content. "Whenever one of these keys fails so that it turns not rightly in the lock," said he to us, "this narrow entrance does not open. The one is more precious; but the other requires exceeding much of art and wit before it unlocks, because it is that which disentangles the knot. From Peter I hold them; and he told me to err rather in opening than in keeping shut, if but the people prostrate themselves at my feet." Then he pushed the valve of the sacred gate, saying: "Enter, but I give you warning that whoso looks backward returns outside."[3] And when the pivots of that sacred portal, which are of metal, sonorous and strong, were turned within their hinges, Tarpeia roared not so loud nor showed herself so harsh, when the good Metellus was taken from her, whereby she afterwards remained lean.

139. I turned away attentive to the first tone, and it seemed to me I heard *"Te Deum laudamus"* in a voice mingled with the sweet sound. That which I heard gave me just such an impression as we are wont to receive when people stand singing with an organ, and the words now are, now are not heard.

CANTO X

1. WHEN we were within the threshold of the gate, which the evil love of souls disuses, be-

cause it makes the crooked way seem straight, I heard by its resounding that it was closed again. And, if I had turned my eyes to it, what excuse would have been befitting for the fault?

7. We were ascending through a cloven rock, which was moving to one side and to the other, even as the wave which retreats and approaches. "Here must be used a little art," began my Leader, "in keeping close, now on this hand, now on that, to the side which recedes." And this made our steps so scant that the waning disk of the moon had regained its bed to go to rest, before we were out from that needle's eye. But when we were free and open above, where the mountain gathers itself back, I weary, and both uncertain of our way, we stopped upon a level more solitary than roads through deserts. From its edge, where it borders the void, to the foot of the high bank which ever rises, a human body three times told would measure; and as far as my eye could stretch its wings, now on the left and now on the right side, such did this cornice seem to me. Our feet had not yet moved upon it, when I perceived the circling bank, which, being perpendicular, allowed no ascent, to be of white marble and adorned with such carvings, that not only Polycletus, but Nature herself would have been shamed there.

34. The Angel who came to earth with the announcement of the peace, many years wept for, which opened Heaven from its long interdict, appeared before us, carved here so truly in a sweet attitude, that he did not seem an image that is silent. One would have sworn that he was saying *"Ave";* for she was imaged there who turned the key to open the exalted love. And on her action she had these words impressed, *Ecce ancilla Dei!*[4] as exactly as a shape is sealed in wax.

46. "Keep not thy mind only on one place," said the sweet Master, who had me on that side where people have their heart. Whereupon I moved my eyes and saw, beyond Mary, upon that side where he was who was moving me, another story imposed upon the rock; wherefore I passed Virgil, and drew near so that it might be set before my eyes. There in the very marble were carved the cart and the oxen draw-

---

[1] The first stair is the symbol of contrition; the second is the symbol of confession; the third is the symbol of the satisfaction rendered by deeds of love, the works of penitence.

[2] The P's stand for *peccati*, the Italian word for sins.

[3] Cf. Aquinas, *Summa Theologica*, Part III, Q 84, A 10; Luke, 9. 62.

[4] "Behold the handmaid of the Lord!" Luke, 1. 38.

ing the holy ark, by reason of which men fear an office not given in charge.[1] In front appeared people; and all of them, divided in seven choirs, of two of my senses made the one say: "No," the other: "Yes, they are singing." In like manner, by the smoke of the incense that was imaged there, my eyes and nose were made in *Yes* and *No* discordant. There, preceding the blessed vessel, dancing, girt up, was the humble Psalmist, and more and less than king was he on that occasion. Opposite, portrayed at a window of a great palace, Michal was looking on, even as a lady scornful and troubled.[2]

70. I moved my feet from the place where I was standing, in order to look from near at another story which, beyond Michal, was gleaming white to me. Here was storied the high glory of the Roman prince, whose worth incited Gregory to his great victory:[3] I speak of Trajan the emperor; and a poor widow was at his bridle in attitude of weeping and of grief. Round about him it seemed trampled and thronged with knights, and above him the eagles in the gold were moving in appearance in the wind. The wretched woman among all these seemed to be saying: "Lord, do me vengeance for my son who is slain, whereat I am broken-hearted." And he to answer her: "Now wait till I return"; and she: "My Lord"—like one in whom grief is urgent—"if thou return not?" And he: "He who shall be where I am will do it for thee." And she: "What will the good deed of another be to thee, if thou art unmindful of thine own?" Whereon he: "Now comfort thee; for it behoves that I discharge my duty ere I go; justice so wills, and pity holds me back." He who never beheld a new thing produced that visible speech, novel to us, because it is not found on earth.

97. While I was delighting myself with looking at the images of such great humilities, and for their Maker's sake dear to see: "Behold," murmured the Poet, "on this side many people, but they make few steps; they will put us on the way to the lofty stairs." My eyes which were intent on gazing, were not slow in turning toward him in order to see novelties, whereof they are fain.

106. I would not, indeed, Reader, that thou be diverted from thy good purpose, through hearing how God wills that the debt be paid. Heed not the form of the suffering; think on what follows; think that, at the worst, beyond the Great Judgment it cannot go!

112. I began: "Master, that which I see moving toward us does not seem to me to be persons, but what I know not, I am so at loss in looking." And he to me: "The heavy condition of their torment bows them to earth, so that my own eyes at first had contention with it. But look fixedly there, and disentangle with thy sight that which is coming beneath those stones; already thou canst discern how each is stricken."

121. O proud Christians, wretched and weary, who, diseased in vision of the mind, have confidence in backward steps, are ye not aware that we are worms born to form the angelic butterfly, which flies unto judgment without defence? Wherefore does your mind float up aloft, since ye are as it were defective insects, even as a worm in which formation fails?

130. As to support ceiling or roof, by way of corbel, a figure is sometimes seen joining its knees to its breast, which out of the unreal gives birth to a real distress in him who sees it, thus fashioned did I see these, when I gave good heed. True it is, that they were more or less bowed down, according as they had more or less upon their backs; and he who had most patience in his looks, weeping, appeared to say: "I can no more."

CANTO XI

1. "O OUR Father, who art in Heaven, not circumscribed, but for the greater love which Thou hast to the first works on high, praised be Thy name and Thy power by every creature, as it is meet to render thanks to Thy sweet effluence. May the peace of Thy Kingdom come unto us, for if it come not, we cannot unto it of ourselves, with all our striving. As Thine angels, singing Hosanna, make sacrifice to Thee of their will, so may men make of theirs, Give us this day the daily manna, without which, in this rough desert, he back-

[1] See II Samuel, 6. 4-7.
[2] See II Samuel, 6. 12-16.
[3] It was believed that Pope Gregory the Great interceded for Trajan, praying that he might be delivered from Hell. See *Paradise*, xx. 106-117.

ward goes, who toils most to go on. And as we forgive to each the wrong that we have suffered, even do Thou, benignant, forgive, and regard not our desert, Our virtue, which is easily overcome, put not to proof with the old adversary, but deliver from him who so assails it. This last prayer, dear Lord, is, indeed, not made for ourselves, for it is not needful, but for those who have remained behind us."[1]

25. Thus praying good speed for themselves and us, those shades were all going under their load, like that of which one sometimes dreams, unequally distressed, round and round and weary, along the first cornice, purging away the sullies of the world. If good is always asked for us there, what can be said and done here for them by those who have a good root to their will? Truly we ought to aid them to wash away the marks which they bore hence, so that pure and light they may issue forth unto the starry wheels.

37. "Ah! so may justice and pity disburden you speedily, that ye may be able to move the wing which may lift you according to your desire, show on which hand is the shortest path toward the stairway; and, if there be more than one passage, point out to us that which least steeply slopes; for this one who comes with me, because of the burden of the flesh of Adam wherewith he is clothed, is chary, against his will, of mounting up."

46. It was not manifest from whom came the words which they returned to these that he whom I was following had spoken, but it was said: "Come with us to the right hand along the bank, and ye will find the pass possible for a living person to ascend. And were I not hindered by the stone which tames my proud neck, so that I needs must carry my face low, I would look at that one who is still alive and has not been named, to see if I know him, and to make him pitiful of this burden. I was an Italian, and the son of a great Tuscan; Guglielmo Aldobrandesco was my father: I know not if his name was ever with you.[2] The ancient blood and the gallant deeds of my ancestors made me so arrogant that, not thinking on the common mother, I held every man in scorn

to such extreme that I died therefor, as the Sienese know, and every child in Campagnatico knows it. I am Omberto: and not only to me pride does harm, for all my kinsfolk has it dragged with it into calamity; and here must I bear this load for it till God be satisfied,— here, among the dead, since I did it not among the living."

73. Listening, I bent down my face; and one of them, not he who was speaking, twisted himself under the weight that hampers him, and saw me, and recognized me, and called out, keeping his eyes with effort fixed on me, who was going along all stooping with them.[3] "Oh," said I to him, "art thou not Oderisi, the honor of Gubbio, and the honor of that art which in Paris is called illuminating?" "Brother," said he, "more smiling are the leaves that Franco of Bologna pencils; the honor is now all his, and mine in part. Truly I should not have been so courteous while I lived, because of the great desire of excelling whereon my heart was intent. Of such pride the fee is paid here; and I should not yet be here, were it not that, still having power to sin, I turned me unto God.

91. "O vainglory of human powers! how short while lasts the green upon the top, if it be not followed by dull ages. Cimabue thought to hold the field in painting, and now Giotto has the cry, so that the fame of him is obscured. In like manner the one Guido has taken from the other the glory of our tongue; and he perhaps is born who shall drive both one and the other from the nest.[4] Worldly renown is naught but a breath of wind, which now comes this way and now comes that, and changes name because it changes quarter. What more repute shalt thou have, if thou strippest thy flesh from thee when it is old, than if thou hadst died before thou hadst left thy pap and thy rattle, ere a thousand years have passed?—which is a shorter space compared to the eternal than a movement of the eyelid to the circle which is slowest turned in Heaven.

109. "With him who takes so little of the road in front of me, all Tuscany resounded, and now is scarce a whisper of him in Siena, whereof he was lord when the Florentine rage

---

[1] Cf. Canto xxvi. 130-132.
[2] See Canto vi. 111. The speaker was murdered, in his own stronghold of Campagnatico, in 1259.

[3] See Canto xiii. 136-138.
[4] The first Guido is Guido Guinicelli; see Canto xxvi. 97-99. The other, Guido Cavalcanti.

was destroyed,[1] which at that time was proud, as now it is prostitute. Your reputation is as the color of grass, which comes and goes, and he discolors it through whom it came up fresh from the earth." And I to him: "Thy true speech fills my heart with good humility, and thou abatest a great swelling in me: but who is he of whom thou now wert speaking?" "That," he answered, "is Provenzan Salvani;[2] and he is here, because he was presumptuous in bringing all Siena to his hands. He has gone thus—and he goes without repose—ever since he died: such coin does every one pay in satisfaction, who is too daring on earth."

127. And I: "If that spirit who awaits the verge of life ere he repent abides there below, and, if good prayer do not assist him, ascends not hither, until as long a time pass as he lived, how has this coming been granted unto him?" "When he was living in greatest boast," said he, "laying aside all shame, he freely stationed himself in the Campo of Siena,[3] and there, to deliver his friend from the punishment he was enduring in the prison of Charles, brought himself to tremble in every vein. More I will not say, and I know that I speak darkly; but little time will pass, before thy neighbors will so act that thou shalt be able to gloss it. This deed removed those limits for him."

CANTO XII

1. WITH even pace, like oxen that go yoked, I went on with that burdened soul so long as the sweet Pedagogue allowed it; but when he said: "Leave him, and pass on, for here it is well for every one to urge his bark, both with the sail and with the oars, as much as he can," I straitened up my body again, as is required for walking, although my thoughts remained both stooping and abased.

10. I had moved on, and was following willingly the steps of my Master, and both were now showing how light we were, when he said to me: "Turn thine eyes downward; it will be

well for thee, in order to cheer the way, to look upon the bed of thy footsteps." As above the buried, so that there may be memory of them, their tombs on the ground bear engraved what they were before—whence often is weeping for them there, through the pricking of remembrance, which only to the pious gives the spur —so I saw figured there, but of better semblance in respect of the workmanship, all that for pathway juts out from the mountain.

25. I saw, on one side, him who was created more noble than any other creature, falling down as lightning from heaven.[4]

28. I saw Briareus,[5] on the other side, transfixed by the celestial bolt, lying heavy upon the earth in mortal chill.

31. I saw Thymbraeus,[6] I saw Pallas and Mars, still armed, around their father, gazing at the scattered limbs of the giants.

34. I saw Nimrod at the foot of his great toil, as if bewildered, and looking round upon the people that had been proud with him in Shinar.

37. O Niobe! with what grieving eyes did I see thee portrayed upon the road between thy seven and seven children slain!

40. O Saul! how on thine own sword didst thou here appear dead on Gilboa, which thereafter felt not rain or dew![7]

43. O foolish Arachne,[8] so did I see thee, already half spider, wretched on the shreds of the work which to thy harm by thee was made!

46. O Rehoboam! here thine image seems not now to threaten, but a chariot bears it away full of terror before anyone pursues it.[9]

49. The hard pavement showed also how costly to his mother Alcmæon made the ill-fated ornament appear.[10]

52. It showed how his sons threw themselves

---

[1] In 1260, at Montaperti.
[2] A chief supporter of the Ghibelline cause in Tuscany. Defeated and taken prisoner at the battle of Colle, in 1269, he was beheaded.
[3] The chief public square. Provenzano's friend is said to have been condemned to death, and his ransom fixed at ten thousand florins. Provenzano, not being able to pay this sum from his own means, took his station in the Campo and begged of the passers-by.

[4] Lucifer. See Luke, 10. 18.
[5] See *Hell*, xxxi. 98.
[6] Apollo, so called from his temple at Thymbra, not far from Troy. See Virgil, *Georgics*, iv. 323.
[7] See I Samuel, 31. 4; II Samuel, 1. 21.
[8] Changed to a spider by Athena, whom she had challenged to a trial of skill at the loom.
[9] See I Kings, 12. 18.
[10] Amphiaraüs, the soothsayer, foreseeing his own death if he went to the Theban war, hid himself. His wife, Eriphyle, bribed by a golden necklace, betrayed his hiding-place and was killed by her son Alcmæon, for thus bringing about his father's death.

upon Sennacherib within the temple, and how, he dead, they left him there.[1]

55. It showed the ruin and the cruel butchery that Tomyris wrought, when she said to Cyrus, "For blood thou hast thirsted, and with blood I fill thee."[2]

58. It showed how the Assyrians fled in rout after Holofernes was killed, and also the remnants of the victim.[3]

61. I saw Troy in ashes, and in caverns: O Ilion, how cast down and abject did the image which is there discerned show thee!

64. What Master has there been of pencil or of style that could draw the shadows and the lines which there would make every subtile genius wonder? Dead seemed the dead, and the living alive. He who saw the truth saw not better than I all that I trod on, while I went bent down.—Now be ye proud, and go your way with haughty look, ye sons of Eve, and bend not down your face so that ye may see your evil path!

73. More of the mountain had now been circled by us, and of the sun's course far more spent, than my mind, not disengaged,[4] was aware, when he, who always went attentive in advance, began: "Lift up thy head; there is no longer time for going thus abstracted. See yonder an Angel, who is making ready to come toward us: see how the sixth hand-maiden is returning from the service of the day.[5] With reverence adorn thine acts and thy face so that it may please him to direct us upward. Think that this day never dawns again."

85. I was well used to his admonition never to lose time,[6] so that on that theme he could not speak to me obscurely.

88. The beautiful creature came toward us, clothed in white, and in his face such as seems the tremulous morning star. His arms he opened, and then he opened his wings; he said: "Come: here at hand are the steps, and easily henceforth does one ascend. Very few come to these tidings. O human race, born to fly upward, wherefore at a little wind dost thou so fall?"

97. He led us to where the rock was cleft; here he struck his wings across my forehead,[7] then promised me secure progress.

100. As on the right hand, to ascend the mountain,[8] where the church sits which above Rubaconte[9] dominates the well-guided city, the bold flight of the ascent is broken by the stairs, which were made in an age when the record and the stave were secure, so the bank which falls here very steeply from the next round is made easier; but on this side and that the high rock grazes. As we turned our persons thither, voices sang *Beati pauperes spiritu* in such wise that speech could not tell it. Ah, how different are these passes from those of Hell! for here one enters with songs, and there below with fierce lamentations.

115. Already we were mounting up over the holy stairs, and it seemed to me I was far more light than I had seemed before upon the plain. Whereon I: "Master, say, what heavy thing has been lifted from me, so that almost no fatigue is felt by me as I go on?" He answered: "When the P's which, almost extinct,[10] still remain on thy forehead shall be, as one is, quite erased, thy feet will be so conquered by good-will that not only will they not feel fatigue, but it will be delight to them to be urged upward." Then I did like those who are going with something on their head unknown to them, unless the signs of others make them suspect; wherefore the hand assists to ascertain, and seeks and finds, and performs that office which cannot be accomplished by the sight; and with the fingers of my right hand outspread, I found six only of those letters which he of the keys had incised upon my temples: looking at which my Leader smiled.

CANTO XIII

1. WE were at the top of the stairway, where the mountain, ascent of which frees one from ill, is for the second time cut back. There a cornice binds the hill round about, in like man-

[1] See II Kings, 19. 37.
[2] See Herodotus, i. 214.
[3] See Judith, 14. 18; 15. 2.
[4] Cf. Canto iv. 7-12.
[5] The sixth hour of the day is coming to its end.
[6] See Canto iii. 78.
[7] See Canto ix. 112-114.
[8] The hill of San Miniato, above the city of Florence.
[9] The upper bridge at Florence across the Arno, named after Rubaconte da Mandello, who laid the first stone of it in 1237.
[10] See Aquinas, *Summa Theologica*, Part 11-11, Q 162, A 7.

ner as the first, except that its arc curves more quickly. No figure is there, nor mark which is apparent; thus the bank appears bare and thus appears the path, with but the livid color of the stone.

10. "If to enquire one waits here for people," said the Poet, "I fear that perhaps our choice will have too much delay." Then he set his eyes fixedly on the sun, made of his right side the centre for his movement, and turned the left part of himself. "O sweet light, with confidence in which I enter on the new road, do thou lead us on it," he said, "as there is need for leading here within. Thou warmest the world, thou shinest upon it; if other reason prompt not to the contrary, thy rays ought ever to be guides."

22. As far as here on earth is reckoned for a mile, so far had we now gone on from there, in short time because of ready will. And toward us were heard flying, not however seen, spirits uttering courteous invitations to the table of love. The first voice which passed flying, said loudly: *Vinum non habent,*[1] and went on behind us reiterating it. And before it had become quite inaudible through distance, another passed by, crying: "I am Orestes,"[2] and also did not stay.

34. "O Father," said I, "what voices are these?" and even as I was asking, lo! the third, saying: "Love them from whom ye have had evil." And the good Master: "This circle scourges the sin of envy, and therefore the lashes of the scourge are drawn from love. The curb must be of the contrary sound; I believe, according to my judgment, that thou wilt hear it, before thou arrivest at the pass of pardon. But fix thine eyes intently through the air, and thou wilt see in front of us people sitting, and each is seated against the cliff." Then more than before I opened my eyes; I looked in front of me, and saw shades with cloaks in color not different from the stone. And when we were a little further forward, I heard cry: "Mary, pray for us!" and a cry on Michael, and Peter, and all the Saints.

52. I do not believe there goes on earth to-day a man so hard that he would not be pierced with compassion at that which I then saw. For when I had approached so near to them that their actions came surely to me, tears were drawn from my eyes by heavy grief. They seemed to me covered with coarse haircloth, and one was supporting the other with his shoulder, and all were supported by the bank. Thus the blind, who lack subsistence, wait at pardons[3] to beg for what they need, and one bows his head upon another, so that pity may quickly be moved in others, not only by the sound of their words, but by the sight which implores no less. And as the sun profits not the blind, so to the shades, in that place of which I was just now speaking, the light of Heaven wills not to make largess of itself; for an iron wire pierces the eyelids of all; even as is done to a wild hawk, because it stays not quiet.

73. It seemed to me I was doing outrage in going on, seeing others, not being seen myself, wherefore I turned me to my sage counsellor. Well did he know what the dumb wished to say, and therefore waited not my asking, but said: "Speak, and be brief and to the point."

79. Virgil was coming with me on that side of the cornice from which one may fall, because it is encircled by no rim. On the other side of me were the devout shades, who through the horrible suture were so pressing out their tears that they bathed their cheeks. I turned me to them, and : "O folk," I began, "assured of seeing the Light on high which your desire has alone in its care, may grace speedily dissolve the scum from off your conscience so that the stream of memory may flow down through it clear,[4] tell me, for it will be gracious and dear to me, if there be a soul here among you that is Italian, and perhaps it will be good for him if I learn it." "O my brother, each of us is a citizen of one true city, but thou meanest one who lived in Italy while a pilgrim."[5]

97. It seemed to me I heard this for answer somewhat farther on than where I was standing; wherefore I made myself heard still more that way. Among the others I saw a shade that

---

[1] "They have no wine." See John, 2. 3.
[2] The words of Pylades, before Aegisthus, when contending with Orestes to be put to death in his stead.

[3] On occasion of special indulgences the beggars gather at the door of churches.
[4] See Ephesians, 2. 19.
[5] See Hebrews, 13. 14.

was expectant in look; and, if anyone should wish to ask: How?—it was lifting up its chin in the manner of a blind man. "Spirit," said I, "that art subduing thyself in order to ascend, if thou art that one which answered me, make thyself known to me either by place or by name."

106. "I was of Siena," it answered, "and with these others I cleanse here my guilty life, weeping to Him that He vouchsafe Himself to us. Sapient I was not, although I was called Sapìa,[1] and I was far more glad of others' harm than of my own good fortune. And that thou mayst not believe that I deceive thee, hear whether I was foolish as I tell thee. When the arch of my years was already descending, my fellow-citizens were joined in battle near to Colle[2] with their adversaries, and I prayed to God for that which He willed. They were routed there, and turned into the bitter passes of flight; and I, seeing the pursuit, experienced a joy unmatched by any other; so much that I turned upward my audacious face, crying out to God: 'Henceforth no more I fear thee'; as the blackbird does because of a little fair weather. At the very end of my life I desired peace with God; and even yet my debt would not have been lessened by penitence, had it not been that Pier Pettinagno,[3] who out of charity was sorry for me, held me in memory in his holy prayers. But who art thou that goest asking of our conditions, and carriest thine eyes loosed as I think, and breathing dost speak?"

133. "My eyes," said I, "will yet be taken from me here; but for a short time, for small is the offence committed through their being turned with envy. Far greater is the fear, with which my soul is in suspense, of the torment below, and the load down there already weighs upon me." And she to me: "Who then hath led thee up here among us, if thou thinkest to return below?" And I: "This one who is with me, and who says not a word: and I am alive; and therefore ask of me, spirit elect, if thou wouldst that on earth I should yet move for

thee my mortal feet." "Oh, this is so strange a thing to hear," she replied, "that it is a great sign that God loves thee; therefore assist me sometimes with thy prayer. And I beseech thee, by that which thou most desirest, that, if ever thou tread the earth of Tuscany, thou restore me to good fame among my kindred. Thou wilt see them among that vain people[4] which hopes in Talamone,[5] and will there lose more hope, than in finding the Diana;[6] but the admirals will there lose even more."

CANTO XIV

1. "Who is this that circles our mountain ere death have given him flight, and opens and shuts his eyes at his own will?"[7] "I know not who he is, but I know that he is not alone. Do thou, who art nearer to him, ask him; and sweetly, so that he may speak, accost him." Thus two spirits, leaning one to the other, discoursed of me there on the right hand, then turned their faces up to speak to me; and one of them said: "O soul, that still fixed in thy body art going on toward heaven, for charity console us, and tell us whence thou comest, and who thou art; for thou makest us so greatly marvel at this thy grace, as needs must a thing that never was before." And I: "Through mid-Tuscany there wanders a little stream, that has its source on Falterona,[8] and a hundred miles of course does not suffice it. From thereupon I bring this body. To tell you who I am would be to speak in vain, for my name as yet makes no great sound." "If I rightly penetrate thy meaning with my understanding," then replied to me he who had spoken first, "thou speakest of the Arno."

25. And the other said to him: "Why did he conceal the name of that river, even as a man does of horrible things?" And the shade of whom this was asked, delivered itself thus: "I

---

[1] A lady said to have been of the Bigozzi family, who held a stronghold about four miles from Colle, in the territory of Siena.

[2] This was the battle in 1269, in which the Florentines routed the Sienese Ghibellines. See Canto xi. 121-123.

[3] A poor comb-dealer of Siena.

[4] Cf. *Hell*, xxix. 122.

[5] A little Tuscan port on which the Sienese wasted toil and money in the vain hope that, by strengthening and enlarging it, they could rival the Pisans and Genoese, at sea.

[6] A subterranean stream supposed to flow beneath the city.

[7] These words are spoken by Guido del Duca and answered by Rinier da Calboli; both of them men of note in the Romagna during the thirteenth century. Guido was a Ghibelline, Rinier a Guelf.

[8] One of the highest of the Tuscan Apennines.

know not, but truly it is fit that the name of such a valley perish, for from its source (where the rugged mountain chain, from which Pelorus is cut off, is so teeming that in few places does it pass beyond that mark),[1] far as there where it renders itself to restore that which heaven sucks up from the sea, whence the rivers have what flows in them, virtue is driven away as an enemy by all men, even as a serpent, either through ill-fortune of the place, or through evil habit that incites them. Wherefore the inhabitants of the wretched valley have so changed their nature that it seems as though Circe had them in her feeding. Among foul hogs,[2] more fit for acorns than for other food made for human use, it first directs its poor path. Then, coming down, it finds curs,[3] more snarling than their power warrants, and from them disdainfully it twists its muzzle. It goes on falling, and the more it swells so much the more does the accursed and ill-fated ditch find the dogs becoming wolves.[4] Descending then through many hollow depths, it finds the foxes[5] so full of fraud, that they fear not wit which may entrap them. Nor will I cease to speak because another may hear me: and well it will be for this man if hereafter he mind him of that which a spirit of truth discloses to me.

58. "I see thy grandson,[6] who becomes a hunter of those wolves upon the bank of the fierce stream, and terrifies them all. He sells their flesh, it being yet alive; then he slaughters them like aged cattle; many of life, himself of honor he deprives. Bloody he comes forth from the dismal wood; he leaves it such, that from now for a thousand years it is not rewooded in its primal state."

67. As at the announcement of grievous ills, the face of him who listens is disturbed, from what quarter soever the peril may assail him,

so I saw the other soul, that was staying turned to hear, become disturbed and sad, when it had gathered to itself the words.

73. The speech of the one and the look of the other made me wishful to know their names, and I made request for it, mixed with prayers. Wherefore the spirit which had first spoken to me began again: "Thou wishest that I condescend to do for thee that which thou wilt not do for me; but since God wills that such great grace of His shine through in thee, I will not be chary to thee; therefore know that I am Guido del Duca. My blood was so inflamed with envy that, had I seen a man becoming joyful, thou wouldst have seen me overspread with hue of spite. Of my own sowing such straw I reap. O human race, why dost thou set thy heart there where exclusion of a companion is needful?

88. "This one is Rinier; this is the glory and the honor of the house of Calboli, where no one since has made himself heir of his worth. And between the Po and the mountain, and the sea and the Reno,[7] not his race only has become stripped of the good requisite for truth and for delight; for within these boundaries the land is full of poisonous stocks, so that slowly would they now die out through cultivation. Where is the good Lizio, and Arrigo Mainardi, Pier Traversaro, and Guido di Carpigna?[8] O men of Romagna turned to bastards! When in Bologna will a Fabbro take root again? When in Faenza a Bernardin di Fosco, the noble scion of a little plant? Marvel not, Tuscan, if I weep, when I remember, with Guido da Prata, Ugolin d' Azzo who lived with us, Federico Tignoso and his company, the house of Traversara, and the Anastagi, (both the one race and the other are without heir), the ladies and the cavaliers, the toils and the repose for which love and courtesy inspired us, there where hearts have become so wicked. O Brettinoro, why dost thou not make away with thyself,[9] since thy family has gone, and many people, in order not to become guilty?

---

[1] The chain of the Apennines—from which Pelorus, the northeastern headland of Sicily, seems cut off—nowhere more teems with waters than on Monte Falterona, where the Tiber, as well as the Arno, has its source.

[2] The people of the Casentino, the upper valley of the Arno.

[3] Of Arezzo.

[4] Of Florence.

[5] Of Pisa.

[6] Fulcieri da Calboli, grandson of Rinieri, to whom Guido del Duca is speaking, was made podestà of Florence in 1302.

[7] That is, in all Romagna.

[8] These and others named afterwards were well-born, honorable, and courteous men in Romagna in the thirteenth century.

[9] Brettinoro is a small town near Forlì. It was the birthplace of Guido del Duca, and the family to which he refers was, perhaps, his own.

Bagnacaval does well that it gets no more sons; and Castrocaro does ill, and Conio worse that it still troubles itself to beget such counts.[1] The Pagani will do well after their demon shall be gone from them,[2] yet not so that a pure testimony can ever remain to them. O Ugolin de' Fantolin, thy name is secure, since no longer is one to be expected who can make it dark by his degeneracy.[3] But go thy way, Tuscan, now; for now it pleases me far more to weep than to speak, so much has our discourse wrung my mind."

127. We knew that those dear souls heard us go on; therefore by their silence they made us confident of the road. After we had become alone as we proceeded, a voice, that seemed like lightning when it cleaves the air, came counter to us, saying: "Everyone that findeth me shall slay me,"[4] and fled like thunder which rolls away, if suddenly the cloud is rent. Soon as our hearing had a truce from it, lo! now another with so great a crash that it resembled a thunder-clap which follows fast: "I am Aglauros who became a stone."[5]

140. And then to press close to the Poet, I took a step backward and not forward. The air was now quiet on every side, and he said to me: "That was the hard curb which ought to hold a man within his bound; but ye take the bait, so that the hook of the old adversary draws you to him, and therefore little avails bridle or lure. Heaven calls you, and revolves around you, displaying to you its eternal beauties, and your eye looks only on the ground; wherefore He who discerns all things scourges you."

CANTO XV

1. As much as, between the beginning of the day and the close of the third hour, appears of the sphere which is ever sporting in manner of a child, so much of his course toward the evening appeared to be now remaining for the sun. It was vespers there, and here midnight; and the rays were striking us full in the face, because the mountain had been so circled by us that we were now going straight toward the sunset, when I felt my forehead weighed down by the splendor far more than at first, and the things not known were a wonder to me: wherefore I lifted my hands toward the top of my brows, and made for myself the visor which lessens the excess of what is seen.

16. As when from water, or from a mirror, the ray leaps to the opposite quarter, mounting up in like manner to that in which it descends, and at equal distance departs as much from the fall of the stone, as experiment and art show; so it seemed to me that I was struck by light reflected there in front of me, wherefore my sight was swift to fly. "What is that, sweet Father, from which I cannot screen my sight so much that it may avail me," said I, "and which seems to be moving toward us?" "Marvel not if the family of Heaven still dazzle thee," he replied to me; "it is a messenger that comes to invite one to ascend. Soon will it be that to see these things will not be grievous to thee, but will be to thee a delight as great as nature has fitted thee to feel."

34. When we had reached the blessed Angel, with a glad voice he said: "Enter ye from here on a stairway far less steep than the others."

37. We were mounting, already departed thence, and *"Beati misericordes"*[6] was sung behind us, and: "Rejoice thou that overcomest."

40. My Master and I, we two alone, were going on upward, and I was thinking, as we went, to win profit from his words; and I addressed me to him, enquiring thus: "What did the spirit from Romagna mean, in speaking of 'exclusion' and a 'companion'?" Wherefore he to me: "Of his own greatest fault he knows the harm, and therefore it is not to be wondered at if he rebuke it, in order that there may be less lamenting for it. Because your desires are directed there, where, through companionship, a share is lessened, envy moves the bellows for your sighs. But if the love of the highest sphere turned your desire upward, that fear would not be in your breast; for the more there are who there say 'Ours,' so much the more of

[1] Bagnacavallo, Castrocaro, and Conio are three little towns in Romagna.
[2] The Pagani were lords of Faenza and Imola; the demon was Maghinardo. Cf. *Hell*, xxvii. 49-51.
[3] Both the sons of Ugolino de' Fantolin had died without offspring. The Fantolini were of Faenza.
[4] The words of Cain. Genesis, 4. 14.
[5] The daughter of Cecrops, changed to stone because of envy of her sister.
[6] "Blessed are the merciful."

good doth each possess, and the more of charity burns in that cloister."[1]

58. "I am more empty of satisfaction," said I, "than if I had at first been silent, and more of doubt I gather in my mind. How can it be that a good distributed can make more possessors richer with itself, than if it be possessed by few?" And he to me: "Because thou fastenest thy mind only on earthly things, thou gatherest darkness from the very light. That infinite and ineffable Good which is on high, runs to love even as a sunbeam comes to a lucid body. So much it gives itself as it finds of ardor; so that how far soever charity extends, over it does the Eternal Valor spread. And the more the people who set their hearts on high the more there are for loving well, and the more love there is, and like a mirror one reflects to the other. And if my discourse appease not thy hunger, thou shalt see Beatrice, and she will fully take from thee this and every other longing. Strive only that soon may be extinct, as are the two already, the five wounds which are closed up by being painful."

82. As I was wishing to say: "Thou dost satisfy me," I saw that I had arrived on the next round, so that my eager eyes made me silent. There it seemed to me I was of a sudden rapt in an ecstatic vision, and saw many persons in a temple, and a lady at the entrance, with the sweet mien of a mother, saying: "My son, why hast thou thus dealt with us? Behold, thy father and I have sought thee, sorrowing." And as here she was silent, that which first appeared, disappeared.

94. Then appeared to me another, with those waters down along her cheeks which grief distils when it is born of great despite toward others, and she was saying: "If thou art lord of the city about whose name was such great strife among the gods, and whence every science sparkles forth, avenge thyself on those audacious arms, which have embraced our daughter, O Pisistratus." And the lord appeared to me, benign and mild, to answer her, with temperate look: "What shall we do to him who desires ill for us, if he who loves us is by us condemned?"

106. Then I saw people inflamed with fire of wrath, killing a youth with stones, loudly crying to each other only: "Slay, slay." And I saw him bowed toward the ground by death, which now was weighing on him, but in such great strife he ever made of his eyes gates for heaven, praying to the high Lord, with that aspect which unlocks pity, that He would pardon his persecutors.[2]

115. When my mind returned outwardly to the things which outside of it are true, I recognized my not false errors. My Leader, who could see me act like a man who looses himself from slumber, said : "What ails thee, that thou canst not support thyself? but art come more than half a league veiling thine eyes, and with thy legs tangled like one whom wine or slumber bends." "O my sweet Father, if thou harkenest to me I will tell thee," said I, "what appeared to me when my legs were thus taken from me." And he: "If thou hadst a hundred masks upon thy face, thy thoughts, howsoever small, would not be hidden from me. That which thou hast seen was in order that thou excuse not thyself from opening thy heart to the waters of peace which are poured forth from the eternal fountain. I did not ask: 'What ails thee?' for the reason that he does who looks only with the eye which has no seeing when the body lies inanimate; but I asked, in order to give vigor to thy foot; thus it behoves to spur the sluggards, slow to use their wakefulness when it returns."

139. We were going on through the vesper time, forward intent so far as the eyes could reach against the late and shining rays; and, lo! little by little, a smoke came toward us, dark as night; nor was there place to shelter ourselves from it. This took from us our eyes and the pure air.

CANTO XVI

1. GLOOM of hell, or of night deprived of every planet, under a poor sky, darkened by clouds as much as it can be, never made so thick a veil to my sight, or of so rough a tissue to my feeling, as that smoke which covered us there; for it suffered not my eye to stay open: wherefore my sage and trusty Escort drew to my side and

---

[1] See Aquinas, *Summa Theologica*, Part I-II, Q 26, A 3. Cf. Milton, *Paradise Lost*, v. 73.

[2] See Acts, 7. 55-60.

offered me his shoulder. Even as a blind man goes behind his guide, in order not to stray, and not to butt against anything that may hurt or perhaps kill him, I went along, through the bitter and foul air, listening to my Leader, who was saying only: "Take care that thou be not parted from me."

16. I heard voices, and each appeared to be praying for peace and for mercy to the Lamb of God that taketh sins away. Only *"Agnus Dei"*[1] were their exordiums: one word there was in all, and one measure; so that there seemed entire concord among them. "Are these spirits, Master, that I hear?" said I. And he to me: "Thou apprehendest truly; and they go loosening the knot of anger."

25. "Now who art thou that cleavest our smoke, and speakest of us even as if thou didst still divide the time by calends?" Thus was it spoken by a single voice: whereon my Master said: "Reply, and ask if by this way one goes up." And I, "O creature, that art cleansing thyself, in order to return beautiful unto Him who made thee, a marvel shalt thou hear if thou accompaniest me." "I will follow thee, for so far as is permitted me," it replied, "and if the smoke allows not seeing, in its stead hearing shall keep us joined." Then I began: "With that swathing band which death unbinds I go upward, and I came hither through the infernal anguish; and since God has so enclosed me in His grace that He wills that I should see His court by a mode wholly out of modern usage, conceal not from me who thou wast before thy death, but tell it to me, and tell me if I am going rightly to the pass; and let thy words be our escorts." "I was a Lombard, and was called Marco; I had knowledge of the world, and I loved that virtue, toward which everyone has now unbent his bow: for mounting upward thou art going rightly." Thus he replied, and added: "I pray thee that thou pray for me when thou shalt be above."

52. And I to him: "I pledge thee my faith to do that which thou askest of me; but I am bursting inwardly with a doubt, if I free not myself of it; at first it was single; and now it is made double by thy opinion which makes certain to me, here and elsewhere, that with

which I couple it. The world is indeed as utterly deserted by every virtue as thou declarest to me, and is big and covered with iniquity; but I pray that thou point out to me the cause, so that I may see it, and that I may show it to others; for one sets it in the heavens, and one here below."

64. A deep sigh which grief wrung into "Ay me!" he first sent forth, and then he began: "Brother, the world is blind, and thou truly comest from it. Ye who are living refer every cause upward to the heavens only, as though they moved all things with them of necessity. If this were so, free will would be destroyed in you, and there would be no justice in having joy for good, and grief for evil. The heavens initiate your movements, I do not say all of them; but, supposing that I said it, light for good and for evil is given to you, and free will, which, though it endure fatigue in the first battles with the heavens, afterwards, if it be well nurtured, overcomes everything. To a greater force, and to a better nature, ye, free, are subject, and that creates the mind in you, which the heavens have not in their charge. Therefore if the present world go astray, the cause is in you, in you it is to be sought; and of this I will now be a true informant for thee.

85. "Forth from the hand of Him who delights in it ere it exists, like to a little maid who, weeping and smiling, wantons childishly, issues the simple little soul, which knows nothing, save that, proceeding from a glad Maker, it turns willingly to that which allures it. At first it tastes the savor of trivial good; by this it is deceived and runs after it, if guide or bridle bend not its love. Hence it was needful to impose law as a bridle; needful to have a king who should discern at least the tower of the true city. The laws exist, but who set hand to them? Not one: because the shepherd who is in advance can chew the cud, but has not his hoofs divided:[2] wherefore the people, who see their guide aim only at that good for which they are greedy, feed upon that, and seek no further. Well canst thou see that the evil guidance is the cause which has made the world guilty, and not that nature is corrupt in you.

[1] "Lamb of God."

[2] See Leviticus, 11. 3-8. Also Cf. Aquinas, *Summa Theologica*, Part I-II, Q 102, A 6.

Rome, which made the world good, was wont to have two Suns, which made visible both one road and the other, that of the world and that of God. One has extinguished the other; and the sword is joined to the crozier; and the two together must perforce go ill, because, being joined, one fears not the other. If thou believest me not, consider the fruit, for every plant is known by its seed.

115. "In the land which the Adige and the Po water, virtue and courtesy were wont to be found before Frederick had his quarrel;[1] now it may be securely traversed by anyone who, out of shame, would avoid speaking with the good, or drawing near them. Three old men are indeed still there, in whom the antique age rebukes the new, and it seems late to them ere God remove them to a better life; Corrado da Palazzo,[2] and the good Gherardo,[3] and Guido da Castel, who is better named, in fashion of the French, the simple Lombard.[4]

127. "Say thou henceforth, that the Church of Rome, through confounding in itself two modes of rule, falls in the mire, and defiles itself and its burden."

130. "O my Marco," said I, "thou reasonest well; and now I discern why the sons of Levi were excluded from the heritage;[5] but what Gherardo is that, who, thou sayest, remains for sample of the extinct folk, in reproach of this barbarous age?" "Either thy speech deceives me, or it is making trial of me," he replied to me, "in that, speaking Tuscan to me, it seems that thou knowest naught of the good Gherardo. By other added name I do not know him, unless I should take it from his daughter Gaia. May God be with you! for farther I come not with you. Behold the brightness which rays already whitening through the smoke; and I must needs depart—the Angel is there—before

---

[1] Before Frederick II had his quarrel with Gregory IX; that is, before Emperor and Pope had failed in their respective duties to each other.

[2] Of Brescia, and in his day of high repute for honorable character.

[3] Gherardo da Camino, "noble in his life, and whose memory will always be noble," says Dante in the *Convito,* iv. 14, 123. Gherardo was a noble soldier of Treviso and its ruler for many years.

[4] It is related that Guido da Castello, who lived at Reggio, generously supplied the French men-at-arms, returning poor from Italy, with all they needed: horses, arms, or money.

[5] See Deuteronomy, 10. 8-9.

I became apparent to him." So he turned, and would not hear me more.

CANTO XVII

1. RECALL to mind, Reader, if ever on the alps a cloud closed round thee, through which thou couldst not see otherwise than the mole through its skin, how, when the humid and dense vapors begin to dissipate, the orb of the sun enters feebly through them; and thy imagination will be swift in coming to see, how at first I saw again the sun, which was already at its setting. Thus matching mine to the trusty steps of my Master, I issued forth from such a cloud to the rays already dead on the low shores.

13. O faculty of imagination, that dost sometimes so steal us from outward things that a man heeds it not, although around him a thousand trumpets are sounding, who moves thee if the sense afford thee naught? A light, which is formed in the heavens, moves thee by itself, or by a will which guides it downward.

19. In my imagination appeared the vestige of the pitilessness of her[6] who changed her form into the bird that most delights in singing. And here was my mind so shut up within itself that from without came nothing which then might be received by it. Then there rained down within my raised fantasy, one crucified,[7] despiteful and fierce in his look, and thus was he dying. Around him were the great Ahasuerus, Esther, his wife, and the just Mordecai, who was so blameless in word and deed. And as this image burst of itself, in manner of a bubble for which the water fails, under which it was formed, there rose in my vision a maiden,[8] weeping bitterly, and she was saying: "O queen, wherefore through anger hast thou willed to be naught? Thou hast slain thyself in order not to lose Lavinia; now thou hast lost me: I am she that grieves, mother, at thy destruction, before that of another."

40. As sleep is broken, when of a sudden the new light strikes the closed eyes, and, broken, quivers before it wholly dies, so my imagining

---

[6] Procne or Philomela, according to one or the other version of the myth, was changed into the nightingale after her anger had led her to take vengeance on Tereus.

[7] See Esther, 8.

[8] See *Aeneid,* xii. 595-607.

fell down, soon as a light, greater by far than that to which we are accustomed, struck my face. I was turning to see where I was, when a voice said: "Here is the ascent": and this withdrew me from every other object of attention, and made my will so eager to behold who it was that was speaking, that it never rests till it is face to face. But, as before the sun which weighs down our sight, and by excess veils its own shape, so here my power failed. "This is a divine spirit who directs us, without our asking, on the way to go up, and with his own light conceals himself. He so deals with us as a man does with himself; for he who waits for asking and sees the need, malignly sets himself already to denial. Now let us accord our feet to such an invitation; let us press forward to ascend before it grow dark, for after, it would not be possible until the day returns."

64. Thus said my Leader; and I and he turned our steps to a stairway; and, soon as I was on the first step, I felt near me a motion as if of a wing, and a fanning on my face, and I heard say: *"Beati pacifici,*[1] who are without evil anger."

70. Already were the last sunbeams, on which the night follows, so lifted above us, that the stars were appearing on many sides. "O my strength, why dost thou so melt away?" I said to myself, for I felt the power of my legs put in truce. We were now where the stair no farther ascended, and we were stayed fast, even as a ship that arrives at the shore: and I listened for a while, if I might hear anything in the new circle. Then I turned to my Master, and said: "My sweet Father, say what offence is purged here in the circle where we are: if our feet be stopped, let not thy discourse be stayed." And he to me: "The love of good, defective in its duty, is here restored; here is plied again the ill-slackened oar. But that thou mayst still more clearly understand, turn thy mind to me, and thou shalt gather some good fruit from our delay.

91. "Neither Creator nor creature," he began, "my son, was ever without love, either natural, or of the mind, and this thou knowest. The natural is always without error; but the other may err either through an evil object, or through little, or through too much vigor.

[1] "Blessed are the peacemakers."

While love is directed on the primal goods, and with due measure on the secondary, it cannot be the cause of ill-delight. But when it is bent to evil, or runs to good with more zeal, or with less, than it ought, against the Creator his own creature is working. Hence thou canst comprehend that love is of necessity the seed in you of every virtue, and of every action that deserves punishment.

106. "Now since love can never turn its sight from the welfare of its subject, all things are secure from hatred of themselves; and since no being can be conceived of as divided from the First and standing by itself, from hating Him every affection is cut off. It follows, if, thus distinguishing, I rightly judge, that the evil which is loved is that of one's neighbor; and in three modes this love has its birth in your clay. There is he who hopes to excel through the abasement of his neighbor, and only on this account longs that from his greatness he may be brought low. There is he who fears loss of power, favor, honor, and fame, because another surmounts; whereat he is so saddened that he loves the contrary. And there is he who seems so resentful for injury that he becomes greedy of vengeance, and such a one must needs coin harm for others. This triform love is wept for down below.

125. "Now I would that thou hear of the other—that which runs to the good in faulty measure. Every one confusedly conceives of a good in which the mind may be at rest, and desires it; wherefore everyone strives to attain to it. If the love be slack that draws you to look on this, or to acquire it, this cornice, after just repentance, torments you for it. Another good there is, which does not make man happy; it is not happiness, it is not the good essence, the fruit and root of every good. The love which abandons itself too much to this is wept for above us in three circles; but how it is reckoned tripartite, of this I am silent, in order that thou seek it out for thyself."

CANTO XVIII

1. THE lofty Teacher had put an end to his discourse, and was looking attentive on my face to see if I appeared content; and I, whom a fresh thirst was already goading, was silent

outwardly and was saying within: "Perhaps the too much questioning I make annoys him." But that true Father, who perceived the timid wish which did not disclose itself, by speaking gave me boldness to speak. Whereupon I: "Master, my sight is so vivified in thy light, that I discern clearly all that thy discourse imports or describes: therefore I pray thee, sweet Father dear, that thou expound to me the love to which thou referrest every good deed and its contrary." "Direct," he said, "toward me the keen eyes of the understanding, and the error of the blind who make themselves leaders will be manifest to thee.

19. "The mind, which is created apt to love, is mobile unto everything that pleases, so soon as by pleasure it is roused to action. Your faculty of apprehension draws an image from a real existence, and displays it within you, so that it makes the mind turn to it; and if, thus turned, the mind incline toward it, that inclination is love; it is nature which is bound anew in you by pleasure.[1] Then, as the fire moves upward by virtue of its form, which is born to ascend thither where it most abides in its own matter,[2] so the captive mind enters into longing, which is a spiritual motion, and never rests until the thing beloved makes it rejoice. Now it may be apparent to thee how far the truth is hidden from the people who aver that every love is in itself a laudable thing, because, perchance, its subject-matter always appears to be good;[3] but not every seal is good although the wax be good."

40. "Thy words, and my wit following them," replied I to him, "have revealed love to me; but that has made me more big with doubt. For if love be offered to us from without, and if the soul go not with other foot, it is not her own merit if she go strait or crooked." And he to me: "So much as reason sees here can I tell thee; beyond that await still for Beatrice; for it is a work of faith. Every substantial form that is distinct from matter, or that is united with it,[4] has a specific virtue collected in itself which is not perceived unless in

operation, nor does it show itself save by its effect, as by green leaves the life in a plant. Therefore, man does not know whence the intelligence of the first cognitions comes, nor whence the affection for the first objects of desire, which exist in you even as zeal in the bee for making honey; and this first will admits not desert of praise or blame.[5] Now in order that to this every other may be gathered, the virtue that counsels is innate in you, and ought to hold the threshold of assent. This is the principle wherefrom the reckoning of desert in you is derived, according as it gathers in and winnows good and evil loves. Those who in reasoning went to the foundation, took note of this innate liberty, wherefore they bequeathed morals to the world. If we assume, then, that every love which is kindled within you arises of necessity, in you exists the power to restrain it. This noble faculty Beatrice understands as free will, and therefore see that thou have it in mind, if she take to speaking of it with thee."[6]

76. The moon, almost at midnight slow, shaped like a bucket that is all ablaze, was making the stars appear fewer to us, and was running counter to the heavens along those paths which the sun inflames, when a man at Rome sees it at its setting between Sardinia and Corsica; and that noble shade, for whom Pietola[7] is more famed than the Mantuan city, had laid down the burden of my loading: so that I, who had harvested his open and plain discourse upon my questions, remained like a man, who, drowsy, wanders. But this drowsiness was taken from me suddenly by folk, who, behind our backs, had now come round to us. And such a fury and a throng as Ismenus and Asopus saw of old along their banks at night if but the Thebans were in need of Bacchus,[8] such curves its way along that circle, according to what I saw, of those coming on whom good will and right love are riding. They were soon upon us; because all that great crowd was moving at a run; and two in front, weeping, were crying out: "Mary ran with

---

[1] For the doctrine in this canto, see Aquinas, *Summa Theologica*, Part I, Q 76, A 1.
[2] *Ibid.*, Part III, Q 13, A 1.
[3] *Ibid.*, Part III, Suppl., Q 98, A 1; Cf. Part I, Q 19, A 9; Q 82, A 2; Part I-II, Q 27, A 1.
[4] *Ibid.*, Part I, Q 3, A 5; Q 76, A 4.

[5] Cf. Canto xvii. 91-97.
[6] See *Paradise*, v. 19-24.
[7] The modern name of Andes, the birthplace of Virgil.
[8] The rivers Ismenus and Asopus ran not far from Thebes, the birthplace of Bacchus.

haste unto the mountain";[1] and: "Cæsar, to subdue Ilerda, thrust at Marseilles, and then ran on to Spain." "Swift, swift, that time be not lost by little love," the others were crying as they followed, "so that zeal in well-doing may make grace green again."

106. "O people, in whom keen fervor now perhaps redeems negligence and delay, shown by you through lukewarmness in well-doing, this one who is alive (and surely I do not lie to you) wishes to go up, if but the sun may shine again for us; therefore tell us where is the opening near at hand." These words were of my Leader; and one of those spirits said: "Come thou behind us, and thou wilt find the gap. We are so full of will to move on that we cannot stay; therefore pardon, if thou hold our duty for churlishness. I was Abbot of San Zeno at Verona, under the empire of the good Barbarossa, of whom Milan, still grieving, talks. And one there is who has one foot already in the grave,[2] who soon shall lament on account of that monastery, and will be sorry for having had power over it; because in place of its true shepherd he has put his son, ill in his whole body and worse in mind, and who was evil-born." I know not if he said more, or if he were silent, so far beyond us had he already run on; but this I heard, and to retain it pleased me.

130. And he who was at every need my succor, said: "Turn thee this way; see two of them coming, giving a bite to sloth." In rear of all they were saying: "The people for whom the sea was opened were dead before the Jordan beheld his inheritors";[3] and: "They who endured not the toil even to the end with the son of Anchises, offered themselves to a life without glory."[4]

139. Then when those shades were so far parted from us that they could no more be seen, a new thought set itself within me, from which many others and diverse were born; and I so rambled from one to another that, with the wandering, I closed my eyes, and transmuted my meditation into dream.

[1] See Luke, 1. 39.
[2] Alberto della Scala, lord of Verona; he died in 1301. See Leviticus, 21. 16-23.
[3] See Numbers, 14. 23-33; Joshua, 5. 6.
[4] See *Aeneid*, v. 700-778.

CANTO XIX

1. AT the hour when the heat of day, vanquished by the Earth or sometimes by Saturn, can no longer warm the coldness of the moon, —when the geomancers see in the east, before the dawn, their Greater Fortune[5] rising along a path which short while stays dark for it,— there came to me in dream[6] a woman stammering, with eyes asquint, and crooked on her feet, with hands lopped off, and pallid in her color. I gazed at her; and as the sun comforts the cold limbs which the night benumbs, so did my look make her tongue nimble, and then in short while set her wholly straight, and so colored her wan face as love requires. Then, when thus she had her speech unloosed, she began to sing, so that with difficulty should I have turned my attention from her. "I am," she sang, "I am the sweet Siren, who bewitch the mariners in mid sea, so full am I of pleasantness to hear. I turned Ulysses from his wandering way by my song; and whoso customs himself with me seldom departs, so wholly do I satisfy him."

25. Not yet was her mouth closed, when at my side a Lady appeared, holy and ready to put her to confusion. "O Virgil, O Virgil, who is this?" she sternly said; and he came with his eyes fixed only on that modest one. She took hold of the other, and in front she opened her, rending her garments, and showed me her belly; this waked me with the stench that issued from it. I turned my eyes to the good Master: "At least three calls have I given thee," he said; "arise and come on; let us find the gate through which thou mayst enter."

37. I rose up, and all the circles of the sacred mountain were already full of the high day, and we went on with the new sun at our backs. Following him, I was bearing my forehead like one who has it laden with thought, and who makes of himself a half arch of a bridge, when I heard: "Come ye! here is the passage," spoken in a mode soft and benign, such as is not

[5] Geomancy is divination by an arrangement of points on the ground, or of pebbles, in certain figures which have special names. One of them, in this form, : : · · , was called the Greater Fortune. The stars forming the figure of the Greater Fortune would be in the east about two hours before sunrise.
[6] Cf. *Hell*, xxvi. 7.

heard in this mortal region. With open wings, which seemed as of a swan, he who had thus spoken to us turned us upward, between two walls of the hard rock. Then he moved his pinions, and fanned us, affirming *qui lugent*[1] to be blessed, for they shall have their souls mistresses of consolation.

52. "What ails thee that thou gazest only on the ground?" my Guide began to say to me, both of us having mounted up a little from the Angel. And I: "With such mistrust a recent vision makes me go, which bends me to itself so that I cannot withdraw me from the thought of it." "Hast thou seen," said he, "that ancient sorceress, who above us henceforth is alone lamented? Hast thou seen how from her man is unbound? Let it suffice thee, and strike thy heels on the ground; turn upward thine eyes to the lure which the eternal King whirls with the great circles."[2]

64. Even as the falcon that first looks at his feet, then turns at the cry, and stretches forward, through desire of the food that draws him thither; such I became, and such, so far as the rock is cleft to afford a way to him who goes up, did I go on to where the circling is begun. When I had come forth on the fifth round, I saw people upon it who were weeping, lying on the earth all turned downwards. "*Adhaesit pavimento anima mea*,"[3] I heard them saying with such deep sighs that the words were hardly understood. "O elect of God, whose sufferings both justice and hope make less hard, direct us toward the high ascents." "If ye come secure from the lying down, and wish to find the way most speedily, let your right hands be always outermost." Thus the Poet prayed, and thus was answer made to us from a little in advance of us; wherefore I, in his speaking, marked the one who was hidden; and then I turned my eyes to my Lord: whereon he granted me, with cheerful sign, that which my look of desire was asking.

88. Then, when I could do with myself according to my pleasure, I drew me above that creature, whose words had first made me note him, saying: "Spirit, in whom weeping ma-

tures that without which one can not turn to God, suspend a little for me thy greater care. Tell me who thou wast; and why ye have your backs turned upward; and if thou wouldst have me obtain aught for thee there whence I alive set forth."

97. And he to me: "Why heaven turns to itself our backs thou shalt know; but first, *scias quod ego fui successor Petri*.[4] Between Sestri and Chiaveri[5] descends a beautiful stream,[6] and of its name the title of my race makes its boast. One month and little more I proved how the great mantle weighs on him who guards it from the mire, so that all the other burdens seem a feather. My conversion, alas! was tardy; but when I became the Roman Shepherd, then I discovered how false is life. I saw that there the heart was not at rest; nor was it possible to rise higher in that life; wherefore the love of this was kindled in me. Up to that time I had been a wretched soul and parted from God, wholly avaricious; now, as thou seest, I am punished for it here. That which avarice does is displayed here in the purgation of these converted souls, and the Mountain has no more bitter penalty. Even as our eye, fixed upon earthly things, was not lifted on high, so justice here has sunk it to earth. As avarice quenched our love for every good, whereby our working was lost, so justice here holds us close, bound and captive in feet and hands; and, so long as it shall be the pleasure of the just Lord, so long shall we stay immovable and outstretched."

127. I had knelt down and was about to speak; but as I began, and he became aware, only by listening, of my reverence: "What cause," said he, "has bent thee thus downward?" And I to him: "Because of your dignity my conscience stung me for standing." "Straighten thy legs, lift thee up, brother," he replied; "err not, I am fellow servant of One Power with thee and with the rest.[7] If ever thou hast understood that holy gospel sound which says *neque nubent*,[8] thou mayst well

---

[1] They that mourn.

[2] Cf. Canto xiv. 148-150.

[3] "My soul cleaveth unto the dust." Psalms, 119. 25.

[4] "Know that I was a successor of Peter." The speaker is Adrian V (Ottobono de' Fieschi), who died in 1276, having been Pope for thirty-eight days.

[5] Little towns on the Genoese coast.

[6] The Lavagna; the Fieschi were Counts of Lavagna.

[7] See Revelation, 19. 10.

[8] "They neither marry." Matthew, 22. 30.

see why I speak thus. Now go thy way; I wish not that thou tarry longer; for thy stay hinders my weeping, with which I mature that which thou hast said. A niece I have on earth who is named Alagia,[1] good in herself, if only our house make her not wicked by example; and she alone remains to me yonder."

CANTO XX

1. AGAINST a better will the will fights ill: wherefore against my own pleasure, in order to please him, I drew from the water the sponge not full.

4. I moved on; and my Leader moved on through the spaces vacant only alongside of the rock, as upon a wall one goes close to the battlements; for, on the other side, the folk, who through their eyes are pouring out drop by drop the evil that possesses all the world, approach too near the edge.

10. Accursed be thou, old she-wolf, that more than all the other beasts hast prey, because of thy hungry hollow without end! O Heaven! by whose revolution it seems that some believe conditions here below are transmuted, when will he come through whom she shall depart?[2]

16. We were going on with slow and scanty steps, and I attentive to the shades whom I heard piteously lamenting and bewailing; and by chance I heard: "Sweet Mary," cried out in front of us in the lament, just as a woman does who is in travail; and in continuance: "So poor wast thou as may be seen by that inn where thou didst lay down thy holy burden." Following this I heard: "O good Fabricius,[3] thou didst wish rather for virtue with poverty, than to possess great riches with vice." These words were so pleasing to me that I drew myself farther on, to have acquaintance with that spirit from whom they seemed to come. It was speaking now of the largess that Nicholas[4]

made to the damsels in order to lead their youth to honor. "O soul that speakest so much good," said I, "tell me who thou wast, and why thou alone dost renew these worthy praises? Thy words will not be without meed, if I return to complete the short journey of that life which is flying to its end."

40. And he: "I will tell thee, not for comfort that I may expect from yonder, but because so great grace shines in thee ere thou art dead. I was the root of the evil plant which overshadows all the Christian land,[5] so that good fruit is seldom plucked from it. But if Douai, Lille, Ghent, and Bruges had power, there would soon be vengeance on it;[6] and I implore it from him who judges all things. Yonder I was called Hugh Capet: of me are born the Philips and the Louises, by whom of late France has been ruled. I was the son of a butcher of Paris. When the ancient kings had all died out, save one, betaken to gray vestments, I found the bridle of the government of the realm fast in my hands, and so much power of new acquest, and such fullness of friends, that to the widowed crown the head of my son was promoted, from whom the consecrated bones of these began.

61. "So long as the great dowry of Provence[7] took not shame away from my race, it was little worth, but still it did not ill. Then it began its rapine with force and with falsehood; and, after, for amends, it took Ponthieu and Normandy and Gascony; Charles came to Italy, and, for amends, made a victim of Conradin,[8] and then pushed Thomas[9] back to heaven, for amends. A time I see, not long after this day, which draws another Charles[10]

[1] Alagia was the wife of the Marquis Moroello Malaspina (Canto viii. 118-132).
[2] Cf. *Hell*, i. 49-54, 101-111.
[3] Caius Fabricius, the famous poor and incorruptible Roman consul, who rejected the bribes of the Samnites, 282 B. C.
[4] St. Nicholas, Bishop of Myra, knowing that, because of their poverty, three maidens were exposed to the risk of leading lives of dishonor, threw secretly, at night, into the window of their house, money enough to provide each with a dowry.

[5] The spirit which is speaking is that of Hugh Capet, whose descendants in 1300 were ruling France, Spain, and Naples.
[6] Philip the Fair gained possession of Flanders by force and fraud, in 1299; but in 1302 the French were driven out of the country, after the signal defeat at Courtrai.
[7] See *Paradise*, vi. 133-135.
[8] The grandson of Frederick II, who, striving to wrest Naples and Sicily, his hereditary possessions, from the hands of Charles of Anjou, was defeated and taken prisoner by him in 1267, and put to death by him in 1268.
[9] Charles was believed to have had St. Thomas Aquinas poisoned, on his journey from Naples to the Council of Lyons, in 1274.
[10] Charles of Valois, brother of Philip the Fair, sent by Boniface VIII, in 1301, to Florence as peace-maker.

forth from France to make both himself and his the better known. Unarmed he goes out thence alone, but with the lance with which Judas jousted; and that he thrusts so that he makes the paunch of Florence burst. Thereby he will gain not land, but sin and shame so much the heavier for himself, as he the lighter reckons such harm. The other,[1] who once went forth a prisoner from his ship, I see selling his daughter, and bargaining over her, as do the corsairs with other female slaves. O Avarice, what more canst thou do with us, since thou hast so drawn my race unto thyself that it cares not for its own flesh? In order that the ill to come and that already done may seem the less, I see the Fleur-de-lis entering Alagna, and in his Vicar Christ made captive.[2] I see him mocked a second time; I see the vinegar and the gall renewed, and, between living thieves,[3] Him put to death. I see the new Pilate[4] so cruel that this does not sate him, but, without decretal, he bears his covetous sails into the Temple.[5] O my Lord, when shall I be glad in seeing the vengeance which, hidden in Thy secret, makes Thine anger sweet?

97. "That which I was saying of that only bride of the Holy Spirit, and which made thee turn toward me for some gloss, is the response to all our prayers so long as the day lasts, but when the night comes, we take up instead thereof a contrary sound. Then we rehearse Pygmalion,[6] whom his gluttonous longing for gold made a traitor and a thief and a parricide; and the misery of the avaricious Midas, which followed on his greedy demand, at which one needs must always laugh. Then of the foolish Achan each bethinks himself, how he stole the spoils, so that the anger of Joshua seems still

to sting him here.[7] Then we accuse Sapphira with her husband;[8] we praise the kicks that Heliodorus received,[9] and in infamy Polymnestor who slew Polydorus[10] circles the whole mountain. Finally our cry here is: 'Crassus, tell us, for thou knowest, what is the taste of gold?'[11] Sometimes one speaks loud, and another low, according to the affection which spurs us to speak now at a greater, and now at a less pace. Therefore in the good which by day is discoursed of here, I was not alone just now, but here near by no other person was raising his voice."

124. We had already departed from him, and were striving to master the road so far as was permitted to our power, when I felt the mountain tremble, like a thing that is falling; whereupon a chill seized me, such as is wont to seize him who is going to death. Surely Delos was not shaken so violently, before Latona made her nest therein, to give birth to the two eyes of heaven.[12] Then from all sides such a cry began that the Master drew towards me, saying: "Distrust not, while I guide thee." *Gloria in excelsis Deo,*[13] all were saying, by what I comprehended from near at hand where the cry could be understood. We stood, motionless and in suspense, like the shepherds who first heard that song, until the trembling ceased, and the song was ended. Then we resumed our holy journey, looking at the shades that were lying on the ground, returned already to their wonted plaint. No ignorance ever with so great a war made me desirous of knowing[14]—if my memory err not in this— as that which I seemed then to have in my

---

[7] See Joshua, 7.

[8] Acts, 5. 1-11.

[9] See II Maccabees, 3. 25.

[10] Priam had entrusted Polydorus, his youngest son, to Polymnestor, King of Thrace, who, when the fortunes of Troy declined, slew Polydorus, that he might take possession of the treasure sent with him. Cf. *Hell*, xxx. 18.

[11] Marcus Licinius Crassus, triumvir (60 B.C.), the richest and most avaricious of men. Having been defeated by the Parthians, he was slain, and their king is said to have poured molten gold down his throat, with the words: "Thou hast thirsted for gold, now drink it."

[12] Delos was a floating island until Jupiter fixed it that it might serve for the birthplace of Apollo and Diana.

[13] "Glory to God in the highest."

[14] Cf. Wisdom of Solomon, 14. 22.

---

[1] Charles II, son of Charles of Anjou. In 1284, he was captured, off Naples, by Ruggieri di Loria, the Admiral of Peter III of Aragon. According to common report, he sold his young daughter in marriage to the old Azzo, Marquis of Este.

[2] This refers to the seizure of Boniface VIII at Anagni, in 1303, by Guillaume de Nogaret and Sciarra Colonna, the emissaries of Philip the Fair.

[3] Boniface died about a month after being made captive. The "living thieves" were Nogaret and Sciarra Colonna.

[4] Philip the Fair.

[5] The suppression of the Order of the Temple in 1312.

[6] See *Aeneid*, i. 353-54.

thought: nor, for our haste, did I dare to ask, nor of myself could I discern anything there: so I went on timid and thoughtful.

CANTO XXI

1. THE natural thirst,[1] which is never satisfied save with the water[2] whereof the poor woman of Samaria besought the grace, was tormenting me, and haste was goading me along the encumbered way behind my Leader, and I was grieving at the just vengeance: and lo! as Luke writes for us that Christ, now risen forth from the sepulchral cave, appeared to the two who were on the way, a shade appeared to us; and it was coming behind us who were looking at the crowd that lay at our feet: nor were we aware of it, so it spoke first, saying, "My brothers, may God give you peace!" We turned suddenly, and Virgil gave back to it the salutation which corresponds thereto; then he began: "In the assembly of the blest, may the righteous court, which relegates me into eternal exile, place thee in peace." "How," said it, —and meanwhile we went on steadily,—"if ye are shades that God deigns not on high, who has guided you so far along his stairs?" And my Teacher: "If thou regard the marks which this one bears, and which the Angel traces, thou wilt clearly see that he is to reign with the good. But, because she who spins day and night[3] had not for him yet drawn the distaff off, which Clotho loads for each one and compacts, his soul, which is thy sister and mine, coming upwards, could not come alone, because it sees not after our fashion. Wherefore I was drawn from out the ample throat of Hell to show him, and I shall show him so far on as my teaching can lead him.

34. "But tell us, if thou knowest, why just now the mountain gave such shocks, and why all seemed to cry with one voice, even down to its moist feet." Thus asking he shot for me through the needle's eye of my desire, so that only with the hope my thirst became less craving.

40. The shade began: "The sacred rule of the mountain can feel nothing which is without due order, or which is beyond its wont. This place is free from every alteration; that which from itself heaven receives into itself, and naught else, can be the cause of this: because neither rain, nor hail, nor snow, nor dew, nor frost, falls higher up than the little stairway of the three short steps; clouds, thick or thin, appear not; nor lightning, nor the daughter of Thaumas[4] who yonder often changes her quarter; dry vapor does not rise farther up than to the highest of the three steps of which I spoke, whereon the vicar of Peter has his feet. It trembles perhaps lower down, little or much; but up here it never trembled because of wind that is hidden, I know not how, in the earth.[5] It trembles here when some soul feels itself pure, so that it rises, or moves to ascend; and such a cry seconds it. Of the purity the will alone gives proof, which surprises the soul wholly free to change its company, and rejoices it with willing. It wills from the first indeed, but the desire,—which, contrary to the will, Divine Justice sets to the torment, as it had been to the sin,— allows it not.[6] And I who have lain in his woe five hundred years and more, only just now felt a free volition for a better seat. Because of this didst thou feel the earthquake, and hear the pious spirits upon the Mountain render praise to that Lord, who, may He speed them upward soon!"

73. Thus he said to us, and since one enjoys drinking in proportion as the thirst is great, I could not say how much he did me good.

76. And the sage Leader: "Now I see the net which snares you here, and how it is unmeshed; and why it trembles here; and for what ye rejoice together. Now may it please thee that I may know who thou wast, and may it be disclosed to me in thy words why for so many centuries thou hast lain here?" "At the time when the good Titus, with the aid of the Most High King, avenged the wounds wherefrom issued the blood sold by Judas,[7] I was famous enough on earth with the name which lasts longest, and honors most," replied that spirit, "but not as yet with faith. So sweet was

[1] Cf. Aristotle, *Metaphysics*, i. 1. 980ᵃ22.
[2] Cf. John, 4. 13-15.
[3] Lachesis.
[4] Iris, the rainbow.
[5] See Aristotle, *Meteorology*, ii. 8.
[6] See Aquinas, *Summa Theologica*, Part III, Suppl., Q 72, A 2.
[7] Titus besieged and destroyed Jerusalem in A. D. 70. Statius was born between A. D. 60 and 65, and probably died about the end of the first century.

the spirit of my voice, that me of Toulouse[1] Rome drew to itself, where I earned the right to adorn my temples with myrtle. Statius the people still name me yonder: I sang of Thebes, and then of the great Achilles, but I fell on the way with my second load. Seed of my ardor were the sparks that warmed me of the divine flame whereby more than a thousand have been kindled; I speak of the *Aeneid,* which was mother to me, and was nurse to me in poesy: without it I balanced not the weight of a drachm; and to have lived yonder, when Virgil lived, I would agree to one sun more than I owe for my issue from ban."

103. These words turned Virgil to me with a look which, silent, said: "Be silent": but the power that wills cannot do everything; for smiles and tears are such followers on the passion from which each springs, that in the most truthful they least follow the will. I only smiled, like a man who makes a sign; whereat the shade became silent, and looked at me in the eyes where the expression is most fixed. And it said: "So mayst thou bring to a good end so great a labor, why did thy face just now display to me a flash of a smile?"

115. Now am I caught on one side and the other; one bids me be silent, the other conjures me to speak: wherefore I sigh, and am understood by my Master, and: "Have no fear to speak," he said to me, "but speak, and tell him what he asks so earnestly." Whereon I: "Perhaps thou marvellest, ancient spirit, at the smile I gave; but I would have more wonder seize thee. This one, who guides my eyes on high, is that Virgil from whom thou didst derive the strength to sing of men and of the gods. If thou didst believe other cause for my smile, leave it as not being true, and believe it was those words which thou saidst of him." Already he was stooping to embrace the feet of my Teacher, but he said to him: "Brother, do it not, for thou art a shade, and thou seest a shade." And he rising: "Now canst thou comprehend the sum of the love that warms me to thee, when I forget our emptiness, treating the shades as if a solid thing."

CANTO XXII

1. ALREADY was the Angel left behind us—the Angel who had turned us to the sixth round, having erased a stroke from my face; and he had said to us that those who have their desire set on justice are *Beati,* and his words completed this with *sitiunt,* without the rest.[2] And I, more light than through the other passes, was so going on, that without any fatigue I was following upward the swift spirits, when Virgil began: "Love kindled by virtue always kindles another, provided that its flame appear outwardly; wherefore from the hour when Juvenal descended among us in the limbo of Hell,[3] and made known to me thy affection, my own good will toward thee has been such that more never bound one to an unseen person; so that these stairs will now seem short to me. But tell me—and as a friend pardon me, if too great confidence let loose my rein, and as a friend henceforth talk with me—how could avarice find a place within thy breast, amid wisdom so great as that wherewith through thy diligence thou wast filled?"

25. These words made Statius at first incline a little to a smile; then he replied: "Every word of thine is to me a dear token of love. Truly often things are apparent which give false material for suspicion, because the true reasons are hidden. Thy question assures me that it is thy belief, perhaps because of that circle where I was, that I was avaricious in the other life; know then that avarice was too far removed from me, and this want of measure thousands of courses of the moon have punished. And had it not been that I set right my care, when I understood the passage where thou dost exclaim, as if indignant with human nature, 'O accursed hunger of gold, through what dost thou not impel the appetite of mortals?'[4] I, rolling, should feel the dismal jousts.[5] Then I perceived that the hands could spread

[1] Statius was actually born at Naples. In Dante's time, there was a confusion between him and a rhetorician of Toulouse of the same name.

[2] That is, the Angel had not recited all the words of the Beatitude, which are as follows in the Vulgate: *Beati qui esuriunt et sitiunt justitiam: quoniam ipsi saturabuntur.* He had omitted *esuriunt,* and said only, "Blessed are they which do *thirst* after righteousness."

[3] In a famous passage of his Seventh Satire, 81-87, Juvenal speaks of Statius with high praise.

[4] See *Aeneid,* iii. 56-57.

[5] See *Hell,* vii. 25-35.

their wings too much in spending; and I repented as well of that as of my other sins. How many shall rise with cropped hair[1] through ignorance, which during life and in the last hours prevents repentance for this sin! And know, that the fault which rebuts any sin with direct opposition, together with it dries up its verdure here. Wherefore if for my purgation I have been among that people who lament their avarice, by reason of its contrary this has befallen me."

55. "Now when thou wast singing the cruel strife of the twofold affliction of Jocasta,"[2] said the Singer of the Bucolic songs, "it does not appear by that which Clio touches with thee there, that the Faith, without which good works do not suffice, had as yet made thee faithful. If this be so, what Sun, or what candles, did so disperse thy darkness that thou didst thereafter set thy sails behind the Fisherman?"

64. And he to him, "Thou first didst direct me on the way toward Parnassus to drink in its grots, and then, on the way to God, thou didst enlighten me. Thou didst like him, who goes by night, and carries the light behind him, and profits not himself, but makes the persons following him wise, when thou saidst, 'The world is renewed; Justice returns, and the primeval time of man, and a new progeny descends from heaven.'[3] Through thee I became a poet, through thee a Christian. But in order that thou mayst better see that which I outline, I will stretch my hand to color it. Already was the whole world teeming with the true belief, sown by the messengers of the eternal realm; and thy words just mentioned were so in harmony with the new preachers, that I adopted the practice of visiting them. Then they came to seem to me so holy, that, when Domitian persecuted them, their lamentations were not without my tears. And so long as I remained in yonder world, I succored them; and their upright customs made me scorn all other sects. And before I had led the Greeks to the rivers of Thebes in my verse, I received baptism; but through fear I was a secret Christian, for a long while making show of pagan-

ism: and this lukewarmness made me circle round the fourth circle, longer than to the fourth century.

94. "Thou, therefore, that didst lift for me the covering that was hiding from me such great good as I say, tell me, while we have remainder of ascent, where is our ancient Terence, Cæcilius, Plautus, and Varro, if thou knowest it; tell me if they are damned, and in what region?" "They, and Persius, and I, and many others," replied my Leader, "are with that Greek whom the Muses suckled more than ever any other, in the first girdle of the blind prison. Often we discourse of the mountain[4] that has our nurses[5] always with itself. Euripides is there with us, and Antiphon, Simonides, Agathon, and many other Greeks who of old adorned their brows with laurel. There of thine own people are seen Antigone, Deïphile and Argia, and Ismene sad as she lived.[6] There she is seen who showed Langia;[7] there is the daughter of Tiresias and Thetis,[8] and Deïdamia with her sisters."[9]

115. Now both the poets became silent, intent afresh on looking around, free from the ascent and from the walls; and four of the handmaids of the day were now remaining behind, and the fifth was at the pole, directing still upward its blazing horn, when my Leader: "I think that it behoves us to turn our right shoulders to the outer edge, circling the Mount as we are wont to do." Thus usage was there our guide, and we took the way with less doubt because of the assent of that worthy soul.

127. They were going on in front, and I solitary behind, and I was listening to their speech which was giving me understanding for poesy. But soon the pleasant converse was interrupted by a tree which we found in the

[1] See *Hell*, vii. 57.
[2] See *Hell*, xxvi. 52-54.
[3] See Virgil, *Eclogues*, iv. 5-7.
[4] Parnassus.
[5] The Muses.
[6] The sisters Antigone and Ismene, daughters of Oedipus and Jocasta; Deïphile and Argia, also sisters, daughters of Adrastus, King of Argos.
[7] Hypsipyle, who showed the fountain Langia to Adrastus and the other kings, when their soldiers were perishing with thirst. See *Hell*, xviii. 92-95, and *Purgatory*, xxvi. 94-96.
[8] But for Manto, the only daughter of Tiresias, mentioned by Statius. See *Hell*, xx. 55.
[9] Deïdamia, the daughter of Lycomedes, king of Scyros, and beloved by Achilles while he was in hiding there. See *Hell*, xxvi. 62. .

mid road, with apples sweet and good to smell.
And as a fir-tree tapers upward from branch
to branch, so downward did that, I think in
order that no one may go up. On the side upon
which our way was closed, a limpid water was
falling from the high rock and spreading itself
over the foliage above. The two poets ap-
proached the tree, and a voice from within the
leaves cried: "Of this food ye shall have
dearth." Then it said: "Mary thought more,
how the wedding[1] should be honorable and
complete, than of her own mouth, which an-
swers now for you; and the ancient Roman
women were content with water for their
drink;[2] and Daniel despised food and gained
wisdom.[3] The primal age was beautiful as
gold; with hunger it made acorns savory, and
with thirst every streamlet nectar. Honey and
locusts were the viands which nourished the
Baptist in the desert, wherefore he is in glory,
and so great as by the Gospel is revealed to
you."[4]

CANTO XXIII

1. WHILE I was fixing my eyes upon the green
leafage, just as he who wastes his life following
the little bird is wont to do, my more than
Father said to me: "Son, come on now, for
the time that is assigned to us must be more
usefully apportioned." I turned my eyes, and
no less quickly my step after the Sages, who
were speaking so that they made the going of
no cost to me; and lo! a lament and song were
heard: *"Labia mea, Domine,"*[5] in such fash-
ion that it gave birth to delight and pain.
"O sweet Father, what is that which I hear?"
I began, and he: "Shades which go, perhaps
loosing the knot of their debt."

16. Even as do pilgrims rapt in thought,
who, overtaking on the road unknown folk,
turn themselves to them, and stay not; so be-
hind us, moving more quickly, coming up and
passing by, a crowd of souls, silent and devout,
was gazing at us. Each was dark and hollow
in the eyes, pallid in the face, and so wasted
that the skin took its shape from the bones. I

do not think that Erisichthon[6] was so dried up
to utter rind by hunger, when he had most
fear of it. I said to myself in thought: "Behold
the people who lost Jerusalem, when Mary
struck her beak into her son." The sockets of
their eyes seemed rings without gems. Whoso
in the face of men reads OMO, would surely
there have recognized the M. Who would be-
lieve that the scent of an apple, and that of a
water, begetting a longing, could so control,
if he knew not how?

37. I was still wondering what so famished
them, the cause of their meagreness and of
their wretched scurf not yet being manifest,
and lo! from the depth of its head, a shade
turned his eyes on me, and looked fixedly, then
cried out loudly: "What grace to me is this!"
Never should I have recognized him by his
face; but in his voice was manifest to me that
which his aspect had annulled in itself. This
spark rekindled in me all my knowledge of the
altered visage, and I recognized the face of
Forese.[7]

49. "Ah, strive not with the dry scab that
discolors my skin," he prayed, "nor with my
lack of flesh, but tell me the truth about thy-
self; and who are those two souls, who yonder
make an escort for thee: stay not thou from
speaking to me." "Thy face," replied I to him,
"which once I wept for dead, now gives me
no less a grief for weeping seeing it so dis-
figured; therefore, tell me, for God's sake,
what so despoils you; make me not speak
while I am marvelling, for ill can he speak
who is full of other wish." And he to me: "By
the eternal counsel a virtue falls into the water
and upon the plant, now left behind, whereby
I grow so lean. All this folk who sing weep-
ing, because of following their appetite beyond
measure, are here in hunger and in thirst mak-
ing themselves holy again. The odor which
issues from the fruit and from the spray which
is spread over the verdure, kindles in us de-
sire to eat and drink. And not once only, as
we circle this floor, is our pain renewed; I say
pain, and ought to say solace, for that will

[1] See Canto xiii. 29.
[2] See Aquinas, *Summa Theologica,* Part II-II, Q
149, A 4.
[3] See Daniel, 1. 8-17.
[4] See Matthew, 11. 11; Luke, 7. 28.
[5] "O Lord, open thou my lips." Psalms, 51. 15.

[6] Punished for sacrilege by Ceres with insatiable
hunger, so that at last he turned his teeth upon him-
self.
[7] Brother of Corso Donati, and related to Dante's
wife, Gemma de' Donati.

leads us to the tree, which led Christ with joy to say: 'Eli,'[1] when with his blood he delivered us."

76. And I to him: "Forese, from that day on which thou didst change world to a better life, up to this time, five years have not rolled round. If the power of sinning further had ended in thee, before the hour supervened of the good sorrow which re-weds us to God, how hast thou come up hither? I thought to find thee still down there below, where time is made good by time."[2] Whereon he to me: "My Nella with her bursting tears has brought me thus speedily to drink of the sweet wormwood of these torments. With her devout prayers and with sighs has she drawn me from the hill-side where one waits, and has delivered me from the other circles. So much the more dear and more precious to God is my poor widow, whom I loved so well, as she is the more solitary in good conduct; for the Barbagia[3] of Sardinia is far more modest in its women than the Barbagia where I left her. O sweet brother, what wouldst thou that I say? A future time is already in my sight, to which this hour will not be very old, when from the pulpit it shall be interdicted to the brazen-faced dames of Florence to go about displaying the bosom with the paps. What barbarian, what Saracen women were there ever for whom either spiritual or other discipline was needed to make them go covered? But if the shameless ones were assured of that which the swift heaven is preparing for them, already would they have their mouths open for howling. For if my foresight here does not deceive me, they will be sad before he who is now consoled with the lullaby shall have bearded cheeks.

112. "Ah brother, now no longer conceal thyself from me; thou seest that not only I, but all these people are gazing there where thou dost veil the sun." Whereon I to him: "If thou bring back to mind what thou wast with me, and what I was with thee, the present remembrance will even now be grievous. From that life he who goes in front of me

turned me the other day, when the sister of him," and I pointed to the sun, "there showed herself round. Through the deep night, from the truly dead, he has led me, with this real flesh which follows him. Thence his encouragements have drawn me upward, ascending and circling the mountain that sets you straight whom the world made crooked. He says that he will bear me company so long till I shall be there where Beatrice will be; there it behoves that I remain without him. Virgil is this one who says thus to me," and I pointed to him, "and this other is that shade for whom just now your realm, which from itself releases him, shook every slope."

CANTO XXIV

1. SPEECH made not the going, nor did the going make that more slow; but, talking, we went on apace, even as a ship urged by a good wind. And the shades, that seemed things doubly dead, through the pits of their eyes drew in wonder at me, perceiving that I was alive.

7. And I, continuing my talk, said: "He goes up for the sake of another perchance more slowly than he would do. But, tell me, if thou knowest, where is Piccarda;[4] tell me if I see any person to be noted among this folk that so gazes at me." "My sister, who, between fair and good, was I know not which the most, triumphs already rejoicing in her crown on high Olympus." So he said first, and then: "Here it is not forbidden to name each one, since our semblance is so milked away by the diet. This," and he pointed with his finger, "is Bonagiunta,[5] Bonagiunta of Lucca; and that face beyond him, more pricked through than the others, had the Holy Church in his arms;[6] he was from Tours; and by fasting he purges the eels of Bolsena, and the Vernaccia wine." Many others he named to me, one by one, and at their naming all appeared content; so that for this I saw not one dark mien. I saw, using their teeth through hunger on emptiness,

---

[1] See Matthew, 27. 46.

[2] See Canto iv. 130-132.

[3] A mountainous district in Sardinia, inhabited by people of barbarous customs.

[4] Forese's sister. See *Paradise,* iii.

[5] Bonagiunta Urbiciani, a poet of Lucca who lived and wrote in the last half of the thirteenth century.

[6] Martin IV, native of Tours, Pope from 1281 to 1285. He is said to have died from a surfeit at Orvieto.

Ubaldin dalla Pila, and Boniface,[1] who shepherded many people with his crook. I saw Messer Marchese, who once had leisure for drinking at Forlì with less thirst, and even so was such that he felt not sated.

34. But as one does who looks, and then makes more account of one than of another, so did I to him of Lucca, who seemed most to wish acquaintance with me. He was murmuring, and I heard something like "Gentucca" from there where he felt the chastisement of the justice which so strips them. "O soul," said I, "who seemest so desirous to speak with me, do so that I can understand thee, and satisfy both thyself and me by thy speech." "A woman is born, and wears not yet the veil," he began, "who will make my city pleasant to thee, however men may blame it. Thou shalt go on with this prevision: if from my murmuring thou hast conceived error, the true things will hereafter clear it up for thee. But tell me, if I here see him, who drew forth the new rhymes, beginning: 'Ladies who have intelligence of Love'?"[2]

52. And I to him: "I am one who, when Love inspires me, notes, and in that mode which he dictates within, I go uttering." "O brother, now I see," said he, "the knot which held back the Notary,[3] and Guittone,[4] and me short of the sweet new style which I hear. I see clearly how your pens go on close following the dictator, which surely was not the case with ours. And he who most sets himself to look farther sees nothing more between one style and the other." And, as if contented, he was silent.

64. As the birds that winter along the Nile sometimes make a troop in the air, then fly in greater haste, and go in file, so all the folk that were there, light both through leanness and through will, turning away their faces, quickened again their pace.

70. And as the man who is weary of running lets his companions go on, and then

walks, until the panting of his chest be abated, so Forese let the holy flock pass on and came along behind with me, saying: "When shall it be that I see thee again?" "I know not," I replied to him, "how long I may live; but truly my return will not be so speedy, that I shall not in desire be sooner at the shore; because the place where I was set to live, strips itself more of good from day to day, and seems ordained to dismal ruin." "Now go," said he, "for I see him who is most to blame for this[5] dragged at the tail of a beast, toward the valley[6] where never is there exculpation. The beast at every step goes faster, with ever increasing speed, till it strikes him, and leaves his body vilely undone. Those wheels have not far to turn," and he raised his eyes to heaven, "ere that will be clear to thee which my speech may not further declare. Now do thou stay behind, for time is so precious in this kingdom, that I lose too much coming thus at even pace with thee."

94. As a cavalier sometimes sets forth at a gallop from a troop which is riding, and goes to win the honor of the first encounter, so with longer strides did he depart from us; and I remained on the way with only those two who were such great marshals of the world.

100. And when he had passed on so far before us that my eyes became such followers of him as my mind was of his words, there appeared to me the laden and living branches of another apple-tree, and not far distant, because only then had I turned thitherward. I saw people beneath it raising their hands and crying, I know not what, toward the leaves, like eager and fond little children who pray, and he to whom they pray does not answer, but, to make their longing the more keen, holds aloft their desire, and conceals it not. Then they departed as if undeceived: and upon this we came to the great tree which rejects so many prayers and tears. "Pass ye farther onward, without drawing near; the tree[7] which was eaten of by Eve is higher up, and

[1] Bonifazio de' Fieschi, Archbishop of Ravenna from 1274 to 1294.
[2] The first verse of the first canzone of *The New Life*.
[3] The Sicilian poet, Jacopo da Lentino.
[4] Guittone d' Arezzo, commonly called Fra Guittone, as one of the order of the Frati Gaudenti, mentioned in *Hell*, xxiii. 103. Also see Canto xxvi. 124. He died probably in 1293.

[5] Corso Donati, the leader of the Black Guelphs. On October 6, 1308, he was compelled to fly from Florence. Near the city he was thrown from his horse and dragged along, till he was overtaken and killed by his pursuers.
[6] "The woful valley of the abyss." See *Hell*, iv. 8.
[7] See Canto xxxii. 38ff.

this plant was raised from it." Thus said I know not who among the branches; wherefore Virgil and Statius and I, drawing close together, proceeded onward along the side that rises. "Bethink ye," the voice was saying, "of the accursed ones,[1] formed in the clouds, who, when glutted, strove against Theseus with their double breasts; and of the Hebrews, who, at the drinking, showed themselves weak,[2] wherefore Gideon had them not for companions, when he went down the hills toward Midian."

127. Thus keeping close to that one of the two margins, we passed by, hearing of sins of gluttony followed, indeed, by miserable gains. Then going at large along the lonely road, full a thousand steps and more had carried us onward, each of us in meditation without a word. "Why go ye thus in thought, ye three alone?" said a sudden voice; whereat I started, as do terrified and timid beasts. I lifted up my head to see who it might be, and never were glass or metals in a furnace seen so shining and ruddy, as one I saw who said: "If it please you to mount upward, here there is need to turn; this way he goes who would go for peace." His aspect had taken my sight from me, wherefore I turned to go behind my teachers, like one who goes according as he hears.

145. And as the breeze of May, a herald of the dawn, stirs and smells sweet, all impregnate with the herbage and with the flowers, such a wind I felt strike upon the middle of my forehead, and I clearly felt the motion of the plumage, which made me perceive the odor of ambrosia. And I heard say: "Blessed are they whom so much grace illumines, that the love of taste kindles not too great desire in their breasts, hungering always so much as is right."[3]

CANTO XXV

1. It was the hour in which the ascent allowed no delay; for the Sun had left the meridian circle to the Bull, and the Night to the Scorpion;[4] wherefore as does the man who, what-

ever may appear to him, does not stop, if the goad of necessity prick him, but goes on his way, so did we enter through the gap, one before the other, taking the stairway which by its narrowness unpairs the climbers.

10. And as the little stork that lifts its wing through will to fly, and dares not abandon the nest, and lets it drop, so was I, with will to ask kindled and quenched, coming as far as to the motion that he makes who proposes to speak. Nor, though our going was swift, did my sweet Father forbear, but he said: "Discharge the bow of speech which up to the iron thou hast drawn." Then I opened my mouth confidently, and began: "How can one become lean, where the need of nourishment is not felt?" "If thou wouldst call to mind," he said, "how Meleager was consumed by the consuming of a brand, this would not be so difficult to thee; and if thou wouldst think, how at your quivering your image quivers within the mirror, that which seems hard would seem easy to thee. But in order that thou mayst be inwardly at ease in respect to thy wish, lo, here is Statius, and I call on him, and pray that he be now the healer of thy wounds."

31. "If I explain to him the eternal view," replied Statius, "where thou art present, let it excuse me that to thee I cannot make denial."

34. Then he began, "If, son, thy mind regards and receives my words, they will be for thee a light unto the 'How,' which thou askest.[5] Perfect blood, which is never drunk up by the thirsty veins, but remains like the food which thou removest from the table, takes in the heart a virtue informative of all the human members, as being that which goes through the veins to become them. Digested still further, it descends to the part whereof it is more becoming to be silent than to speak; and from there, afterwards, it drops upon another's blood in the natural vessel. There one and the other meet together; the one ordained to be passive, and the other to be active because of the perfect place wherefrom it is pressed out; and, conjoined with the former, the latter begins to operate, first by coagulating, and then it quickens that to which it gives consistency for its own material. The active virtue having

[1] The centaurs, said to have been born of Ixion and a phantom cloud. They fought with Theseus at the marriage feast of Peirithous.
[2] See Judges, 7. 4-7.
[3] See Matthew, 5. 6. Also Cf. Canto xxii. 5-6.
[4] The hour indicated is about 2 p. m.
[5] See Aquinas, *Summa Theologica*, Part I, QQ 118, 119.

become a soul, like that of a plant[1] (in so far different that this is on the way, and that already arrived), then so works, that now it moves and feels, as a sea-fungus does; and then it proceeds to organize the powers of which it is the germ. Now, son, the virtue is displayed, now it is diffused, which issues from the heart of the begetter, where nature is intent on all the members.

61. "But how from an animal it becomes a rational being, thou as yet seest not; this is such a point that once it made one wiser than thou to err, so that in his teaching he separated from the soul the potential intellect, because he saw no organ assumed by it.[2] Open thy breast to the truth which is coming, and know that, so soon as the articulation of the brain is perfect in the embryo, the Primal Motor turns to it with joy over such art of nature, and breathes into it a new spirit replete with virtue, which draws into its own substance that which it finds active there, and becomes one single soul which lives and feels and circles on itself. And that thou mayst the less wonder at my words, consider the warmth of the sun which, combining with the juice that flows from the vine, becomes wine.[3]

79. "And when Lachesis has no more thread, this soul is loosed from the flesh, and virtually bears away with itself both the human and the divine; the other faculties all of them mute, but memory, understanding, and will far more acute in action than before. Without a stop, it falls of itself, marvellously, to one of the banks.[4] Here it first knows its own roads. Soon as the place there circumscribes it, the formative virtue rays out around it, in like shape and size, as in the living members. And as the air when it is full of rain becomes adorned with divers colors, by reason of the rays of another which are reflected in it, so here the neighboring air shapes itself in that form which the soul

that has stopped virtually imprints upon it. And then like the flamelet which follows the fire whithersoever it shifts, so does its new form follow the spirit. Since thereafter it has its aspect from this, it is called a shade; and thence it organizes every sense even to the sight; thence we speak, and thence we laugh, thence we make the tears and the sighs, which thou mayst have heard on the mountain. According as our desires and our other affections impress us, the shade is shaped; and this is the cause of that at which thou wonderest."

109. And now we had come to the last circuit, and had turned to the right hand, and were intent upon another care. Here the bank shoots forth flame, and the ledge breathes a blast upward which drives it back, and sequesters a path from it. Wherefore it was needful to go one by one along the open side; and on the one hand I was afraid of the fire, and on the other I was afraid of falling off. My Leader said, "Along this place, one must keep tight the rein upon the eyes, because for little one might go astray."

121. *"Summae Deus clementiae,"*[5] I then heard being sung, in the bosom of the great burning, which made me care not less to turn. And I saw spirits going through the flame; wherefore I looked at them and at my own steps, apportioning to each my sight from moment to moment. After the end that is made to that hymn, they loudly cried: *"Virum non cognosco";*[6] then began again the hymn with low voice; this finished, they cried anew: "To the wood Diana kept herself, and drove therefrom Helice,[7] who had tasted the poison of Venus." Then they returned to their singing; then they cried aloud wives and husbands who were chaste, as virtue and marriage enjoin upon us. And I believe this mode suffices them for all the time that the fire burns them. With such cure it is needful, and with such diet, that the last wound of all should be closed up.

---

[1] See Aquinas, *Summa Theologica,* Part I, Q 118, A 1; Aristotle, *Generation of Animals,* ii. 3.
[2] The "one wiser than thou" is generally understood to refer to Averroes, whose error was in his exposition of Aristotle's doctrine as set forth in *On the Soul,* iii. 4-5.
[3] See Aquinas, *Summa Theologica,* Part I, Q 76, A 4.
[4] Of Acheron (see *Hell,* iii. 78), or of Tiber (see *Purgatory,* ii. 100-105), according as the soul is damned or saved.

[5] "God of clemency supreme," the beginning of a hymn, sung at Matins on Saturday, containing a prayer for purity.
[6] "I know not a man." See Luke, 1. 34.
[7] Or Callisto, a nymph attendant on Diana. She bore a son to Jupiter, and, having been changed into a bear by Juno, she was by Jove transferred with her child to the heavens, where they are seen as the Great and Little Bear.

CANTO XXVI

1. WHILE we were thus going on along the edge, one before the other, the good Master was often saying: "Take heed! let it avail that I warn thee." The sun, which now, with his radiance, was changing all the west from azure to a white aspect, was striking me on the right shoulder; and with my shadow I was making the flame appear more ruddy, and only to that indication I saw many shades, as they went on, giving heed. This was the occasion which gave them a beginning to speak of me, and they began to say: "He does not seem a fictitious body"; then certain of them came toward me, so far as they could do so, always with regard not to come out where they would not be burned.

16. "O thou, who goest behind the others, not from being slower, but perhaps from reverence, reply to me, who am burning in thirst and fire: nor by me only is thy reply needed, for all these have a greater thirst for it than Indian or Ethiop for cold water. Tell us how it is that thou makest of thyself a wall to the sun, as if thou hadst not yet entered within the net of death." Thus spoke one of them to me; and I should at once have made myself known, if I had not given attention to another new thing which then appeared; for along the middle of the burning road were coming people with their faces opposite to these, which held me engaged to look at them. There I see, on either side, each shade making haste and one kissing the other, without stopping, content with a brief greeting. Thus within their brown troop one ant touches muzzle with another, perchance to spy out their way and their fortune.

37. Soon as they end the friendly salutation, before the first step runs onward by, each strives to outcry the other; the new-come folk: "Sodom and Gomorrah," and the other: "Into the cow enters Pasiphaë, that the bull may run to her lust." Then like cranes, which should fly part to the Riphaean mountains,[1] and part toward the sands,[2] these shunning the frost and those the sun, the one folk goes, the other comes on, and, weeping, they return to their first chants,[3] and to the cry which most befits them. And those same who had prayed me drew near to me as before, intent in their looks to listen.

52. I, who twice had seen their desire, began: "O souls, secure of having, whenever it may be, a state of peace, my limbs have not remained yonder, either unripe nor mature, but are here with me, with their blood, and with their joints. I go hence upward in order to be no longer blind. A Lady is on high who wins grace for us,[4] whereby I bring my mortal body through your world. But so may your greatest wish soon become satisfied, in such wise that that heaven may harbor you which is full of love, and most amply spreads,[5] tell me, in order that I may yet rule the paper for it, who are ye, and who are that crowd which go their way behind your backs."

67. Not otherwise is the astonished mountaineer confused, and gazing round is dumb, when rough and rustic he enters the town, than each shade became in its appearance; but, after they were unburdened of their astonishment, which in high hearts is quickly abated: "Blessed thou," began again the one who first had questioned me, "who, in order the better to die, dost ship experience of our regions. The people who do not come with us offended in that for which once Cæsar in his triumph heard 'Queen' shouted out against him; therefore they go off crying 'Sodom,' upbraiding themselves, as thou hast heard, and they help the burning by their shame. Our sin was hermaphrodite; but because, following our appetite like beasts, we did not observe human law, when we part from them we recite, in opprobrium of ourselves, the name of her who bestialized herself in the beast-shaped planks. Now thou knowest our deeds, and of what we were guilty; if, perchance, thou wishest to know by name who we are, there is not time to tell, and I should not know. I will indeed make thee short of wish about myself; I am Guido Guinicelli;[6] and I am purging myself already, because I truly repented before my last hour."

[1] Mountains vaguely placed by the early geographers in the far north.
[2] The deserts of Libya.
[3] See Canto xxv. 121.
[4] See *Hell*, ii. 94-96.
[5] The Empyrean, the seat of Paradise.
[6] The most illustrious of the Italian poets before Dante; the date of his death is uncertain, but he was living in 1274. See Canto xi. 97.

94. Such as in the frenzy of Lycurgus her two sons became at seeing again their mother,[1] such I became, but I rise not so far, when I hear name himself the father of me, and of the others my betters who ever used sweet and gracious rhymes of love; and without hearing or speaking, full of thought, I went on, gazing a long time upon him; nor, for the fire, did I draw nearer to him.

103. When I was fed with looking, I offered myself wholly ready for his service, with the affirmation which makes another believe. And he to me: "By what I hear, thou leavest such impression on me, and so clear, that Lethe cannot take it away nor make it dim. But, if thy words just now swore truth, tell me what is the reason why thou displayest in speech and look that thou dost hold me dear?" And I to him, "The sweet ditties of yours, which, so long as the modern use shall endure, will still make dear their ink."

115. "O brother," said he, "this one whom I point out to thee with my finger," and he pointed to a spirit in advance,[2] "was a better smith of his mother tongue. In verses of love and proses of romances he surpassed all; and let the foolish talk who think that he of Limoges[3] excels him; to rumor more than to the truth they turn their faces, and thus establish their opinion, before art or reason is listened to by them. Thus did many of old concerning Guittone,[4] from cry to cry giving the prize only to him, until the truth prevailed with more persons. Now if thou hast such ample privilege that it is permitted thee to go unto the cloister in which Christ is abbot of the college, say to Him for me one paternoster, so far as is needful for us in this world, where power to sin is no longer ours."

133. Then, perhaps to give place to one who was near behind him, he disappeared through the fire, like a fish going through the water to the bottom. I moved forward a little to him who had been pointed out to me, and said, that for his name my desire was preparing a gracious place. He readily began to say: "Your courteous request so pleases me that I cannot, nor do I wish to hide me from you. I am Arnaut, who weep and go singing; contrite I see my past folly, and glad I see before me the joy I hope for. Now I pray you, by that Power which guides you to the summit of this stairway, at due time be mindful of my pain."[5] Then he hid himself in the fire which refines them.

CANTO XXVII

1. As when he darts forth his first rays there where his Maker shed His blood (Ebro falling under the lofty Scales, and the waves in the Ganges scorched by noon) so the sun was now standing;[6] and thus the day was departing, when the glad Angel of God appeared to us. Outside the flame he was standing on the bank, and was singing: Beati mundo corde,[7] in a voice far more living than ours. Then: "No one goes farther, ye holy souls, if first the fire sting not: enter into it, and to the song beyond be ye not deaf," he said to us, as we drew near to him: whereat I became such, when I heard him, as is he who is put in the pit. I stretched forward above my clasped hands, looking at the fire, and vividly imagining human bodies I had once seen burnt.

19. My good Escorts turned toward me, and Virgil said to me: "My son, here may be torment, but not death. Bethink thee! bethink thee! . . . lo, if I even upon Geryon guided thee safe, what shall I do now that I am nearer God? Believe for certain that if within the belly of this flame thou shouldst stand full a thousand years it could not make thee bald of a single hair. And if perchance thou believest that I am deceiving thee, draw towards it, and make trial for thyself with thine own hands upon the hem of thy garments. Put aside now, put aside every fear, turn hitherward, and come on secure."

[1] When Hypsipyle was about to be put to death by Lycurgus, king of Nemea, enraged with her for leaving his infant child, who was killed by a serpent while she was showing the river Langia to the Argives (see Canto xxii. 112), she was found and rescued by her own sons.

[2] Arnaut Daniel, a famous Provençal troubadour of the end of the twelfth century.

[3] Giraut de Borneil, another famous poet, contemporary with Arnaut Daniel.

[4] See Canto xxiv. 56.

[5] The words of Arnaut are in the Provençal tongue.

[6] It was near sunrise at Jerusalem, and consequently near sunset in Purgatory, midnight in Spain, and midday at the Ganges.

[7] "Blessed are the pure in heart."

33. And I still motionless and against conscience!

34. When he saw me still stand motionless and obdurate, he said, disturbed a little: "Now see, son, between Beatrice and thee is this wall."

37. As at the name of Thisbe, Pyramus, at point of death, opened his eyelids and looked at her, what time the mulberry became dark red, so, my obduracy becoming softened, I turned to my wise Leader, hearing the name that in my memory is ever welling up. Whereat he nodded his head, and said: "How? do we want to stay on this side?" then he smiled as one does at a child who is conquered by an apple.

46. Then within the fire he set himself in front of me, praying Statius, that he would come behind, who previously, for a long way, had divided us. When I was within, I would have thrown myself into boiling glass to cool me, so without measure was the burning there. My sweet Father, to encourage me, went talking only of Beatrice, saying: "I seem already to see her eyes."

55. A voice which was singing on the other side was guiding us, and we, attentive ever to it, came forth where the ascent began. *"Venite, benedicti patris mei,"*[1] sounded within a light that was there such that it overcame me, and I could not look on it. "The sun is going," it added, "and the evening comes; tarry not, but hasten your steps so long as the west grows not dark."

64. The way mounted straight, through the rock, in such direction that in front of me I cut off the rays of the sun which was already low. And of few stairs had we made essay ere, by the vanishing of my shadow, both I and my Sages perceived the setting of the sun behind us. And before the horizon in all its immeasurable regions had become of one aspect, and night had all her dispensations, each of us made his bed of a stair; for the nature of the mountain took from us the power, more than the delight, of ascending.

76. As goats, that have been swift and wanton on the peaks ere they were fed, become tranquil while they ruminate, hushed in the shade so long as the sun is hot, watched by the shepherd, who on his staff is leaning and, leaning, tends them; and as the herdsman, who lodges out of doors, passes the night beside his quiet flock, watching that the wild beast may not scatter it: such were we all three then, I like a goat, and they like shepherds, hemmed in on this side and on that by the high rock.

88. Little of the outside could there be seen, but in that little I saw the stars both brighter and larger than their wont. Thus ruminating, and thus gazing upon them, sleep overcame me, sleep which oft before the deed be done knows news thereof.

94. At the hour, I think, when from the east Cytherea, who with fire of love seems always burning, first beamed upon the mountain,[2] I seemed in dream to see a lady, young and beautiful, going through a meadow gathering flowers, and singing she was saying: "Let him know, whoso asks my name, that I am Leah, and I go moving my fair hands around to make me a garland. To please me at the mirror I here adorn me, but my sister Rachel never departs from her looking-glass, and sits all day. She is as fain to look at her fair eyes as I to adorn me with my hands. Her, seeing, and me, doing satisfies."[3]

109. And now before the splendors which precede the sun, and rise the more grateful unto pilgrims as in returning they lodge less far away, the shadows were fleeing on every side, and my sleep with them; whereupon I rose, seeing the great Masters already risen. "That sweet fruit which the care of mortals goes seeking upon so many branches, today shall set at peace thy hungerings." These words did Virgil use toward me, and never were there gifts which for pleasure were equal to these. Such great wish upon wish came to me to be above, that at every step thereafter I felt my wings growing for the flight.

124. When beneath us all the stairway had been run over, and we were on the topmost step, Virgil fixed his eyes on me, and said: "The temporal fire and the eternal thou hast seen, Son, and art come to a place where of my-

[1] "Come, ye blessed of my Father." Matthew, 25. 34.

[2] Venus, the morning star, was rising. Cf. Canto i. 19, 20.
[3] Leah and Rachel are the types of the active and the contemplative life.

self I discern no farther. I have brought thee here with understanding and with art; thine own pleasure take thou henceforward for guide: forth art thou from the steep ways, forth art thou from the narrow. See there the sun, which is shining on thy front; see the young grass, the flowers, and the shrubs, which here the earth of itself alone produces. Until the beautiful eyes come rejoicing, which weeping made me come to thee, thou canst sit down and thou canst go among them. Expect no more or word or sign from me. Free, upright, and sound is thine own will, and it would be wrong not to act according to its choice; wherefore thee over thyself I crown and mitre."

CANTO XXVIII

1. FAIN now to search within and round about the divine forest dense and living, which was tempering the new day to my eyes, without longer waiting I left the bank, taking the level ground very slowly, over the soil which on every side breathed fragrance. A sweet breeze that had no variation in itself smote me on the brow, not with heavier stroke than a soft wind; at which the branches, readily trembling, one and all were bending toward the quarter where the holy mountain casts its first shadow; yet not so swayed from their uprightness, that the little birds among the tops had to leave the practice of their every art; but, singing with full joy, they received the early breezes among the leaves, which were keeping a burden to their rhymes, such as gathers from bough to bough through the pine forest on the shore of Chiassi,[1] when Aeolus lets forth the Scirocco.[2]

22. Now had my slow steps carried me within the ancient wood so far that I could not see back to where I had entered it: and lo, a stream took from me further progress, which with its little waves was bending toward the left the grass that sprang up on its bank. All the waters, that are purest here on the earth, would seem to have some mixture in them, compared with that which hides nothing, although it moves along dusky under the perpetual shad-

ow, which never lets the sun or moon shine there.

34. With my feet I stood still, and with my eyes I passed to the other side of the streamlet, to gaze at the great variety of the fresh blossoms; and there, even as a thing appears suddenly which turns aside through wonder every other thought, appeared to me a solitary lady, who was going along, singing, and culling flower from flower, wherewith all her path was painted. "Ah, fair Lady, who warmest thyself in the rays of love, if I may trust to looks which are wont to be witnesses of the heart, may the will come to thee," said I to her, "to draw forward toward this stream, so far that I may hear what thou art singing. Thou makest me remember where and what was Proserpine, at the time when her mother lost her, and she the spring."

52. As a lady who is dancing turns, with feet close to the ground and to each other, and hardly sets foot before foot, she turned on the red and the yellow flowerets toward me, not otherwise than a virgin who lowers her modest eyes, and made my prayers content, approaching so that the sweet sound came to me with its meaning. So soon as she was there where the grasses are just bathed by the waves of the fair stream, she gave me the boon of lifting her eyes. I do not believe that so great a light shone beneath the eyelids of Venus, when transfixed by her son quite out of his custom. She was smiling upon the right bank opposite, gathering with her hands the many colors which that high land brings forth without seed. The stream made us three paces apart; but the Hellespont where Xerxes passed it—still a curb on all human pride—endured not more hatred from Leander for swelling between Sestos and Abydos, than that from me because it did not then open.

76. "Ye are new come," she began, "and, perchance, why I smile in this place chosen for human nature as its nest, some doubt holds you marvelling; but the psalm *Delectasti*[3] affords light which may uncloud your understanding. And thou who art in front, and didst pray to

---

[1] Classe, the old port of Ravenna, from which the sea long since receded.
[2] The southeast wind.

[3] Psalms, 92. 4, *Delectasti me, Domine, in factura tua, et in operibus manuum tuarum exultabo.* "For thou, Lord, hast made me glad through thy work; I will triumph in the works of thy hands."

me, say, if aught else thou wouldst hear, for I came ready for every question of thine, so far as may suffice."

85. "The water," said I, "and the sound of the forest impugn within me recent faith in something which I heard contrary to this."[1] Whereon she: "I will tell how that which makes thee wonder proceeds from its own cause; and I will clear away the mist which falls upon thee.

91. "The supreme Good, which Itself alone is pleasing to Itself, made man good, and for good, and gave to him this place for earnest of eternal peace. Through his own default he dwelt here little while; through his own default he changed honest laughter and sweet sport to tears and to toil. In order that the disturbance, which the exhalations of the water and of the earth (that follow after the heat so far as they can) produce down below, should not make any war on man, this mountain rose so high toward heaven, and is free from them, from there where it is locked in. Now because the whole air revolves in a circuit with the primal revolution,[2] if its circling be not broken by some obstacle, upon this height, which is wholly disengaged in the living air, this motion strikes, and makes the wood, because it is thick-set, resound; and the plant thus struck has such power that with its virtue it impregnates the breeze, and this in its whirling then scatters it around; and the rest of the earth, according as it is fit in itself, or through its sky, conceives and brings forth divers trees of divers virtues. It should not then, this being heard, appear a marvel on earth, when some plant takes root there without apparent seed. And thou must know that the holy plain where thou art is full of every seed, and has within itself fruit which is never gathered yonder upon earth.

121. "The water which thou seest does not rise from a vein which vapor condensed by the frost restores, like a stream that gains and loses breath; but it issues from a constant and sure fountain, which by the will of God regains as

much as it pours forth open on two sides. On this side it descends with virtue that takes from one the memory of sin; on the other it restores that of every good deed. On this side it is called Lethe,[3] so on the other Eunoë; and it works not if first it be not tasted on this side then on that. To all other savors this is superior.

134. "And though thy thirst may be fully sated even if I reveal no more to thee, I will yet give thee a corollary as a favor; nor do I think my speech will be less dear to thee, if it extend with thee beyond my promise. Those who in old time sang of the Golden Age, and of its happy state, perchance, upon Parnassus, dreamed of this place: here was the root of mankind innocent; here is always spring, and every fruit; this is the nectar of which each one of them tells."

145. I turned me backward then wholly to my Poets, and saw that with a smile they had heard the last words; then to the beautiful Lady I turned again my eyes.

CANTO XXIX

1. SINGING like a lady enamored, she, at the ending of her words, continued: *Beati, quorum tecta sunt peccata.*[4] And, like the nymphs who were wont to go solitary through the sylvan shades, one desiring to see and one to avoid the sun, she then moved on counter to the stream, going up along the bank, and I at even pace with her, following her little step with little. Of her steps and mine there were not a hundred, when the banks both alike gave a turn, in such wise that I faced again toward the east. Nor even thus had our way been long, when the lady turned wholly round to me, saying: "My brother, look and listen."

16. And lo, a sudden lustre ran through the great forest on every side, so that it made me question if it were lightning. But because the lightning stays even as it comes, and this, lasting, became more and more resplendent, in my thought I said, "What thing is this?" And a sweet melody ran through the luminous air; whereupon a righteous zeal made me reproach the hardihood of Eve, who, there, where the

---

[1] Cf. Canto xxi. 43-53.
[2] With the movement given to it by the revolution of the crystalline heaven, the so-called *Primum Mobile,* from which the other heavenly spheres derive their motion.

[3] See *Hell,* xxxiv. 127-132.
[4] "Blessed are they whose transgressions are forgiven." Psalms, 32. 1.

earth and the heavens were obedient, the only woman, and but just now formed, did not endure to stay under any veil; under which if she had stayed devout, I should have tasted those ineffable delights before, and for a longer time.

31. While I was going on amid so many first fruits of the eternal pleasure, all enrapt, and still desirous of more joys,[1] in front of us the air, beneath the green branches, became like a blazing fire, and the sweet sound was now heard as a song.

37. O Virgins sacrosanct! if for you I have ever endured hunger, cold, or vigils, the occasion spurs me that I claim reward therefor. Now it behoves that Helicon pour forth for me, and that Urania aid me with her choir to put into verse things difficult to think.

43. A little farther on, the long tract of space which was still between us and them shewed falsely in their seeming seven trees of gold. But when I had come so near to them that the common object, which deceives the sense, lost not through distance any of its attributes, the power which supplies discourse to reason[2] distinguished them as candlesticks,[3] and in the voices of the song, *Hosanna*. On high the fair array was flaming, brighter by far than the moon in the clear sky at midnight, in the middle of her month. I turned me round full of wonder to the good Virgil, and he replied to me with a look charged not less with amazement. Then I turned back my gaze to the high things, which were moving toward us so slowly that they would have been outstripped by new-made brides.

61. The lady chided me: "Why art thou only thus ardent in gazing on the living lights, and dost not look at that which comes behind them?" Then I saw folk coming behind, as if after their leaders, clothed in white, and such whiteness there never was on earth.[4] The water was resplendent on the left flank, and reflected to me my left side, if I looked in it, even as a mirror. When I had such position on my bank that only the stream separated me, in order to see better, I gave halt to my steps, and I saw the flamelets go forward leaving the air behind

them painted, and they had the semblance of streaming pennons, so that it remained divided overhead by seven stripes, all in those colors whereof the sun makes his bow, and Delia her girdle.[5] These banners stretched to the rear beyond my sight, and according to my judgment the outermost were ten paces apart. Under so fair a sky as I describe, twenty-four elders,[6] two by two, were coming crowned with flower-deluce. All were singing: "Blessed art thou among the daughters of Adam, and blessed forever be thy beauties."

88. After the flowers and the other fresh herbage, opposite to me on the other bank, were free from those folk elect, there came behind them, even as light follows light in heaven, four living creatures, each crowned with green leaves. Each was feathered with six wings, the feathers full of eyes; and the eyes of Argus, if they were living, would be such. To describe their forms, Reader, I scatter rhymes no more, for other spending so constrains me that in this I cannot be liberal. But read Ezekiel, who depicts them as he saw them coming from the cold quarter with wind, with cloud, and with fire; and such as thou wilt find them in his pages such were they here, save that as to the wings John is with me, and differs from him.[7]

106. The space between these four contained a triumphal chariot upon two wheels, which came drawn along by the neck of a Griffon.[8] And he stretched up the one and the other of his wings between the midmost stripe, and the three and three others, so that he did harm to no one of them by cleaving it: so high they rose that they were lost to sight. His members were of gold so far as he was bird, and the rest were white mixed with crimson. Not Africanus, or indeed Augustus, gladdened Rome with so beautiful a chariot; but even that of the Sun would be poor to it—that of the Sun, which, going astray,[9] was consumed at the prayer of the devout Earth, when Jove in his secrecy was

[1] Cf. Canto vi. 46-48.
[2] See Canto xviii. 22.
[3] See Revelation, 1. 12; 4, 5; Isaiah, 11. 2.
[4] See Mark, 9. 3.
[5] Delia, the moon, and her girdle the halo.
[6] See Revelation, 4. 4.
[7] These four living creatures represent the four Evangelists. See Ezekiel, 1. 6; Revelation, 4. 8.
[8] The griffon, half eagle and half lion, represents Christ in his double nature, divine and human. See Song of Solomon, 5. 10, 11. The chariot he draws is the Church.
[9] When driven by Phaëthon.

just. Three ladies,[1] at the right wheel, came
dancing in a circle; one so ruddy that hardly
would she have been noted within the fire; the
next was as if her flesh and bones had been
made of emerald; the third seemed as snow
fresh fallen. And now they seemed led by the
white, now by the red, and the others took
their step both slow and swift from the song of
her who led. On the left, four,[2] robed in pur-
ple, made festival, following the measure of
one of them who had three eyes in her head.

133. Behind all the group thus described, I
saw two old men, unlike in dress, but like in
demeanor, both dignified and staid. The one
showed himself one of the familiars of that su-
preme Hippocrates whom Nature made for
the creatures that she holds most dear;[3] the
other showed the contrary care,[4] with a shin-
ing and sharp sword, such that it caused me
fear on the hither side of the stream. Then I
saw four of humble aspect, and behind all an
old man alone, coming asleep with a keen
countenance.[5] And these seven were robed like
the first band; but they made not a crown of
lilies round their heads, rather of roses, and of
other red flowers. The sight at little distance
would have sworn that all were aflame above
their brows.

151. And when the chariot was abreast of
me, a peal of thunder was heard, and those
worthy people seemed to have their farther
progress interdicted, stopping there with the
first ensigns.[6]

CANTO XXX

1. WHEN the Septentrion of the first heaven[7]
(which never knew setting nor rising, nor veil
of other cloud than sin, and which was making
every one there acquainted with his duty, as

the lower[8] makes him who turns the helm to
come to port) stopped still, the truthful people
who had come first between the Griffon and it,
turned to the chariot as to their peace, and one
of them, as if sent from heaven, singing, cried
thrice: *Veni, sponsa, de Libano,*[9] and all the
others after.

13. As the blessed at the last trump will arise
swiftly, each from his tomb, singing Hallelu-
jah with reinvested voice,[10] so, upon the divine
wagon, *ad vocem tanti senis,*[11] rose up a hun-
dred ministers and messengers of life eternal.
All were saying: *Benedictus, qui venis,*[12] and,
scattering flowers above and around, *Manibus
o date lilia plenis.*[13]

22. I have seen ere now at the beginning of
the day the eastern region all rosy, and the rest
of heaven beautiful with fair clear sky, and the
face of the sun rising shaded, so that through
the tempering of vapors the eye sustained it a
long while; thus within a cloud of flowers,
which was ascending from the angelic hands
and falling down again within and without, a
lady, with wreath of olive over a white veil, ap-
peared to me, robed with the color of living
flame under a green mantle. And my spirit
which now for so long a time had not been
broken down, trembling with awe at her pres-
ence, without having more knowledge by the
eyes, through occult virtue that proceeded
from her, felt the great potency of ancient love.

40. Soon as the lofty virtue smote my sight,
which already had transfixed me ere I was out
of boyhood, I turned me to the left, with the
confidence with which the little child runs to
his mother when he is frightened, or when he
is troubled, to say to Virgil: "Less than a
drachm of blood remains in me that does not
tremble; I recognize the signals of the ancient
flame."[14] But Virgil had left us deprived of
himself; Virgil, sweetest Father; Virgil, to
whom for my salvation I gave me. Nor did all

[1] The theological virtues, Faith, Hope, and Charity.
[2] The four cardinal virtues, Prudence, Justice, Tem-
perance, and Fortitude. See Aquinas, *Summa Theo-
logica,* Part III, Q 85, A 3.
[3] Acts, represented under the type of its author,
St. Luke, See Colossians, 4. 14.
[4] The Pauline Epistles, typified by their writer,
whose sword is the symbol of war and martyrdom.
[5] The four "humble in appearance" are the repre-
sentatives in their writers of the minor Epistles, and
they are followed by St. John, as the writer of Revela-
tion.
[6] Cf. Canto xxxii. 29.
[7] The seven candlesticks of the first heaven, the
Empyrean.

[8] The lower septentrion, or the seven stars of the
Great or Little Bear.
[9] "Come with me from Lebanon, my spouse." The
Song of Solomon, 4. 8.
[10] See Revelation, 19. 1.
[11] "At the voice of so great an elder."
[12] "Blessed thou that comest," words derived from
Psalms, 118. 26; Cf. Matthew, 21. 9.
[13] "Oh, give lilies with full hands"; words from the
Aeneid, vi, 883.
[14] See *Aeneid,* iv. 23.

which the ancient mother lost avail unto my cheeks, cleansed with dew,[1] that they should not turn dark again with tears.

55. "Dante, though Virgil be gone away, weep not yet, weep not yet, for by another sword thou needst must weep."

58. Like an admiral who, on poop or on prow, comes to see the people that are serving on the other ships, and encourages them to do well, upon the left-hand border of the chariot —when I turned me at the sound of my own name, which of necessity is registered here,— I saw the Lady, who had first appeared to me veiled beneath the angelic festival, directing her eyes toward me across the stream. Although the veil, which descended from her head, circled by the leaf of Minerva, did not allow her to appear distinctly, royally, still severe in her mien, she went on, as one who speaks, and keeps back her warmest words. "Look at me well: I am, indeed, I am, indeed, Beatrice. How hast thou deigned to approach the mountain? Didst thou not know that here man is happy?" My eyes fell down to the clear fount; but seeing myself in it I drew them to the grass, such great shame weighed on my brow. As to her son the mother seems haughty, so she seemed to me; for somewhat bitter tastes the savor of tart pity.

82. She was silent, and the angels sang of a sudden: *In te, Domine, speravi;* but beyond *pedes meos*[2] they did not pass. Even as the snow, among the living rafters upon the back of Italy, is congealed, blown and packed by Sclavonian winds, then melting, trickles through itself, if only the land which loses shadow breathe, so that it seems as fire melting the candle; thus was I without tears and sighs before the song of them who always sing following the notes of the eternal spheres; but when I heard in their sweet melodies their compassion for me, more than if they had said: "Lady, why dost thou so confound him?" the ice that was bound tight around my heart became breath and water, and with anguish issued from my breast, through my mouth and through my eyes.

100. She, still standing motionless on the aforesaid side of the chariot, then turned her words to those pious beings thus: "Ye watch in the eternal day, so that nor night nor slumber robs from you one step the world may make along its ways; wherefore my reply is with greater care, that he who is weeping yonder may understand me, in order that fault and grief may be of one measure. Not only through the working of the great wheels, which direct every seed to some end according as the stars are its companions, but through largess of divine graces, which have for their rain vapors so lofty that our sight goes not near thereto— this man was virtually such in his new life, that every right disposition would have made admirable proof in him. But so much the more malign and wild does the ground become with bad seed and untilled, as it has the more of good earthly vigor.

121. "Some time did I sustain him with my face; showing my youthful eyes to him, I led him with me turned in right direction. So soon as I was on the threshold of my second age, and had changed life, he took himself from me, and gave himself to others. When I had risen from flesh to spirit, and beauty and virtue were increased in me, I was less dear and less pleasing to him; and he turned his steps along a way not true, following false images of good, which pay no promise in full. Nor did it avail me to obtain inspirations with which, both in dream and otherwise, I called him back; so little did he heed them. So low he fell that all means for his salvation were already short, save showing him the lost people. For this I visited the gate of the dead, and to him, who has conducted him up hither, my prayers were borne with weeping. The high decree of God would be broken, if Lethe should be passed, and such viand should be tasted, without some scot of repentance which may pour forth tears."

CANTO XXXI

1. "O THOU, who art on the farther side of the sacred river," turning her speech to me with the point, which only with the edge had seemed to me keen, she began anew, going on without delay, "Say, say, if this is true; to so heavy a charge thine own confession must needs be conjoined." My faculties were so confused that the voice moved, and became extinct

---

[1] See Canto i. 121-129.
[2] See Psalms, 31. 1-8.

before it had been released from its organs. A little while she waited, then said: "What thinkest thou? Reply to me; for the sad memories in thee are not yet injured by the water." Confusion and fear mingled together forced such a "Yes" from out my mouth, that the eyes were needed for the hearing of it.

16. As a cross-bow breaks its cord and its bow when it shoots with too great tension, and the shaft hits the mark with less force, so did I burst under that heavy load, pouring forth tears and sighs, and the voice slackened along its passage. Whereupon she to me: "Within those desires of mine that were leading thee to love the Good beyond which there is nothing to which one may aspire, what trenches running traverse, or what chains didst thou find, for which thou shouldst thus have despoiled thyself of the hope of passing onward? And what satisfactions, or what advantages were displayed on the brow of the others, for which thou shouldst have lingered before them?"

31. After the drawing of a bitter sigh, hardly had I the voice to make answer, and the lips with difficulty gave it form. Weeping, I said: "The present things with their false pleasure turned my steps, soon as your face was hidden." And she: "Hadst thou been silent, or hadst thou denied that which thou dost confess, thy fault would not be less known, by such a Judge is it known. But when the accusation of the sin bursts from one's own mouth, in our court the wheel turns itself back against the edge.

43. "Yet still, that thou mayst now bear shame for thy error, and that another time, hearing the Sirens, thou mayst be stronger, lay aside the sowing of tears,[1] and listen; so shalt thou hear how my buried flesh should have moved thee in opposite direction. Never did nature or art present to thee pleasure such as the fair limbs wherein I was enclosed, and which are scattered in earth. And if the supreme pleasure thus failed thee through my death, what mortal thing should afterward have drawn thee into its desire? Forsooth thou oughtest, at the first arrow of things fallacious, have risen upward after me, who was no longer such. Nor oughtest thou to have weighed thy wings downward to await more blows,

either of some young girl or other vanity of so brief a use. The young bird awaits two or three; but before the eyes of the full-fledged, the net is spread in vain, or the arrow shot."[2]

64. As children, silent in shame, with their eyes upon the ground, stand listening and conscience-stricken and repentant, so was I standing. And she said: "Since thou art grieved through hearing, lift up thy beard, and thou shalt take greater grief from seeing." With less resistance is a sturdy oak uprooted by a native wind, or by one from the land of Iarbas,[3] than I raised my chin at her command; and when by the beard she asked for my eyes, truly I recognized the venom of the argument.

76. And when my face was lifted up, my sight perceived that those primal creatures were resting from their strewing, and my eyes, still little assured, saw Beatrice turned toward the animal that is one person only in two natures. Beneath her veil, and beyond the stream, she seemed to me more to surpass her ancient self, than she seemed to surpass all others here when she was here. So pricked me there the nettle of repentance that of all other things the one which most had turned me to its love became the most my foe.

88. Such self-conviction stung my heart that I fell overcome; and what I then became she knows who afforded me the cause.

91. Then, when my heart restored my outward faculties, I saw above me the lady whom I had found alone, and she was saying: "Hold me, hold me." She had drawn me into the stream up to the throat, and dragging me after her was moving over the water, light as a shuttle. When I was near the blessed shore, I heard "Asperges me"[4] so sweetly that I cannot remember it, far less can write it. The beautiful lady opened her arms, clasped my head, and immersed me where I had perforce to swallow of the water. Then she took me, and presented me, thus bathed, within the dance of the four beautiful ones, and each of them covered me with her arm. "Here we are nymphs, and in heaven we are stars:[5] before Beatrice had de-

---

[1] See Psalms, 126. 5.

[2] See Proverbs, 1. 17.
[3] From the south; the land of Iarbas, the son of Jupiter Ammon, was Libya. See *Aeneid*, iv. 196.
[4] Cf. Psalms, 51. 7.
[5] See Canto, i. 23.

scended to the world we were ordained unto her for her handmaids. We will lead thee to her eyes; but for the joyous light which is within them, the three yonder who look more deeply shall sharpen thine own."

112. Thus singing, they began; and then to the breast of the Griffon they led me with them, where Beatrice was standing turned toward us. They said: "See that thou spare not thy sight: we have placed thee before the emeralds, whence Love of old drew his darts against thee." A thousand desires hotter than flame bound fast my eyes to the reluctent eyes which ever stayed fixed upon the Griffon. Not otherwise than as the sun in a mirror, was the twofold animal gleaming therewithin, now with one, now with the other mode of being.

124. Think, Reader, if I marvelled when I saw the thing stay quiet in itself, and in its image transmuting itself.

127. While, full of awe and glad, my soul was tasting that food which, sating in itself, causes longing for itself, the other three, showing themselves of the loftier order in their bearing, came forward dancing to their angelic carol. "Turn, Beatrice, turn thy holy eyes," was their song, "upon thy faithful one, who to see thee has taken so many steps. Of thy grace do us the grace that thou unveil to him thy mouth, so that he may discern the second beauty which thou dost conceal."[1]

139. O splendor of living light eternal! Who has become so pallid under the shadow of Parnassus, or has so drunk at its cistern, that he would not seem to have his mind encumbered, trying to render thee as thou didst appear there where with its harmony the heaven hangs over thee, when in the open air thou didst thyself disclose?

CANTO XXXII

1. So fixed and intent were my eyes to relieve their ten years' thirst, that my other senses were all extinct: and they themselves, on one side and the other, had a wall of indifference, so did the holy smile draw them to itself with the an-

cient net; when perforce my sight was turned toward my left by those goddesses, because I heard from them a "Too fixedly." And the condition which exists for seeing, in eyes but just now smitten by the sun, caused me to be for a while without sight. But when my vision reshaped itself to the lesser sensation (I say to the lesser, in respect to the great one wherefrom by force I had removed myself), I saw that the glorious army had wheeled upon its right flank, and was returning with the sun and with the seven flames in its face.

19. As under its shields to protect itself a troop turns and wheels with its banner, before it all can change about, that soldiery of the celestial realm which was in advance had wholly gone past us, before its front beam had bent the chariot round. Then to the wheels the ladies returned, and the Griffon moved his blessed burden, in such wise however that no feather of him shook. The beautiful lady who had drawn me at the ford, and Statius and I were following the wheel which made its orbit with the smaller arc. Thus passing through the lofty wood, empty through fault of her who trusted to the serpent, an angelic song set the time to our steps.

34. Perhaps an arrow loosed from the string had traversed in three flights as great a distance as we had advanced, when Beatrice descended. I heard "Adam!" murmured by all:[2] then they encircled a plant despoiled of flowers and of other leafage on every bough. Its tresses, which the wider spread the higher up they are, would be wondered at for height by the Indians in their woods.

43. "Blessed art thou, Griffon, that thou dost not break off with thy beak of this wood sweet to the taste, since the belly is ill racked thereby." Thus around the sturdy tree the others cried; and the animal of two natures: "Thus is preserved the seed of all righteousness."[3] And turning to the pole which he had drawn, he dragged it to the foot of the widowed trunk, and that which was of it[4] he left bound to it.

52. As when the great light falls downward mingled with that which shines behind the ce-

---

[1] "The eyes of Wisdom are her demonstrations by which one sees the truth most surely; and her smile is her persuasions in which the interior light of Wisdom is displayed without any veil; and in these two is felt that loftiest pleasure of Beatitude, which is the chief good in Paradise." Dante, *Convito*, iii. 15.

[2] See 2 Esdras, VII. 48.

[3] See Romans, 5. 19, 21.

[4] The pole, the mystic type of the cross of Christ, which was, according to an old legend, made of the wood of this tree.

lestial Carp,[1] our plants become swollen, and then renew themselves, each in its own color, before the sun yokes his coursers under another star, so, disclosing a color less than of roses and more than of violets, the plant renewed itself, which at first had its boughs so bare.

61. I did not understand, nor here is sung, the hymn which that folk then sang, nor did I bear the melody to the end.

64. If I could portray how the pitiless eyes[2] sank to slumber, while hearing of Syrinx—the eyes to which much watching cost so dear— like a painter who paints from a model I would depict how I fell asleep; but whoso would, let him be one who can represent slumber well. Therefore I pass on to when I awoke, and I say that a splendor rent for me the veil of sleep, and a call: "Arise, what doest thou?"

73. As, to see some of the flowerets of the apple tree[3] which makes the Angels greedy for its fruit, and makes perpetual marriage feasts in Heaven,[4] Peter and John and James were led,[5] and being overcome, came to themselves at the word by which greater slumbers were broken, and saw their band diminished alike by Moses and Elias, and the raiment of their Master changed, so I came to myself, and saw that compassionate one standing above me, who had before been conductress of my steps along the stream; and all in doubt I said: "Where is Beatrice?" And she: "Behold her under the new leafage, sitting upon its root. Behold the company which surrounds her; the rest are going on high behind the Griffon, with sweeter song and more profound."[6]

91. And if her speech was further poured forth I know not, because already in my eyes was she who from attending to aught else had closed me in. She was sitting alone upon the bare ground, like a guard left there of the chariot which I had seen bound by the biform animal. In a circle the seven Nymphs were making of themselves an enclosure for her, with those lights in their hands which are secure from Aquilo and from Auster.

100. "Here shalt thou be short time a forester; and thou shalt be with me without end a citizen of that Rome whereof Christ is a Roman. Therefore for profit of the world which lives ill, keep now thine eyes upon the chariot; and what thou seest, mind that thou write when thou hast returned to earth." Thus Beatrice; and I, who at the feet of her commands was all devout, gave my mind and my eyes where she willed.

109. Never with so swift a motion did fire descend from a dense cloud, when it falls from that region which stretches most remote, as I saw the bird of Jove swoop down through the tree, breaking the bark, as well as the flowers and new leaves; and he struck the chariot with all his force, whereat it reeled, like a ship in a tempest beaten by the waves now to starboard, now to larboard. Then I saw a she fox,[7] which seemed fasting from all good food, leap into the body of the triumphal vehicle; but, rebuking her for her ugly sins, my Lady turned her to such flight as her fleshless bones allowed. Then, from there whence he had first come, I saw the eagle descend down into the ark of the car and leave it feathered from himself. And a voice, such as issues from a heart that is afflicted, issued from Heaven, and thus spoke: "O little bark of mine, how ill art thou laden!"

130. Then it seemed to me that the earth opened between the two wheels, and I saw a dragon issue from it, who fixed his tail upward through the chariot: and, like a wasp that retracts its sting, drawing to himself his malignant tail, he drew out part of the floor, and went wandering away. That which remained covered itself again, as lively soil with grass, with the plumage, offered perhaps with sane and benign intention; and both one and the other wheel and the pole were again covered with it in such time that a sigh holds the mouth open longer. Thus transformed, the holy structure put forth heads upon its parts, three upon the pole, and one on each corner.[8] The first were horned like oxen, but the four

[1] In the spring, when the Sun is in the sign of the Ram, which follows that of the Fishes, here termed the Carp.
[2] The hundred eyes of Argus, who, when watching Io, fell asleep while listening to the tale of the loves of Pan and Syrinx, and was then slain by Mercury.
[3] See The Song of Solomon, 2. 3.
[4] See Revelation, 19. 9.
[5] See Matthew, 17. 1-8.
[6] Christ having ascended, Beatrice, typifying Revelation, is left seated by the chariot, the type of the Church on earth.

[7] The early heresies.
[8] See Revelation, 12. 3.

had a single horn upon the forehead. A like monster was never seen before. Secure, as a fortress on a high mountain, there appeared to me a dishevelled harlot sitting upon it, with bold brows glancing round.[1] And, as if in order that she should not be taken from him, I saw a giant standing at her side, and now and then they kissed each other. But because she turned her lustful and roving eye on me that fierce paramour scourged her from head to foot. Then full of jealousy, and cruel with anger, he loosed the monster, and dragged it through the wood so far, that he made of that alone a shield from me for the harlot and for the strange beast.[2]

CANTO XXXIII

1. *Deus, venerunt gentes,*[3] the ladies began, alternating, now three now four, a sweet psalmody, and weeping; and Beatrice, sighing and pitiful, was listening to them with such aspect that scarce was Mary at the cross more changed. But when the other virgins gave place to her to speak, risen upright upon her feet, she answered, colored like fire: *Modicum, et non videbitis me, et iterum,* my beloved Sisters, *modicum, et vos videbitis me.*[4] Then she set all the seven in front of her; and behind her, by a sign only, she placed me, and the Lady, and the Sage who had remained. Thus she moved on; and I do not think her tenth step had been set upon the ground, when with her eyes she smote mine, and with tranquil aspect said to me: "Come more forward, so that if I speak with thee, thou mayst be well placed for listening to me." So soon as I was with her as I should be, she said to me: "Brother, why dost thou not venture to question me, now thou art coming with me?"

25. As befalls those who with exceeding reverence are speaking in presence of their superiors, that they drag not their voice living to the teeth, it befell me that without perfect utterance I began: "My Lady, you know my need, and that which is good for it." And she to me: "From fear and from shame I wish that thou henceforth disentangle thyself, so that thou mayst speak no more like one who dreams.

34. "Know thou, that the vessel which the serpent broke was, and is not;[5] but let him who has the blame thereof think that the vengeance of God fears not sops.[6] The eagle that left its feathers on the car, whereby it became a monster, and then a prey, shall not be for all time without an heir; for I see surely, and therefore I tell it, stars already close at hand, secure from every obstacle and from every hindrance, to give to us a time in which a Five hundred, Ten, and Five sent by God shall slay the abandoned woman together with that giant who is sinning with her.[7] And perchance my narration, dark like that of Themis and the Sphinx, less persuades thee, because after their fashion it clouds the understanding. But soon the facts will be the Naiades[8] which shall solve this difficult enigma, without harm of flocks or of harvest. Do thou note; and even as these words are uttered by me, so do thou teach them to those alive with that life which is a running unto death; and bear in mind when thou writest them, not to conceal what thou hast seen the plant, which here has now been twice despoiled.[9] Whoever robs or breaks it, with blasphemy of deed offends God, who for His own use alone created it holy. For biting it, the first soul, in pain and in desire, for five thousand years and more, longed for Him who punished on Himself the bite.

64. "Thy wit sleeps, if it deem not that for a special reason it is so lofty and so inverted at

---

[1] See Revelation, 17. 3.
[2] The harlot and the giant stand respectively for the Pope and the king of France. The dragging of the car, transformed into a monster, through the wood, so far as to hide it from the poet, may be taken as typifying the removal of the seat of the Papacy from Rome to Avignon, in 1305.
[3] Cf. Psalms, 79. "O God, the heathen are come . . ."
[4] "A little while and ye shall not see me: and again, a little while and ye shall see me." John, 15. 16.

[5] See Revelation, 17. 8.
[6] According to a belief that, if a murderer could contrive, within nine days of the murder, to eat a sop of bread dipped in wine, above the grave of his victim, he would escape from the vengeance of the murdered man's family.
[7] Beatrice sees near at hand a 515, in Roman numerals a DXV, which letters by transposition form DVX, "a leader," sent by God, who shall reëstablish the Divine order upon earth.
[8] According to a blunder in the manuscripts of Ovid's *Metamorphoses,* vii. 759, the Naiades solved the riddles of the oracles, at which Themis, offended, sent forth a wild beast to ravage the flocks and fields. The correct reading is Laiades, that is, Oedipus, the son of Laius.
[9] See Canto xxxii. 51, 158.

.

its top.[1] And if thy vain thoughts had not been as water of Elsa[2] round about thy mind, and their pleasantness as Pyramus to the mulberry,[3] by so many circumstances alone thou wouldst have recognized morally the justice of God in the interdict upon the tree. But though I see thee in thy understanding made of stone, and thus stony, dark, so that the light of my speech dazzles thee, I yet would have thee bear it hence within thee, even if not written, at least depicted, for the reason that the pilgrim's staff is carried wreathed with palm."

79. And I: "Even as wax, which does not change the figure imprinted by a seal, is my brain now stamped by you. But why do your desired words fly so far above my sight, that the more it strives the more it loses them?" "In order that thou mayst know," she said, "that school which thou hast followed, and mayst see how its doctrine can follow my word; and mayst see that your way is distant so far from the divine, as the heaven which highest hastens on is remote from earth."[4] Whereon I replied to her: "I do not remember that I ever estranged myself from you, nor have I conscience of it that reproaches me." "And if thou canst not remember it," she replied smiling, "now call to mind how this very day thou hast drunk of Lethe; and if from the smoke fire is inferred, this thy forgetfulness clearly proves fault in thy will intent elsewhere. Truly my words shall henceforth be naked so far as it is befitting to uncover them to thy rude sight."

103. And more flashing, and with slower steps, the sun was holding the circle of the meridian, which appears here or there accord-

ing to the point of view, when, as he, who goes in advance of people as a guide, halts if he find some strange thing on his track, the seven ladies halted at the edge of a pale shadow, such as beneath green leaves and black boughs the Alp casts over its cold streams. In front of them, it seemed to me I saw Euphrates and Tigris issue from one fountain, and, like friends, depart slowly from one another.

115. "O light, O glory of the human race, what water is this which here pours forth from one source, and from itself divides itself a-away?" To this prayer answer was made to me: "Pray Matilda that she tell it to thee." And hereupon the beautiful Lady answered, as one who frees himself from blame: "This and other things have been told to him by me; and I am sure that the water of Lethe has not hidden them from him." And Beatrice: "Perhaps a greater care, which oftentimes takes the memory away, has darkened the eyes of his mind. But behold Eunoë,[5] which flows forth yonder, lead him to it, and, as thou art wont, revive his lifeless power." As a gentle soul which makes not excuse, but makes its own will of another's will, soon as by a sign it is outwardly disclosed, even so, when I had been taken by her, the beautiful Lady moved on, and to Statius she said, with manner of a lady, "Come with him."

136. If I had, Reader, longer space for writing, I would in part at least sing of the sweet draught which never would have sated me; but, because all the leaves destined for this second canticle are full, the curb of my art lets me go no farther.

142. I returned from the most holy wave, reanimate, even as new plants renewed with new foliage, pure and disposed to mount unto the stars.

[1] See Canto xxxii. 40-41.
[2] A Tuscan river, whose waters have a petrifying quality.
[3] The blood of Pyramus dyed the mulberry.
[4] See Isaiah, 55. 9.

[5] Eunoë, "the memory of good," which its waters restore to the purified soul. See Canto xxviii. 129-131.

·: PARADISE :·

CANTO I

THE glory of Him who moves everything penetrates through the universe, and is resplendent in one part more and in another less. In the heaven which receives most of His light I have been,[1] and have seen things which he who descends from thereabove neither knows how nor has power to recount; because, drawing near to its own desire,[2] our intellect enters so deep, that the memory cannot follow after. Truly whatever of the Holy Realm I could treasure up in my mind shall now be the theme of my song.

13. O good Apollo, for this last labor make me such a vessel of thy worth as thou demandest for the gift of the beloved laurel. Thus far one summit of Parnassus has been enough for me, but now with both[3] I need to enter the remaining arena. Enter into my breast, and breathe thou in such wise as when thou drewest Marsyas from out the sheath of his limbs. O divine Power, if thou lend thyself to me so that I may make manifest the image of the Blessed Realm imprinted within my head, thou shalt see me come to thy chosen tree, and crown myself then with those leaves of which the theme and thou will make me worthy. So rarely, Father, are they gathered for triumph or of Cæsar or of poet, (fault and shame of human wills,) that the Peneian leaf[4] should bring forth joy unto the joyous Delphic deity, whenever it makes any one to long for it. Great flame follows a little spark: perhaps after me prayer shall be made with better voices, whereto Cyrrha[5] may respond.

38. The lamp of the world rises to mortals through different passages, but from that which joins four circles with three crosses it issues with better course and conjoined with a better star, and it tempers and seals the mundane wax more after its own fashion.[6] Almost such a passage had made morning there and evening here;[7] and there all that hemisphere was white, and the other part black, when I saw Beatrice turned to her left side, and gazing upon the sun: never did eagle so fix himself upon it. And even as a second ray is wont to issue from the first, and mount upward again, like a pilgrim who wishes to return; so from her action, infused through the eyes into my imagination, mine was made, and I fixed my eyes upon the sun beyond our wont. Much is permitted there which here is not permitted to our faculties, by virtue of the place made for the human race as its proper seat. Not long did I endure it, nor so little that I did not see it sparkle round about, like iron that issues boiling from the fire. And on a sudden, day seemed to be added to day, as if He who has the power had adorned the heaven with another sun.

64. Beatrice was standing with her eyes wholly fixed on the eternal wheels, and on her I fixed my eyes from thereabove removed. Looking at her I inwardly became such as Glaucus[8] became on tasting of the grass which made him consort in the sea of the other gods.

---

[1] The Empyrean.

[2] See Aquinas, *Summa Theologica,* Part I-II, Q 3, A 8.

[3] Parnassus was supposed to have two peaks; the Muses dwelt upon one, Apollo upon the other.

[4] Daphne, changed into the laurel, was the daughter of Peneus.

[5] Cyrrha, a city sacred to Apollo, not far from the foot of Parnassus, and here used as synonymous with Delphi, of which it was the port.

[6] At the vernal equinox the sun rises from a point on the horizon where the four great circles, namely, the horizon, the zodiac, the equator, and the equinoctial colure, meet, and, cutting each other, form three crosses. The sun is in the sign of Aries "a better star," because the influence of this constellation was supposed to be benignant.

[7] The last indication of time given in the *Purgatory* is in Canto xxxiii. 104: "the sun was holding the circle of the meridian."

[8] A fisherman changed to a sea-god.

Transhumanizing cannot be signified in words; therefore let the example suffice him for whom grace reserves the experience. If I was only that of me which Thou didst the last create,[1] O Love that governest the heavens, Thou knowest, who with Thy light didst lift me. When the revolution which Thou, being desired, makest eternal,[2] made me attent unto itself with the harmony which Thou dost attune and modulate, so much of the heaven then seemed to me enkindled by the flame of the sun, that rain or river never made so widespread a lake.

82. The novelty of the sound and the great light kindled in me a desire concerning their cause, never before felt with such keenness. Whereon she, who saw me as I see myself, to quiet my perturbed mind opened her mouth, ere I mine to ask, and began: "Thou thyself makest thyself dull with false imagining, so that thou seest not what thou wouldst see, if thou hadst shaken it off. Thou art not on earth, as thou believest; but lightning, flying from its proper site, never ran as thou who art returning thereunto."

94. If I was divested of my first doubt by these brief little smiled-out words, within a new one was I the more enmeshed. And I said: "Already I rested content concerning a great wonder; but now I wonder how I can transcend these light bodies." Whereon she, after a pitying sigh, directed her eyes toward me, with that look which a mother turns on her delirious child, and she began: "All things whatsoever have order among themselves; and this is the form which makes the universe like unto God.[3] Herein the exalted creatures see the imprint of the Eternal Power, which is the end for which the aforesaid rule is made. In the order of which I speak, all natures are disposed, by diverse lots, more or less near to their source;[4] wherefore they are moved to different ports over the great sea of being, and each with the instinct given to it which bears it on. This bears the fire upward toward the moon; this is the motive force in mortal hearts; this binds together and unites the earth. Nor does this bow shoot forth only the created things which are without intelligence, but also those which have understanding and love.

121. "The Providence that ordains all this makes always quiet with its own light the heaven within which that one which has the greatest speed revolves. And thither now, as to a site decreed, the virtue of that bowstring is bearing us on, which directs to a joyful mark whatever it shoots. It is true, that as the form often does not accord with the intention of the art, because the material is deaf to respond, so the creature sometimes deviates from this course; for it has power, though thus impelled, to bend in another direction (even as the fire of a cloud may be seen to fall), if the first impetus, diverted by false pleasure, turn it earthwards. Thou shouldst not, if I deem aright, wonder more at thy ascent, than at a stream if it descends from a high mountain to the base. It would be a marvel in thee, if, deprived of hindrance, thou hadst sat below, even as quiet in living fire on earth would be."

142. Thereon she turned again her face toward heaven.

CANTO II

O YE who in a little bark, desirous to listen, have followed behind my craft which singing passes on, turn to see again your shores; put not out upon the deep; for haply, losing me, ye would remain astray. The water which I take was never crossed. Minerva breathes, and Apollo guides me, and nine Muses point out to me the Bears.

10. Ye other few, who have lifted up your necks betimes for the bread of the Angels, on which one here subsists, but never becomes sated of it, ye may well put forth your vessel over the deep brine, keeping my wake before you on the water which turns smooth again. Those glorious ones who passed over to Colchos wondered not when they saw Jason become a ploughman, as ye shall do.[5]

---

[1] See *Purgatory*, xxv. 67-75; Cf. II Corinthians, 12.3.
[2] "The Empyrean . . . is the cause of the most swift motion of the First Moving Heaven, because of the most ardent desire of every part of the latter to be conjoined with every part of that most divine and quiet heaven." Dante, *Convito*, ii. 4, 19-25.
[3] See Aquinas, *Summa Theologica*, Part I, Q 45, A 3; Q 50, A 1.
[4] *Ibid.*, Part I, Q 45, A 3; Q 49, A 1.
[5] When, to obtain the golden fleece, Jason yoked the two fire-breathing oxen, and ploughed with them, sowing the dragon's teeth in the furrows.

19. The concreate and perpetual thirst for the deiform realm[1] was bearing us on swift almost as ye see the heavens. Beatrice was gazing upward, and I upon her, and perhaps in such time as a quarrel[2] rests, and flies, and from the notch is unlocked, I saw myself arrived where a wonderful thing drew my sight to itself; and therefore she, from whom the working of my mind could not be hid, turning toward me, glad as beautiful, said to me: "Uplift thy grateful mind to God, who has united us with the first star."

31. It seemed to me that a cloud had covered us, lucid, dense, solid, and polished, as if a diamond which the sun had struck. Within itself the eternal pearl had received us, even as water receives a ray of light, remaining undivided. If I was body (and here[3] it is not conceivable how one dimension brooked another, which needs must be if body enter body), the desire ought the more to kindle us to see that Essence, in which is seen how our nature and God were united. There will be seen that which we hold by faith, not demonstrated, but it will be known of itself like the first truth which man believes.

46. I replied: "My Lady, devoutly, to the utmost that I can, do I thank Him who has removed me from the mortal world. But tell me, what are the dusky marks of this body, which there below on earth make people fable about Cain?"[4]

52. She smiled a little, and then she said to me: "If the opinion of mortals errs where the key of sense does not unlock, surely the shafts of wonder ought not to pierce thee now, since thou seest that the reason following the senses has short wings. But tell me what thou thyself thinkest of it." And I: "That which up here appears to us diverse, I believe is caused by bodies rare and dense."

61. And she: "Surely thou shalt see that thy belief is quite submerged in error, if thou listen well to the argument that I shall make

against it. The eighth sphere[5] displays to you many lights, which may be noted of different aspects in quality and quantity. If rarity and density effected all this, one single virtue, more or less or equally distributed, would be in all. Different virtues must needs be fruits of formal principles;[6] and these, all but one, would, in pursuance of thy reasoning, be destroyed. Further, if rarity were the cause of that duskiness about which you ask, this planet would either be thus deficient of its matter in part quite through and through, or else, as a body divides the fat and the lean, so this would interchange the leaves in its volume. If the first were the case, it would be manifest in the eclipses of the sun, by the shining through of the light, as when it is poured upon any other rare body.

82. "This is not so; therefore we must look at the other supposition, and if it happen that I quash this, thy opinion will be proved false. If it be that this rarity does not pass through, there must needs be a limit, beyond which its contrary allows it not to pass farther; and thence the ray from another body is thrown back, just as color returns through a glass which hides lead behind itself. Now thou wilt say that the ray shows itself dimmer there than in the other parts, because it is reflected there from farther back. From this objection experiment, which is wont to be the fountain to the streams of your arts, may deliver thee, if ever thou try it. Thou shalt take three mirrors, and set two of them at an equal distance from thee, and let the other, more remote, meet thine eyes between the first two. Turning toward them, cause a light to be placed behind thy back, which may shine upon the three mirrors, and return to thee reflected from all. Although the more distant image may not reach thee so great in quantity, thou wilt there see how it must needs be of equal brightness with the others.

106. "Now, as beneath the blows of the warm rays that which lies under the snow remains bare both of the former color and the cold, thee, thus remaining in thy intellect, will I inform with light so living that it shall tremble in its aspect to thee.

[1] Cf. Paradise, i. 105.
[2] The bolt for a cross-bow.
[3] See Aquinas, Summa Theologica, Part III, Suppl., Q 85, A 2.
[4] Fancying the dark spaces on the surface of the moon to represent Cain carrying a thorn-bush for the fire of his sacrifice.

[5] The heaven of the fixed stars.
[6] See Aquinas, Summa Theologica, Part I-II, Q 9, A 1.

112. "Within the heaven of the divine peace revolves a body, in whose virtue lies the being of all that it contains. The following heaven, which has so many sights, distributes that being through divers essences distinct from it, and contained by it. The other circles, by various differences, dispose the distinctions which they have within themselves unto their ends and their sowings. These organs of the world thus proceed, as thou now seest, from grade to grade; for they receive from above, and operate below.

124. "Observe me well, how I advance through this place to the truth which thou desirest, so that hereafter thou mayst know to keep the ford alone. The motion and the virtue of the holy spheres must needs be inspired by blessed motors,[1] as the work of the hammer by the smith. And the heaven, which so many lights make beautiful, takes its image from the deep mind which revolves it, and makes thereof a seal. And as the soul within your dust is diffused through different members, and conformed to divers potencies, so does the Intelligence[2] display its goodness multiplied through the stars, itself circling upon its own unity. Divers virtue makes divers alloy with the precious body that it quickens, wherein it is bound, even as life in you. Because of the glad nature whence it flows, the mingled virtue shines through the body, as gladness through the living pupil. From this comes what seems different between light and light, not from density and rarity; this is the formal principle which produces, conformably with its own goodness, the dark and the bright."

CANTO III

THAT sun which first had heated my breast with love had uncovered to me, proving and disproving, the sweet aspect of fair truth; and I, to confess myself corrected and assured, so far as was needful raised my head more erect to speak. But a sight appeared which held me so fast to itself, to look on it, that I did not bethink me of my confession.

10. As through transparent and polished glasses, or through clear and tranquil waters,

not so deep that their bed be lost, the lineaments of our faces return so faintly, that a pearl on a white brow comes not less readily to our eyes, such I saw many faces eager to speak; wherefore I ran into the contrary error to that which kindled love between the man[3] and the fountain. At once, as soon as I was aware of them, supposing them mirrored faces, I turned round my eyes to see of whom they were, and saw nothing; and I turned them forward again, straight into the light of my sweet guide who, with a smile, was glowing in her holy eyes. "Do not wonder that I smile," she said to me, "at thy childish thought, since thy foot does not trust itself yet upon the truth, but turns thee, as it is wont, to emptiness. These which thou seest are real substances,[4] relegated here for failure in their vows. Therefore speak with them, and hear, and believe; for the veracious light which satisfies them does not allow them to turn their feet from itself."

34. And I directed myself to the shade that seemed most eager to speak, and I began, like a man whom an excessive desire confuses: "O well-created spirit, who in the rays of life eternal art tasting the sweetness, which if not tasted is never understood, it will be gracious to me, if thou content me with thy name, and with your lot." Whereon she promptly, and with smiling eyes: "Our charity does not lock its door to a just wish, any more than that which wills that all its court be like itself. In the world I was a virgin Sister, and if thy memory look back well, my being more beautiful will not conceal me from thee; but thou wilt recognize that I am Piccarda,[5] who, placed here with these other blessed ones, am blessed in the slowest sphere. Our affections, which are inflamed only in the pleasure of the Holy Spirit, rejoice in being formed according to His order; and this lot, which appears so far down, is given to us, because our vows were neglected and void in some particular."

58. Whereon I to her: "In your marvellous aspects there shines I know not what divine

---

[1] Angels, which are called Intelligences.
[2] Cf. xxviii. 78.

[3] Narcissus.
[4] See Aquinas, *Summa Theologica*, Part I, Q 3, A 5.
[5] The sister of Corso and Forese Donati; see *Purgatory*, xxiv. 10-15. She was a nun, of the order of St. Clare.

which transmutes you from our former conceptions; therefore I was not swift in remembering;[1] but now that which thou sayest to me assists me, so that to reshape is easier to me. But tell me, ye who are happy here, do ye desire a more exalted place, in order to see more, or to make for yourselves more friends?"

67. With those other shades she first smiled a little, then answered me so glad, that she seemed to burn in the first fire of love: "Brother, virtue of charity quiets our will, and makes us wish only for that which we have, and quickens not our thirst for aught else. If we desired to be more on high, our desires would be discordant with the will of Him who assigns us here, which thou wilt see is not possible in these circles, if to exist in charity is here of necessity, and if thou dost well consider its nature. Nay, it is the essence of this blessed existence to hold itself within the divine will, whereby our wills themselves are made one. So that as we are, from seat to seat throughout this realm, to all the realm is pleasing, as to the King who inwills us with His will; and His will is our peace; it is that sea whereunto everything is moving which It creates and which nature makes."

88. Then was it clear to me, how everywhere in Heaven is Paradise, even if the grace of the Supreme Good does not there rain down in one measure.

91. But as it happens, if one food sates, and for another the appetite still remains, that this is asked for, and thanks returned for that; even thus did I, with act and with word, to learn from her, what was the web wherein she had not drawn the shuttle to the end. "Perfect life and high desert enheaven a lady[2] higher up," she said to me, "according to whose rule, in your world below, there are who vest and veil themselves, in order that, even till death, they may wake and sleep with that Spouse Who accepts every vow which love conforms unto His pleasure. A young girl, I fled from the world to follow her, and in her garb I enclosed myself, and pledged me to the pathway of her Order. Afterward men, more used to ill than

good, dragged me forth from the sweet cloister; and God knows what then my life became.

109. "And this other splendor, which shows itself to thee at my right side, and which is enkindled with all the light of our sphere, understands of herself that which I say of me. She was a Sister; and from her head in like manner the shadow of the sacred veil was taken. But after she too was returned unto the world, against her liking and against good usage, she was never loosed from the veil of the heart. This is the light of the great Constance,[3] who from the second wind of Swabia conceived the third and the last power."

121. Thus she spoke to me, and then began singing "Ave Maria," and singing vanished, as through deep water some heavy thing. My sight, that followed her so far as was possible, after it lost her, turned to the mark of greater desire, and wholly reverted to Beatrice; but she so flashed upon my gaze that at first my sight endured it not: and this made me more slow in questioning.

CANTO IV

BETWEEN two viands, distant and attractive in equal measure, a free man would die of hunger, before he would bring one of them to his teeth. Thus a lamb would stand between two ravenings of fierce wolves, fearing both alike; thus would stand a dog between two does. Wherefore if, urged in equal measure by my doubts, I was silent, I do not blame myself; nor, since it was necessary, do I commend.

10. I was silent, but my desire was depicted on my face, and my questioning with that far more fervent than by distinct speech. Beatrice did what Daniel did,[4] when he lifted Nebuchadnezzar from anger, which had made him unjustly cruel, and she said: "I see well how one and another desire draws thee, so that thy care so binds itself that it breathes not forth. Thou reasonest: 'If the good will endure, by what reckoning does the violence of others lessen for me the measure of desert?' Further, that the souls appear to return to the stars, in accordance with the opinion of Plato, gives

---

[1] Cf. *Hell*, vi. 43-45.
[2] Chiara Sciffi (St. Clare), the friend of St. Francis, who, in 1212, established under his direction a religious order for virgins, of extreme austerity. The order bore her name.

[3] Constance, daughter of Roger II of Sicily; married, in 1186, to the Emperor, Henry VI, the second of the three great Swabian emperors.
[4] Cf. Daniel, 11. 1-45.

thee occasion for doubt.[1] These are the questions that thrust equally upon thy wish; and therefore I will treat first of that which has the most venom.

28. "Of the Seraphim he who is most in God, Moses, Samuel, and whichever John thou wilt take, I say even Mary, have not their seats in another heaven than those spirits who just now appeared to thee, nor have they more or fewer years for their existence; but all make the first circle beautiful, yet have sweet life diversely, through feeling more or less the eternal breath. These showed themselves here, not because this sphere is allotted to them, but to afford sign of the celestial grade which is least exalted. It is needful to speak thus to your wit, since only through objects of sense does it apprehend that which it afterward makes worthy of the intellect. For this the Scripture condescends to your capacity, and attributes feet and hands to God, and means otherwise; and Holy Church represents to you Gabriel and Michael with human aspect, and the other who made Tobias whole again.[2]

49. "That which Timaeus argues of the souls is not like this which is seen here, since it seems that he thinks as he says. He says that the soul returns to its own star, believing it to have been severed thence, when nature gave it for form.[3] But perhaps his opinion is of other guise than his words sound, and may be of a meaning not to be derided. If he means that the honor of their influence and the blame return to these wheels, perhaps his bow hits some truth. This principle, ill understood, formerly turned awry almost the whole world, so that it ran astray in naming Jove, Mercury, and Mars.

64. "The other dubitation which disturbs thee has less venom, for its malice could not lead thee from me elsewhere. That our justice seems unjust in the eyes of mortals is argument of faith,[4] and not of heretical iniquity. But because your intelligence can well penetrate to this truth, I will make thee content, as thou desirest. If it be violence when he who suffers contributes nothing to what forces him,

these souls were not by reason of that excused; for will, unless it wills, is not quenched, but does as nature does in fire, though violence a thousand times may wrest it; because if it bend much or little, it follows the force; and thus did these, when they had power to return to the holy place. If their will had been entire, such as held Lawrence[5] on the gridiron, and made Mucius[6] severe to his own hand, it would have urged them back, so soon as they were loosed, along the road on which they had been dragged; but will so firm is too rare. And by these words, if thou hast gathered them up as thou shouldst, is the argument quashed which would have given thee annoy yet many times.

91. "But now another pass runs traverse before thine eyes, such that by thyself thou wouldst not issue from it ere thou wert weary. I have put it in thy mind for certain, that a soul in bliss cannot lie, since it is always near to the Primal Truth; and then thou mightst hear from Piccarda that Constance retained affection for the veil; so that she seems in this to contradict me. Many a time ere now, brother, has it happened that, in order to escape peril, that which it was not meet to do has been done against one's liking; even as Alcmæon (who, thereto entreated by his father, slew his own mother), not to lose piety, pitiless became.[7] On this point, I wish thee to think that the force mingles itself with the will, and they so act that the offences cannot be excused. Will absolute does not consent to the wrong; but it consents in so far thereto, as it fears, if it draw back, to fall into greater trouble. Therefore when Piccarda says this, she means it of the absolute will; and I of the other: so that we both speak truth together."

115. Such was the rippling of the holy stream which issued from the fount whence every truth flows forth; and such it set at rest one and the other desire.

118. "O beloved of the First Lover, O divine one," said I then, "whose speech overflows me and warms, so that it quickens me more and more, my affection is not so deep that it can suffice to render to you grace for grace, but may He Who sees and can, respond for this.

---

[1] Cf. Plato, *Timaeus*, 41, 42.
[2] See Tobit, 3. 25; 6. 16.
[3] See Aquinas, *Summa Theologica*, Part I, Q 76, A 1.
[4] *Ibid.*, Part III, Q 7, A 3.

[5] St. Lawrence, martyred thus A. D. 258.
[6] See Dante, *Convito*, iv. 5, 107-118.
[7] See *Purgatory*, xii. 49-51.

I clearly see that our intellect is never satisfied unless the Truth illume it, beyond which nothing true extends. In that it reposes, as a wild beast in his lair, so soon as it has reached it: and it can reach it; otherwise every desire would be in vain. Because of this, doubt springs up like a shoot, at the foot of the truth; and it is nature which urges us to the summit from height to height. This invites me, this gives me assurance, Lady, with reverence to question you of another truth which is obscure to me. I wish to know if man can so make satisfaction to you for defective vows with other goods, that in your scales they may not be light?"

139. Beatrice looked at me with eyes so divine, full of the sparks of love, that my power, vanquished, turned its back, and I almost lost myself with eyes cast down.

CANTO V

"IF I flame upon thee in the heat of love, beyond the measure that is seen on earth, so that I vanquish the valor of thine eyes, marvel not, for it proceeds from perfect vision, which, according as it apprehends, so does it move its foot to the apprehended good. I see clearly how already in thy intellect is shining the eternal light,[1] which, only seen, always enkindles love; and if any other thing seduce your love, it is naught but some vestige of that light, ill-recognized, which therein shines through. Thou wishest to know if for an unfulfilled vow so much can be paid with other service as may secure the soul from suit."

16. So Beatrice began this chant, and as one who breaks not off his speech, she thus continued her holy discourse: "The greatest gift which God in His bounty bestowed in creating, and the most conformed to His own goodness, and that which He prizes the most, was the freedom of the will, with which the creatures that have intelligence, they all and they alone, were and are endowed. Now, if thou argue from this, the high worth of the vow will appear to thee, if it be such that God consent when thou consentest; for, in closing the compact between God and man, victim is made of this treasure, such as I say, and made by its own act. What then can be rendered in

[1] See Canto iv. 124-126.

compensation? If thou think to make good use of that which thou hast offered, thou wishest to do good work with ill-gotten gain.

34. "Thou art now assured as to the greater point; but since Holy Church in this grants dispensation, which seems contrary to the truth that I have disclosed to thee, it behoves thee still to sit a little at table, because the tough food which thou hast taken requires still some aid for thy digestion. Open thy mind to that which I reveal to thee, and shut it therewithin; for to have heard without retaining does not make knowledge.

43. "Two things combine in the essence of this sacrifice; the one is that in respect to which it is made, the other is the covenant. This last is never cancelled if not kept; and concerning this was my preceding speech so precise. Therefore it was only imperative on the Hebrews to make offering, while the special thing offered might be changed, as thou shouldst know.[2] The other, which is known to thee as the matter, may indeed be such that there is no fault if it be exchanged for some other matter. But let not any one shift the load upon his shoulder at his own will, without the turning both of the white and of the yellow key.[3] And let him deem every permutation foolish, if the thing laid down be not contained in that which is taken up, as four in six.[4] Therefore, whatever thing weighs so much, through its own worth, that it can drag down every balance, cannot be made good with other spending.

64. "Let not mortals take a vow as a trifle: be faithful, and not awry in so doing, as Jephthah was in his first offering;[5] to whom it rather behoved to say: 'I have done ill,' than, by keeping his vow, to do worse.[6] And thou mayst find the great leader of the Greeks in like manner foolish;[7] wherefore Iphigenia wept for her fair face, and made weep for her both the simple and the wise, who heard tell of such like observance. Be ye, Christians, more grave in moving; be not like a feather to every wind, and think not that every water may wash you.

[2] See Leviticus, 27, in respect to commutation allowed.
[3] See *Purgatory,* ix. 118-126.
[4] Cf. Leviticus, 27.
[5] See Judges. 11. 30-39.
[6] Cf. Shakespeare's *King John,* III. 1.270-73.
[7] See Lucretius, *Nature of Things,* i. 85ff; *Aeneid,* ii. 116ff.

Ye have the Old and the New Testament, and the Shepherd of the Church who guides you; let this suffice you for your salvation. If evil covetousness cry aught else to you, be ye men, and not silly sheep, so that the Jew among you may not laugh at you. Do not ye as the lamb, which leaves its mother's milk, and, simple and wanton, at its own pleasure combats with itself."

85. Thus Beatrice to me, even as I write; then all desireful turned again to that region where the world is most alive. Her silence and her changed look imposed silence on my eager mind, which already had new questions in advance. And as an arrow that hits the mark before the bowstring is quiet, so we ran into the second realm.[1] Here I saw my lady so joyous as she entered into the light of that heaven, that the planet itself became the brighter for it. And if the star was changed and smiled, what did I become, who even by my nature am transmutable in every wise!

100. As in a fishpond, which is still and clear, the fish draw to that which comes in such manner from without that they deem it their food, so I saw full more than a thousand splendors drawing toward us, and in each was heard: "Lo, one who shall increase our loves!" And as each one came to us, the shade was seen full of joy by the bright effulgence that issued from it.

109. Think, Reader, if that which is here begun should not proceed, how thou wouldst have a grievous craving to know more; and by thyself thou wilt see what my desire was to hear from these of their conditions, soon as they became manifest to mine eyes.

115. "O well-born, to whom Grace concedes to see the thrones of the eternal triumph ere the warfare is abandoned, with the light which spreads through the whole heaven we are enkindled, and therefore if thou desirest to enlighten thyself by means of us, sate thyself at thy pleasure." Thus was it said to me by one of those pious spirits; and by Beatrice: "Speak, speak securely, and trust even as to gods."[2] "I see clearly, how thou dost nest thyself in thine own light, and that thou drawest it through

thine eyes, because they sparkle as thou smilest; but I know not who thou art, nor why, O worthy soul, thou hast the grade of the sphere which is veiled to mortals by another's rays."

130. This I said, addressed to the light which first had spoken to me; whereon it became far more lucent than it had been. Even as the sun, which, when the heat has consumed the tempering of the dense vapors, conceals itself by excess of light, so, by reason of more joy, did the holy shape hide itself from me within its own radiance, and thus close enclosed, it answered me in the fashion which the following canto sings.

CANTO VI

"AFTER Constantine turned the Eagle counter to the course of the heavens which it had followed behind the ancient[3] who took to wife Lavinia, a hundred and a hundred years and more the bird of God held itself on the verge of Europe, near to the mountains from which it first came forth, and there it governed the world beneath the shadow of its sacred wings, from hand to hand, and thus changing, descended unto mine. Cæsar I was, and am Justinian, who, by will of the primal Love which I feel, drew out from among the laws the superfluous and the vain. And before I was intent on this work, I believed one nature to be in Christ, not more, and with such faith was I content; but the blessed Agapetus,[4] who was the supreme pastor, directed me to the pure faith with his words. I believed him; and that which was in his faith I now see clearly, even as thou seest that every contradiction is both false and true. Soon as with the Church I moved my feet, it pleased God, through grace, to inspire me with this high task, and I gave myself wholly to it. And I entrusted my arms to my Belisarius, with whom the right hand of Heaven was so conjoined that it was a sign that I should rest me.

28. "Now here to the first question my answer comes to the stop; but its condition constrains me to add a sequel to it, in order that thou mayst see with how much reason he moves against the sacrosanct ensign, who appropriates it to himself, and he too who op-

[1] The Heaven of Mercury.
[2] See Aquinas, *Summa Theologica*, Part III, Q 16,
A 1.
[3] Aeneas.
[4] Agapetus was Pope, 535-536.

poses himself to it.[1] See how great virtue has made it worthy of reverence." And he began from the hour when Pallas[2] died to give it a kingdom.

37. "Thou knowest that it made its abode in Alba for three hundred years and more, till at the end when the three against the three[3] fought for it still. And thou knowest what it did, from the wrong of the Sabine women down to the woe of Lucretia, in seven kings, conquering the neighboring peoples round about. Thou knowest what it did when borne by the illustrious Romans against Brennus, against Pyrrhus, and against the other princes and confederates; whereby Torquatus, and Quinctius who was named from his neglected locks, the Decii and the Fabii acquired the fame which willingly I embalm. It struck to earth the pride of the Arabs,[4] who, following Hannibal, passed the Alpine rocks from which thou, Po, dost glide. Under it, in their youth, Scipio and Pompey triumphed, and to that hill beneath which thou wast born, it seemed bitter.[5]

55. "Afterward, near the time when all Heaven willed to bring the world to its own serene mood, Cæsar, by the will of Rome, took it; and what it did from the Var even to the Rhine, the Isère beheld, and the Saône, and the Seine beheld, and every valley whence the Rhone is filled. That which it did after it came forth from Ravenna, and leaped the Rubicon, was of such flight that neither tongue nor pen could follow it. Toward Spain it wheeled its troop; then toward Durazzo, and smote Pharsalia so that to the warm Nile the pain was felt. It saw again Antandros and the Simois, whence it had set forth, and there where Hector lies;[6] and ill for Ptolemy then it shook itself. Thence it swooped flashing down on Juba; then wheeled again unto your west, where it heard the Pompeian trumpet. Of what it did with its next standard-bearer,[7] Brutus with

Cassius howls in Hell; and it made Modena and Perugia woful. Because of it the sad Cleopatra is still weeping, who, fleeing before it, took from the asp sudden and black death. With him it ran far as the Red Sea shore; with him it set the world in such peace that his temple was locked up on Janus.[8]

82. "But what the ensign which makes me speak had done before, and after was to do, through the mortal realm which is subject to it, becomes in appearance little and obscure, if it be looked on in the hand of the third Cæsar[9] with clear eye and with pure affection; for the Living Justice which inspires me granted to it, in the hand of him of whom I speak, the glory of doing vengeance for Its own wrath. Now marvel here at that which I unfold to thee: afterward with Titus it sped to do vengeance for the vengeance of the ancient sin.[10]

94. "And when the Lombard tooth bit the Holy Church, under its wings Charlemagne, conquering, succored her.

97. "Now canst thou judge of such as those whom I accused above, and of their misdeeds, which are the cause of all your ills. To the public ensign one opposes the yellow lilies, and the other appropriates it to a party, so that it is hard to see which is most at fault. Let the Ghibellines practise, let them practise their art under another ensign, for this one he ever follows ill who parts justice and it. And let not this new Charles[11] strike it down with his Guelfs, but let him fear the talons, which have stripped the fell from a loftier lion. Many a time ere now the sons have wept for the sin of the father; and let him not believe that for his lilies God will change His arms.

112. "This little star is adorned with good spirits who have been active in order that honor and fame may follow them. And when the desires thus deviating mount thitherward, the rays of the true love must needs mount upward less living. But in the equal measure of our wages with our desert is part of our joy, because we see them neither less nor greater. Hereby the Living Justice makes our affection

---

[1] The Ghibelline and the Guelf, respectively.
[2] See *Aeneid*, xii. 940-50.
[3] The Horatii and Curiatii.
[4] In Dante's time the territory of Carthage was held by the Arabs.
[5] According to an old tradition, Fiesole, which lies on a hill overlooking Florence, had been the headquarters of Catiline's army, and was destroyed by the Romans after his defeat and death.
[6] See *Aeneid*, iii. 5.   [7] Augustus.

[8] The doors of the temple of Janus were closed only in time of peace.
[9] Tiberius.
[10] Cf. *Purgatory*, xxi. 82-84.
[11] Charles II, King of Naples, son of Charles of Anjou.

so sweet within us, that it can never be bent aside to any iniquity. Divers voices make sweet melodies; thus in our life divers seats render sweet harmony among these wheels.

127. "And within the present pearl shines the light of Romeo, whose beautiful and great work was ill requited.[1] But the Provençals who wrought against him have not the laugh; and forsooth he goes an ill road who makes harm for himself of another's good deed. Four daughters, and each a queen, had Raymond Berenger, and Romeo, a humble person and a pilgrim, did this for him. And then crooked words moved him to demand a reckoning of this just man, who had rendered to him seven and five for ten. Thereon he departed, poor and old, and if the world but knew the heart he had, while begging his livelihood bit by bit, much as it lauds him it would laud him more."

CANTO VII

"*Osanna sanctus Deus Sabaoth, superillus-trans claritate tua felices ignes horum mala-choth!*"[2]—thus, revolving to its own melody, that substance,[3] upon which a double light is twinned,[4] was seen by me to sing; and it and the others moved in their dance, and like swiftest sparks veiled themselves to me with sudden distance. I was in doubt, and was saying: "Tell her, tell her," within myself, "tell her," I was saying, "my Lady, who slakes my thirst with her sweet distillings"; but that reverence which is wholly mistress of me, only by BE and by ICE, bowed me again like one who drowses.

16. Short while did Beatrice suffer me thus, and she began, irradiating me with a smile such as would make a man in the fire happy: "According to my infallible advisement, how a just vengeance could be justly avenged has set

[1] Romeo, a pilgrim to Rome, came to the court of Raymond Berenger IV, Count of Provence (who died in 1245), and winning the count's favor, served him with such wisdom and fidelity that by his means his master's revenues were greatly increased, and his four daughters married to four kings. The Provençal nobles, jealous of Romeo, procured his dismissal, and he departed, with his mule and his pilgrim's staff and scrip, and was never seen again.
[2] "Hosanna! Holy God of Sabaoth, illuminating from above with thy brightness the blessed fires of these realms."
[3] See Aquinas, *Summa Theologica*, Part I, Q 3, A 5.
[4] See Canto v. 131-137.

thee thinking; but I will quickly loose thy mind: and do thou listen, for my words will make thee the gift of a great doctrine.

25. "By not enduring a curb for his own good upon the power which wills, that man who was not born, damning himself, damned all his offspring; wherefore the human race lay sick down there for many centuries, in great error, until it pleased the Word of God to descend where He, by the sole act of His eternal love, united with Himself in person the nature which had estranged itself from its Maker.

34. "Now turn thy sight to that which now I say: This nature, thus united with its Maker, was pure and good such as it was created; but by itself it had been banished from Paradise, because it turned aside from the way of truth and from its own life. The penalty therefore which the cross afforded, if it be measured by the nature assumed, — none ever so justly stung; and, so, none was ever of such great wrong, if we regard the Person who suffered, in whom this nature was contracted. Therefore from one act issued things diverse; for one death was pleasing to God and to the Jews: at it the earth trembled and the heaven was opened. Henceforth it ought no longer to seem difficult to thee, when it is said that a just vengeance was afterward avenged by a just court.

52. "But I see now thy mind bound up, from thought to thought, within a knot, the loosing of which is awaited with great desire. Thou sayest: 'I discern clearly that which I hear; but why God willed only this mode for our redemption is hidden from me.' This decree, brother, lies buried to the eyes of every one whose wit is not matured in the flame of love. Yet, inasmuch as on this mark there is much gazing, and little is discerned, I will tell why such mode was the most worthy.

64. "The Divine Goodness, which from Itself spurns all envy, burning in Itself so sparkles that It displays the eternal beauties. That which distils immediately from It, thereafter has no end, for when It seals Its imprint can never be removed. That which rains down immediately from It is wholly free, because it is not subject to the power of the new things. It is the most conformed to It, and therefore pleases It the most; for the Holy Ardor which

irradiates everything is most living in what is most like Itself.

76. "With all these things[1] the human creature is advantaged, and if one fail, he needs must fall from his nobility. Sin alone is that which disfranchises him, and makes him unlike the Supreme Good, so that he is little illumined by Its light; and to his dignity he never returns, unless, where fault empties, he fill up with just penalties against evil delight. Your nature, when it sinned totally in its seed, was removed from these dignities, even as from Paradise; nor could it recover them, if thou considerest full subtly, by any way, without passing by one of these fords: either that God, solely by His courtesy, should have remitted; or that man by himself should have made satisfaction for his folly.[2]

94. "Fix now thine eye within the abyss of the eternal counsel, as closely fastened on my words as thou art able. Man within his own limits could never make satisfaction, through not being able to descend in humility, by subsequent obedience, so far as in his disobedience he had intended to ascend; and this is the reason why man was shut off from power to make satisfaction by himself. Therefore it was needful for God with His own ways[3] to restore man to his perfect life—I mean with one way, or else with both. But because the deed of the doer is so much the more prized, the more it displays of the goodness of the heart whence it issues, the Divine Goodness which sets its impress on the world was content to proceed by all Its ways to lift you up again; nor between the last night and the first day has there been or will there be so exalted and so magnificent a procedure either by the one way or by the other. For God was more bounteous in giving Himself to make man sufficient to uplift himself, than if He only of Himself had remitted; and all the other modes were scanty in respect to justice, if the Son of God had not humbled Himself to become incarnate.

121. "Now to fulfil for thee every desire, I return to a certain place to make it clear, in order that there thou mayst see as I do. Thou sayest:

'I see the water, I see the fire, the air, and the earth, and all their mixtures come to corruption, and endure short while, and yet these things were created things'; so that, if what I have said[4] has been true, they ought to be secure against corruption. The Angels, brother, and the pure country in which thou art, may be called created, just as they are, in their entire being; but the elements which thou hast named, and those things which are made of them, are informed by a created virtue. The matter of which they consist was created; the informing virtue in these stars which go round about them was created. The ray and the motion of the holy lights draw out from its potentiate elements the soul of every brute and of the plants; but the Supreme Benignity inspires your life without intermediary, and enamors it of Itself so that ever after it desires It. And hence thou further canst infer your resurrection, if thou reflect how the human flesh was made when the first parents were both made."

CANTO VIII

THE world in its peril was wont to believe that the beautiful Cyprian[5] revolving in the third epicycle rayed out mad love; wherefore the ancient people in their ancient error not only unto her did honor with sacrifice and with votive cry, but they honored Dione also and Cupid, the one as her mother, the other as her son, and they said that he had sat in Dido's lap;[6] and from her, from whom I take my beginning, they took the name of the star which the sun woos, now behind her now before. I was not aware of the ascent to it; but of being in it, my Lady gave me full assurance, whom I saw become more beautiful.

16. And as a spark is seen within a flame, and as within a voice a voice is distinguished when one is steady and the other goes and returns, I saw within that light other lamps moving in a circle, speeding more or less, according to the measure, I believe, of their eternal vision. From a cold cloud winds, whether visible or not,[7] never descended so swiftly, that they would not seem impeded and slow to him who had seen these divine lights coming to us, leav-

---

[1] Cf. Canto v. 19-24.
[2] See Ecclesiastes, 7. 25.
[3] See Psalms, 25. 10. Cf. Aquinas, *Summa Theologica*, Part I, Q 21, A 2.

[4] See line 67, *supra*.
[5] Venus, who was born in Cyprus.
[6] See *Aeneid*, i. 657ff., 715ff.
[7] Cf. Aristotle, *Meteorology*, iii. 1.

ing the circling begun first in the exalted Sera-
phim. And within those who appeared most
in front was sounding *Hosanna,* in such
wise that never since have I been without de-
sire of hearing it again.

31. Then one drew nearer to us, and alone
began: "We all are ready at thy pleasure, that
thou mayst have joy of us. With one circle,
with one circling, and with one thirst, we re-
volve with the celestial Princes, to whom thou
in the world once didst say: *Ye whose intelli-
gence moves the third heaven;*[1] and we are so
full of love that, in order to please thee, a little
quiet will not be less sweet to us."

40. After my eyes had offered themselves
reverently to my Lady, and she had made them
of herself contented and assured, they turned
again to the light which had promised so
much; and: "Say who ye are," was my utter-
ance, imprinted with great affection. Ah! how
much greater in quantity and quality did I see
it become, through the new gladness which
was added to its gladnesses when I spoke!

49. Thus become, it said to me:[2] "The world
held me below but short while; and had it been
longer much evil had not been which will be-
fall.[3] My joy, which rays around me, holds me
concealed from thee, and hides me like a crea-
ture swathed in its own silk. Much didst thou
love me, and hadst good reason why; for had I
stayed below I had shown thee of my love
more than the leaves. That left bank which is
bathed by the Rhone, after it has mingled with
the Sorgue, awaited me in due time for its
lord;[4] as well as that horn of Ausonia[5] which
has for suburbs Bari, and Gaeta, and Catona,[6]
from where the Tronto and the Verde disgorge

into the sea. Already was shining on my brow
the crown of that land which the Danube wa-
ters after it abandons its German banks;[7] and
the fair Trinacria[8] (which between Pachynus
and Pelorus, on the gulf which receives great-
est annoy from Eurus, is darkened, not by
Typhœus but by nascent sulphur) would be
still awaiting its kings sprung through me
from Charles and Rudolph,[9] if evil rule,
which always embitters the subject people, had
not moved Palermo to shout: 'Die! Die!'[10]

76. "And if my brother had forenoted this,[11]
he would ere now be flying from the greedy
poverty of Catalonia, in order that it might not
do him harm: for truly it is needful for him
or for some other to provide, so that on his
laden bark more load be not put. His own na-
ture, which descended niggardly from a liberal
one, would have need of such a soldiery as
should not care for putting into a chest."

85. "Because I believe that the deep joy
which thy speech, my lord, infuses in me, is
seen by thee there where every good has end
and has beginning, even as I see it, it is the
more grateful to me; and this also I hold dear,
that thou discernest it, gazing upon God. Thou
hast made me glad; and so now do thou make
clear to me (since in speaking thou has moved
me to doubt) how from sweet seed can issue
bitterness."

[1] The first verse of the first canzone of Dante's
Convito.
[2] It is Charles Martel, eldest son of Charles II of
Naples, who speaks. He died in 1295, predeceasing his
father.
[3] On the death of Charles II in 1309, the kingdom of
Naples, to which Martel would have succeeded, was
secured by his brother Robert, who brought many ills
upon the country. See lines 76-84, *infra.*
[4] Charles of Anjou, grandfather of Charles Martel,
had received a part of Provence as dowry of his wife
Beatrice, the youngest daughter of Raymond Berenger.
Cf. Canto vi. 133-136.
[5] Italy.
[6] Bari on the Adriatic, Gaeta on the Mediterranean,
and Catona at the toe of Italy, together with the two
rivers named, give roughly the boundaries of the king-
dom of Naples.
[7] The mother of Charles Martel was sister of Ladis-
laus IV, king of Hungary. He died without offspring,
and Charles II claimed the kingdom by right of his
wife.
[8] Sicily; the gulf darkened by sulphurous fumes is
the Bay of Calabria, which, lying between Cape
Pachynus, the extreme southeastern point of the island,
and Cape Pelorus, the extreme northeastern, is ex-
posed to the full violence of Eurus, or the east wind.
Clouds of smoke from Ætna sometimes darken it. The
eruptions of Ætna were ascribed by Ovid to the strug-
gles of Typhœus, one of the Giants who make war
upon the Gods, and who, being overthrown by Zeus,
was buried under Mount Ætna.
[9] From his father, Charles II, or his grandfather,
Charles of Anjou, and from the Emperor Rudolph of
Hapsburg, his wife's father.
[10] By the insurrection which began at Palermo in
1282—the famous Sicilian Vespers—the French were
driven from the island, and the rule over it of Charles
of Anjou was brought to an end. The sovereignty was
conferred by the people on Peter III of Aragon, the
husband of the daughter of Manfred, the illegitimate
son of the Emperor Frederick II.
[11] Robert, the third son of Charles II. He had been
kept as a hostage in Catalonia from 1288 to 1295, and
when he became king of Naples in 1309 he introduced
into his service many Catalonian officials.

94. This I to him; and he to me: "If I can make one truth plain to thee, thou wilt hold thy face toward that which thou askest, as thou dost now hold thy back. The Good which revolves and contents all the realm that thou art ascending, makes its foresight to be a power in these great bodies. And not only are the natures foreseen in the Mind which by itself is perfect, but they together with their well-being. Wherefore whatsoever this bow shoots falls disposed to its foreseen end, even as a thing directed to its aim. Were this not so, the heaven through which thou art journeying would produce its effects in such wise that they would not be works of art but ruins; and that cannot be, if the Intelligences which move these stars are not defective, and defective the Prime Intelligence in that it did not make them perfect. Dost thou wish that this truth be made still clearer to thee?"

113. And I: "No, truly; because I see it to be impossible that Nature should weary in that which is needful." Whereupon he again: "Now, say, would it be worse for man on earth if he were not a citizen?" "Yes," answered I, "and here I ask not the reason." "And can he be so, unless he live there below diversely for diverse duties? No; if your master[2] writes well of this." Thus he came deducing far as here; then he concluded: "Therefore the roots of your works must needs be diverse; on which account one is born Solon, and another Xerxes, another Melchisedech, and another he who, flying through the air, lost his son.[3] The circular nature, which is the seal of the mortal wax, performs its art well, but does not distinguish one inn from another. Hence it happens that Esau differs in seed from Jacob, and Quirinus comes from so mean a father that he is ascribed to Mars. A begotten nature would always make its course like its begetters, if the divine foresight did not overcome.

136. "Now that which was behind thee is before thee, but that thou mayst know that I have joy in thee, I will that thou cloak thyself with a corollary. Ever does a nature, if it find fortune discordant with itself, like every other seed out of its region, come to ill result. And

if the world there below would fix attention on the foundation which Nature lays, following that, it would have its people good. But ye wrest to religion one who shall have been born to gird on the sword, and ye make a king of one who is for preaching; so that your track is outside of the road."

CANTO IX

AFTER thy Charles, O beautiful Clemence,[4] had enlightened me, he told me of the frauds which his seed must experience;[5] but he said: "Keep silence, and let the years revolve"; so that I can say nothing, except that just lamentation shall follow on your wrongs.

7. And now the life of that holy light had turned again unto the Sun which fills it, as that Good which suffices for every thing. Ah, souls deceived, and creatures impious, who from such Good turn away your hearts, directing your foreheads unto vanity!

13. And lo! another of those splendors made towards me, and by brightening outwardly was signifying its will to please me. The eyes of Beatrice, which were fixed upon me, as before,[6] made me assured of dear assent to my desire. "Pray, blessed spirit," I said, "afford speedy satisfaction to my wish, and give me proof that what I think I can reflect on thee." Whereon the light which was still new to me, from out its depth, wherein before[7] it was singing, proceeded, as one whom doing good delights:

25. "In that part[8] of the wicked Italian land which lies between Rialto and the founts of the Brenta and the Piave, rises a hill,[9] and mounts not very high, wherefrom a torch descended which made a great assault upon that district. From one root both I and it were born; I was called Cunizza; and I am refulgent here because the light of this star overcame me. But gladly do I grant myself indulgence for the oc-

[1] Cf. Aristotle, *Politics*, i. 1, 2; iii. 9; vii. 8.
[2] Aristotle.
[3] Daedalus and Icarus.

[4] The widow of Charles Martel.
[5] Frauds by which his son Caroberto was deprived of his rights of succession to the throne of Naples.
[6] See Canto viii. 42.
[7] See Canto viii. 28-30.
[8] The March of Treviso, lying between Venice (Rialto) and the Alps.
[9] The hill on which stood the little stronghold of Romano, the birthplace of the tyrant Azzolino. See *Hell*, xii. 109. Cunizza was his sister.

casion of my lot, and it does not trouble me; which perhaps would seem a hard saying to your vulgar. Of this resplendent and precious jewel of our kingdom,[1] which is nearest to me, great fame has remained, and ere it die away this hundredth year shall yet come round five times. See if man ought to make himself excellent, so that the first life may leave another! And this the present crowd, which the Tagliamento and the Adige shut in, considers not; nor yet, though it be scourged, does it repent. But it will soon come to pass that because her people are stubborn against duty,[2] Padua at the marsh will change the water which bathes Vicenza. And where the Sile and the Cagnano unite, one lords it, and goes with his head high, for catching whom the web is already made.[3] Feltro will yet weep the crime of its impious shepherd, which will be so shameful, that, for a like, none ever entered Malta.[4] Too large would be the vat which should receive the Ferrarese blood, and weary he who should weigh it ounce by ounce, which this courteous priest will give to show himself of his party; and such gifts will be conformed to the living of the country. Above are mirrors, ye call them Thrones, wherefrom God in judgment shines on us, so that these words seem good to us." Here she was silent, and had to me the semblance of being turned elsewhither by the wheel in which she set herself as she was before.[5]

67. The other joy, which was already known to me as an illustrious thing, became to my sight like a fine ruby whereon the sun should strike. Through joy effulgence is gained there on high, even as a smile here; but below the shade darkens outwardly, as the mind is sad.

73. "God sees everything, and thy vision, blessed spirit, is in Him," said I, "so that no wish can steal itself away from thee. Thy

voice, then, which forever charms the heavens, together with the song of those devout fires which make a cowl for themselves with their six wings,[6] why does it not satisfy my desires? Surely I should not wait for thy request if I intheed myself, as thou thyself in-meest."

82. "The greatest valley in which the water spreads,"[7] began then his words, "except of that sea which garlands the earth, extends between its discordant shores so far counter to the sun, that it makes a meridian where first it is wont to make the horizon. I was a dweller on the shore of that valley, between the Ebro and the Macra,[8] which, with short course, divides the Genoese from the Tuscan. With almost the same sunset and the same sunrise sit Buggea and the city whence I was, which once made its harbor warm with its own blood.[9] That people to whom my name was known called me Folco, and this heaven is imprinted by me, as I was by it. For the daughter of Belus,[10] wronging both Sichaeus and Creüsa, burned not more than I, so long as it befitted my locks; nor she of Rhodope who was deluded by Demophoön;[11] nor Alcides when he had enclosed Iole in his heart.[12] Yet here we repent not, but smile; not for the fault, which does not return to the memory, but for the Power which ordained and foresaw. Here we gaze on the art which adorns so great a work, and we discern the good whereby the world below turns to that above.

109. "But in order that thou mayst bear away all fulfilled thy wishes which have been born in this sphere, I must needs proceed still further. Thou wouldst know who is in this light, which beside me here so sparkles, as a sunbeam on clear water. Now know that there-

---

[1] Folco, or Folquet, of Marseilles, once a dissolute troubadour, then bishop of Toulouse.

[2] The Paduan Guelfs were defeated more than once, near Vicenza, by Can Grande, the Imperial Vicar, staining with their blood the waters of the marsh.

[3] At Treviso, whose lord, Riccardo da Camino, was assassinated in 1312.

[4] An act of treachery in 1314 on the part of Alessandro Novello, Bishop and Lord of Feltre, in delivering up certain Ghibelline refugees from Ferrara. Some of them were beheaded; others hanged. Malta was a prison.

[5] See Canto viii. 19-21; 34-35.

[6] See Isaiah, 6. 2.

[7] The Mediterranean.

[8] Between the Ebro in Spain and the Macra in Italy lies Marseilles, under almost the same meridian as Buggea (now Bougie), on the African coast.

[9] When the fleet of Cæsar defeated that of Pompey with its contingent from Marseilles, 49 B. C.

[10] Dido. See Aeneid, iv. 2, 68, 101.

[11] Phyllis, daughter of the king of Thrace, hanged herself, believing herself deserted by Demophoön, the son of Theseus. Rhodope was a chain of mountains between Thrace and Macedonia.

[12] Iole was the daughter of a king of Thessaly, and the love of Hercules (Alcides) for her so excited the jealousy of his wife Dejaneira that she brought about his death.

within Rahab[1] is at rest, and being joined with our order it is sealed by her in the supreme degree. By this heaven, in which the shadow that your world makes comes to a point, she was taken up before any other soul of the triumph of Christ. It was well befitting to leave her in some heaven, as a palm of the high victory which was acquired with one palm and the other, because she favored the first glory of Joshua in the Holy Land,[2] which little touches the memory of the Pope.[3]

127. "Thy city, which was planted by him who first turned his back on his Maker, and whose envy has been so bewept,[4] produces and scatters the accursed flower[5] which has caused the sheep and the lambs to stray, because it has made a wolf of the shepherd. For this the Gospel and the great Doctors are deserted, and there is study only of the Decretals, as is apparent by their margins. On this the Pope and the Cardinals are intent; their thoughts go not to Nazareth, there where Gabriel spread his wings. But the Vatican, and the other chosen parts of Rome, which have been the burial place for the soldiery that followed Peter, shall soon be free from this adultery."[6]

CANTO X

LOOKING upon His Son with the Love which the one and the other eternally breathe forth, the primal and ineffable Power made everything which revolves through the mind or through space with such order that he who contemplates it cannot be without taste of Him.

7. Lift then thy sight, Reader, with me to the lofty wheels, straight to that region where the one motion strikes on the other;[7] and there begin to gaze with delight on the art of that Master who within Himself so loves it that His eye never departs from it. See how from that point the oblique circle which bears the planets branches off, to satisfy the world which calls on them; and if their road were not bent, much virtue in the heavens would be in vain, and well-nigh every potency dead here below; and if its departure were more or less distant from the straight line, much of the order of the world, both below and above, would be defective.

22. Now remain, Reader, upon thy bench, pursuing in thought that which is foretasted if thou wouldst be glad far sooner than weary. I have set before thee; henceforth feed thou thyself, for that theme whereof I have been made the scribe wrests all my care unto itself.

28. The greatest minister of nature, which imprints the world with the worth of the heavens, and with his light measures the time for us, conjoined with that region which is mentioned above, was circling through the spirals in which from day to day he earlier presents himself. And I was with him; but of the ascent I was not aware, otherwise than is a man, before his first thought, aware of its coming. It is Beatrice who thus conducts from good to better, so instantaneously that her act does not extend through time.

40. How lucent in itself must that have been which was apparent not by color but by light within the sun where I had entered! Though I should call on genius, art, and use, I could not tell it so that it could ever be imagined; but one may believe it, and let him long to see it. And if our fancies are low for such loftiness, it is no marvel, for beyond the sun there was never eye could go. Such was here the fourth family of the exalted Father, who always satisfies it, showing how He breathes forth, and how He begets. And Beatrice began: "Give thanks, give thanks to the Sun of the Angels, who to this visible one has raised thee by His grace."

55. Heart of mortal was never so disposed to devotion, and so ready, with its whole will, to render itself up to God, as I became at those words; and all my love was so set on Him that it eclipsed Beatrice in oblivion. It did not displease her; but she so smiled thereat that the splendor of her smiling eyes divided upon many things my mind intent on one.

64. I saw many living and surpassing efful-

---

[1] See Hebrews, 11. 31. Cf. Joshua, 2. 1-21; 6. 17; James, 2. 25.

[2] See Joshua, 2. 6.

[3] Boniface VIII, Cf. *Hell,* xxvii. 85-87.

[4] See Wisdom of Solomon, 2. 24.

[5] The lily on the florin.

[6] By the removal in 1305 of the papal court to Avignon.

[7] At the equinox, the sun in Aries is at the intersection of the ecliptic and the equator of the celestial sphere, and his apparent movement, in his annual revolution in the zodiac, cuts his apparent diurnal motion, which is parallel to the equator.

gences make of us a centre, and make of themselves a crown; more sweet in voice than shining in aspect. Thus girt we sometimes see the daughter of Latona, when the air is so impregnate that it holds the thread which makes her zone.[1] In the court of Heaven, wherefrom I return, are found many jewels so precious and beautiful that they cannot be brought from the kingdom, and of these was the song of those lights. Let him who does not wing himself so that he may fly up thither, await tidings thence from the dumb.

76. After those blazing suns, thus singing, had circled three times round about us, like stars near to the fixed poles, they seemed to me as ladies not released from a dance, but who stop silent, listening till they have caught the new notes.

82. And within one I heard begin: "Since the ray of grace, by which true love is kindled, and which then in loving grows multiplied, so shines on thee that it conducts thee upward by that stair which, without reascending, no one descends,[2] he who should deny to thee the wine of his flask for thy thirst, would not be more at liberty than water which descends not to the sea. Thou wishest to know with what plants this garland is enflowered, which, round about her, gazes with delight upon the beautiful Lady who strengthens thee for heaven. I was of the lambs of the holy flock which Dominic leads along the way where they fatten well if they do not stray. This one who is nearest to me on the right was my brother and master; and he was Albert of Cologne,[3] and I Thomas of Aquino.

100. "If thus of all the rest thou wouldst be informed, come, following my speech, with thy sight circling around upon the blessed wreath. That next flaming issues from the smile of Gratian, who so aided one court and the other that it pleases in Paradise.[4] The next, who at his side adorns our choir, was that Peter who, like the poor woman, offered his treasure to Holy Church.[5] The fifth light, which is most

beautiful among us,[6] breathes from such love that all the world there below is greedy to know tidings of it: within it is the lofty mind wherein wisdom so profound was put, that, if the truth be true, to see so much no second has arisen.[7] At its side behold the light of that candle which, below in the flesh, saw most inwardly the angelic nature, and its ministry.[8] In the next little light smiles that advocate of the Christian times, with whose discourse Augustine provided himself.[9]

121. "Now if thou leadest the eye of the mind, following my praises, from light to light, thou stayest already thirsting for the eighth. Therewithin, through seeing every good, the holy soul rejoices which makes the fallacious world manifest to him who hearkens to it well.[10] The body whence it was chased out lies below in Cieldauro,[11] and from martyrdom and from exile it came to this peace. Beyond, see flaming the glowing breath of Isidore, of Bede, and of Richard who in contemplation was more than man.[12] This one from whom thy look returns to me is the light of a spirit to whom, in his grave thoughts, it seemed that death came slow. It is the eternal light of Siger,[13] who, reading in the Street of Straw, syllogized invidious truths."

139. Then, as a horologe which calls us at the hour when the Bride of God rises to sing

---

known for his compilation of extracts from the works of the Fathers relating to the chief doctrines of the Church: the *Sententiarum libri IV.* In the proem he says that he desired, "like the poor widow" (Luke, 21. 1-4), "to cast something from his penury into the treasury of the Lord."

[6] Solomon.

[7] See I Kings 3. 12.

[8] Dionysius the Areopagite, the disciple of St. Paul (Acts, 17. 34), to whom was ascribed a book of great repute, written probably in the fifth or sixth century, *On the Celestial Hierarchy.*

[9] Paulus Orosius, who lived in the fourth and fifth centuries, and wrote, at the request of St. Augustine, his *History against the Pagans.*

[10] Boethius, statesman and philosopher; his work, *De Consolatione philosophiae,* was held in high esteem by Dante.

[11] Boethius, put to death in Pavia, in 525, was buried in the church of S. Pietro in Cielo d' Oro—St. Peter's of the Golden Ceiling.

[12] Isidore, bishop of Seville, died 636; the Venerable Bede, died 735; Richard, prior of the Monastery of St. Victor, at Paris, a mystic of the twelfth century; all eminent theologians.

[13] Siger of Brabant, who in the last half of the thirteenth century, as doctor in the University of Paris, gave instruction in the Rue du Fouarre.

[1] When the air is so full of vapor that it forms a halo.

[2] Cf. *Purgatory,* ii. 91, 92.

[3] Albertus Magnus, styled *Doctor universalis.*

[4] Gratian, an Italian Benedictine monk of the twelfth century, compiled the *Decretum Gratiani,* composed of texts designed to establish the agreement of the civil and canon law.

[5] Peter Lombard, a theologian of the twelfth century,

matins to her Bridegroom that he may love
her, in which the one part draws and urges the
other, sounding *ting! ting!* with such sweet
note that the well-disposed spirit swells with
love, so did I see the glorious wheel move, and
render voice to voice in concord and in sweet-
ness which cannot be known save there where
joy is everlasting.

CANTO XI

O INSENSATE care of mortals! how defective
are those syllogisms which make thee down-
ward beat thy wings! One was going after the
laws, and one after the aphorisms,[1] and one fol-
lowing the priesthood, and one to reign by
force or by sophisms, and one to rob, and one
to civic business, one, involved in pleasure of
the flesh, was wearying himself, and one was
giving himself to idleness, when I, loosed from
all these things, with Beatrice, up in Heaven
was thus gloriously received.

13. After each had returned to that point of
the circle at which it was at first, it stayed still,
as a candle in a candlestick. And within that
light which first had spoken to me I heard, as
making itself more clear, it smiling began:
"Even as I am resplendent with its radiance,
so, looking into the Eternal Light, I apprehend
whence is the occasion of thy thoughts. Thou
art perplexed, and hast the wish that my speech
be explained in language so open and so full
that it may be level to thy sense, where I said
just now: 'Where they fatten well,'[2] and there
where I said: 'No second has been born';[3] and
here is need that one distinguish well.

28. "The Providence which governs the
world with that counsel, in which every cre-
ated vision is vanquished ere it reach its depth,
in order that the Bride of Him, who with loud
cries[4] espoused her with His blessed blood,
might go toward her beloved, secure in herself
and also more faithful to Him, ordained two
princes in her favor, who on this side and that
should be to her for guides. The one was all
seraphic in ardor,[5] the other, through wisdom,
was on earth a splendor of cherubic light.[6] I

will speak of one, because in praising one,
whichever be taken, both are spoken of, for to
one end were their works.

43. "Between the Tupino and the water[7]
which descends from the hill chosen by the
blessed Ubald, hangs the fertile slope of a high
mountain, wherefrom Perugia at Porta Sole[8]
feels cold and heat, while behind it Nocera and
Gualdo weep because of their heavy yoke.[9]
From this slope, where it most breaks its steep-
ness, a Sun rose upon the world, as this one
sometimes does from the Ganges. Wherefore
let him who talks of this place not say Ascesi,[10]
which were to speak short, but Orient,[11] if he
would speak properly. He was not yet very far
from his rising when he began to make the
earth feel some comfort from his great virtue;
for, while still a youth, he ran into strife with
his father for sake of a lady[12] such as to whom,
as unto death, no one unlocks the gate of pleas-
ure; and before his spiritual court *et coram
patre*[13] he was united to her; and thereafter
from day to day he loved her more ardently.
She, deprived of her first husband,[14] for eleven
hundred years and more, despised and obscure,
even till him had remained unwooed; nor had
it availed to hear, that he, who caused fear to
all the world, found her undisturbed with
Amyclas at the sound of his voice;[15] nor had it
availed to have been constant and undaunted,
so that, where Mary remained below, she
mounted on the cross with Christ.

73. But that I may not proceed too obscurely,
henceforth in my diffuse speech take Francis
and Poverty for these lovers. Their concord
and their glad semblances made love, and won-
der, and sweet regard to be the cause of holy
thoughts; so that the venerable Bernard first

---

[1] Of Hippocrates.
[2] See Canto x. 96.
[3] Cf. Canto x. 114.
[4] See Matthew, 27. 46, 50.
[5] St. Francis of Assisi.
[6] St. Dominic.

[7] The Chiassi, which flows from the hill near Gub-
bio chosen for his hermitage by St. Ubald.
[8] The gate of Perugia, which fronts Monte Subasio,
on which Assisi lies.
[9] Little towns, southeast of Assisi, held in subjection
by Perugia.
[10] So the name of Assisi was sometimes spelled, and
here with a play on *ascesi* "I rose."
[11] As the place where this new Sun of righteousness
arose.
[12] Poverty.
[13] "In presence of his father."
[14] Christ.
[15] When Cæsar knocked at the door of Amyclas, his
voice caused no alarm, because Poverty made the
fisherman secure.

bared his feet,[1] and ran following such great peace, and, running, it seemed to him that he was slow. O unknown riches! O fertile good! Egidius bares his feet and Sylvester bares his feet,[2] following the bridegroom; so pleasing is the bride. Then that father and that master goes on his way with his lady, and with that family which the humble cord was now girding. Nor did baseness of heart weigh down his brow for being the son of Pietro Bernardone, nor for appearing marvellously despised; but royally he opened his hard intention to Innocent, and from him received the first seal for his Order.[3]

94. "After the poor folk had increased behind him, whose marvellous life would be better sung in the glory of the heavens, the holy purpose of this archimandrite was adorned with a second crown by the Eternal Spirit, through Honorius.[4] And after that, through thirst for martyrdom, he had preached Christ and the others who followed him, in the proud presence of the Sultan,[5] and because he found the people too unripe for conversion, and in order not to stay in vain, had returned to the fruit of the Italian herbage, on the harsh rock,[6] between the Tiber and the Arno, he received from Christ the last seal,[7] which his limbs bore for two years. When it pleased Him, Who had allotted him to such great good, to draw him up to the reward which he had gained in making himself lowly,[8] he commended his most dear lady to his brethren as to rightful heirs, and commanded them to love her faithfully; and from her bosom his illustrious soul willed to depart, returning to its realm, and for his body he willed no other bier.

118. "Think now what he was, who was a worthy colleague to keep the bark of Peter on the deep sea to its right aim! And this was our Patriarch:[9] wherefore thou canst see that whoever follows him as he commands loads good merchandise. But his flock has become so greedy of strange food that it cannot but be scattered over diverse meadows; and the farther his sheep, remote and vagabond, go from him, the more empty of milk do they return to the fold. Some of them indeed there are who fear the harm, and keep close to the shepherd; but they are so few that little cloth furnishes their cowls. Now if my words are not faint, if thy hearing has been attentive, if thou recallest to mind that which I have said, thy wish will be content in part, because thou wilt see the plant wherefrom they are hewn, and thou wilt see how the wearer of the thong reasons— 'Where they fatten well if they do not stray.'"

CANTO XII

Soon as the blessed flame took to speaking its last word the holy mill-stone began to revolve, and had not wholly turned in its gyration before another enclosed it with a circle, and matched motion with motion, song with song; song which in those sweet pipes as much surpasses our Muses, our Sirens, as a primal splendor that which it reflected. As two bows parallel and like in colors are turned across a thin cloud, when Juno gives the order to her handmaid,[10] the one without born of the one within (in manner of the speech of that wandering one[11] whom love consumed, as the sun does vapors), and make the people here to be presageful, by reason of the covenant which God established with Noah concerning the world, that it shall nevermore be flooded; so the two garlands of those sempiternal roses were turning around us, and so did the outer correspond to the inner.

22. After the dance and the exalted great festivity, alike of the singing and of the flaming, light with light joyous and bland, had become quiet together at one instant and with one will, even as the eyes which must needs close and lift themselves together at the pleasure that moves them, from the heart of one of the new lights there came a voice, which made me seem as the needle to the star in turning me to

[1] Bernard, a wealthy citizen of Assisi, was St. Francis's first disciple. After the death of Francis he was chosen head of the Order.
[2] Egidius, the blessed Giles of Assisi, and Sylvester were two of Francis's most devoted followers.
[3] Pope Innocent III approved the Rule of St. Francis.
[4] In 1223, Honorius III confirmed the sanction of the Order.
[5] Francis, with some of his followers, in 1219, accompanied the Crusaders of the Fifth Crusade to Egypt.
[6] Mount Alvernia, in the Casentino.
[7] The Stigmata.
[8] See Matthew, 18. 6, 10, 14; Mark, 9. 42; Luke, 12. 32; 17. 2.

[9] St. Dominic.
[10] Iris.
[11] The nymph Echo.

its whereabout; and it began:[1] "The love which makes me beautiful draws me to discourse of the other leader, by whom so well it has been spoken here of mine. It is fit that where one is the other be led in, so that as they waged war united, so together may their glory shine.

37. "The army of Christ, which it cost so dear to arm afresh, was moving behind the standard, slow, mistrustful, and scanty, when the Emperor who forever reigns made provision for His soldiery that were in peril, of His grace only, not because it was worthy, and, as has been said, succored His Bride with two champions, by whose deeds, by whose words, the people gone astray were brought back.

46. "In that region where the sweet Zephyr rises to open the new leaves wherewith Europe is seen to reclothe herself, not very far from the beating of the waves behind which, over their long course, the sun sometimes hides himself from every man,[2] sits the fortunate Callaroga, under the protection of the great shield on which the Lion is subject and subjugates.[3] Therein was born the amorous lover of the Christian faith, the holy athlete, benignant to his own, and harsh to his enemies;[4] and so soon as it was created, his mind was so replete with living virtue, that in his mother it made her a prophetess.[5] After the espousals between him and the Faith were completed at the sacred font, where they dowered each other with mutual salvation, the lady who gave the assent for him saw in a dream the marvellous fruit which should issue from him and from his heirs; and in order that he might be construed as he was, a spirit went forth from here to name him with the possessive of Him whose he wholly was. Dominic[6] was he called; and I speak of him as of the husbandman whom Christ elected to His garden to assist Him. Truly he seemed the messenger and familiar of Christ; for the first love that was manifest in him was for the first counsel which Christ gave.[7] Oftentimes was he found by his nurse upon the ground silent and awake, as though he would say: 'I am come for this.' O father of him truly Felix! O mother of him truly Joanna, if this, being interpreted, means as is said![8]

82. "Not for the world, for which men now toil, following him of Ostia and Thaddeus,[9] but for love of the true manna, he became in short time a great teacher, such that he set himself to go about the vineyard, which quickly grows white if the vinedresser be at fault; and of the Seat, which was formerly more benign unto the righteous poor (not by reason of itself but by reason of him who sits there and is degenerate), he asked not to dispense or two or three for six, not the fortune of the first vacancy, *non decimas, quae sunt pauperum Dei*,[10] but leave to fight against the errant world for that seed[11] of which four and twenty plants surround thee. Then with doctrine and with will, together with the apostolic office, he went forth like a torrent which a lofty vein presses out, and on the heretical stocks his onset smote with most vigor there where the resistance was the greatest. From him proceeded thereafter divers rills whereby the catholic garden is watered, so that its bushes are more living.

106. "If such was the one wheel of the chariot on which the Holy Church defended herself and vanquished in the field her civil strife, surely the excellence of the other should be very plain to thee, concerning whom Thomas before my coming was so courteous. But the track which the highest part of its circumference made is derelict; so that there is mould where the crust was.[12] His household, which set out aright with their feet upon his footprints, are so turned round that they set the

---

[1] It is St. Bonaventura, the biographer of St. Francis, who speaks.

[2] Cf. *Hell*, xxvi. 117.

[3] Callaroga, now Calahorra, a city in Old Castile. On the shield of Castile two lions and two castles are quartered, one lion below and one above.

[4] St. Dominic, born in 1170.

[5] His mother dreamed that she gave birth to a dog, black and white in color, with a lighted torch in its mouth, which set the world on fire; symbols of the black and white robe of the Order, and of the flaming zeal of its brethren.

[6] *Dominicus*, the possessive of *Dominus*, "Belonging to the Lord."

[7] See Matthew, 19. 21.

[8] Felix, signifying "happy," and Joanna, said to mean, "the grace of the Lord."

[9] Henry of Susa, cardinal of Ostia, who wrote a much studied commentary on the Decretals, and Taddeo d' Alderotto of Bologna, called "the greatest physician in Christendom."

[10] "Not the tithes which belong to God's poor."

[11] See Luke, 8. 11.

[12] Good wine makes a crust; bad wine makes mould in the cask.

forward foot on that behind; and soon shall there be sight of the harvest of the ill culture, when the tare will complain that the bin is taken from it.[1] Nevertheless, I say, he who should search our volume leaf by leaf might still find a page where he would read: 'I am that which I am wont.' But it will not be from Casale nor from Acquasparta,[2] whence come such to the writing that one evades it, and the other contracts it.

127. "I am the life of Bonaventura of Bagnoregio, who in great offices always set the sinister[3] care behind. Illuminato and Augustin are here, who were among the first barefoot poor that in the cord made themselves friends to God. Hugh of St. Victor[4] is here with them, and Peter Mangiadore, and Peter of Spain,[5] who down below shines in twelve books; Nathan the prophet, and the Metropolitan Chrysostom,[6] and Anselm,[7] and that Donatus[8] who deigned to set his hand to the first art; Raban[9] is here, and at my side shines the Calabrian abbot Joachim,[10] endowed with prophetic spirit.

142. "The flaming courtesy of Brother Thomas, and his well advised discourse, moved me to envy so great a paladin; and with me moved this company."

CANTO XIII

LET him imagine, who desires to understand well that which I now saw (and let him retain the image like a firm rock, while I am speaking), fifteen stars which in different regions vivify the heaven with brightness so great that it overcomes every thickness of the air; let him imagine that Wain[11] for which the bosom of our heaven suffices both night and day, so that with the turning of its pole it does not disappear; let him imagine the mouth of that horn[12] which begins at the point of the axle on which the primal wheel goes round—to have made of themselves two signs in the heavens, like that which the daughter of Minos made, when she felt the frost of death,[13] and one to have its rays within the other, and both to revolve in such manner that one should go first and the other after; and he will have, as it were, the shadow of the true constellation, and of the double dance, which was circling round the point where I was; since it is as much beyond our wont as the motion of the heaven which outspeeds all the rest is swifter than the movement of the Chiana.[14] There was sung not Bacchus, not Pæan, but three Persons in the divine nature, and It and the human in one Person. The singing and the revolving completed each its measure, and those holy lights gave heed to us, making themselves happy from care to care.

31. Then the light[15] within which the marvellous life of the poor man of God had been narrated to me broke the silence among those concordant divinities, and said: "Since one straw is threshed, since its seed is now garnered, sweet love invites me to beat out the other. Thou believest that into the breast, wherefrom the rib was drawn to form the beautiful cheek of her whose palate costs dear to all the world, and into that which, pierced by the lance, both after and before made such satisfaction that it overcomes the balance of all sin, whatever of light it is allowed to human nature to have was all infused by that Power which made one and the other; and therefore thou wonderest at that which I said above, when I told that the good which is inclosed in the fifth light had no second. Now open thine eyes to that which I

[1] See Matthew, 13. 30.
[2] Frate Ubertino of Casale, the leader of a party of zealots among the Franciscans, enforced the written Rule of the Order with excessive strictness; Matteo of Acquasparta, general of the Franciscans in 1287, relaxed it.
[3] Care for temporal things. Cf. Proverbs, 3. 16.
[4] A noted theologian of the mystic school, of the abbey of St. Victor at Paris.
[5] Peter Mangiador, or Comestor, "the Eater," so called as being a devourer of books. He was chancellor of the University of Paris, and died toward the end of the twelfth century. Peter of Spain wrote a compendium of logic, Summae logicales, in twelve books. He was chosen Pope in 1276, taking the name of John XXI.
[6] A Greek Father of the Church, patriarch of Constantinople.
[7] Archbishop of Canterbury, died in 1109.
[8] The compiler of a treatise on grammar in use throughout the Middle Ages.
[9] Rabanus Maurus, Archbishop of Mainz in the ninth century; a great scholar and writer.
[10] Joachim, Abbot of Flora, in Calabria. He died in 1202. He wrote apocalyptic and prophetic treatises.
[11] The Great Bear.
[12] The Lesser Bear.
[13] Dionysus bore Ariadne, deserted by Theseus, to heaven, and changed her crown into a constellation: Ariadne's Crown.
[14] The Chiana was a sluggish Tuscan stream.
[15] Of St. Thomas Aquinas.

answer to thee, and thou wilt see thy belief and
my speech become in the truth as the centre in
a circle.

52. "That which dies not and that which can
die are naught but the splendor of that idea
which in His love our Sire brings to birth;[1]
for that living Light, which so streams from its
Lucent Source that It is not disunited from It,
nor from the Love which with them is in-
trined, doth of Its own goodness collect Its
rays, as it were mirrored, in nine subsistences,
Itself eternally remaining one. Thence It de-
scends to the ultimate potentialities, downward
from act to act, becoming such that finally It
makes naught save brief contingencies: and
these contingencies I understand to be the gen-
erated things which the moving heavens pro-
duce with seed and without it. The wax of
these, and that which moulds it, are not of one
mode, and therefore under the signet of the
idea It more or less shines through; whence it
comes to pass that one same plant in respect to
species bears better or worse fruit, and that ye
are born with diverse dispositions.

73. "If the wax were exactly worked, and the
heavens were supreme in their power, the
whole light of the seal would be apparent. But
nature always gives it defective, working like
the artist who has the practice of his art and a
hand that trembles. Yet if the fervent Love dis-
poses and imprints the clear Vision of the
primal Power, complete perfection is acquired
there. Thus of old the earth was made worthy
of the complete perfection of the living being;
thus was the Virgin made impregnate; so that
I commend thy opinion that human nature
never was, nor will be, what it was in those
two persons.

88. "Now, if I should not proceed farther,
'How then was that one without a peer?'
would thy words begin. But, in order that that
which is not apparent may clearly appear, con-
sider who he was, and the cause which moved
him to make request, when it was said to him:
'Ask.'[2] I have not so spoken that thou canst not
clearly see that he was a king, who asked for
wisdom, in order that he might be a worthy
king; not to know the number of the motors
here on high, or if *necese* with a contingent

ever made *necesse;*[3] *non si est dare primum
motum esse,*[4] or if in the semicircle a triangle
can be made so that it should not have one
right angle. Wherefore if thou notest what I
said and also this, a kingly prudence is that
peerless seeing, on which the arrow of my inten-
tion strikes. And if thou directest clear eyes to
the 'has arisen,' thou wilt see it has respect only
to kings, who are many, and the good are rare.
With this distinction take thou my saying, and
thus it can stand with that which thou believest
of the first father, and of our Beloved one.[5]

112. "And let this ever be as lead to thy feet,
to make thee move slowly as a weary man,
both to the *yea* and to the *nay* which thou seest
not; for he is very low down among the fools
who affirms or denies without distinction,
alike in the one and in the other case; because
it happens that oftentimes the hasty opinion
bends in false direction, and then self-love binds
the intelligence. Far more than in vain does he
leave the bank, since he returns not such as he
sets out, who fishes for the truth, and has not
the art; and of this Parmenides, Melissus,
Bryson,[6] are manifest proofs to the world, and
many others who went on and knew not
whither. Thus did Sabellius, and Arius,[7] and
those fools who were as swords unto the Scrip-
tures in making their straight faces crooked.

130. "Let not the folk be yet too confident in
judgment, like him who reckons up the ears in
the field ere they are ripe; for I have seen the
briar first show itself stiff and rugged all win-
ter long, then bear the rose upon its top; and
once I saw a bark run straight and swift over
the sea through all her course, and perish at
last at entrance of the harbor. Let not dame
Bertha or master Martin, seeing one rob, and
another make offering, believe to see them
within the Divine counsel; for the one may
rise and the other may fall."

CANTO XIV

FROM the centre to the rim, and so from the
rim to the centre, the water in a round vessel

[1] The nine orders of the Angelic Hierarchy.
[2] See I Kings, 3. 5-9.
[3] If from two premises, one necessary and one con-
tingent, a necessary conclusion is to be deduced.
[4] "If a prime motion is to be granted," that is, a
motion not the effect of another.
[5] The Lord Jesus.
[6] Heathen philosophers.
[7] Sabellius denied the Trinity, Arius denied the con-
substantiality of the Father and the Son.

moves, according as it is struck from without or within. This which I say fell suddenly into my mind as the glorious life of Thomas became silent, because of the similitude which was born of his speech and that of Beatrice, whom after him it pleased thus to begin: "This man has need, and he tells it not to you, neither with his voice nor as yet in thought, of going to the root of another truth. Tell him if the light wherewith your substance blossoms will remain with you eternally even as it is now; and if it remain, tell how, after ye shall be again made visible, it can be that it will not hurt your sight."

19. As, when urged and drawn on by increase of delight, those who are dancing in a ring all at once lift their voice and gladden their motions, so, at that ready and devout petition, the holy circles showed new joy in their turning and in their marvellous melody. Whoso laments because we die here to live there on high, has not seen here the refreshment of the eternal rain.

28. That One and Two and Three which ever lives, and ever reigns in Three and Two and One, uncircumscribed, and circumscribing all things, was thrice sung by each of those spirits with such a melody that for every merit it would be adequate reward. And I heard in the divinest light of the smaller circle a modest voice,[1] perhaps such as was that of the Angel to Mary, make answer: "As long as the festival of Paradise shall be, so long will our love radiate around us such a garment. Its brightness will follow our ardor, the ardor our vision, and that is great in proportion as it receives of grace above its own worth. When the flesh, glorious and sanctified, shall be clothed on us again, our persons will be more acceptable through being all complete; wherefore whatever of gratuitous light the Supreme Good gives us will be increased—light which enables us to see Him; so that our vision must needs increase, our ardor increase which by that is kindled, our radiance increase which comes from this.

52. But even as a coal which gives forth flame, and by a vivid glow surpasses it, so that

its own aspect is defended, thus this effulgence, which already encircles us, will be vanquished in appearance by the flesh which all this while the earth covers; nor will so great a light have power to fatigue us, for the organs of the body will be strong for everything which can delight us." So sudden and ready both one and the other choir seemed to me in saying "Amen," that truly they showed desire for their dead bodies, perhaps not only for themselves, but also for their mothers, for their fathers, and for the others who were dear before they became sempiternal flames.

67. And lo! round about, of a uniform brightness, arose a lustre, beyond that which was there, like an horizon, which is growing bright. And as at rise of early evening new appearances begin in the heavens, so that the sight seems and seems not true, it seemed to me that there I began to see new subsistences, and a circle forming outside the other two circumferences. O true sparkling of the Holy Spirit! how sudden and glowing it became to my eyes, which, vanquished, endured it not! But Beatrice showed herself to me so beautiful and smiling that it must be left among those sights which followed not my memory.

82. Therefrom my eyes regained power to raise themselves again, and I saw myself, alone with my Lady, translated to more exalted salvation. That I was more uplifted I perceived clearly by the fiery smile of the star, which seemed to me ruddier than its wont. With all my heart and with that speech which is one in all men, I made to God a holocaust such as was befitting to the new grace; and the ardor of the sacrifice was not yet exhausted in my breast before I knew that offering had been accepted and propitious; for with such a glow and such a ruddiness splendors appeared to me within two rays, that I said: "O Helios, who dost so adorn them!"

97. Even as, distinct with less and greater lights, the Galaxy so whitens between the poles of the world that it makes even the wise to question, thus, constellated in the depth of Mars, those rays made the venerable sign which joining of quadrants in a circle make. Here my memory overcomes my genius, for that Cross was flashing forth Christ, so that I know not to find worthy example. But he who

[1] Probably that of Solomon, who in Canto x. 109, is said to be "the light which is the most beautiful among us."

takes his cross and follows Christ shall yet ex-
cuse me for that which I omit, when he be-
holds Christ lightening in that glow.

109. From horn to horn,[1] and between the
top and the base, lights were moving, brightly
scintillating as they met together and in their
passing by. Thus here are seen the atoms of
bodies, straight and athwart, swift and slow,
changing appearance, long and short, moving
through the sunbeam, wherewith sometimes
the shade is striped which people with skill and
art contrive for their protection.

118. And as a viol or harp, strung in accord
of many strings, makes a sweet tinkling to one
by whom the tune is not caught, thus from the
lights which there appeared to me a melody
was gathered through the Cross, which rapt
me without my understanding the hymn. I
was indeed aware that it was of lofty praise,
because there came to me: "Arise and con-
quer!" as to one who understands not, and yet
hears. I was so enamoured therewith that un-
til then there had not been anything which had
fettered me with such sweet bonds. Perchance
my word appears too daring, in setting lower
the pleasure from the beautiful eyes, gazing
into which my desire has repose. But he who
considers that the living seals of every beauty
have more effect the higher they are, and that
I had not there turned round to those eyes,[2]
may excuse me for that whereof I accuse my-
self in order to excuse myself, and may see that
I speak truth; for the holy pleasure is not ex-
cluded here, because it becomes the purer as
it mounts.

CANTO XV

A BENIGN will, wherein the love which right-
eously inspires always manifests itself, as cu-
pidity[3] does in the evil will, imposed silence on
that sweet lyre, and quieted the holy strings
which the right hand of heaven slackens and
draws tight. How shall those beings be deaf
to righteous prayers, who, in order to give me
the will to pray to them, were concordant in
silence? Well is it that he should grieve with-
out end, who, for the love of thing which
does not last, despoils himself forever of this
love.

13. As, through the tranquil and pure eve-
ning skies, a sudden fire shoots from time to
time, moving the eyes which were steady, and
seems to be a star which changes place, save
that from the region whence it was kindled
nothing is lost, and it lasts short while; so from
the arm which extends on the right, ran a star
of the constellation which is resplendent there,
down to the foot of that Cross. Nor from its
ribbon did the gem depart, but through the ra-
dial strip it ran along and seemed like fire be-
hind alabaster. With like affection did the
shade of Anchises stretch forward (if our great-
est Muse merits belief), when in Elysium he
perceived his son.[4]

28. *O sanguis meus! a superinfusa gratia
Dei! sicut tibi, cui bis unquam coeli janua re-
clusa?*[5] Thus that light; whereat I gave heed
to it; then I turned back my sight to my Lady,
and on the one side and the other I was awe-
struck; for within her eyes was glowing such a
smile, that with my own I thought to touch the
depth of my grace and of my Paradise.

37. Then, joyous to hearing and to sight, the
spirit added to his beginning things which I
did not understand, so deep was his speech.
Nor did he hide himself from me by choice, but
by necessity, for his conception was set above
the mark of mortals. And when the bow of his
ardent affection was so relaxed that his speech
descended towards the mark of our under-
standing, the first thing that was understood by
me was: "Blessed be Thou, Trine and One,
who art so greatly courteous in my seed."

49. And he went on: "A pleasing and long-
felt hunger, derived from reading in the great
volume where white or dark is never changed,
thou hast relieved, my son, within this light
in which I speak to thee, thanks to her who
clothed thee with plumes for the lofty flight.

---

[1] From arm to arm of the cross.

[2] "The eyes of this Lady," says Dante, speaking of
philosophy in the *Convito,* "are her demonstrations,
which, directed to the eyes of the understanding,
enamour the delivered soul. O sweetest and ineffable
looks, the sudden captors of the minds of men,
which appear in the demonstrations in the eyes of
Philosophy when she discourses with her lovers! Truly
in you is the salvation by which he is made blessed
who looks on you, and is saved from the death of ig-
norance and sin." *Convito,* ii. 16, 27-37.

[3] See *Purgatory,* xviii. 62-75.

[4] See *Aeneid,* vi. 684-7.

[5] "O blood of mine! O overflowing grace of God!
To whom, as to thee, was ever the gate of Heaven
twice opened?" It is the spirit of Cacciaguida, the
great-great-grandfather of Dante, who thus speaks.

Thou believest that thy thought flows to me from Him who is First, even as from the unit, if that be known, ray out the five and six;[1] and therefore who I am, and why I appear to thee more joyful than any other in this blithe throng, thou askest me not. Thou believest the truth; for the lesser and the great of this life gaze upon the mirror in which, before thou thinkest, thou dost display thy thought. But in order that the sacred Love, in which I watch with perpetual vision, and which makes me thirst with sweet desire, may be fulfilled the better, let thy voice, secure, bold, and glad, sound forth the will, sound forth the desire, to which my answer is already decreed."

70. I turned me to Beatrice, and she heard before I spoke, and granted me a sign which made grow the wings to my desire. Then I began thus: "When the Prime Equality appeared to you, the affection and the intelligence became of one weight for each of you; because the Sun which illumined and warmed you with its heat and with its light is of such equality that all similitudes are defective. But will and discourse in mortals, for the reason which is manifest to you, are diversely feathered in their wings. Wherefore I, who am mortal, feel myself in this inequality, and therefore I give not thanks, save with my heart, for thy paternal welcome. Truly I beseech thee, living topaz, that dost ingem this precious jewel, that thou make me content with thy name?"

88. "O leaf of mine, in whom, while only awaiting, I took pleasure, I was thy root." Such a beginning he, answering, made to me.

91. Then he said to me: "He from whom thy family is named,[2] and who for a hundred years and more has circled the mountain on the first ledge, was my son and was thy great-grandsire; truly it behoves that thou shorten for him his long fatigue with thy works. Florence, within the ancient circuit of her walls wherefrom she still takes both tierce and nones,[3] was abiding in peace, sober and modest.

She had not necklace nor coronal, nor dames with ornamented shoes, nor girdle which was more to be looked at than the person. Not yet did the daughter at her birth cause fear to the father, for the time and dowry did not outrun due measure on this side and that. She has not houses empty of families; nor had Sardanapalus[4] yet arrived there to show what may be done in a chamber. Not yet by your Uccellatoio was Montemalo surpassed, which, as it has been surpassed in its rise, shall be so in its fall.[5] I saw Bellincion Berti[6] go girt with leather and bone, and his dame come from her mirror without a painted face. And I saw him of the Nerli, and him of the Vecchio,[7] contented with the unlined skin, and their dames with the spindle and the thread. O fortunate women! Each one was sure of her burial place; and as yet no one was deserted in her bed for France. One over the cradle kept her careful watch, and, comforting, she used the idiom which first amuses fathers and mothers. Another, drawing the tresses from her distaff, told to her household tales of the Trojans, of Fiesole, and of Rome. A Cianghella, a Lapo Salterello[8] would then have been held as great a marvel as Cincinnatus or Cornelia would be now.

130. "To so reposeful, to so fair a life of citizens, to such a trusty community, to such a sweet inn, Mary, called on with loud cries,[9] gave me; and in your ancient Baptistery I became at once a Christian and Cacciaguida. Moronto was my brother, and Eliseo; my dame came to me from the valley of the Po, and thence was thy surname. Afterward I followed the emperor Conrad,[10] and he belted me of his soldiery, so much by good deeds did I come into his favor. Behind him I went against the

---

[4] A symbol of luxury and effeminacy.
[5] The view from Montemalo (Monte Mario) of Rome in its splendor was not yet surpassed by that of Florence from the height of Uccellatoio.
[6] Bellincion Berti was "an honorable citizen of Florence" and "a noble soldier."
[7] Two ancient and honored families.
[8] Cianghella was a contemporary of Dante: "a most arrogant and intolerable woman, and very wanton in her life." Lapo Salterello was a lawyer and judge: "a rash and bad citizen, a litigious and tonguey man." Cf. Canto xvii. 61-63.
[9] The Virgin, called on in the pains of childbirth. Cf. *Purgatory*, xx. 19-21.
[10] Conrad III of Swabia. In 1147 he joined in the disastrous Second Crusade.

---

[1] See Canto ix. 73-75.
[2] Alighiero, from whom, it would appear from his station in Purgatory, Dante inherited the sin of pride, as well as his name.
[3] The bell of the church called the Badìa, or Abbey, measured the time for the Florentines. Tierce is the first division of the canonical hours of the day, from six to nine; nones, the third, from twelve to three.

iniquity of that law[1] whose people usurp your jurisdiction,[2] through fault of the Pastors. There by that foul folk was I released from the deceitful world, the love of which debases many souls, and I came from martyrdom to this peace."

CANTO XVI

O our petty nobility of blood! If thou makest folk glory in thee down here, where our affection languishes, it will nevermore be a marvel to me; for there, where appetite is not perverted, I mean in Heaven, I myself gloried in thee. Truly art thou a cloak which quickly shortens, so that, if naught be added from day to day, Time goes round about thee with his shears.

10. With the *You*,[3] which Rome was first to tolerate, in which her family least perseveres, my words began again. Whereat Beatrice, who was a little withdrawn, smiling, seemed like her, who coughed at the first fault that is written of Guenever.[4] I began: "You are my father, you give me all confidence to speak; you uplift me so that I am more than I. By so many streams is my mind filled with gladness that it makes of itself a joy, in that it can bear this and not burst. Tell me then, my beloved forefather, who were your ancestors, and what were the years that were reckoned in your boyhood. Tell me of the sheepfold of St. John,[5] how large it was then, and who were the people within it worthy of the highest seats."

28. As a coal is quickened into flame at the breathing of the winds, so I saw that light glow at my blandishments; and as it became more beautiful to my eyes, so with voice more sweet and soft, but not with this modern speech, it said to me: "From that day on which *Ave* was said, unto the child-birth in which my mother, who now is sainted, was lightened of me with whom she had been burdened, this fire had come to its Lion[6] five hundred, fifty, and thirty

times to reinflame itself beneath his paw.[7] My ancestors and I were born in the place where the last ward is first reached by him who runs in your annual game.[8] Let it suffice thee to hear this of my elders; as to who they were, and whence they came hither, silence is more becoming than speech.

46. "All those able to bear arms who at that time were there, between Mars and the Baptist,[9] were the fifth of them who are living. But the citizenship, which is now mixed with Campi, with Certaldo, and with Fighine,[10] was to be seen pure in the lowest artisan. Oh, how much better it would be that those folk of whom I speak were neighbors, and to have your boundary at Galluzzo and at Trespiano,[11] than to have them within, and to endure the stench of the churl of Aguglione,[12] and of him of Signa, who already has his eye sharp for barratry!

58. "If the folk who are the most degenerate in the world had not been as a stepdame unto Cæsar, but like a mother benignant to her son, there is one who has become a Florentine, and is a money-changer and trader, who would have been turned back to Simifonti,[13] where his grandsire used to go about begging; Montemurlo would still belong to its Counts, the Cerchi would be in the parish of Acone, and perhaps the Buondelmonti in Valdigreve.[14] The intermingling of persons was ever the beginning of harm to the city, as the food which is loaded on is to the body. And a blind bull falls more headlong than the blind lamb; and

---

[1] The law of Mahomet.
[2] In the Holy Land.
[3] The plural pronoun, used as a mark of respect.
[4] Beatrice is observant, like the Dame de Malehaut, who coughed at seeing the first kiss received by Queen Guenever from Sir Lancelot.
[5] Florence, whose patron saint was St. John the Baptist.
[6] The sign Leo in the zodiac, appropriate to Mars.

[7] Five hundred and eighty revolutions of Mars are accomplished in a few months more than ten hundred and ninety years.
[8] The races run along the Corso on June 24, the festival of St. John the Baptist.
[9] Between the Ponte Vecchio, at the head of which stood the statue of Mars, and the Baptistery—two points marking the circuit of the ancient walls.
[10] Small towns in the territory of Florence.
[11] Galluzzo and Trespiano are villages two or three miles from Florence.
[12] The churl of Aguglione was a lawyer named Baldo, who became one of the priors of Florence in 1311. He of Signa is supposed to have been one Bonifazio, who "sold his favors and offices."
[13] A stronghold in the Val d'Elsa.
[14] The Conti Guidi, unable to defend their stronghold of Montemurlo from the Pistoians, had been compelled to sell it to the Florentines. The Cerchi and the Buondelmonti had been forced by the Florentine Commune to surrender their fortresses and to take up their abode in the city.

oftentimes one sword cuts more and better than five.

73. If thou regard Luni and Urbisaglia, how they have gone, and how Chiusi and Sinigaglia are going their way after them, it will not appear to thee a strange thing or a hard, to hear how families are undone, since even cities have their term. All things of yours have their death even as yourselves; but it is concealed in some that last long, while lives are short. And as the revolution of the heaven of the Moon covers and uncovers the shores without a pause, so Fortune does with Florence. Wherefore what I shall tell of the high Florentines, whose fame is hidden by time, should not appear to thee a marvellous thing. I saw the Ughi, and I saw the Catellini, Filippi, Greci, Ormanni, and Alberichi, even in their decline, illustrious citizens; and I saw, as great as they were old, with him of La Sannella, him of L' Arca, and Soldanieri, and Ardinghi, and Bostichi. Over the gate (which at present is laden with new felony[1] of such great weight that soon there will be jettison from the bark), were the Ravignani, from whom the Count Guido is descended, and whosoever has since taken the name of the high Bellincionje.[2] He of La Pressa knew already how one should rule, and Galigaio already had in his house the gilded hilt and pummel. Great were already the column of the Vair,[3] the Sacchetti, Giuochi, Fifanti, and Barucci, and Galli, and they who blush for the bushel.[4] The stock from which the Calfucci sprang was already great,[5] and already the Sizii and Arrigucci had been drawn to the curule chairs.

109. "Oh, how great did I see those who have been undone by their pride![6] and the balls of gold[7] made Florence flourish with all

their great deeds. So did the fathers of those who, whenever your church is vacant, become fat by staying in consistory.[8] The overweening race which is as a dragon behind him who flies, and to him who shows tooth or purse is gentle as a lamb,[9] already was coming up, but from small folk, so that it did not please Ubertin Donato that this father-in-law afterward made him their kinsman. Already had Caponsacco descended into the market place down from Fiesole, and already was Giuda a good citizen, and Infangato.[10] I will tell a thing incredible and true; into the little circle one entered by a gate which was named for those of La Pera.[11] Everyone who bears the beautiful ensign of the great baron[12] whose name and whose worth the feast of Thomas keeps fresh, from him had knighthood and privilege; although to-day he who binds it with a border unites himself with the populace.[13] Already there were Gualterotti and Importuni; and the Borgo[14] would even now be more quiet, if they had gone fasting of new neighbors. The house of which was born your weeping,[15] by reason of its just indignation which has slain you, and put an end to your glad living, was honored, both itself and its consorts. Oh Buondelmonte, how ill didst thou flee its nuptials through the persuasions of another![16] Many would be glad

[8] The Visdomini and the Tosinghi, guardians of the bishopric of Florence, who had the right, during any vacancy of the see, of administering its revenues, and thus after the death of a bishop, by securing delay in the appointment of his successor, grew fat on the episcopal revenues.
[9] The Adimari.
[10] These three names mean "Head in bag," "Judas," and "Bemired."
[11] The Peruzzi, who bore the pear as a charge upon their scutcheon.
[12] Hugh, imperial vicar of Tuscany in the time of Otho II and Otho III. He died on St. Thomas's Day, December 21, 1006.
[13] Giano della Bella, the great leader of the Florentine commonalty in the latter years of the thirteenth century. He bore the arms of Hugh with a border of gold.
[14] The Borgo Santi Apostoli would have been more tranquil if the Buondelmonti had not come to take up their abode in it after the destruction of their stronghold of Montebuono.
[15] The Amidei had a long and bitter feud with the Buondelmonti that divided the whole city.
[16] The quarrel between the Amidei and the Buondelmonti arose from Buondelmonte dei Buondelmonti's slighting a daughter of the former house, to whom he was betrothed, for a daughter of the Donati, induced thereto by her mother. This was in 1215.

[1] Above the Gate of St. Peter rose the walls of the abode of the Cerchi, who, making themselves the head of the White faction, became chief promoters of civil strife in Florence.
[2] See Canto xv. 112, and Hell, xvi. 37.
[3] The family of the Pigli, whose scutcheon was divided longitudinally by a stripe of the heraldic representation of the fur called vair.
[4] One of the Chiaramontesi, being the officer in charge of the sale of salt for the Commune, had cheated both the Commune and the people by using a false measure. See Purgatory, xii. 104, 105.
[5] The house of the Donati.
[6] The Uberti (see Hell, x).
[7] The Lamberti, who bore golden balls on their shields. See Hell, xxviii. 103-111.

who now are sorrowful, if God had conceded thee to the Ema[1] the first time that thou camest to the city. But it behoved that Florence in her last hour of peace should offer a victim to that mutilated stone which guards the bridge.[2]

148. "With these families, and with others with them, I saw Florence in such repose that she had no occasion why she should weep. With these families I saw her people so glorious and so just that the lily was never set reversed upon the staff, nor made vermilion by divisions."

CANTO XVII

As HE who still makes fathers chary toward their sons came to Clymene, to ascertain concerning that which he had heard against himself;[3] such was I, and such was I perceived to be both by Beatrice, and by the holy lamp which previously for my sake had changed its station. Wherefore my Lady said to me: "Send forth the flame of thy desire in such wise that it may issue imprinted well by the internal stamp; not in order that our knowledge may increase through thy speech, but in order that thou accustom thyself to tell thy thirst, so that one may give thee drink."

13. "O dear root of me, who so upliftest thyself that, even as earthly minds see that two obtuse angles can not be contained in a triangle, so thou, gazing upon the Point to which all times are present, dost see contingent things, ere in themselves they are; while I was conjoined with Virgil, up over the mountain which cures the souls, and while descending in the dead world, grave words were said to me of my future life; although I feel myself truly four-square against the blows of chance. Wherefore my wish would be contented by hearing what fortune is drawing near for me; for arrow foreseen comes more slack." Thus said I unto that same light which had spoken to me

before, and, as Beatrice willed, was my wish confessed.

31. Not with ambiguous terms in which the foolish folk of old were entangled, before the Lamb of God which taketh away sins had been slain, but with clear words and with plain speech that paternal love, enclosed and made manifest by its own smile, made answer:

37. "Contingency, which does not extend outside the volume of your matter, is all depicted in the Eternal Vision. Yet thence it does not take necessity, more than does a ship which is going down the stream from the eye in which it is mirrored. Therefrom, even as sweet harmony comes to the ear from an organ, comes to my sight the time that is preparing for thee. As Hippolytus departed from Athens, by reason of his pitiless and perfidious stepmother, so from Florence thou must needs depart. This is willed, this is already sought for, and will soon be brought to pass, by him[4] who meditates it there where every day Christ is bought and sold. The blame will follow the injured party, in outcry, as is wont; but the vengeance will be testimony to the truth which dispenses it. Thou shalt leave everything beloved most dearly; and this is the arrow which the bow of exile shoots first. Thou shalt make proof how the bread of others savors of salt, and how hard a path is the descending and the mounting of another's stairs. And that which will weigh heaviest upon thy shoulders will be the evil and senseless company[5] with which thou wilt fall into this valley; which all ungrateful, all mad and malevolent will turn against thee; but short while after, it, not thou, shall have the forehead red therefor. Of its bestiality, its own proceduce will afford the proof; so that it will be well-becoming for thee to have made thee a party by thyself.

70. "Thy first refuge and first inn shall be the courtesy of the great Lombard[6] who bears the holy bird upon the ladder, who will have for thee such benign regard that, in doing and in asking, between you two, that will be first, which between others is the slowest. With him

---

[1] A little stream that has to be crossed in coming from Montebuono to Florence.

[2] That victim was Buondelmonte himself, slain by the outraged Amidei, at the foot of the mutilated statue of Mars.

[3] Phaëthon, son of Clymene by Apollo, having been told that Apollo was not his father, went to his mother to ascertain the truth—with calamitous results. See *Hell*, xvii. 107; *Purgatory*, iv. 72.

[4] Boniface VIII.

[5] The other Florentine exiles of the party of the Whites.

[6] Bartolommeo della Scala, lord of Verona, whose armorial bearings were the imperial eagle upon a ladder.

shalt thou see one,[1] who was so impressed, at his birth, by this strong star,[2] that his deeds will be notable. Not yet are the people aware of him, because of his young age; for these wheels have revolved around him only nine years. But ere the Gascon cheat the lofty Henry[3] some sparkles of his virtue shall appear, in his caring not for money nor for toils. His magnificences shall hereafter be so known, that his enemies will not be able to keep their tongues mute about them. Look thou to him, and to his benefits; by him shall many people be transformed, rich and mendicant changing condition. And thou shalt bear hence written of him in thy mind, but thou shalt not tell it,"—and he told things incredible to those who shall be present. Then he added: "Son, these are the glosses on which was said to thee: behold the snares which are hidden behind few revolutions. Yet I would not that thou hate thy neighbors, because thy life has a future far beyond the punishment of their perfidies."

100. When by its silence that holy soul showed it had finished putting the woof into that web which I had held out to it, warped, I began, as he who, in doubt, longs for counsel from a person who sees, and wills uprightly, and loves: "I see well, my Father, how the time spurs on toward me to give me such a blow as is heaviest to him who most deserts himself; wherefore it is good that I arm me with foresight, so that if the place most dear be taken from me, I may not lose the others by my songs. Down through the world of endless bitterness, and over the mountain from whose fair summit the eyes of my Lady uplifted me, and then through heaven from light to light, I have learned that which, if I tell again, will have for many a savor of great bitterness; and if I am a timid friend to the truth, I fear to lose life among those who will call this time ancient."

121. The light, within which my treasure that I had found there was smiling, first became flashing as a mirror of gold in the sun-

beam; then it replied: "A conscience dark, either with its own or with another's shame, will indeed feel thy speech to be harsh; but nevertheless, all falsehood laid aside, make thy whole vision manifest, and let then the scratching be where the itch is; for if at the first taste thy voice shall be molestful, afterwards, when it shall be digested, it will leave vital nourishment. This cry of thine shall do as the wind, which strikes hardest the loftiest summits; and that is no little argument of honor. Therefore only the souls which are known of fame have been shown to thee within these wheels, upon the mountain, and in the woeful valley; for the mind of him who hears rests not, nor confirms its faith, by an example which has its root unknown and hidden, nor by other argument which is not apparent."

CANTO XVIII

Now was that blessed mirror enjoying only its own thoughts,[1] and I was tasting mine, tempering the bitter with the sweet, and that Lady who was leading me to God said: "Change thy thought; think that I am near to Him who lightens the burden of every wrong." I turned me round at the loving sound of my Comfort, and what love I then saw in the holy eyes, I here leave it; not only because I distrust my own speech, but because of the memory which cannot return so far above itself, unless another guide it. Thus much of that moment can I recount, that, again beholding her, my affection was free from every other desire.

16. While the Eternal Pleasure, which was raying directly upon Beatrice, was contenting me with its second aspect from her fair face, vanquishing me with the light of a smile, she said to me: "Turn thee, and listen, for not only in my eyes is Paradise."

22. As sometimes here the affection is seen in the countenance, if it be so great that the whole soul is taken up by it, so in the flaming of the holy effulgence to which I turned me, I recognized the will in it still to discourse somewhat with me. It began: "In this fifth seat[5] of the tree, which has life from its top, and always bears fruit, and never loses leaf, are blessed

---

[1] Can Grande della Scala, the youngest brother of Bartolommeo, and his successor as lord of Verona. He was made Imperial Vicar in 1311, and on him the hopes of the Ghibellines rested.

[2] Mars.

[3] Before the Gascon Pope Clement V, under whom the papal see was established at Avignon, shall deceive Henry VII.

[4] See Aquinas, *Summa Theologica*, Part I, Q 34, A 1.

[5] The Heaven of Mars, the fifth resting-place in the ascent of Heaven.

spirits, who below, before they came to heaven, were of great renown, so that every Muse would be rich with them. Therefore gaze upon the arms of the Cross; he, whom I shall name, will there do the act which in a cloud its own swift fire does." At the naming of Joshua, even as it was done, I saw a light drawn along the Cross; nor was the word noted by me before the fact. And at the name of the lofty Maccabeus[1] I saw another move revolving, and gladness was the whip of the top. Thus for Charlemagne and for Roland my attentive gaze followed two of them, as the eye follows its falcon as he flies. Afterward William, and Renouard,[2] and the duke Godfrey,[3] and Robert Guiscard[4] drew my sight along that Cross. Then, moving, and mingling among the other lights, the soul which had spoken with me showed me how great an artist it was among the singers of the heaven.

52. I turned me round to my right side to see in Beatrice my duty signified either by speech or by act, and I saw her eyes so clear, so joyous, that her semblance surpassed her other and her latest wont. And even as, through feeling more delight in doing well, a man from day to day becomes aware that his virtue makes advance, so I, seeing that miracle more adorned, became aware that my circling round together with the heaven had increased its arc. And such as is the change, in brief passage of time, in a pale lady, when her countenance discharges itself of the load of bashfulness, such was there to my eyes, when I turned, because of the whiteness of the temperate sixth star which had received me within itself.[5] I saw, within that torch of Jove, the sparkling of the love which was there, shaping out our speech to my eyes.

73. And as birds, risen from the shore, as if rejoicing together at their pasture, make of themselves a troop now round, now of other shape, so within the lights holy creatures were singing as they flew, and in their figures made of themselves now D, now I, now L.[6] At first, as they sang, they moved to their own notes, then as they became one of these characters, they stopped a little, and were silent.

82. O divine Pegasea,[7] who makest the wits of men glorious, and renderest them long-lived, as they, through thee, the cities and the kingdoms, illumine me with thyself that I may set forth their shapes, as I have conceived them; let thy power appear in these brief verses!

88. They showed themselves then in five times seven vowels and consonants; and I noted the parts as they seemed as if spoken to me. *Diligite justitiam* were the first verb and noun of all the picture; *qui judicatis terram*[8] were the last. Then in the M of the fifth word they remained arranged, so that Jove seemed silver patterned there with gold. And I saw other lights descending where the top of the M was, and become quiet there, singing, I believe, the Good which moves them to Itself. Then, as on the striking of burning logs rise innumerable sparks, wherefrom the foolish are wont to draw auguries, so thence there seemed to rise again more than a thousand lights, and mount, some much and some little, according as the Sun which kindles them allotted to them; and, each having become quiet in its place, I saw the head and the neck of an eagle represented by that patterned fire. He who paints there, has none who may guide Him, but He Himself guides, and from Him is recognized that virtue which is form for the nests. The rest of the blessed spirits, which at first seemed content to lily themselves on the M, with a slight motion followed out the imprint.

115. O sweet star, what and how many gems made plain to me that our justice is the effect of that heaven which thou dost ingem! Wherefore I pray the Mind, in which thy motion and thy virtue have beginning, that It look down there whence issues the smoke which vitiates thy radiance, so that now, a second time, It may be wroth at the buying and the selling in the temple, which was built up with blood and

---

[1] See I Maccabees, 2-9.
[2] William, Count of Orange, and Renouard his companion in arms, paladins of Charlemagne.
[3] Godfrey of Bouillon, the leader of the First Crusade.
[4] The founder of the Norman kingdom of Naples.
[5] The change was from the red light of Mars to the white light of Jupiter, a planet called by astrologers "temperate," as lying between the heat of Mars and the coldness of Saturn.

[6] See line 91, *infra*.
[7] An appellation of the Muses in general, whose fountain, Hippocrene, sprang up at the stamp of Pegasus.
[8] "Love righteousness, ye that be judges of the earth." Wisdom of Solomon, 1. 1.

martyrdoms. O soldiery of Heaven whom I contemplate, pray ye for those on earth who are all gone astray after the bad example! Of old it was the wont to make war with swords, but now it is made by taking away, now here now there, the bread which the pitying Father locks up from none.

130. But thou that writest only in order to cancel, bethink thee that Peter and Paul, who died for the vineyard which thou art laying waste, are still alive. Thou canst say indeed: "I have my desire set so on him[1] who willed to live alone, and for a dance was dragged to martyrdom, that I know not the Fisherman nor Paul."

CANTO XIX

WITH outspread wings appeared before me the beautiful image which the interwoven souls, joyful in their sweet fruition, were making. Each of them appeared as a little ruby on which a ray of the sun should glow so enkindled as to reflect him into my eyes. And that which it now behoves me to retrace, never did voice report, nor ink write, nor was it ever comprised by fancy; for I saw, and also heard the beak speaking, and uttering with its voice both *I* and *My*, when in conception it was *We* and *Our*.

13. And it began: "Through being just and pious am I here exalted to that glory which allows not itself to be surpassed by desire; and on earth I left my memory such that the evil people there commend it, but follow not its story." Thus one sole heat makes itself felt from many embers, even as from many loves one sole sound issued from that image. Whereon I at once: "O perpetual flowers of the eternal gladness, ye which make all your odors seem to me only one, solve for me, by your breath, the great fast which long has held me hungering, not finding for it any food on earth. Well do I know that if the Divine Justice makes another realm in heaven its mirror,[2] yours does not apprehend it through a veil. Ye know how intently I prepare myself to listen; ye know what is that doubt which is so old a fast to me."

34. As a falcon which, issuing from the hood, moves its head, and claps its wings, showing its will, and making itself fine; so I saw this emblem, which was woven of praise of the Divine Grace, become, with songs such as he knows who thereabove rejoices. Then it began: "He who turned the compasses at the verge of the world, and distributed within it so much occult and manifest, could not so imprint His Power on all the universe that His Word should not remain in infinite excess. And this makes certain that the first proud one, who was the top of every creature, through not awaiting light, fell immature. And hence it appears, that every lesser nature is a scant receptacle for that Good which has no end, and measures Itself by Itself. Therefore our vision, which must needs be one of the rays of the Mind with which all things are replete, cannot in its own nature be so potent as not to discern its origin far beyond that which is apparent to it.

58. "Therefore the sight into the Eternal Justice which your world receives penetrates within as the eye into the sea; which, though from the shore it can see the bottom, on the main it sees it not, and nevertheless it is there, but the depth conceals it. There is no light but that which comes from the serene which is never clouded; nay, rather there is darkness, either shadow of the flesh, or its poison. The hiding-place is now open enough to thee, which concealed from thee the living Justice concerning which thou didst make such frequent question; for thou saidst: 'A man is born on the bank of the Indus, and no one is there who may tell of Christ, nor who may read, nor who may write; and all his wishes and acts are good, so far as human reason sees, without sin in life or in speech. He dies unbaptized, and without faith; where is this Justice which condemns him? where is his sin if he does not believe?' Now who art thou, that, with the short vision of a single span, wouldst sit upon a bench to judge a thousand miles away? Assuredly, for him who subtilizes with me, if the Scripture were not above you, there would be marvellous occasion for doubting. Oh earthly animals! oh gross minds![3]

86. "The primal Will, which of Itself is good, has never moved from Itself, which is the

[1] St. John the Baptist, whose image was on the florin. Cf. Matthew, 14. 1-12; Mark, 6. 21-28.
[2] See Canto ix. 61f.
[3] Cf. *Hell*, xxxiv. 92.

Supreme Good. So much is just as is consonant with It; no created good draws It to itself, but It, raying forth, is the cause of that good."

91. As the stork circles above her nest, after she has fed her brood, and as the one that has been fed looks up at her, such became the blessed image, which impelled by so many counsels moved its wings, and I so raised my brows. Wheeling it sang, and said: "As are my notes to thee who understandest them not, such is the Eternal Judgment to you mortals."

100. After those shining flames of the Holy Spirit became quiet, still in the sign which made the Romans reverend to the world, it began again: "To this kingdom no one ever ascended, who had not believed in Christ either before or after he was nailed to the tree. But behold, many cry Christ, Christ, who, at the Judgment, shall be far less near to him, than some one who knows not Christ; and the Ethiop will condemn such Christians when the two companies shall be separated, the one forever rich, and the other poor. What may the Persians say to your kings, when they shall see that volume open in which was written all their dispraises?

115. "There shall be seen among the deeds of Albert that which will soon set the pen in motion, by which the kingdom of Prague shall be made a desert.[1] There shall be seen the woe which he who shall die by the blow of a wild boar is bringing upon the Seine by falsifying the coin.[2] There shall be seen the pride that quickens thirst, which makes the Scot and the Englishman mad, so that neither can keep within his own bounds. The luxury shall be seen, and the effeminate living of him of Spain, and of him of Bohemia, who never knew valor, nor wished it.[3] The goodness of the cripple of Jerusalem shall be seen marked with an I, while an M shall mark the contrary.[4] The

avarice and the cowardice shall be seen of him who guards the island of the fire, where Anchises ended his long life; and, to give to understand how paltry he is, the writing for him shall be in abridged letters which shall note much in little space.[5] And to every one shall be apparent the foul deeds of his uncle and of his brother,[6] who have dishonored so eminent a race and two crowns. And he of Portugal,[7] and he of Norway[8] shall be known there; and he of Rascia,[9] who, to his harm, has seen the coin of Venice. Oh happy Hungary, if she allow herself no longer to be maltreated! and happy Navarre, if she arm herself with the mountains which bind her round! And all should believe that, for earnest of this, Nicosia and Famagosta are now lamenting and complaining because of their beast which departs not from the side of the others."[10]

CANTO XX

WHEN he who illumines all the world descends from our hemisphere so that the day on every side is spent, the heaven, which before is enkindled by him alone, suddenly makes itself again conspicuous with many lights, wherein one alone is shining. And this act of heaven came to my mind when the ensign of the world and of its leaders became silent in its blessed beak; because all those living lights, shining far more, began songs which have lapsed and fallen from my memory.

13. O sweet Love, that mantlest thyself with a smile, how ardent didst thou appear in those flutes which had the breath alone of holy thoughts!

16. After the precious and shining stones, wherewith I saw the sixth luminary, ingemmed, imposed silence on their angelic chime, I seemed to hear the murmur of a

---

[1] The devastation of Bohemia in 1304, by Albert of Austria (Purgatory, vi. 97ff.).

[2] After his defeat at Courtrai, in 1302, Philip the Fair, to provide himself with means, debased the coin of the realm. He died in 1314 from the effects of a fall from his horse, overthrown by a wild boar in the forest of Fontainebleau.

[3] Respectively, Ferdinand IV of Castile and Wenceslaus IV of Bohemia. Cf. Purgatory, vii. 102.

[4] The virtues and vices of the lame Charles II, king of Naples, titular king of Jerusalem, shall be marked in Roman numerals. See Canto viii. 82.

[5] Frederick of Aragon, king of Sicily. See Purgatory, vii. 119.

[6] James, king of Majorca and Minorca, and James, king of Aragon. See Purgatory, vii. 120.

[7] Dionysius, king of Portugal, to whom a base love of money-getting was ascribed.

[8] Hakon V, who cruelly warred with Denmark.

[9] Rascia, so called from a Slavonic tribe, which occupied a region south of the Danube, embracing a part of the modern Servia and Bosnia. King Stephen Ouros, who died in 1307, imitated the coin of Venice with a debased coinage.

[10] Cities in Cyprus, which are now lamenting under the rule of Henry II, of the house of Lusignan.

stream which falls down clear from rock to rock, showing the abundance of its mountain source. And as the sound takes its form at the cithern's neck, and as at the vent of the bag-pipe wind which enters it, thus, without pause of waiting, that murmer of the Eagle rose up through its neck, as if it were hollow. There it became voice, and thence it issued through its beak in form of words, such as the heart where-on I wrote them was waiting.

31. "The part in me which in mortal eagles sees and endures the sun," it began to me, "must now be gazed at fixedly, because of the fires whereof I make my shape, those with which the eye in my head is sparkling are the chief of all their grades. He who shines in the middle, as the pupil, was the singer of the Holy Spirit, who bore about the ark from town to town;[1] now he knows the merit of his song, so far as it was the effect of his own counsel, by the remuneration which is proportioned to it. Of the five which make a circle for my brow, he who is nearest to my beak consoled the poor widow for her son;[2] now he knows, by the ex-perience of this sweet life and of its opposite, how dear it costs not to follow Christ. And he who on the rising arc comes next in the cir-cumference of which I speak, by true peni-tence delayed death;[3] now he knows that the eternal judgment is not transmuted, when worthy prayer there below makes to-morrow's that which was to-day's. The next who follows, with a good intention which bore bad fruit, made himself Greek, together with the laws and me, in order to give place to the Pastor;[4] now he knows how the ill deduced from his good action is not hurtful to him, although thereby the world be destroyed. And he whom thou seest in the down-bent arc was William,[5] whom that land deplores which weeps for Charles and Frederick living;[6] now he knows how heaven is enamoured of a just king, and by the aspect of his effulgence makes it still seen. Who, down in the erring world, would

believe that Rhipeus the Trojan[7] was the fifth of the holy lights in this circle? Now he knows much of that which the world cannot see of the divine grace, although his sight cannot discern the bottom."

73. Like a little lark that in the air expati-ates, first singing, and then is silent, content with the last sweetness which satisfies her, such seemed to me the image of the imprint of the Eternal Pleasure, according to whose desire everything becomes that which it is.

79. And though I was there, in respect to my doubt,[8] like glass to the color which it clothes, it endured not to bide its time in silence, but with the force of its own weight urged from my mouth: "What things are these?" whereat I saw great festival of flashing. Then at once, with its eye more enkindled, the blessed ensign answered me, in order not to keep me in won-dering suspense:

88. "I see that thou believest these things be-cause I say them, but thou seest not how; so that, although believed in, they are hidden. Thou dost as one who fully apprehends a thing by name, but cannot see its quiddity unless an-other explain it. *Regnum coelorum*[9] suffers vi-olence from fervent love, and from living hope which vanquishes the divine will; not in such wise as man overcomes man, but van-quishes it, because it wills to be vanquished, and, vanquished, vanquishes with its own be-nignity. The first life of the eyebrow and the fifth make thee marvel, because thou seest the region of the Angels painted with them. From their bodies they did not issue Gentiles, as thou believest, but Christians, with firm faith, one in the Feet that were to suffer, one in the Feet that had suffered. For the one came back unto his bones from Hell, where there is never return to righteous will; and that was the re-ward of living hope; of living hope, which put its power into the prayers made to God to raise him up, so that it might be possible for his will to be moved.

112. "The glorious soul, of whom I speak, returning to the flesh, in which it was but little while, believed in Him Who had power to aid it; and in believing was kindled to such fire of

---

[1] David. See II Samuel, 6; Cf. *Purgatory,* x. 64-67.
[2] Trajan. See *Purgatory,* x. 73-93.
[3] King Hezekiah. See II Kings, 20. 1-6; Isaiah, 38, 1-5.
[4] Constantine the Great ceded Rome to the Pope and transferred the seat of empire to Constantinople.
[5] William 11 called "the Good," king of Sicily and Apulia.
[6] See Canto xix. 127-135.

[7] See *Aeneid,* ii. 426-427.
[8] See Canto xix. 103-105.
[9] "The kingdom of Heaven." Matthew, 11. 12.

true love, that at its second death it was worthy to come unto this festivity. The other, through grace which distils from a fount so deep that creature never pushed the eye far as its primal wave, there below set all his love on righteousness; wherefore from grace to grace God opened his eye to our future redemption, so that he believed in it, and thenceforth endured no more the stench of paganism, and reproved therefor the perverse folk. Those three Ladies whom thou hast seen at the right wheel[1] were to him for baptism, more than a thousand years before baptizing. O predestination, how remote is thy root from the vision of those who see not the First Cause entire! And ye, mortals, keep yourselves restrained in judging; for we who see God know not yet all the elect; and to us such defect is sweet, for our good is perfected in this good—that what God wills we also will."

139. Thus, to make my short sight clear, sweet medicine was given to me by that divine image. And as a good lutanist makes the vibration of the string accompany a good singer, whereby the song acquires more pleasantness, so I remember that, while it spake, I saw the two blessed lights moving their flamelets to the words, just as the winking of the eyes concords.

CANTO XXI

ALREADY were my eyes fixed again upon the countenance of my Lady, and my mind with them, and from every other intent it was withdrawn; and she was not smiling, but: "If I should smile," she began to me, "thou wouldst become such as Semele was when she became ashes; for my beauty, which along the stairs of the eternal palace is kindled the more, as thou hast seen, the higher the ascent, is so resplendent that, were it not tempered, at its effulgence thy mortal power would be as a bough shattered by thunder. We are lifted to the seventh splendor, which beneath the breast of the burning Lion now radiates downward mingled with his strength.[2] Fix thy mind behind thine eyes, and make of them mirrors for the figure which in this mirror shall be apparent to thee."

[1] See *Purgatory,* xxix. 121.
[2] Saturn, which was in the sign of the Lion.

19. He who should know what was the pasture of my sight in her blessed aspect, when I transferred me to another care, would know, by counterpoising one side with the other, how pleasing it was to me to obey my celestial escort.

25. Within the crystal which, circling round the world, bears the name of its illustrious leader, under whom all wickedness lay dead,[3] I saw, of the color of gold on which a sunbeam is shining, a ladder rising up so high that my eye followed it not. I saw, moreover, so many splendors descending along the steps, that I thought every light which appears in heaven had been poured down from it.

34. And as, by their natural custom, the daws, at the beginning of the day, move about together, in order to warm their cold feathers; then some go away without return, others wheel round to whence they started, and others, circling, make a stay; such fashion it seemed to me was here in that sparkling which came together, so soon as it struck on a certain step; and that one which stopped nearest to us became so bright that I said in my thought: "I see well the love which thou dost signify to me. But she, from whom I await the how and the when of speech and of silence, stays still; wherefore I, contrary to desire, do well not to ask." Whereupon she, who saw my silence, in the sight of Him who sees everything, said to me: "Let loose thy warm desire."

52. And I began: "My own merit does not make me worthy of thy answer; but for her sake who concedes to me the asking, O blessed life, that art hidden within thine own joy, make known to me the cause which has placed thee so near me; and tell why in this wheel the sweet symphony of Paradise is silent, which below through the others so devoutly sounds."

61. "Thou hast thy hearing mortal, as thy sight," it replied to me; "therefore no song is here for the same reason that Beatrice has no smile. Down over the steps of the holy stairway I have descended so far, only to give thee glad welcome with my speech and with the light that mantles me; nor has more love made me to be more ready, for as much and more love is burning up there, even as the flaming manifests to thee; but the high charity, which makes

[3] Saturn, in the golden age.

us prompt servants to the Counsel that governs the world, allots here, even as thou observest."

73. "I see well," said I, "O sacred lamp, how free love suffices in this Court for following the eternal Providence; but this is what seems to me hard to discern, why thou alone among thy consorts wert predestined to this office."' I had not come to the last word before the light made a centre of its middle, whirling itself like a swift millstone.

82. Then the love that was within it answered: "A divine light is directed on me, penetrating through this wherein I embosom me; the virtue of which, conjoined with my vision, lifts me above myself so far that I see the Supreme Essence from which it emanates. Thence comes the joy wherewith I flame, because to my vision, in proportion as it is clear, I match the clearness of my flame. But that soul in Heaven which is most enlightened, that Seraph who has his eye most fixed on God, could not satisfy thy demand; because that which thou askest lies so deep within the abyss of the eternal statute, that from every created sight it is cut off. And when thou returnest to the mortal world, carry this back, so that it may no longer presume to move its feet toward such a goal. The mind which shines here, on earth is smoky; wherefore consider how can it do there below that which it cannot do though Heaven assume it."

103. So did its words prescribe to me, that I left the question, and drew me back to ask it humbly who it was. "Between the two shores of Italy, and not very distant from thy native land, rise rocks so high that the thunders sound far lower down, and they form a ridge which is called Catria, beneath which a hermitage is consecrated which was wont to be devoted to worship only."[2]

112. Thus it began again to me with its third speech, and then, continuing, said: "There in the service of God I became so steadfast, that, only with food of olive juice, lightly I used to pass the heats and frosts, content in contemplative thoughts. That cloister was wont to render in abundance to these heavens; and now it is become so empty as needs must soon be re-

vealed. In that place was I Peter Damian,[3] and Peter the sinner had I been in the house of Our Lady on the Adriatic shore. Little of mortal life was remaining for me, when I was sought for and dragged to that hat which ever is passed down from bad to worse. Cephas[4] came, and the great vessel of the Holy Spirit[5] came, lean and barefoot, taking the food of whatsoever inn. Now the modern pastors require one to prop them up on this side and that, and one to lead them, so heavy are they, and one to hold up their trains behind. They cover their palfreys with their mantles, so that two beasts go under one hide. O Patience, that dost endure so much!"

136. At these words I saw more flamelets from step to step descending and whirling, and every whirl made them more beautiful. Round about this one they came, and stopped, and uttered a cry of such deep sound that here could be none like it; nor did I understand it, the thunder so overcame me.

CANTO XXII

OPPRESSED with amazement, I turned me to my Guide, like a little child who always runs back thither where he most confides; and she, like a mother who quickly succors her pale and breathless son with her voice, which is wont to reassure him, said to me: "Knowst thou not that thou art in Heaven? and knowst thou not that Heaven is all holy, and whatever is done here comes from righteous zeal? How the song would have transformed thee, and I by smiling, thou canst now conceive, since the cry has so greatly moved thee; in which, if thou hadst understood its prayers, already would be known to thee the vengeance which thou shalt see before thou diest. The sword of here on high cuts not in haste, nor tardily, save to the seeming of him who, desiring or fearing, awaits it. But turn thee round now toward the others; for many illustrious spirits thou shalt see, if, as I bid, thou carry back thy look."

22. As was her pleasure I directed my eyes, and saw a hundred little spheres, which together were making themselves more beautiful with

---

[1] Cf. Canto iii. 52-87.

[2] Catria is a high offshoot to the east from the Apennines, between Urbino and Gubbio. On its side was the Camaldolite monastery of Fonte Avellana.

[3] A doctor of the Church in the eleventh century. For years abbot of Fonte Avellana, in 1058 he, much against his will, was made cardinal bishop of Ostia.

[4] St. Peter. See John, 1. 42.

[5] St. Paul. See Acts, 9. 15.

their mutual rays. I was standing as one who within himself represses the point of his desire, and attempts not to ask, he so fears the too-much. And the largest and most lustrous of those pearls[1] came forward to make my wish concerning itself content. Then within it I heard: "If thou couldst see, as I do, the charity which burns among us, thy thoughts would be expressed; but that thou, by waiting, mayst not retard thy high end, I will make answer to thee, even to the thought about which thou so restrainest thyself.

37. "That mountain on whose slope Cassino is, was of old frequented on its summit by the deluded and ill-disposed people, and I am he who first bore up there the name of Him Who brought to earth the truth which so high exalts us: and such grace shone upon me that I drew away the surrounding villages from the impious worship which seduced the world. All these other fires were contemplative men, kindled by that heat which brings to birth holy flowers and fruits. Here is Macarius, here is Romualdus,[2] here are my brothers, who fixed their feet within the cloisters, and held their heart steadfast."

52. And I to him: "The affection which thou displayest in speaking with me, and the good semblance which I see and note in all your ardors, have expanded my confidence as the sun does the rose, when she becomes open as wide as she has power to be. Therefore I pray thee, and do thou, Father, assure me if I am capable of receiving so great grace, that I may see thee with uncovered shape."

61. Whereon he: "Brother, thy high desire shall be fulfilled up in the last sphere,[3] where are fulfilled all others and my own. There every desire is perfect, mature, and whole; in that alone is every part there where it always was: for it is not in space, and it has not poles; and our ladder reaches up to it, so that thus from thy sight it steals itself. Far up as there the patriarch Jacob saw it stretch its upper part, when it appeared to him so laden with Angels.

73. "But no one now lifts his feet from earth

to ascend it; and my Rule remains for waste of paper. The walls, which used to be an abbey. have become dens, and the cowls are sacks full of bad meal. But heavy usury is not levied so counter to God's pleasure, as that fruit which makes the heart of the monks so mad; for whatsoever the Church has in keeping is all for the folk that ask it in God's name, not for kindred, or for others more vile. The flesh of mortals is so soft that on earth a good beginning does not suffice from the springing of the oak to the forming of the acorn. Peter began without gold and without silver, and I with prayers and with fasting, and Francis his convent with humility; and if thou lookest at the beginning of each, and then lookest again to where it has run astray, thou wilt see the white changed to dark. Truly, Jordan turned back, and the sea fleeing when God willed, were more marvellous to behold than to see succor here."

97. Thus he said to me, and then drew back to his company, and the company closed together; then like a whirlwind all gathered itself upward.

100. The sweet Lady urged me behind them, with only a sign, up over that ladder; so did her virtue overcome my nature. But never here below, where one mounts and descends naturally, was there motion so rapid that it could be compared unto my wing. So may I return, Reader, to that devout triumph, for the sake of which I often bewail my sins and beat my breast, thou hadst not drawn out and put thy finger in the fire so quickly as I saw the sign which follows the Bull,[4] and was within it.

112. O glorious stars, O light impregnate with great virtue, from which I acknowledge all my genius, whatever it may be; with you was born and with you was hiding himself he who is father of every mortal life, when I first felt the Tuscan air; and then, when grace was bestowed on me to enter within the lofty wheel which turns you, your region was allotted to me. To you[5] my soul now devoutly sighs that it may acquire virtue for the hard pass which draws her to itself.

124. "Thou art so near the ultimate salvation," began Beatrice, "that thou oughtest to

---

[1] St. Benedict.
[2] St. Macarius of Alexandria, a disciple of St. Antony, who did much to promote the monastic rule in the East. St. Romualdus founded the Order of Camaldoli in 1012.
[3] The Empyrean.

[4] The sign of the Gemini, or Twins, in the Heaven of the Fixed Stars.
[5] The Gemini.

have thine eyes clear and keen. And therefore ere thou enter farther into it, look back downward, and see how great a world I have already set beneath thy feet, in order that thy heart may present itself joyous to its utmost unto the triumphant throng which comes glad through this round ether."

133. With my sight I returned through all and each of the seven spheres, and saw this globe such that I smiled at its mean semblance; and that counsel I approve as best which holds it of least account; and he who thinks of other things may be called truly righteous. I saw the daughter of Latona[1] enkindled without that shadow which had been the cause why I once believed her rare and dense. The aspect of thy son, Hyperion,[2] here I endured, and I saw how Maia and Dione[3] move around and near him. Then appeared to me the temperateness of Jove, between his father and his son, and then was clear to me the varying which they make in their position. And all the seven were displayed to me—how great they are and how swift they are, and how far apart they are in their abodes. While I was revolving with the eternal Twins, the little threshing-floor which makes us so fierce all appeared to me, from its hills to its river-mouths.

154. Then I turned back my eyes to the beautiful eyes.

CANTO XXIII

As the bird, among the beloved leaves, having reposed on the nest of her sweet brood through the night which hides things from us, who, in order to see this longed-for looks and to find the food wherewith she may feed them, in which her heavy toils are pleasing to her, anticipates the time, upon the open twig, and with ardent affection awaits the sun, fixedly looking till the dawn may break; so was my Lady, standing erect and expectant, turned toward the region beneath which the sun shows least haste; so that I, seeing her rapt and eager, became such as he who in desire would fain have something else and in hope is satisfied. But

short while was there between one and the other *when;* of my awaiting, I mean, and of my seeing the heavens become more and more resplendent.

19. And Beatrice said: "Behold the hosts of the Triumph of Christ, and all the fruit harvested by the revolution of these spheres." It seemed to me her face was all aflame, and her eyes were so full of joy that I must needs pass on without description.

25. As in the clear skies at the full moon Trivia[4] smiles among the eternal nymphs who paint the heaven through all its depths, I saw, above thousands of lamps, a Sun that was enkindling each and all of them, as ours kindles the supernal shows; and through its living light the lucent Substance[5] gleamed so bright upon my face that I sustained it not.

34. Oh Beatrice, sweet guide and dear!

35. She said to me: "That which overcomes thee is a virtue against which naught defends itself. Here is the Wisdom and the Power that opened the roads between heaven and earth, for which there erst had been such long desire."

40. As fire is unlocked from a cloud, by dilating so that it has not room there, and contrary to its own nature falls down to earth, so my mind, becoming greater amid those feasts, issued from itself, and what it became it cannot remember.

46. "Open thine eyes and look on what I am; thou hast seen things such as thou art become able to sustain my smile." I was as one who comes to himself from a forgotten vision and endeavors in vain to bring it back to mind, when I heard this invitation, worthy of such gratitude that it is never to be effaced from the book which records the past. If now all those tongues which Polyhymnia and her sisters made most rich with their sweetest milk should sound to aid me, it would not come to a thousandth of the truth in singing the holy smile and how it lighted up the holy face. And thus, depicting Paradise, the consecrated poem must needs make a leap, even as one who finds his way cut off. But whoso should consider the ponderous theme and the mortal shoulder which is laden therewith would not blame it if under this it

[1] The Moon. Cf. Canto ii. 49-148.

[2] The Titan Hyperion was the father of Helios, the Sun.

[3] Maia and Dione were respectively the mothers of Mercury and Venus, and by their names these planets are here designated.

[4] An appellation of Diana, and hence of the moon.

[5] Christ in His glorified body.

tremble. It is no voyage for a little barque, this
which my venturous prow goes cleaving, nor
for a pilot who would spare himself.

70. "Why does my face so enamour thee that
thou turnest not to the fair garden which blos-
soms beneath the rays of Christ? Here is the
Rose, in which the Divine Word became flesh:
here are the lilies[1] by whose odor the good way
was taken."

76. Thus Beatrice: and I, who to her coun-
sels was wholly ready, again gave myself up to
the battle of the feeble brows.

79. As my eyes, covered with a shadow, have
ere now seen a meadow of flowers under a sun-
beam which streams bright through a rifted
cloud, so saw I many throngs of splendors
flashed upon from above by burning rays,
though I saw not the source of the gleams. O
benignant Power which dost so imprint them,
thou didst raise thyself on high to bestow scope
there for my eyes, which were powerless.

88. The name of the fair flower[2] which I ev-
er invoke, both morning and evening, wholly
constrained my mind to gaze upon the great-
er fire. And when the brightness and the mag-
nitude of the living star, which up there con-
quers as it conquered here below, were de-
picted in both my eyes, from within the mid
heavens a torch, formed in a circle in fashion
of a crown, descended and engirt her, and re-
volved around her. Whatever melody sounds
sweetest here below, and to itself most draws
the soul, would seem a cloud which, being
rent, thunders, compared with the sound of
that lyre wherewith was crowned the beaute-
ous sapphire by which the brightest Heaven is
ensapphired.

103. "I am Angelic Love, and I circle round
the lofty joy which breathes from out the womb
which was the hostelry of our Desire; and I
shall circle, Lady of Heaven, until thou shalt
follow thy Son and make the supreme sphere
more divine because thou enterest it." Thus
the circling melody sealed itself, and all the
other lights made the name of Mary resound.

112. The royal mantle[3] of all the revolutions
of the world, which is most fervid and most
quickened in the breath of God and in His

ways, had its inner shore so distant above us
that sight of it, there where I was, did not yet
appear to me. Therefore my eyes had not power
to follow the crowned flame, which mounted
upward after her offspring. And as an infant
which, when it has taken the milk, stretches
its arms toward its mother, because of its af-
fection which flames up outwardly, each of
these splendors stretched upward with its flame,
so that the exalted love which they had for
Mary was manifest to me. Then they remained
there in my sight, singing *Regina coeli*[4] so
sweetly that never has the delight departed
from me. Oh how great is the abundance which
is heaped up in those most rich coffers which
were good fields for sowing here below! Here
they live and enjoy the treasure which was ac-
quired while they wept in the exile of Baby-
lon, where the gold was left aside. Here, under
the exalted Son of God and of Mary, together
with the ancient and with the new council, he
triumphs in his victory who holds the keys of
such glory.[5]

CANTO XXIV

"O FELLOWSHIP elect to the great supper of
the blessed Lamb, who feeds you so that your
desire is always full, since by grace of God this
man foretastes of that which falls from your
table, before death prescribe the time for him,
give heed to his immense longing, and some-
what bedew him; ye drink ever of the fount
whence comes that of which he is thinking."
Thus Beatrice; and those glad souls made them-
selves spheres upon fixed poles, flaming bright-
ly after the manner of comets. And as wheels
within the fittings of clocks revolve, so that to
him who gives heed the first seems quiet, and
the last to fly, so these carols, differently danc-
ing, swift and slow, made me rate their riches.

19. From the one which I noted of greatest
beauty, I saw issue a fire so happy that it left
there none of greater brightness; and it re-
volved three times round Beatrice with a song
so divine that my fancy repeats it not to me;
wherefore my pen makes a leap, and I write

---

[1] See II Corinthians, 2. 14.
[2] The Virgin.
[3] Probably the Empyrean.

[4] "O Queen of Heaven," the first words of an
antiphon sung in the office of the Virgin at compline
on certain days after Easter. "O Queen of Heaven, re-
joice, for He whom thou wert worthy to bear rose
as He promised; pray to God for us. Hallelujah."
[5] St. Peter.

it not, for our imagination, much more our speech, is of too vivid color for such folds. "O holy sister mine, who dost so devoutly pray to us, by thine ardent affection thou dost unloose me from that fair sphere": after it had stopped, the blessed fire directed to my Lady its breath, which spoke thus as I have said:

34. And she: "O light eternal of the great man to whom our Lord left the keys, which he bore below, of this marvellous joy, test this man on points light and grave, as pleases thee, concerning the Faith, through which thou didst walk upon the sea. If he loves rightly, and hopes rightly, and believes, is not hidden from thee, for thou hast thy sight there where everything is seen depicted. But since this realm has made citizens by the true faith, it is well that to glorify it speech of it should fall to him."

46. Even as the bachelor arms himself—and dost not speak, until the master propounds the question—in order to adduce the proof, not to decide it, so, while she was speaking, I was arming me with every reason, in order to be ready for such a questioner, and for such a profession.

52. "Speak, good Christian, declare thyself; Faith, what is it?" Whereon I raised my brow to that light whence this was breathed forth, then turned me to Beatrice, and she made prompt signals to me that I should pour the water forth from my internal fount. "May the Grace," I began, "which grants to me that I confess myself to the chief centurion cause my conceptions to be well expressed." And I went on: "As the veracious pen, Father, of thy dear brother[1] (who with thee set Rome on the good track) wrote of it, Faith is the substance of things hoped for, and evidence of things not seen;[2] and this appears to me its essence."

67. Then I heard: "Rightly dost thou think, if thou understandest well why he placed it among the substances, and then among the evidences." And I thereon: "The deep things which grant unto me here the sight of themselves, are so hidden to eyes below that there their existence is in belief alone, upon which the lofty hope is founded, and therefore it takes the designation of substance; and from this belief we needs must syllogize, without having

other sight, wherefore it receives the designation of evidence."[3] Then I heard: "If all that is acquired down below for doctrine, were so understood, the wit of sophist would have no place there."

82. These words were breathed forth from that enkindled love; then it added: "Very well have the alloy and the weight of this coin been now gone over, but tell me if thou hast it in thy purse?" Whereupon I: "Yes, I have it so shining and so round that in its stamp nothing is doubtful to me." Then issued from the deep light which was shining there: "This precious jewel, whereon every virtue is founded, whence came it to thee?" And I: "The abundant rain of the Heavenly Spirit, which is shed over the Old and over the New parchments, is a syllogism which has proved it to me with such acuteness, that in comparison with this every demonstration seems to me obtuse." I heard then: "The Old proposition and the New which are so conclusive to thee—why dost thou hold them for Divine speech?" And I: "The proof which discloses the truth to me are the works that followed, for which nature never heated iron, nor beat anvil."

103. It was replied to me: "Say, what assures thee that these works were? The very thing itself which requires to be proved, naught else, affirms it to thee." "If the world were converted to Christianity," said I, "without miracles, this alone is such that the others are not the hundredth part; for thou didst enter poor and fasting into the field to sow the good plant, which once was a vine and now has become a bramble."

112. This ended, the high holy Court resounded through the spheres a "We praise thee, O God," in the melody which up there is sung.

115. And that Baron[4] who thus from branch to branch, examining, had now drawn me on, so that we were approaching the last leaves, began again: "The Grace that holds courteous converse with thy mind has opened thy mouth thus far as it should be opened, so that I approve that which has issued forth, but now it is

[1] St. Paul.
[2] See Hebrews, 11. 1.

[3] See, for this signification of substance, Aquinas, *Summa Theologica*, Part I, Q 29, A 2.
[4] During the Middle Ages a term not infrequently applied to the most eminent among the saints, and even to Christ Himself.

befitting to express what thou believest, and whence it was offered to thy belief."

124. "O holy father, spirit who seest that which thou didst so believe that thou, toward the sepulchre, didst outdo younger feet,[1] began I, "thou wishest that I should here declare the form of my ready belief, and also thou hast asked the cause of it. And I answer: I believe in one God, sole and eternal, who, unmoved, moves all the Heavens with love and with desire; and for such belief I have not only proofs physical and metaphysical, but that truth also gives it to me which hence rains down through Moses, through Prophets, and through Psalms, through the Gospel, and through you who wrote after the fiery Spirit made you reverend. And I believe in three Eternal Persons, and these I believe to be one essence, so one and so threefold that it will admit to be conjoined with *are* and *is*. Of the profound divine condition on which I touch, the evangelic doctrine many times sets the seal upon my mind. This is the beginning, this is the spark which afterwards dilates into a vivid flame, and like a star in heaven scintillates within me."

148. Even as a lord who hears what pleases him, thereon, rejoicing in the news, embraces his servant, soon as he is silent, thus, blessing me as he sang, the apostolic light, at whose command I had spoken, thrice encircled me when I was silent; so had I pleased him in my speech.

CANTO XXV

IF it ever happen that the sacred poem to which both heaven and earth have so set hand, that it has made me lean for many years, should overcome the cruelty which bars me out of the fair sheepfold, where a lamb I slept, foe to the wolves that give it war, then with other voice, with other fleece, a Poet will I return, and on the font of my baptism will I take the crown; because there I entered into the Faith which makes the souls known to God; and afterward Peter, for its sake, thus encircled my brow.

13. Then a light moved toward us from that sphere whence had issued the first-fruit which Christ left of His vicars; and my Lady, full of gladness, said to me: "Look, look! behold the Baron for whose sake there below Galicia is visited."[2]

19. As when the dove alights near his mate, and each, circling and cooing, displays its affection to the other, so by the one great Prince glorious I saw the other greeted, praising the food which feeds them thereabove. But after their gratulation was completed, silent *coram me*[3] each stopped, so blazing that it overcame my sight. Then Beatrice, smiling, said: "Illustrious life, by whom the bounty of our basilica was written,[4] do thou make Hope resound upon this height; thou knowest that thou dost represent it as many times as Jesus displayed most brightness to the three."[5] "Lift up thy head, and mind thou reassure thyself; for that which comes up here from the mortal world needs must be ripened in our rays." This comfort came to me from the second fire; whereon I lifted up my eyes unto the mountains which had bent them down before with excess of weight.

40. "Since, through grace, our Emperor wills that thou, before thy death, come face to face with his Counts in His most secret hall, so that, having seen the truth of this Court, thou mayest therewith confirm in thyself and others the Hope which there below rightly enamours, say what it is, and how thy mind blossoms with it, and say whence it came to thee"; thus further did the second light proceed.

49. And that compassionate one, who guided the feathers of my wings to such lofty flight, thus in the reply anticipated me: "The Church militant has not any child possessed of more hope, as is written in the Sun which irradiates all our band; therefore it is conceded to him that from Egypt he should come to Jerusalem, to behold, before his term of warfare is completed. The other two points which are asked not for sake of knowing, but that he may report how greatly this virtue is pleasing to thee, I leave to him, for they will not be difficult to him, nor of vainglory, and let him answer there-

[1] Cf. John, 20. 4-6.

[2] St. James, the brother of St. John, is believed to be buried at Compostella, in Galicia.
[3] "Before me."
[4] The reference is to the Epistle of James, which Dante wrongly attributes to St. James the Greater. See James, 1. 5, 17.
[5] Cf. Matthew, 17. 1ff.; 25. 37; Mark, 9. 1; Luke, 8. 51; 9. 28.

to, and may the grace of God accord this to him."

64. As a scholar who follows his teacher, prompt and glad in that wherein he is expert, so that his worth may be disclosed: "Hope," said I, "is a sure expectation of future glory, which divine grace produces, and preceding merit.[1] From many stars this light comes to me, but he first instilled it into my heart who was the supreme singer of the Supreme Leader. 'Let them hope in Thee, who know Thy name,' he says in his theody;[2] and who knows it not, if he has my faith? Thou afterwards in thy Epistle[3] didst instil it into me together with his instilling, so that I am full, and upon others shower down your rain."

79. While I was speaking, within the living bosom of that fire a flash was trembling, sudden and frequent, in the manner of lightning. Then it breathed: "The love wherewith I still glow toward the virtue which followed me even to the palm, and to the issue of the field, wills that I breathe again to thee, who dost delight in it; and it is my pleasure, that thou tell that which Hope promises to thee." And I: "The new and the old Scriptures set up the mark, and that points it out to me. Of the souls whom God hath made his friends, Isaiah says that each one should be clothed in his own land with a double garment,[4] and his own land is this sweet life; and thy brother, far more explicitly, there where he treats of the white robes, makes manifest to us this revelation.[5]

97. At first, close on the end of these words, *Sperent in te*[6] was heard above us, to which all the carols made answer; then among them a light became so bright that, if the Crab had one such crystal, winter would have a month of one sole day. And as a glad maiden rises and goes and enters in the dance, only to do honor to the new bride, and not for any failing, so did I see the brightened splendor come to the two who were turning in a wheel, such as was befitting their ardent love. It set itself there into the song and into the measure, and my

Lady kept her gaze upon them, even as a bride silent and motionless. "This is he who lay upon the breast of our Pelican,[7] and who was chosen from upon the cross for the great office."[8]

115. Thus my Lady; but no more after than before her words did she move her look from its fixed attention. As is he who gazes and endeavors to see the sun a little eclipsed, and who through seeing becomes sightless, so did I become in respect to that last fire, till it was said: "Why dost thou dazzle thyself in order to see a thing which has no place here?[9] On earth my body is earth; and it will be there with the others until our number corresponds with the eternal purpose. With the two robes in the blessed cloister are only those two lights which ascended;[10] and this thou shalt carry back unto your world."

130. At this word the flaming gyre became quiet, together with the sweet mingling made of the sound of the trinal breath, even as, for avoiding of fatigue or danger, the oars, erst driven through the water, all stop at the sound of a whistle.

136. Ah! how greatly was I disturbed in mind, when I turned to see Beatrice, at not being able to see her, although I was near her, and in the happy world.

CANTO XXVI

WHILE I was apprehensive because of my quenched sight, a breath which made me attentive issued from the effulgent flame that had quenched it, saying: "While thou art regaining the sense of sight which thou hast consumed on me, it is well that thou make up for it by discourse. Begin then, and tell at what thy soul is aimed, and make thy recokoning that thy sight is confounded in thee and not dead; because the Lady who conducts thee through

[7] Christ. It was believed that the pelican killed its brood, and then revived them with its blood.
[8] See John, 19. 27.
[9] Dante seeks to see whether St. John is present in the earthly as well as the spiritual body; his desire having its source in the words of the Gospel: "Jesus saith unto him, If I will that he tarry till I come, what is that to thee? . . . Then went this saying abroad among the brethren, that that disciple should not die." See John, 21. 22, 23. From these words arose a legend that, immediately on his apparent death, St. John, still in the body, was taken up to heaven.
[10] Jesus and Mary. See Canto xxiii. 86, 120.

[1] These words are taken directly from Peter Lombard, *Liber Sententiarum*, iii. 26.
[2] See Psalms, 9. 10.
[3] See James, 1. 12; 2. 5; 4. 8.
[4] See Isaiah, 59. 7.
[5] See Revelation, 7. 9-17.
[6] "They will put their trust in thee." Psalms, 9. 10.

this divine region has in her look the virtue which the hand of Ananias had."[1]

13. I said: "At her pleasure, or soon or late, let the cure come to the eyes which were the gates when she entered with the fire wherewith I ever burn. The Good which makes this court content is Alpha and Omega of every scripture that Love reads to me, either low or loud."[2]

19. That same voice which had taken from me fear in regard to the sudden dazzling, laid on me the charge to speak further, and said: "Surely with a finer sieve it behoves thee to sift; it behoves thee to tell who directed thy bow to such a target."

25. And I: "By philosophic arguments and by authority that descends from here, such love must needs be impressed on me; for the good, inasmuch as it is good, so soon as it is understood, kindles love; and so much the greater as the more of goodness it comprises in itself. Therefore, to the Essence (wherein is such supremacy that every good which is found outside of It is naught else than a beam of Its own radiance), more than to any other, the mind of everyone who discerns the truth on which this argument is founded must needs be moved in love. This truth does he make plain to my intelligence, who demonstrates to me the first love of all the sempiternal substances.[3] The voice of the true Author makes it plain who, speaking of Himself, says to Moses: 'I will make thee see all goodness.'[4] Thou, too, makest it plain to me, beginning the lofty announcement which below on earth, above all other trump, proclaims the secret of this place on high."[5]

46. And I heard: "By human understanding, and by authorities concordant with it, thy sovran love looks unto God; but say, further, if thou feelest other cords draw thee towards Him, so that thou mayst declare with how many teeth this love doth bite thee."

52. The holy intention of the Eagle of Christ was not latent to me; nay, rather I perceived whither he wished to lead my profession; therefore, I began again: "All those bitings which can make the heart turn to God have been concurrent unto my love; for the existence of the world, and my own existence, the death which He endured that I may live, and that which all the faithful hope even as I do, together with the aforesaid living consciousness, have drawn me from the sea of perverted love, and have set me on the shore of the right. The leaves, wherewith all the garden of the Eternal Gardener is enleaved, I love in measure of the good borne unto them from Him."

67. Soon as I was silent a most sweet song resounded through the heavens, and my Lady said with the others: "Holy, Holy, Holy."

70. And as at a keen light sleep is broken by the spirit of sight, which runs to the splendor that goes from coat to coat, and he who awakes shrinks from what he sees, so ignorant is his sudden wakening, until his judgment comes to his aid; thus Beatrice chased away every mote from my eyes with the radiance of her own, which were refulgent more than a thousand miles; so that I then saw better than before; and, as one amazed, I asked concerning a fourth light which I saw with us. And my Lady: "Within those rays the first soul which the First Power ever created gazes with joy upon its Maker."

85. As the bough which bends its top at passing of the wind, and then uplifts itself by its own virtue which raises it, so did I, in amazement, while she was speaking; and then a desire to speak, wherewith I was burning, gave me again assurance, and I began: "O fruit, that wast alone produced mature, O ancient Father, to whom every bride is daughter and daughter-in-law, devoutly as I can, I supplicate thee that thou speak to me; thou seest my wish, and that I may hear thee speedily, I do not tell it."

97. Sometimes an animal, when covered up, so stirs, that its impulse must needs be apparent because of the corresponding movement which its wrapping makes; and in like manner the first soul made evident to me, through its covering, how gladly it came to do me pleasure.

103. Then it breathed forth: "Without its being uttered to me by thee, I better discern thy wish, than thou whatever thing is most certain to thee; because I see it in the truthful Mirror which makes of Itself a reflection of other things, while nothing makes of itself a reflec-

---

[1] See Acts, 9. 18.
[2] See Revelation, 1. 8.
[3] Aristotle.
[4] See Exodus, 33. 19.
[5] See Revelation, 1. 8.

tion of It. Thou wouldst hear how long it is since God placed me in the lofty garden where this Lady made thee ready for so long a stairway; and how long it was a delight to my eyes; and the proper cause of the great wrath; and of the idiom which I used and which I made.

115. "Now, my son, the tasting of the tree was not by itself the cause of so great an exile, but only the overpassing of the bound. In that place whence thy Lady moved Virgil, I longed for this assembly during four thousand three hundred and two revolutions of the sun; and while I was on earth I saw him return to all the lights of his path nine hundred and thirty times. The tongue which I spoke was all extinct long before the people of Nimrod attempted their unaccomplishable work; for never was any product of the reason durable for ever, because of human liking, which alters, following the heavens. That man speaks is work of nature; but, thus or thus, nature then leaves to you to do according as it pleases you. Before I descended to the infernal anguish, the Supreme Good, whence comes the gladness that swathes me, was on earth called *I;* afterwards it was called *El;*[1] and that must needs me, for the custom of mortals is as a leaf on a branch, which goes away and another comes. On the mountain which rises highest from the wave I was, with pure life and sinful, from the first hour to that which follows the sixth, when the sun changes quadrant."

CANTO XXVII

"To the Father, to the Son, and to the Holy Spirit be glory," all Paradise began, so that the sweet song was inebriating me. That which I was seeing seemed to me a smile of the universe; for my inebriation was entering through the hearing and through the sight. O joy! O ineffable gladness! O life entire of love and of peace! O riches secure, without longing!

10. Before my eyes the four torches were standing enkindled, and that which had come first began to make itself more vivid, and in its semblence became such as Jupiter would become, if he and Mars were birds, and should exchange plumage. The Providence which here assigns turn and office, had imposed silence

[1] *I* is here to be pronounced *jah;* see Psalms, 68. 4.

on the blessed choir on every side, when I heard: "If I change color, marvel not; for, as I speak, thou shalt see all these change color. He who on earth usurps my place, my place, my place, which is vacant in the presence of the Son of God,[2] has made of my cemetery a sewer of blood and of filth, wherewith the Perverse One who fell from here above, below there is placated."

28. With that color which, by reason of the opposite sun, paints the cloud at evening and at morning, I then saw the whole Heaven overspread. And as a modest lady who abides sure of herself, and at the fault of another, on only hearing of it, becomes timid, thus did Beatrice change semblance; and such eclipse, I believe, there was in heaven when the Supreme Power suffered.

37. Then his words proceeded, in a voice so transmuted from itself that his countenance was not more changed: "The Bride of Christ was not nurtured on my blood, and that of Linus and of Cletus, to be employed for acquist of gold; but for acquist of this glad life Sixtus and Pius and Calixtus and Urban[3] shed their blood after much weeping. It was not our intention that part of the Christian people should sit on the right hand of our successors, and part on the other; nor that the keys which were entrusted to me should become a device upon a banner which should fight against the baptized;[4] nor that I should be made a figure on a seal to venal and mendacious privileges, whereat I often redden and flash. Rapacious wolves, in garb of shepherd, are seen from here on high over all the pastures: O defence of God, why dost thou yet lie still! To drink our blood Cahorsines and Gascons are making ready;[5] O good beginning, to what vile end must thou fall! But the high Providence, which with Scipio defended for Rome the glory of the world, will succor speedily, as I conceive. And thou, son, who because of thy mortal

[2] Dante held that Boniface VIII had no right to the papal throne, because his election had taken place while Celestine V, his predecessor, was still alive, and had been secured by bribery and deception.

[3] Early Popes.

[4] In Boniface VIII's war against the Colonna family. See *Hell,* xxvii. 85-111.

[5] John XXII, Pope from 1316 to 1334, was a native of Cahors; his immediate predecessor, Clement V, 1305-1314, was a Gascon.

weight wilt again return below, open thy mouth, and conceal not that which I conceal not."

67. Even as our air snows down flakes of frozen vapors, when the horn of the Goat of heaven is touched by the sun, so I saw the æther become adorned, and flaked upward with the triumphant vapors which had made sojourn there with us. My sight was following their semblances, and followed, till the intermediate space by its vastness took from it the power of passing farther onward. Whereon my Lady, who saw me freed from gazing upward, said to me: "Cast down thy sight, and look how thou hast revolved."

79. I saw that, since the hour when I had first looked,[1] I had moved through the whole arc which the first climate makes from its middle to its end; so that beyond Cadiz I saw the mad track of Ulysses, and on the other side almost the shore[2] on which Europa became a sweet burden. And more of the site of this little threshing-floor would have been discovered to me, but the sun was proceeding beneath my feet, a sign and more removed.

88. My enamoured mind, that ever pays court to my Lady, was more than ever burning to bring back my eyes to her. And if nature or art has made bait in human flesh or in paintings of it, to catch the eyes in order to possess the mind, all united would seem naught compared to the divine pleasure which shone upon me when I turned me to her smiling face. And the virtue which that look vouchsafed to me, tore me from the fair nest of Leda,[3] and impelled me to the swiftest heaven.

100. Its parts, most living and lofty, are so uniform that I cannot tell which of them Beatrice chose for a place for me. But she, who saw my desire, began, smiling so glad that God seemed to rejoice in her countenance: "The nature of the universe which holds the centre quiet, and moves all the rest around it, begins here as from its starting-point. And this heaven has no other Where than the Divine Mind, wherein is kindled the love that revolves it, and the virtue which it rains down. Light and love enclose it with one circle, even as it does the others, and of that cincture He who girds it is the sole Intelligence. The motion of this heaven is not marked out by another, but the others are measured by this, just as ten by its half and by its fifth. And how time can have its roots in such a flower-pot and in the others its leaves, may now be manifest to thee.

121. "O covetousness, which dost so whelm mortals beneath thee, that no one has power to withdraw his eyes from out thy waves! Well does the will blossom in men, but the continual rain converts the true plums into blighted fruit. Faith and innocence are found only in children; then each flies away before the cheeks are covered. One, so long as he lisps, keeps the fasts, who afterward, when his tongue is loosed, devours whatever food under whatever moon; and one, while he lisps, loves his mother and listens to her, who afterward, when his speech is perfect, desires to see her buried. So the skin of the fair daughter of him who brings morning and leaves evening, white in its first aspect, becomes black.[4] Do thou, in order that thou make no marvel of it, reflect that on earth there is no one who governs; wherefore the human family goes thus astray. But ere January be all un-wintered by that hundredth part which is down there neglected,[5] these supernal circles shall so roar that the storm which has been so long awaited shall turn round the sterns to where the prows are, so that the fleet shall run straight, and true fruit shall come after the flower."[6]

CANTO XXVIII

AFTER she who imparadises my mind had disclosed the truth counter to the present life of wretched mortals; as one who sees in a mirror the flame of a torch which is lighted behind him, ere he has it in sight or in thought, and turns round to see if the glass tell him the truth, and sees that it accords with it as the note with its measure; so my memory recollects that I did, looking into the beautiful eyes, wherewith Love made the cord to capture me. And when I turned, and mine were touched

---

[1] See Canto xxii. 133-153.
[2] The coast of Phoenicia, whence Europa was carried off by Jupiter.
[3] From Gemini, the constellation of Castor and Pollux, the twin sons of Leda.

[4] See Aristotle. *Physics,* ii. 2. 194[b]13.
[5] By an error in the calendar, by which the year was lengthened by about a day in each century.
[6] Cf. lines 125, 126, *supra.*

by what is apparent in that sphere whenever one gazes fixedly on its circling, I saw a Point which was raying out light so keen that the sight on which it blazes must needs close because of its intense keenness. And whatever star seems smallest from here would seem a moon if placed beside it, as star with star is placed.

22. Perhaps as near as a halo seems to girdle the light which paints it, when the vapor that bears it is most dense, at such distance around the Point a circle of fire was whirling so rapidly that it would have surpassed that motion which most swiftly girds the world; and this was girt around by another, and that by the third, and the third then by the fourth, by the fifth the fourth, and then by the sixth the fifth. Thereon the seventh followed, so widespread now in compass that the messenger of Juno entire would be narrow to contain it. So the eighth and the ninth; and each was moving more slowly, according as it was in number more distant from the unit. And that one had the clearest flame from which the Pure Spark was least distant; I believe because it partakes more of Its truth.

40. My Lady, who saw me deeply suspense in heed, said: "On that Point Heaven and all nature are dependent. Look on that circle which is most conjoined to It, and know that its motion is so swift because of the burning love whereby it is spurred." And I to her: "If the world were disposed in the order which I see in those wheels, that which is set before me would have satisfied me; but in the world of sense the revolutions may be seen so much the more divine as they are more remote from the centre. Wherefore if my desire is to have end in this marvellous and angelic temple, which has for confine only love and light, I need yet to hear why the example and the exemplar go not in one fashion, because by myself I contemplate this in vain." "If thy fingers are insufficient for such a knot, it is no wonder, so hard has it become through not being tried."

61. Thus my Lady; then she said: "Take that which I shall tell thee, if thou wouldest be satisfied and sharpen thy wit about it. The corporeal circles are wide or narrow according to the more or less of virtue which is diffused

through all their parts. Greater goodness must work greater weal; the greater body, if it has its parts equally complete, contains the greater weal. Hence this one, which sweeps along with itself all the rest of the universe, corresponds to the circle which loves most, and knows most. Therefore, if thou draw thy measure round the virtue, not round the appearance of the beings which seem circular to thee, thou wilt see in each heaven a marvellous agreement with its Intelligence, of greater to more and of smaller to less."

79. As the hemisphere of the air remains splendid and serene when Boreas blows from that cheek wherewith he is mildest, whereby the mist which before troubled it is cleared and dissolved, so that the heaven smiles to us with the beauties of its every region, so I became after my Lady had provided me with her clear answer, and, like a star in heaven, the truth was seen.

88. And after her words had stopped, not otherwise does molten iron throw out sparks than the circles sparkled. Every scintillation followed its blaze, and they were so many that their number was of more thousands than the doubling of the chess.[1] I heard Hosannah sung from choir to choir to the fixed Point that holds them, and will forever hold them, at the *Ubi*[2] in which they have ever been. And she, who saw the questioning thoughts within my mind,[3] said: "The first circles have shown to thee the Seraphim and the Cherubim. Thus swiftly they follow their own bonds, in order to liken themselves to the Point as most they can, and they can in proportion as they are exalted to see. Those other loves, which go around them, are called Thrones of the divine aspect, because they terminated the first triad.[4]

[1] This alludes to the story that the inventor of the game asked, as his reward from the King of Persia, a grain of wheat for the first square of the board, two for the second, four for the third, and so on with successive duplication to the last or sixty-fourth square, the number reached by this process extending to twenty figures.

[2] The *where*.

[3] His questioning thoughts were in regard to the arrangement of the Orders of the Heavenly Hierarchy, which Beatrice now proceeds to declare to him, following the treatise *Concerning the Heavenly Hierarchy*, generally ascribed during the Middle Ages to Dionysius the Areopagite (see Acts, 17. 34; II Corinthians, 12. 2-4).

[4] See Canto IX. 61.

And thou shouldst know that all have delight in proportion as their vision penetrates into the Truth in which every understanding is at rest. Hence may be seen how beatitude is founded on the act which sees, not on that which loves, which follows after. And the merit, to which grace and good-will give birth, is the measure of this seeing; thus is the progress from grade to grade.

115. "The next triad, that in like manner bourgeons in this sempiternal spring which the nightly Aries despoils not, perpetually sing Hosannah with three melodies, which sound in the three orders of joy wherewith it is threefold. In this hierarchy are the three divinities, first Dominations, and then Virtues; the third order is of Powers. Then, in the two penultimate dances, the Principalities and Archangels circle; the last is wholly of Angelic sports. These orders all gaze upward, and downward so prevail, that toward God all are drawn, and all draw. And Dionysius with such great desire set himself to contemplate these orders, that he named and divided them, as I. But Gregory[1] afterward separated from him; wherefore, so soon as he opened his eyes in this Heaven, he smiled at himself. And if a mortal declared on earth so much of secret truth, I would not have thee wonder, for he who saw it here on high disclosed it to him, with much else of the truth of these circles."

CANTO XXIX

WHEN the two children of Latona, covered by the Ram and by the Scales, both at one moment make a zone of the horizon, as long as from the instant the zenith holds them in balance, till one and the other, changing their hemisphere, are unbalanced from that girdle, so long, with her countenance painted with a smile, was Beatrice silent, looking fixedly upon the Point which had overcome me.

10. Then she began: "I tell, not ask, what thou wishest to hear, for I have seen it where every *where* and every *when* are centred. Not for the gain of good unto Himself, which cannot be, but that His splendor might, in resplendence say, *I am;* in His own eternity, outside of time, outside of every other limit, as it pleased Him, the Eternal Love disclosed Himself in new loves. Nor before, as if inert, did He lie; for neither before nor after[2] did the moving of God upon these waters proceed.

22. "Form and matter, conjoined and simple, came into being which had no defect, as three arrows from a three-stringed bow; and as in glass, in amber, or in crystal a ray shines so that there is no interval between its coming and its being complete, so did the triform effect ray forth from its Lord into its being all at once, without distinction of beginning. Order was concreate and established for the substances; and those in which pure act was produced were top of the world.[3] Pure potentiality held the lowest part; in the middle such a bond tied up potentiality with act, that it is never unbound. Jerome wrote for you of the Angels, as being created a long tract of centuries before the rest of the world was made; but this truth[4] is written on many pages by the writers of the Holy Spirit, and thou wilt thyself discern it there, if thou watchest well for it; and also the reason sees it somewhat, which would not admit that the motors could be so long without their perfection. Now thou knowest where and when these Loves were created, and how; so that three flames of thy desire are already quenched.

49. "One would not reach to twenty, in counting, so quickly as a part of the Angels disturbed the lowest of your elements.[5] The rest remained and began this art which thou beholdest, with such great delight that they never cease from circling. The origin of the fall was the accursed pride of him whom thou hast seen opprest by all the weights of the world. Those whom thou seest here were modest to recognize themselves as from the Goodness which had made them apt for intelligence so great; wherefore their vision was exalted by illuminating grace and by their merit, so that they have a full and steadfast will. And I would not that thou doubt, but be certain, that

---

[1] Pope St. Gregory differed slightly from Dionysius in his arrangement of the Orders of the Heavenly Host.

[2] See Genesis, 1. 2.
[3] See Aquinas, *Summa Theologica*, Part I, Q 50, A 1.; Part II-II, Q 113, A 6.
[4] *Ibid.*, Part I, Q 61, A 3.
[5] See *Hell*, xxxiv. 122-126.

to receive grace is meritorious in proportion as the affection is open to it.

67. "Henceforth, if my words have been harvested, thou canst contemplate much in regard to this consistory without other assistance. But since on earth it is taught in your schools that the angelic nature is such that it understands, and remembers, and wills, I will speak further, in order that thou mayest see the simple truth, which there below is confused, by the equivocation in such like teaching. These substances, since first they were gladdened by the face of God, have not turned their sight from it, from which nothing is concealed; therefore they have not a vision interrupted by new objects, and therefore do not need to remember by a divided conception. So that down there men dream when not asleep, believing and not believing to speak truth; but in the one is more fault and more shame.

85. "Ye below go not along one path in philosophizing; so much do the love of display and the thought of it transport you; and yet this is endured here on high with less indignation than when the divine Scripture is set aside, or when it is perverted. Men think not there how much blood it costs to sow it in the world, or how much he pleases who humbly keeps close to it. Every one strives for display, and makes his own inventions, and those are treated of by the preachers, and the Gospel is silent. One says that the moon turned back at the passion of Christ and interposed herself, so that the light of the sun reached not down; and others that the light hid itself of its own accord, so that this eclipse answered for the Spaniards and for the Indians as well as for the Jews. Florence has not so many Lapi and Bindi[1] as fables such as these that are shouted the year long from the pulpits, on every side; so that the poor flocks, who know naught, return from the pasture fed with wind; and not seeing the harm does not excuse them.

109. "Christ did not say to his first company: 'Go, and preach idle stories to the world,' but he gave to them the true foundation; and that alone sounded in their mouths, so that to fight for kindling of the faith they made shield and lance of the Gospel. Now men go forth to preach with jests and with buffooneries, and so there be only a good laugh the cowl puffs up, and nothing more is asked; but such a bird is nesting in the tail of the hood, that if the crowd should see it, they would see in what pardoning they are trusting; wherefore such great folly has grown on earth, that, without proof of any testimony, men would flock to every promise. On this the pig of St. Antony fattens,[2] and others also, who are far more pigs, paying with money that has no stamp of coinage.

127. "But because we have digressed enough, turn back thine eyes now toward the straight path, so that the way be shortened with the time. This nature[3] so exceedingly extends in number, that never was there speech or mortal concept that can go so far. And if thou consider that which is revealed by Daniel thou wilt see that in his thousands[4] a determinate number is concealed. The Primal Light that irradiates it all is received in it by as many modes as are the splendors with which It pairs Itself. Wherefore, since the affection follows upon the act that conceives, in this nature the sweetness of love diversely glows and warms. Behold now the height and the breadth of the Eternal Goodness, since it has made for itself so many mirrors on which it is broken, One in itself remaining as before."

CANTO XXX

THE sixth hour is glowing perhaps six thousand miles distant from us, and this world now inclines its shadow almost to a level bed, when the mid-heaven, deep above us, begins to become such that some one star loses its show so far as to this depth; and as the brightest handmaid of the sun comes farther on, so the heaven is closed from light to light, even to the most beautiful. Not otherwise the Triumph, that plays forever round the Point which vanquished me, seeming enclosed by that which

[1] Common nicknames in Florence.

[2] St. Antony of Egypt, the patriarch of monks, is represented with a hog under his feet, as a symbol of his mastery of sensual temptations. The monks of his order kept swine, fed at public charge; it was a profanation to steal or kill them. Dante gives the name of pigs to his degenerate followers, many of whom grew fat on the sale of false indulgences.
[3] See Aquinas, *Summa Theologica*, Part I, Q 50, A 3.
[4] See Daniel, 7. 10.

it encloses, was extinguished little by little to my sight; wherefore my seeing nothing and my love constrained me to turn with my eyes to Beatrice. If what has been said of her so far as here were all included in a single praise, it would be little to furnish forth this turn. The beauty which I saw transcends measure not only beyond our reach, but surely I believe that its Maker alone can enjoy it all.

22. By this pass I concede myself vanquished more than ever comic or tragic poet was overcome by crisis of his theme. For as the sun does to the sight which trembles most, even so remembrance of the sweet smile deprives my memory of its very self. From the first day when in this life I saw her face, until this sight, the following with my song has not been cut off for me, but now needs must my pursuit desist from further following her beauty in my verse, as at his utmost every artist.

34. Such, as I leave her for a greater heralding than that of my trumpet, which is bringing its arduous theme to a close, with act and voice of a leader whose talk is accomplished she began again: "We have issued forth from the greatest body to the Heaven which is pure light: light intellectual full of love, love of true good full of joy, joy which transcends every sweetness. Here thou shalt see the one and the other soldiery of Paradise; and the one in those aspects which thou shalt see at the Last Judgment."

46. As a sudden flash which scatters the spirits of the sight so that it deprives the eye of the action of the strongest objects; so did a vivid light shine round about me, leaving me swathed with such a veil of its own effulgence that nothing was visible to me.

52. "The Love which quieteth this Heaven always welcomes to itself with such a salutation, in order to make the candle fit for its flame." No sooner had these brief words come within me than I comprehended that I was surmounting above my own power; and I rekindled me with a new vision, such that no light is so pure that my eyes could not have withstood it. And I saw light in form of a river glowing with effulgence, between two banks painted with marvellous spring. From this stream were issuing living sparks, and on every side were setting themselves in the flowers,

like rubies which gold encompasses. Then, as if inebriated by the odors, they plunged again into the wonderful flood, and as one was entering another was issuing forth.

70. "The high desire which now inflames and urges thee to have knowledge concerning that which thou seest, pleases me the more the more it swells; but thou must needs drink of this water before so great a thirst in thee be slaked." Thus the Sun of my eyes said to me; then added: "The stream, and the topazes which enter and issue, and the smiling of the herbage, are shadowy prefaces of their truth; not that these things are difficult in themselves, but there is defect on thy part that thou hast not yet vision so exalted."

82. There is no babe who so hastily springs with face toward the milk, if he awake much later than his wont, as I did, to make yet better mirrors of my eyes, stooping to the wave which flows in order that we may be bettered in it. And even as the eaves of my eyelids drank of it, so it seemed to me from its length to have become round. Then as folk who have been under masks, who seem other than before, if they divest themselves of the semblance not their own wherein they disappeared, in such wise for me the flowers and the sparks were changed into greater festival, so that I saw both the Courts of Heaven made manifest.

97. O splendor of God, through which I saw the high triumph of the true kingdom, give to me power to tell how I saw it!

100. Light is thereabove which makes the Creator visible to that creature which has its peace only in seeing Him; and it spreads in circular shape so far that its circumference would be too large a girdle for the sun. Its whole appearance is made of a ray reflected from the summit of the First Moving Heaven, which from it takes its life and potency. And as a hill mirrors itself in water at its base, as if to see itself adorned, when it is rich with verdure and with flowers, so, above the light, round and round about, on more than a thousand seats, I saw mirrored, as they rose, all that of us have made return on high. And if the lowest row gather within itself so great a light, how vast is the spread of this rose in its outermost leaves! My sight lost not itself in the breadth and in the height, but took in all the

quantity and quality of that joy. There near and far nor add nor take away; for where God governs without intermediary the natural law is of no relevancy.

124. Into the yellow of the sempiternal rose, which spreads wide, rises in tiers, and breathes forth odor of praise unto the Sun that makes perpetual spring. Beatrice, like one who is silent and wishes to speak, drew me and said, "Behold, how vast is the convent of the white stoles;[1] See our city, how wide its circuit! See our benches so full that few people are now wanting here. On that great seat, on which thou holdest thine eye because of the crown which already is set above it, ere thou dost sup at this wedding-feast, shall sit the soul (which on earth will be imperial) of the lofty Henry who, to set Italy straight, will come ere she is ready.[2] The blind cupidity which bewitches you has made you like the little child who dies of hunger, and drives away his nurse; and such a one will then be prefect in the divine forum that openly or covertly he will not go with him along one road;[3] but short while thereafter shall he be endured by God in the holy office; for he shall be thrust down there where Simon Magus is for his deserts, and shall make him of Anagna[4] go lower."

CANTO XXXI

In form then of a pure white rose the holy host was shown to me, which, in His own blood, Christ made His bride. But the other, which, flying, sees and sings the glory of Him who enamours it, and the goodness which made it so great, like a swarm of bees which one while inflower themselves and one while return to where their work acquires savor, were descending into the great flower which is adorned with so many leaves, and thence rising up again to where their love always abides. They had their faces all of living flame, and their wings of gold, and the rest so white that no snow reaches that limit. When they descended into the flower, from bench to bench, they imparted of the peace and of the ardor which they acquired as they fanned their sides. Nor did the interposing of so great a flying plenitude, between what was above and the flower, impede the sight or the splendor; for the divine light penetrates through the universe, according as it is worthy, so that naught can be an obstacle to it. This secure and joyous realm, thronged with ancient and with modern folk, had its look and love all on one mark.

28. O Trinal Light, which in a single star, scintillating on their sight, dost so satisfy them, look down here upon our tempest!

31. If the Barbarians, coming from a region such that every day it is covered by Helice,[5] revolving with her son of whom she is fond, when they beheld Rome and her lofty work— what time Lateran rose above mortal things— were wonder-struck, I, who to the divine from the human, to the eternal from the temporal, had come, and from Florence to a people just and sane, with what amazement must I have been full! Truly what with it and with the joy I was well pleased not to hear, and to stand mute. And as a pilgrim who is refreshed within the temple of his vow as he looks around, and hopes some day to report how it was, so, journeying through the living light, I carried my eyes over the ranks, now up, now down, and now circling about. I saw faces persuasive to love, beautified by the light of Another and by their own smile, and actions graced with every dignity.

52. My look had now comprehended the general form of Paradise as a whole, and on no part had my sight as yet been fixed; and I turned me with rekindled wish to ask my Lady about things as to which my mind was in suspense. One thing I purposed, and another answered me; I was thinking to see Beatrice, and I saw an old man, robed like the people in glory. His eyes and his cheeks were overspread with benignant joy, his mien kindly such as befits a tender father. And: "Where is she?" on a sudden said I.

65. Whereon he: "To terminate thy desire, Beatrice urged me from my place, and if thou lookest up to the third circle from the highest rank, thou wilt again see her upon the throne

[1] See Revelation, 3. 5.
[2] Henry VII.
[3] Pope Clement V for a time ostensibly supported Henry VII in his Italian expedition, but gradually in underhand fashion turned against him. He died in 1314, eight months after the death of Henry.
[4] Anagni, where Boniface VIII was born.

[5] See *Purgatory*, xxv. 130-137.

which her merits have allotted to her." Without answering I lifted up my eyes, and saw her as she had made for herself a crown reflecting from herself the eternal rays. From that region which thunders highest up no mortal eye is so far distant, in whatsoever sea it lets itself sink deepest, as there from Beatrice was my sight. But this was naught to me, for her image did not descend to me blurred by aught between.

79. "O Lady, in whom my hope is strong, and who, for my salvation, didst endure to leave thy footprints in Hell, of all those things which I have seen through thy power and through thy goodness, I recognize the grace and the virtue. Thou hast drawn me from servitude to liberty by all those ways, by all the modes whereby thou hadst the power to do it. Guard thou in me thine own magnificence so that my soul, which thou hast made whole, may, pleasing to thee, be unloosed from the body." Thus I prayed; and she, so distant, as it seemed, smiled and looked at me; then turned to the eternal fountain.

94. And the holy old man said: "In order that thou mayst complete perfectly thy journey, for which end prayer and holy love sent me, fly with thine eyes through this garden; for seeing it will prepare thy look to mount further through the divine radiance. And the Queen of Heaven, for whom I burn wholly with love, will grant us every grace, because I am her faithful Bernard."[1]

103. As is he who comes perchance from Croatia to see our Veronica,[2] who by reason of its ancient fame is never sated, but says in thought, so long as it is shown: "My Lord Jesus Christ, true God, was then your semblance like to this?" such was I, gazing on the living charity of him who, in this world, in contemplation, tasted of that peace.

112. "Son of Grace, this glad existence," began he, "will not be known to thee holding thine eyes only down here at the base, but look on the circles even to the most remote, until thou seest upon her seat the Queen to whom this realm is subject and devoted."

118. I lifted up my eyes; and as at morning the eastern parts of the horizon surpass that where the sun declines, thus, as if going with my eyes from valley to mountain, I saw a part on the extreme verge vanquishing in light all the rest of the front. And even as there where the pole which Phaëthon guided ill is awaited, the glow is brightest, and on this side and that the light diminishes, so that pacific oriflamme[3] was vivid at the middle, and on each side in equal measure the flame slackened. And at that mid-part I saw more than a thousand jubilant Angels with wings outspread, each distinct both in effulgence and in act. I saw there, smiling at their sports and at their songs, a Beauty which was joy in the eyes of all the other saints. And if I had such wealth in speech as in imagining, I should not dare attempt the least of its delightfulness.

139. Bernard, when he saw my eyes fixed and intent upon the object of his own burning glow, turned his own with such affection to it, that he made mine more ardent to gaze anew.

CANTO XXXII

WITH affection set on his Delight, that contemplator freely assumed the office of a teacher, and began these holy words: "The wound which Mary closed up and anointed, that one who is so beautiful at her feet is she who opened it and who pierced it. Beneath her, in the order which the third seats make, sits Rachel with Beatrice, as thou seest. Sara, Rebecca, Judith, and she[4] who was great-grandmother of the singer who, through sorrow for his sin, said *Miserere mei*,[5] thou mayst see thus from rank to rank in gradation downward, as with the name of each I go downward through the rose from leaf to leaf. And from the seventh row downwards, even as down to it, Hebrew women follow in succession, dividing all the tresses of the flower; because these are the wall by which the sacred stairs are separated ac-

---

[1] St. Bernard of Clairvaux, to whom the Blessed Virgin had appeared during his life.
[2] The likeness of the Saviour miraculously impressed upon the kerchief presented to Him by a holy woman, on His way to Calvary, wherewith to wipe the sweat and dust from His face.

[3] This oriflamme is the part of the rose of Paradise where the Virgin is seated; its mid-point is the Virgin herself. It is called "pacific" in contrast with the war-like oriflamme, the banner given by the archangel Gabriel to the ancient kings of France, which bore a flame on a field of gold (*aurea flamma*).
[4] Ruth.
[5] "Have mercy upon me." Psalms, 51. 1.

cording to the look which faith turned on Christ."

22. "On this side, where the flower is mature with all its leaves, are seated those who believed in Christ about to come. On the other side, where the semicircles are broken by empty spaces, are those who turned their faces on Christ already come. And as on this side the glorious seat of the Lady of Heaven, and the other seats below it, make so great a division, thus, opposite, does the seat of the great John, who, ever holy, endured the desert and martyrdom, and then Hell for two years;[1] and beneath him Francis and Benedict and Augustine and others are allotted thus to divide, far down as here from circle to circle.

37. "Now behold the high divine foresight; for one and the other aspect of the faith will fill this garden equally. And know that downwards from the row which midway cleaves the two divisions, they are seated for no merit of their own, but for that of others, under certain conditions; for all these are spirits absolved ere they had true power of choice. Well canst thou perceive it by their faces, and also by their childish voices, if thou lookest well upon them and if thou listenest to them. Now thou art perplexed, and in perplexity art silent; but I will loose for thee the strong bond in which thy subtle thoughts fetter thee. Within the amplitude of this realm a casual point can have no place, any more than sadness, or thirst, or hunger; for whatever thou seest is established by eternal law, so that here the ring answers exactly to the finger. And therefore this folk, hastened to true life, is not *sine causa* more and less excellent here among themselves.

61. "The King, through whom this realm reposes in such great love and in such great delight that no will dares for more, creating all the minds in His own glad aspect, endows with grace diversely according to His pleasure; and here let the fact suffice. And this is expressly and clearly noted for you in the Holy Scripture in the case of those twins who, within their mother, had their anger stirred.[2] Therefore, according to the color of the hair of such

grace,[3] the highest light must needs befittingly crown them. Without, then, merit from their own ways, they are placed in different grades, differing only in their primary keenness of vision. In the early centuries, indeed, the faith of parents alone sufficed, together with innocence, to secure salvation; after the first ages were complete, it was needful for males, through circumcision, to acquire power for their innocent wings. But after the time of grace had come, without perfect baptism in Christ, such innocence was held back there below.

85. "Look now upon the face which most resembles Christ, for only its brightness can prepare thee to see Christ."

88. I saw raining down on her such great joy, borne in the holy minds created to fly across through that height, that whatsoever I had seen before held me not suspended in such great wonder, nor showed to me such likeness unto God. And that Love which had before descended to her,[4] in front of her spread wide his wings, singing, *Ave, Maria, gratia plena*. The blessed Court responded to the divine song from all sides, so that every countenance became thereby the more serene.

100. O holy Father, who for me endurest to be here below, leaving the sweet place in which thou sittest by eternal allotment, who is that Angel who with such joy looks into the eyes of our Queen, so enamoured that he seems of fire?" Thus did I again recur to the teaching of him who was deriving beauty from Mary, as the morning star from the sun. And he to me, "Confidence and grace as much as there can be in Angel and in soul, are all in him, and we would have it so, for he it is[5] who bore the palm down to Mary, when the Son of God willed to load Himself with our burden.

115. "But come now with thine eyes; as I shall proceed speaking, and note the great patricians of this most just and pious empire. Those two who sit there above, most happy through being nearest to the Empress, are, as it were, two roots of this rose. He who on the left is next her is the Father because of whose audacious tasting the human race tastes so much bitterness. On the right see that ancient Father of

---

[1] The two years from the death of John to the death of Christ; these he passed in limbo.
[2] Jacob and Esau. See Genesis, 25. 22; Romans, 9. 11-12.

[3] See Genesis, 25. 25.
[4] See Canto xxiii. 94.
[5] The angel Gabriel; see Luke, 1. 26.

Holy Church, to whom Christ entrusted the keys of this lovely flower. And he[1] who saw before his death all the grievous times of the fair bride, who was won with the spear and with the nails, sits at his side; and by the other rests that leader, under whom the ingrate, fickle and stubborn people lived on manna. Opposite Peter see Anna sitting, so content to gaze upon her daughter, that she moves not her eyes as she sings Hosannah; and opposite the eldest father of a family sits Lucia,[2] who moved thy Lady, when thou didst bend thy brow to rush downward.[3]

139. "But because the time flies which holds thee slumbering,[4] here will we make a stop, like a good tailor who makes the gown according as he has cloth, and we will direct our eyes to the First Love, so that, looking towards Him, thou mayst penetrate so far as is possible through His effulgence. But, lest perchance, moving thy wings, thou go backward, believing to advance, it is needful that grace be obtained by prayer; grace from her who has the power to aid thee; and do thou follow me with thy affection so that thy heart depart not from my speech."

151. And he began this holy prayer.

CANTO XXXIII

"Virgin Mother, daughter of thine own Son, humble and exalted more than any creature, fixed term of the eternal counsel, thou art she who didst so ennoble human nature that its own Maker disdained not to become its creature. Within thy womb was rekindled the Love through whose warmth this flower has thus blossomed in the eternal peace. Here thou art to us the noonday torch of charity, and below, among mortals, thou art the living fount of hope. Lady, thou art so great, and so availest, that whoso would have grace, and has not recourse to thee, would have his desire fly without wings. Thy benignity not only succors him who asks, but oftentimes freely foreruns the asking. In thee mercy, in thee pity, in thee magnificence, in thee whatever of goodness is in any creature, are united. Now doth this man, who, from the lowest abyss of the universe, far even as here, has seen one after one the spiritual lives, supplicate thee of grace, for power such that he may be able with his eyes to uplift himself higher toward the Ultimate Salvation. And I, who never for my own vision burned more than I do for his, proffer to thee all my prayers, and pray that they be not scant, that with thy prayers thou wouldst dispel for him every cloud of his mortality, so that the Supreme Pleasure may be displayed to him. Further I pray thee, Queen, who canst whatso thou wilt, that, after so great a vision, thou wouldst preserve his affections sound. May thy guardianship vanquish human impulses. Behold Beatrice with all the Blessed for my prayers clasp their hands to thee."[5]

40. The eyes beloved and venerated by God, fixed on the speaker, showed to us how pleasing unto her are devout prayers. Then to the Eternal Light were they directed, to which it may not be believed that eye so clear of any creature enters in.

46. And I, who to the end of all desires was approaching, even as I ought, ended within myself the ardor of my longing. Bernard made a sign to me, and smiled, that I should look upward; but I was already, of myself, such as he wished; for my sight, becoming pure, was entering more and more through the radiance of the lofty Light which in Itself is true.

55. Thenceforward my vision was greater than our speech, which yields to such a sight, and the memory yields to such excess.

58. As is he who dreaming sees, and after the dream the passion remains imprinted, and the rest returns not to the mind, such am I; for my vision almost wholly departs, which the sweetness that was born of it yet distils within my heart. Thus the snow is by the sun unsealed; thus by the wind, on the light leaves, was lost the saying of the Sibyl.

67. O Supreme Light, that so high upliftest Thyself from mortal conceptions, re-lend to my mind a little of what Thou didst appear, and make my tongue so powerful that it may be able to leave one single spark of Thy glory for the folk to come; for, by returning somewhat to my memory and by sounding a little in

---

[1] St. John the Evangelist.
[2] See *Hell*, ii. 97-108; *Purgatory*, ix. 55-63.
[3] See *Hell*, i. 61.
[4] Cf. Cantos i. 73-75; ii. 37-39.

[5] Cf. Chaucer, in *The Second Nun's Tale*, for a paraphrase of the larger part of this prayer.

these verses, more of Thy victory shall be conceived.

76. I think that by the keenness of the living ray which I endured, I should have been dazed if my eyes had been averted from it; and I remember that on this account I was the more hardy to sustain it till I conjoined my gaze with the Infinite Goodness.

82. O abundant Grace, whereby I presumed to fix my look through the Eternal Light till that there I consummated the seeing!

85. I saw that in its depth is enclosed, bound up with love in one volume, that which is dispersed in leaves through the universe; substance and accidents and their modes, fused together, as it were, in such wise, that that of which I speak is one simple Light. The universal form of this knot[1] I believe that I saw, because, in saying this, I feel that I rejoice more spaciously. One single moment only is greater oblivion for me than five and twenty centuries to the emprise which made Neptune wonder at the shadow of Argo.[2]

97. Thus my mind, wholly rapt, was gazing fixed, motionless, and intent, and ever with gazing grew enkindled. In that Light one becomes such that it is impossible he should ever consent to turn himself from it for other sight; because the Good which is the object of the will is all collected in it, and outside of it that is defective which is perfect there.

106. Now will my speech fall more short, even in respect to that which I remember, than that of an infant who still bathes his tongue at the breast. Not because more than one simple semblance was in the Living Light wherein I

was gazing, which is always such as it was before; but through my sight, which was growing strong in me as I looked, one sole appearance, as I myself changed, was altering itself to me.

115. Within the profound and clear subsistence of the lofty Light appeared to me three circles of three colors and of one dimension; and one seemed reflected by the other, as Iris by Iris, and the third seemed fire which from the one and from the other is equally breathed forth.

121. O how inadequate is speech, and how feeble toward my conception! and this toward what I saw is such that it suffices not to call it little.

124. O Light Eternal, that sole abidest in Thyself, sole understandest Thyself, and, by Thyself understood and understanding, lovest and smilest on Thyself! That circle, which appeared in Thee generated as a reflected light, being awhile surveyed by my eyes, seemed to me depicted with our effigy within itself, of its own very color; wherefore my sight was wholly set upon it. As is the geometer who wholly applies himself to measure the circle, and finds not by thinking that principle of which he is in need, such was I at that new sight. I wished to see how the image was conformed to the circle, and how it has its place therein; but my own wings were not for this, had it not been that my mind was smitten by a flash in which its wish came.

142. To the high fantasy here power failed; but now my desire and my will were revolved, like a wheel which is moved evenly, by the Love which moves the sun and the other stars.

---

[1] See Aquinas, *Summa Theologica,* Part. I, Q 4, A 2.
[2] Because it was the first vessel that sailed the sea.

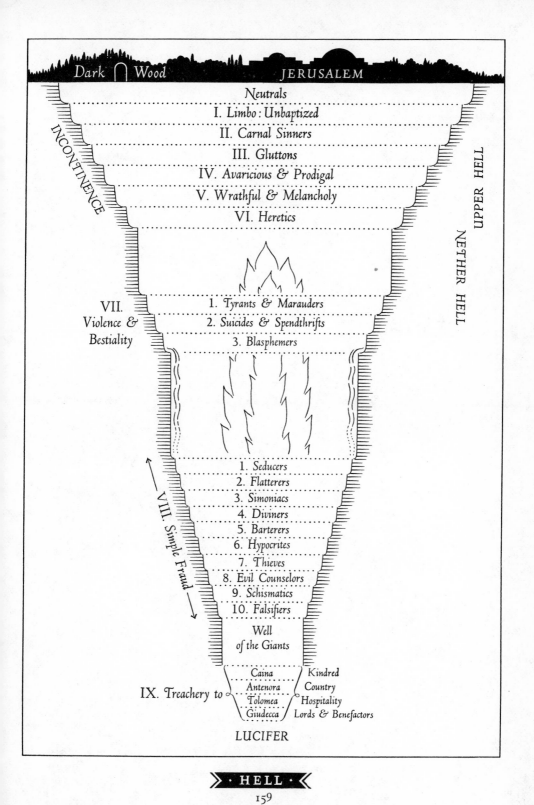

Dark ∩ Wood   JERUSALEM

Neutrals

I. Limbo: Unbaptized

II. Carnal Sinners

III. Gluttons

IV. Avaricious & Prodigal

V. Wrathful & Melancholy

VI. Heretics

INCONTINENCE

UPPER HELL

NETHER HELL

VII.
Violence &
Bestiality

1. Tyrants & Marauders

2. Suicides & Spendthrifts

3. Blasphemers

VIII. Simple Fraud

1. Seducers

2. Flatterers

3. Simoniacs

4. Diviners

5. Barterers

6. Hypocrites

7. Thieves

8. Evil Counselors

9. Schismatics

10. Falsifiers

Well
of the Giants

IX. Treachery to

Caina — Kindred
Antenora — Country
Tolomea — Hospitality
Giudecca — Lords & Benefactors

LUCIFER

HELL

159

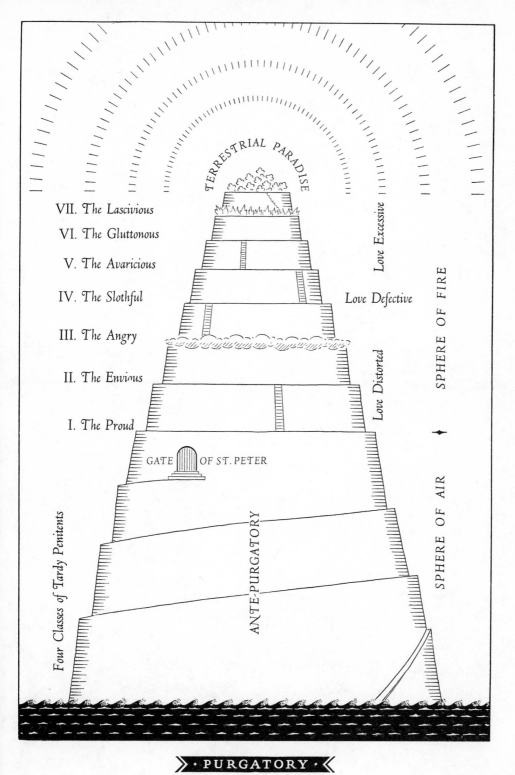

VII. The Lascivious

VI. The Gluttonous

V. The Avaricious

IV. The Slothful

III. The Angry

II. The Envious

I. The Proud

TERRESTRIAL PARADISE

Love Excessive

Love Defective

Love Distorted

SPHERE OF FIRE

GATE OF ST. PETER

SPHERE OF AIR

Four Classes of Tardy Penitents

ANTE-PURGATORY

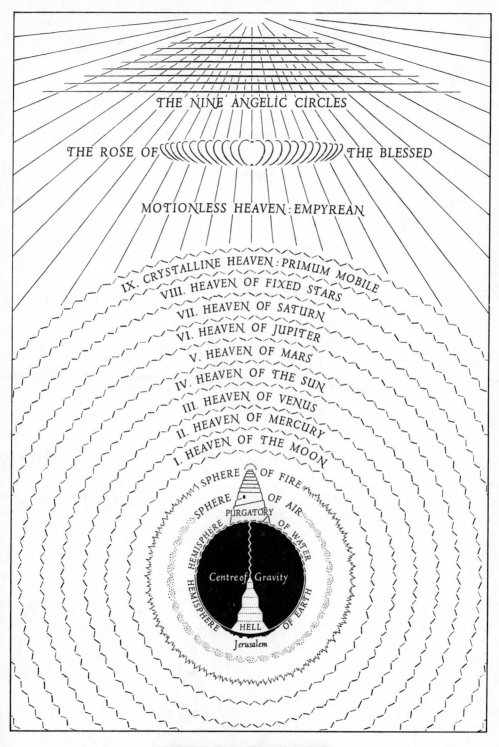

THE NINE ANGELIC CIRCLES

THE ROSE OF THE BLESSED

MOTIONLESS HEAVEN : EMPYREAN

IX. CRYSTALLINE HEAVEN : PRIMUM MOBILE

VIII. HEAVEN OF FIXED STARS

VII. HEAVEN OF SATURN

VI. HEAVEN OF JUPITER

V. HEAVEN OF MARS

IV. HEAVEN OF THE SUN

III. HEAVEN OF VENUS

II. HEAVEN OF MERCURY

I. HEAVEN OF THE MOON

SPHERE OF FIRE

SPHERE OF AIR

PURGATORY

HEMISPHERE OF WATER

HEMISPHERE OF EARTH

Centre of Gravity

HELL

Jerusalem

> · THE UNIVERSE · ◀

THE GREAT IDEAS, *Volumes 2 and 3*